Benchmark Series

Microsoft® Excel® 2010

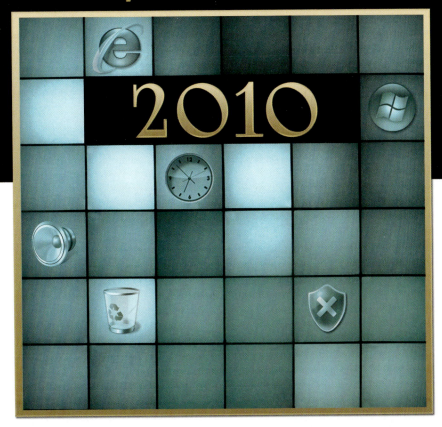

Denise Seguin

Fanshawe College
London, Ontario

St. Paul • Indianapolis

Managing Editor	Sonja Brown
Senior Developmental Editor	Christine Hurney
Production Editor	Donna Mears
Copy Editor	Susan Capecchi
Cover and Text Designer	Leslie Anderson
Desktop Production	Ryan Hamner, Julie Johnston, Jack Ross
Proofreader	Laura Nelson
Indexer	Sandi Schroeder

Acknowledgements: The authors, editors, and publisher thank the following instructors for their helpful suggestions during the planning and development of the books in the Benchmark Office 2010 Series: Somasheker Akkaladevi, Virginia State University, Petersburg, VA; Ed Baker, Community College of Philadelphia, Philadelphia, PA; Lynn Baldwin, Madison Area Technical College, Madison, WI; Letty Barnes, Lake Washington Technical College, Kirkland, WA; Richard Bell, Coastal Carolina Community College, Jacksonville, NC; Perry Callas, Clatsop Community College, Astoria, OR; Carol DesJardins, St. Clair County Community College, Port Huron, MI; Stacy Gee Hollins, St. Louis Community College--Florissant Valley, St. Louis, MO Sally Haywood, Prairie State College, Chicago Heights, IL; Dr. Penny Johnson, Madison Technical College, Madison, WI; Jan Kehm, Spartanburg Community College, Spartanburg, SC; Jacqueline Larsen, Asheville Buncombe Tech, Asheville, NC; Sherry Lenhart, Terra Community College, Fremont, OH; Andrea Robinson Hinsey, Ivy Tech Community College NE, Fort Wayne, IN; Bari Siddique, University of Texas at Brownsville, Brownsville, TX; Joan Splawski, Northeast Wisconsin Technical College, Green Bay, WI; Diane Stark, Phoenix College, Phoenix, AZ; Mary Van Haute, Northeast Wisconsin Technical College, Green Bay, WI; Rosalie Westerberg, Clover Park Technical College, Lakewood, WA.

The publishing team also thanks the following individuals for their contributions to this project: checking the accuracy of the instruction and exercises—Robertt (Rob) W. Neilly, Traci Post, and Lindsay Ryan; developing lesson plans, supplemental assessments, and supplemental case studies—Jan Davidson, Lambton College, Sarina, Ontario; writing rubrics to support end-of-chapter and end-of-unit activities—Robertt (Rob) W. Neilly, Seneca College, Toronto, Ontario; writing test item banks—Jeff Johnson; writing online quiz item banks—Trudy Muller; and developing PowerPoint presentations—Janet Blum, Fanshawe College, London, Ontario.

Trademarks: Access, Excel, Internet Explorer, Microsoft, PowerPoint, and Windows are trademarks or registered trademarks of Microsoft Corporation in the United States and/or other countries. Some of the product names and company names included in this book have been used for identification purposes only and may be trademarks or registered trade names of their respective manufacturers and sellers. The authors, editors, and publisher disclaim any affiliation, association, or connection with, or sponsorship or endorsement by, such owners.

We have made every effort to trace the ownership of all copyrighted material and to secure permission from copyright holders. In the event of any question arising as to the use of any material, we will be pleased to make the necessary corrections in future printings. Thanks are due to the aforementioned authors, publishers, and agents for permission to use the materials indicated.

ISBN 978-0-76384-312-0 (Text)
ISBN 978-0-76384-315-1 (Text + CD)

© 2011 by Paradigm Publishing, Inc.
875 Montreal Way
St. Paul, MN 55102
Email: educate@emcp.com
Website: www.emcp.com

Printed in the United States of America

19 18 17 16 15 14 13   6 7 8 9 10

Contents

Chapter 6 Protecting and Sharing Workbooks   181

Chapter 7 Automating Repetitive Tasks and Customizing Excel   215

Benchmark Microsoft Excel 2010 is designed for students who want to learn how to use this powerful spreadsheet program to manipulate numerical data in resolving issues related to finances or other numbers-based information. No prior knowledge of spreadsheets is required. After successfully completing a course using this textbook, students will be able to

- Create and edit spreadsheets of varying complexity
- Format cells, columns, and rows as well as entire workbooks in a uniform, attractive style
- Analyze numerical data and project outcomes to make informed decisions
- Plan, research, create, revise, and publish worksheets and workbooks to meet specific communication needs
- Given a workplace scenario requiring a numbers-based solution, assess the information requirements and then prepare the materials that achieve the goal efficiently and effectively

In addition to mastering Excel skills, students will learn to import and export files between Excel and other programs in the Office 2010 suite. Upon completing the text, they can expect to be proficient in using Excel to organize, analyze, and present information.

Achieving Proficiency in Excel 2010

Since its inception several Office versions ago, the Benchmark Series has served as a standard of excellence in software instruction. Elements of the book function individually and collectively to create an inviting, comprehensive learning environment that produces successful computer users. The following visual tour highlights the text's features.

UNIT OPENERS display the unit's four chapter titles. Each level has two units, which conclude with a comprehensive unit performance assessment.

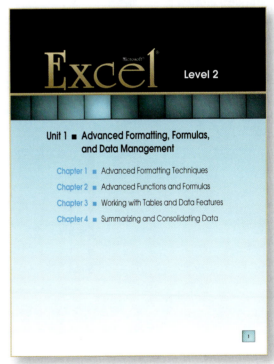

Excel
Microsoft®
Level 2

Unit 1 ■ Advanced Formatting, Formulas, and Data Management

Chapter 1 ■ Advanced Formatting Techniques
Chapter 2 ■ Advanced Functions and Formulas
Chapter 3 ■ Working with Tables and Data Features
Chapter 4 ■ Summarizing and Consolidating Data

CHAPTER OPENERS present the performance objectives and an overview of the skills taught.

SNAP interactive tutorials are available to support chapter-specific skills at www.snap2010.emcp.com.

DATA FILES are provided for each chapter. A prominent note reminds students to copy the appropriate chapter data folder and make it active.

PROJECT APPROACH: Builds Skill Mastery within Realistic Context

MODEL ANSWERS provide a preview of the finished chapter projects and allow students to confirm they have created the materials accurately.

MULTIPART PROJECTS provide a framework for the instruction and practice on software features. A project overview identifies tasks to accomplish and key features to use in completing the work.

Between project parts, the text presents instruction on the features and skills necessary to accomplish the next section of the project.

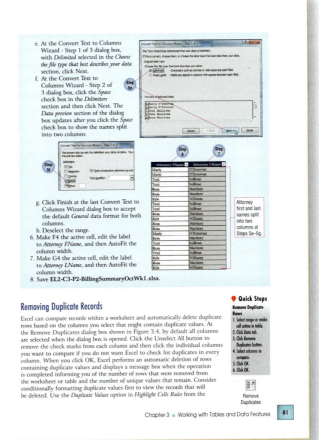

STEP-BY-STEP INSTRUCTIONS guide students to the desired outcome for each project part. Screen captures illustrate what the student's screen should look like at key points.

Typically, a file remains open throughout all parts of the project. Students save their work incrementally.

HINTS provide useful tips on how to use features efficiently and effectively.

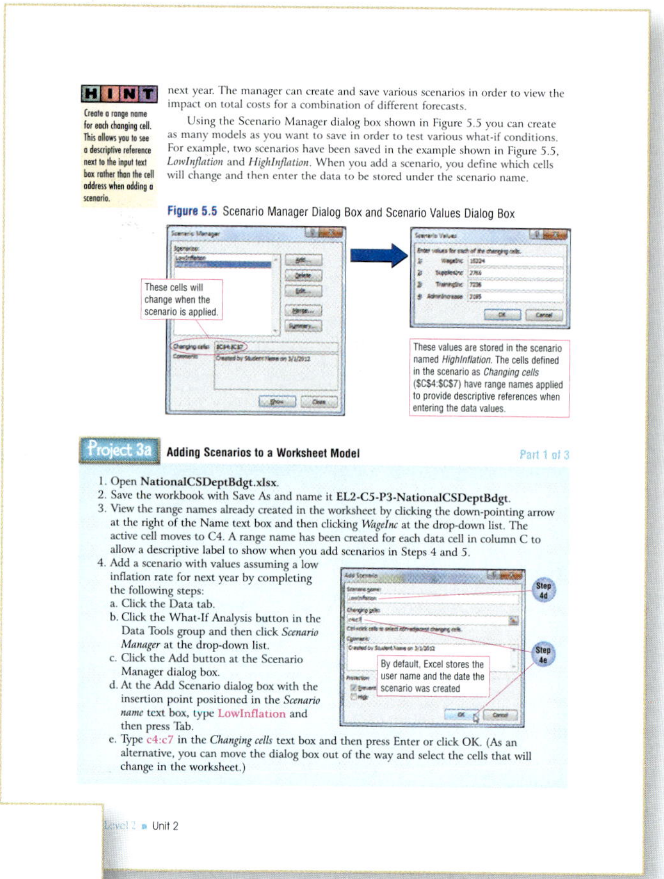

MAGENTA TEXT identifies material to type.

QUICK STEPS provide feature summaries for reference and review.

First sample page content:

HINT

Create a range name for each changing cell. This allows you to see a descriptive reference next to the input text box rather than the cell address when adding a scenario.

next year. The manager can create and save various scenarios in order to view the impact on total costs for a combination of different forecasts.

Using the Scenario Manager dialog box shown in Figure 5.5 you can create as many models as you want to save in order to test various what-if conditions. For example, two scenarios have been saved in the example shown in Figure 5.5, *LowInflation* and *HighInflation*. When you add a scenario, you define which cells will change and then enter the data to be stored under the scenario name.

Figure 5.5 Scenario Manager Dialog Box and Scenario Values Dialog Box

These cells will change when the scenario is applied.

These values are stored in the scenario named *HighInflation*. The cells defined in the scenario as *Changing cells* ($C$4:$C$7) have range names applied to provide descriptive references when entering the data values.

Project 3a Adding Scenarios to a Worksheet Model
Part 1 of 3

1. Open **NationalCSDeptBdgt.xlsx**.
2. Save the workbook with Save As and name it **EL2-C5-P3-NationalCSDeptBdgt**.
3. View the range names already created in the worksheet by clicking the down-pointing arrow at the right of the Name text box and then clicking *WageInc* at the drop-down list. The active cell moves to C4. A range name has been created for each data cell in column C to allow a descriptive label to show when you add scenarios in Steps 4 and 5.
4. Add a scenario with values assuming a low inflation rate for next year by completing the following steps:
   a. Click the Data tab.
   b. Click the What-If Analysis button in the Data Tools group and then click *Scenario Manager* at the drop-down list.
   c. Click the Add button at the Scenario Manager dialog box.
   d. At the Add Scenario dialog box with the insertion point positioned in the *Scenario name* text box, type **LowInflation** and then press Tab.
   e. Type **c4:c7** in the *Changing cells* text box and then press Enter or click OK. (As an alternative, you can move the dialog box out of the way and select the cells that will change in the worksheet.)

Step 4d

Step 4e

By default, Excel stores the user name and the date the scenario was created

---

Second sample page content:

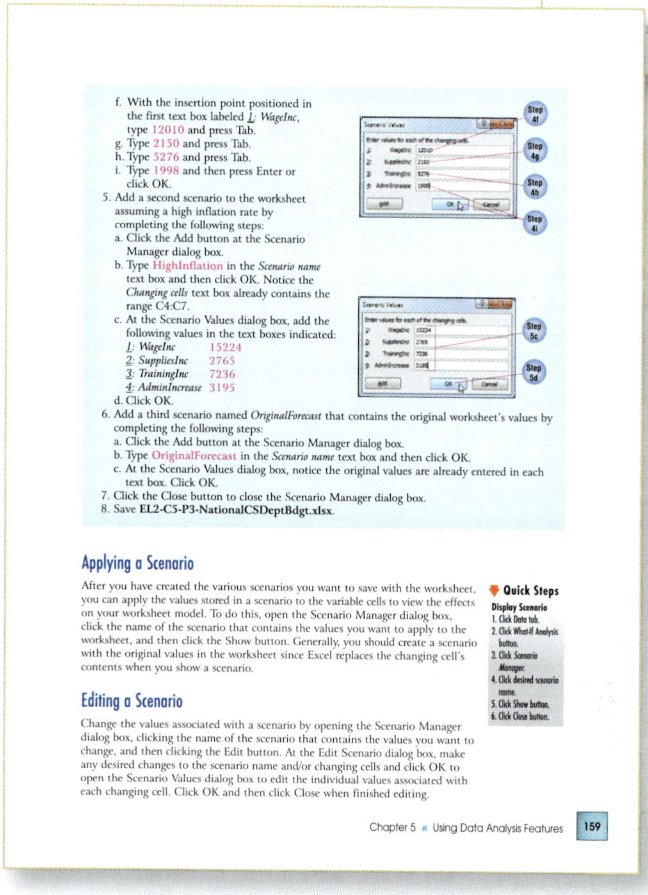

   f. With the insertion point positioned in the first text box labeled *1: WageInc*, type **12010** and press Tab.
   g. Type **2150** and press Tab.
   h. Type **5276** and press Tab.
   i. Type **1998** and then press Enter or click OK.

Step 4f
Step 4g
Step 4h
Step 4i

5. Add a second scenario to the worksheet assuming a high inflation rate by completing the following steps:
   a. Click the Add button at the Scenario Manager dialog box.
   b. Type **HighInflation** in the *Scenario name* text box and then click OK. Notice the *Changing cells* text box already contains the range C4:C7.
   c. At the Scenario Values dialog box, add the following values in the text boxes indicated:
      1: WageInc   15224
      2: SuppliesInc 2765
      3: TrainingInc 7236
      4: AdminIncrease 3195
   d. Click OK.

Step 5c
Step 5d

6. Add a third scenario named *OriginalForecast* that contains the original worksheet's values by completing the following steps:
   a. Click the Add button at the Scenario Manager dialog box.
   b. Type **OriginalForecast** in the *Scenario name* text box and then click OK.
   c. At the Scenario Values dialog box, notice the original values are already entered in each text box. Click OK.
7. Click the Close button to close the Scenario Manager dialog box.
8. Save **EL2-C5-P3-NationalCSDeptBdgt.xlsx**.

Applying a Scenario

After you have created the various scenarios you want to save with the worksheet, you can apply the values stored in the variable cells to view the effects on your worksheet model. To do this, open the Scenario Manager dialog box, click the name of the scenario that contains the values you want to apply to the worksheet, and then click the Show button. Generally, you should create a scenario with the original values in the worksheet since Excel replaces the changing cell's contents when you show a scenario.

▼ **Quick Steps**

Display Scenario
1. Click Data tab.
2. Click What-If Analysis button.
3. Click Scenario Manager.
4. Click desired scenario name.
5. Click Show button.
6. Click Close button.

Editing a Scenario

Change the values associated with a scenario by opening the Scenario Manager dialog box, clicking the name of the scenario that contains the values you want to change, and then clicking the Edit button. At the Edit Scenario dialog box, make any desired changes to the scenario name and/or changing cells and click OK to open the Scenario Values dialog box to edit the individual values associated with each changing cell. Click OK and then click Close when finished editing.

CHAPTER REVIEW ACTIVITIES: A Hierarchy of Learning Assessments

Chapter Summary

- A table in Excel is a range of cells similar in structure to a database in which no blank rows exist and the first row of the range contains column headings.
- Define a range as a table using the Table button in the Tables group of the Insert tab.
- Columns in a table are called fields and rows are called records.
- The first row of a table contains column headings and is called the field names row or header row.
- A table automatically expands to include data typed in a row or column immediately adjacent to a range that has been defined as a table.
- Typing a formula in the first row of a new column causes Excel to define the column as a calculated column and automatically copy the formula to the remaining rows in the table.
- The contextual Table Tools Design tab contains ...
- The Table Styles gallery contains several ... the visual appearance of a table.
- Banding rows or columns formats every ... make reading a large table easier.
- You can add emphasis to the first column ... generally formats the column with a dark ... font and borders depending on the Table ...
- The row containing field names in a table ... Header Row option in the Table Style Options ...
- Adding a Total row to a table causes Excel ... column and create a Sum function in the ... can add additional functions by clicking ... and selecting a function from the pop-up ...
- Excel includes a filter arrow button automatically ... a table with which you can filter and sort ...
- A column containing text that you want ... columns using the Text to Columns button ... tab. The Convert Text to Columns wizard ... how to split the data.
- Using the Remove Duplicates dialog box, ... records within a worksheet and automatically ...
- Data can be validated as it is being entered ... data can be prevented from being stored ... that data has been entered that does not ...
- At the Settings tab in the Data Validation ... criteria for the cell entry. You can allow ... length, or restrict the entries to values within ...
- At the Input Message tab in the Data Validation ... message that pops up when a cell for which ...

94 Excel Level 2 ■ Unit 1

- At the Error Alert tab in the Data Validation dialog box you define the type of error alert to display and the content of the error message.
- Convert a table to a normal range to use the Subtotal feature or when you no longer need to treat a range of cells independently from the rest of the worksheet.
- Sort a worksheet by the column(s) for which you want to group data for subtotals before opening the Subtotals dialog box.
- The Subtotals button is located in the Outline group of the Data tab.
- Excel adds a subtotal automatically at each change in content for the column you specify as the subtotal field. A grand total is also automatically added to the bottom of the range.
- You can display more than one subtotal row for a group to calculate multiple functions such as Sum and Average.
- A subtotaled range is outlined and detail records can be collapsed or expanded using level number, Hide Detail, and Show Detail buttons.
- Use the Group and Ungroup buttons when a worksheet is outlined to manage the display of individual groups.

Commands Review

FEATURE	RIBBON TAB, GROUP	BUTTON	KEYBOARD SHORTCUT
Convert Text to Columns	Data, Data Tools		
Convert to Range	Table Tools Design, Tools		
Create Table	Insert, Tables		Ctrl + T
Data Validation	Data, Data Tools		
Group Data	Data, Outline		Shift + Alt + Right arrow key
Remove Duplicates	Data, Data Tools OR Table Tools Design, Tools		
Table Styles	Table Tools Design, Table Styles		
Sort & Filter table	Home, Editing		
Subtotals	Data, Outline		
...ions			Ctrl + Shift + T
			Shift + Alt + Left arrow key

Chapter 3 ■ Working with Tables and Data Features 95

Concepts Check Test Your Knowledge

Completion: In the space provided at the right, indicate the correct term, command, or number.

1. The first row of a table that contains the column headings is called the field names row or this row.

2. Typing a formula in the first row of a column in a table causes Excel to define the field as this type of column.

3. This is the term that describes the formatting feature in a table in which even rows are formatted differently than odd rows.

4. Change the visual appearance of a table using this gallery in the Table Tools Design tab.

5. Clicking this button causes the Convert Text to Columns wizard to appear.

6. Open this dialog box to instruct Excel to compare the entries in the columns you specify and automatically delete rows that contain repeated data.

7. Open this dialog box to restrict entries in a cell to those that you set up in a drop-down list.

8. This option in the *Allow* list box is used to force data entered into a cell to be a specific number of characters.

9. This is the default error alert style that prevents invalid data from being entered into a cell.

10. The Convert to Range button is found in this tab.

11. Prior to creating subtotals using the Subtotal button in the Outline group of the Data tab, arrange the data in this order.

12. In a worksheet with subtotal rows only displayed, click this button next to a subtotal row in order to view the grouped rows.

13. Click this button in an outlined worksheet to collapse the rows for a group.

14. In an outlined worksheet, this button collapses all records and displays only the Grand Total row.

15. Clicking this button in an outlined worksheet will cause the Hide Detail button for the selected rows to be removed.

96 Excel Level 2 ■ Unit 1

CHAPTER SUMMARY captures the purpose and execution of key features.

COMMANDS REVIEW summarizes visually the major features and alternative methods of access.

CONCEPTS CHECK questions assess knowledge recall.

Skills Check — Assess Your Performance

Assessment 1: CREATE AND FORMAT A TABLE

1. Open **VantageClassics.xlsx**.
2. Save the workbook with Save As and name it **EL2-C3-A1-VantageClassics**.
3. Select A4:L30 and create a table using *Table Style Medium 12* (fifth option in second row in *Medium* section).
4. Add a calculated column to the table in column M. Type the label Total Cost as the column hea... the number of co...
5. Adjust the three r... through M.
6. Adjust all column...
7. Band the columns... table.
8. Add a Total row t... number of copies...
9. Format the average... decimals.
10. The video *Blue Ha...* would like to rem... the record with St...
11. Format the *Total C...*
12. Save, print, and th...

Assessment 2: USE DATA TOOLS

1. Open **EL2-C3-A1...**
2. Save the workboo...
3. Remove the band...
4. Insert a new blank...
5. Split the director... Director FName...
6. Use the Remove D... using *Title* as the...
7. Create the followi...
   a. Create a validat... are seven chara... the user that st... title and messag...
   b. The manager w... of any individu... restricts entries... appropriate inp...

SKILLS CHECK exercises ask students to create a variety of documents using multiple features without how-to directions.

Visual Benchmark — Demonstrate Your Proficiency

FORMAT A BILLING SUMMARY

1. Open **BillingsOct8to12.xlsx**.
2. Save the workbook with Save As and name it **EL2-C1-VB-BillingsOct8to12**.
3. Format the worksheet to match the one shown in Figure 1.9 using the following information:
   - The data in the *Billing Code* column is custom formatted to add the text *Amicus#-* in front of the code number in blue font color.
   - Icon sets are used in the *Attorney Code* column and the same icon set should be applied in the Attorney Code Table section of the worksheet.
   - The Data bars added to the values in the *Legal Fees* column have been edited to change the bar appearance to *Turquoise, Accent 3* gradient fill. **Hint: Select More Rules in the Data Bars side menu.**
   - Values below 1500.00 in the *Total Due* column have been conditionally formatted and then the worksheet is sorted by the font color used for the conditional format.
4. Save, print, then close **EL2-C1-VB-BillingsOct8to12.xlsx**.

Figure 1.9 Visual Benchmark

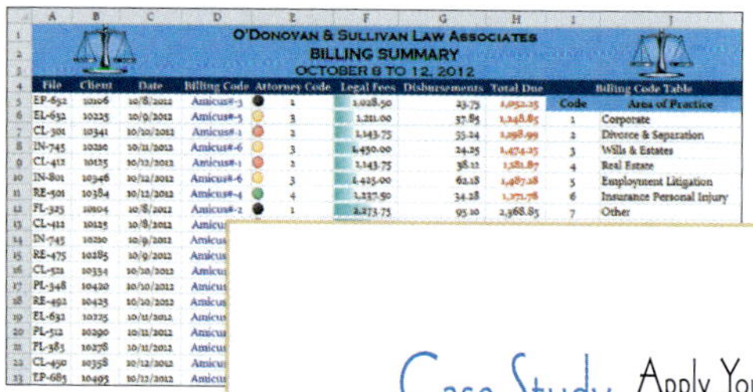

VISUAL BENCHMARK assessments test students' problem-solving skills and mastery of program features.

Case Study — Apply Your Skills

Part 1
Yolanda Robertson of NuTrends Market Research is continuing to work on the franchise expansion plan for the owners of Pizza By Mario. Yolanda has received a new workbook from the owners with profit information by store. Yolanda would like the data summarized. Open the workbook named **PizzaByMarioSales&Profits.xlsx** and review the structure of the data. Yolanda would like a PivotTable report that provides the average gross sales and the average net income by city by state. You determine how to organize the layout of the report. *Hint: You can add more than one numeric field to the Values list box.* Remove the grand totals at the right of the report so that a grand total row appears only at the bottom of the PivotTable. *Hint: Use the Grand Totals button in the Layout group of the PivotTable Tools Design tab.* Apply formatting options to improve the report's appearance and make sure the report prints on one page in landscape orientation. Rename the worksheet containing the report *PivotTable*. Save the revised workbook and name it **EL2-C4-CS-P1-PizzaByMarioRpt**.

Part 2
Yolanda would like a chart that graphs the average net income data for the state of Michigan only. Create a PivotChart in a new sheet named *PivotChart* and filter the chart appropriately to meet Yolanda's request. You determine an appropriate chart style and elements to include in the chart. Yolanda will be using this chart at an upcoming meeting with the franchise owners and wants the chart to be of professional quality. Print the chart. Save the revised workbook and name it **EL2-C4-CS-P2-PizzaByMarioRpt** and then close the workbook.

Part 3
Open **EL2-C4-CS-P1-PizzaByMarioRpt.xlsx**. Use the Help feature to find out how to modify a numeric field setting to show values as ranked numbers from largest to smallest. For example, instead of seeing the average value next to a city, you will see the city's ranking as it compares to other cities in the same state. Ranking from largest to smallest means the highest value in the state is ranked as 1. Using the information you learned in Help, change the display of the average sales to show the values ranked from largest to smallest using *City* as the base field. Remove the *Net Income* field from the PivotTable. Remove the grand total row at the bottom of the PivotTable. Make any other formatting changes to the report you think will improve the appearance. Print the PivotTable. Save the revised workbook and name it **EL2-C4-CS-P3-PizzaByMarioRpt**.

Part 4
Yolanda would like you to do some comparison research of another pizza franchise. Use the Internet to research the sales and net income information of a pizza franchise with which you are familiar. Create a new workbook that compares the total annual sales and net income values of the pizza franchise you researched with the Pizza By Mario information in **EL2-C4-CS-P1-PizzaByMarioRpt.xlsx**. Provide the URL of the website from which you obtained the competitive data. Create a chart that visually presents the comparison data. Save the workbook and name it **EL2-C4-CS-P4-PizzaFranchiseComparison**. Print the comparison data and the chart. Close **EL2-C4-CS-P4-PizzaFranchiseComparison.xlsx**.

CASE STUDY requires analyzing a workplace scenario and then planning and executing multipart projects.

Students search the Web and/or use the program's Help feature to locate additional information required to complete the Case Study.

UNIT PERFORMANCE ASSESSMENT: Cross-Disciplinary, Comprehensive Evaluation

 **Microsoft**

UNIT 2

Performance Assessment

ASSESSING PROFICIENCY checks mastery of features.

WRITING ACTIVITIES involve applying program skills in a communication context.

 Excel2010L2U2

Note: Before beginning unit assessments, copy to your storage medium the Excel2010L2U2 subfolder from the Excel2010L2 folder on the CD that accompanies this textbook and then make Excel2010L2U2 the active folder.

Assessing Proficiency

In this unit, you have learned to use features in Excel that facilitate performing what-if analysis, identifying relationships between worksheet formulas, collaborating with others by sharing and protecting workbooks, and automating repetitive tasks using macros. You also learned how to customize the Excel environment to suit your preferences and integrate Excel data by importing from and exporting to external resources. Finally, you learned how to prepare and distribute a workbook to others by removing items that are private or confidential, by marking the workbook as final, by checking for features incompatible with earlier versions of Excel, and by saving and sending a worksheet in various formats.

Assessment 1 Use Goal Seek and Scenario Manager to Calculate Investment Proposals

1. Open **HillsdaleInvtPlan.xlsx**.
2. Save the workbook with Save As and name it **EL2-U2-A1-HillsdaleInvtPlan**.
3. Use Goal Seek to find the monthly contribution amount the client must make in order to increase the projected value of the plan to $65,000 at the end of the term. Accept the solution Goal Seek calculates.
4. Assign the range name *AvgReturn* to E8.
5. Create three scenarios for changing E8 as follows:

Scenario name	Interest rate
Moderate	5.5%
Conservative	4.0%
Aggressive	12.5%

6. Apply the *Aggressive* scenario and then print the worksheet.
7. Edit the *Moderate* scenario's interest rate to 8.0% and then apply the scenario.
8. Create and then print a Scenario Summary report.
9. Save and then close **EL2-U2-A1-HillsdaleInvtPlan.xlsx**.

Writing Activities

The Writing, Internet Research, and Job Study activities give you the opportunity to practice your writing skills while demonstrating an understanding of some of the important Excel features you have mastered in this unit. Use appropriate word choices and correct grammar, capitalization, and punctuation when setting up new worksheets. Labels should clearly describe the data that is presented.

Create a Computer Maintenance Template
The Computing Services department of National Online Marketing Inc. wants to create a computer maintenance template for Help Desk employees to complete electronically and save to a document management server. This system will make it easy for a technician to check the status of any employee's computer from any location within the company. The Help Desk department performs the following computer maintenance tasks at each computer twice per year.

- Delete temporary Internet files
- Delete temporary document files that begin with a tilde (~)
- Update hardware drivers
- Reconfirm all serial numbers and asset records
- Have employee change password
- Check that automatic updates for the operating system is active
- Check that automatic updates for virus protection is active
- Confirm that automatic backup to the computing services server is active
- ...m that employee ... mail messages

Internet Research

Apply What-If Analysis to a Planned Move
Following graduation, you plan to move out of the state/province for a few years to gain experience living on your own. Create a new workbook to use as you plan this move to develop a budget for expenses in the first year. Research typical rents for apartments in the city in which you want to find your first job. Estimate other living costs in the city including transportation, food, entertainment, clothes, telephone, cable/satellite, cell phone, Internet, and so on. Calculate total living costs for an entire year. Next, research annual starting salaries for your chosen field of study in the same area. Estimate the take home pay at approximately 70% of the annual salary you decide to use. Using the take-home pay and the total living costs for the year, calculate if you will have money left over or have to borrow money to meet expenses.

Next, assume you want to save enough money to go on a vacation at the end of the year. Use Goal Seek to find the take-home pay you need to earn in order to have $2,000 left over at the end of the year. Accept the solution that Goal Seek provides and then create two scenarios in the worksheet as follows:

- A scenario named *LowestValues* in which you adjust each value down to the lowest amount you think is reasonable.
- A scenario named *HighestValues* in which you adjust each value up to the highest amount you think is reasonable.

Apply each scenario and watch the impact on the amount left over at the en... of the year. Display the worksheet in the *HighestValues* scenario and then create a scenario summary report. Print the worksheet applying print optio... as n... ...imize the pages re... ...he scenario summa...

INTERNET RESEARCH project reinforces research and word processing skills.

JOB STUDY at the end of Unit 2 presents a capstone assessment requiring critical thinking and problem solving.

Job Study

Prepare a Wages Budget and Link the Budget to a Word Document
You work at a small, independent, long-term care facility named Gardenview Place Long-Term Care. As assistant to the business manager, you are helping with the preparation of next year's hourly wages budget. Create a worksheet to estimate next year's hourly wages expense using the following information about hourly paid workers and the average wage costs in Table U2.1:

- The facility runs three 8-hour shifts, 7 days per week, 52 weeks per year.

  6 a.m. to 2 p.m.

  2 p.m. to 10 p.m.

  10 p.m. to 6 a.m.

- Each shift requires two registered nurses, four licensed practical nurses, and two health-care aid workers.
- At each shift, one of the registered nurses is designated as the charge nurse and is paid a premium of 15% of his or her regular hourly rate.
- The 6 a.m.-to-2 p.m. and 2 p.m.-to-10 p.m. shifts require one custodian; the 10 p.m.-to-6 a.m. shift requires two custodians.
- Each shift requires the services of an on-call physician and an on-call pharmacist. Budget for the physician and the pharmacist at 4 hours per shift.
- Add 14% to each shift's total wage costs to cover the estimated costs of benefits such as vacation pay, holiday pay, and medical care coverage plans for all workers *except* the on-call physician and on-call pharmacist...who do ...ive these benefi...

Student Courseware

Student Resources CD Each Benchmark Series textbook is packaged with a Student Resources CD containing the data files required for completing the projects and assessments. A CD icon and folder name displayed on the opening page of chapters reminds students to copy a folder of files from the CD to the desired storage medium before beginning the project exercises. Directions for copying folders are printed on the inside back cover.

Internet Resource Center Additional learning tools and reference materials are available at the book-specific website at www.emcp.net/BenchmarkExcel10. Students can access the same files that are on the Student Resources CD along with study aids, web links, and tips for using computers effectively in academic and workplace settings.

SNAP Training and Assessment SNAP is a web-based program offering an interactive venue for learning Microsoft Office 2010, Windows 7, and Internet Explorer 8.0. Along with a web-based learning management system, SNAP provides multimedia tutorials, performance skill items, document-based assessments, a concepts test bank, an online grade book, and a set of course planning tools. A CD of tutorials teaching the basics of Office, Windows, and Internet Explorer is also available if instructors wish to assign additional SNAP tutorial work without using the web-based SNAP program.

eBook For students who prefer studying with an eBook, the texts in the Benchmark Series are available in an electronic form. The web-based, password-protected eBooks feature dynamic navigation tools, including bookmarking, a linked table of contents, and the ability to jump to a specific page. The eBook format also supports helpful study tools, such as highlighting and note taking.

Instructor Resources

Instructor's Guide and Disc Instructor support for the Benchmark Series includes an *Instructor's Guide and Instructor Resources Disc* package. This resource includes planning information, such as Lesson Blueprints, teaching hints, and sample course syllabi; presentation resources, such as PowerPoint slide shows with lecture notes and audio support; and assessment resources, including an overview of available assessment venues, live model answers for chapter activities, and live and PDF model answers for end-of-chapter exercises. Contents of the *Instructor's Guide and Instructor Resources Disc* package are also available on the password-protected section of the Internet Resource Center for this title at www.emcp.net/BenchmarkExcel10.

Computerized Test Generator Instructors can use the EXAMVIEW® Assessment Suite and test banks of multiple-choice items to create customized web-based or print tests.

Blackboard Cartridge This set of files allows instructors to create a personalized Blackboard website for their course and provides course content, tests, and the mechanisms for establishing communication via e-discussions and online group conferences. Available content includes a syllabus, test banks, PowerPoint presentations with audio support, and supplementary course materials. Upon request, the files can be available within 24–48 hours. Hosting the site is the responsibility of the educational institution.

System Requirements

This text is designed for the student to complete projects and assessments on a computer running a standard installation of Microsoft Office 2010, Professional Edition, and the Microsoft Windows 7 operating system. To effectively run this suite and operating system, your computer should be outfitted with the following:

- 1 gigahertz (GHz) processor or higher; 1 gigabyte (GB) of RAM
- DVD drive
- 15 GB of available hard-disk space
- Computer mouse or compatible pointing device

Office 2010 will also operate on computers running the Windows XP Service Pack 3 or the Windows Vista operating system.

Screen captures in this book were created using a screen resolution display setting of 1280 × 800. Choose the resolution that best matches your computer; however, be aware that using a resolution other than 1280 × 800 means that your screens may not match the illustrations in this book.

About the Authors

Denise Seguin has been teaching at Fanshawe College in London, Ontario, since 1986. She has taught a variety of software applications to learners in postsecondary Information Technology diploma programs and in Continuing Education courses. In addition to co-authoring books in the *Benchmark Office 2010* series, she has authored *Microsoft Outlook 2010, 2007, 2003, 2002,* and *2000*. She has also co-authored *Our Digital World*; *Marquee Series: Microsoft Office 2010, 2007,* and *2003*; *Office 2003*; *Office XP*; and *Using Computers in the Medical Office 2007* and *2003* for Paradigm Publishing, Inc.

Microsoft® Excel

Level 2

Unit 1 ■ Advanced Formatting, Formulas, and Data Management

Advanced Formatting Techniques

PERFORMANCE OBJECTIVES

Upon successful completion of Chapter 1, you will be able to:

- Apply conditional formatting by entering parameters for a rule
- Apply conditional formatting using a predefined rule
- Create and apply a new rule for conditional formatting
- Edit, delete, and clear conditional formatting rules
- Apply conditional formatting using an icon set, data bars, and color scale
- Apply conditional formatting using a formula
- Apply fraction and scientific formatting
- Apply a special format for a number
- Create a custom number format
- Apply wrap text and shrink to fit text control options
- Filter a worksheet using a custom AutoFilter
- Filter and sort a worksheet using conditional formatting or cell attributes

Tutorials

1.1 Applying Conditional Formatting

1.2 Applying Conditional Formatting Using Icon Sets

1.3 Applying Conditional Formatting Using Data Bars and Color Scales

1.4 Applying Conditional Formatting Using a Formula

1.5 Using Fraction, Scientific, and Special Numbers Formatting

1.6 Creating a Custom Number Format

1.7 Wrapping and Shrinking Text to Fit within a Cell

1.8 Filtering a Worksheet Using a Custom AutoFilter

1.9 Filtering and Sorting Data Using Conditional Formatting and Cell Attributes

Although many worksheets can be formatted using buttons available in the Font, Alignment, and Number groups in the Home tab of the ribbon or in the Mini toolbar, some situations require format categories that are not represented with a button. In other worksheets you may want to make use of Excel's advanced formatting techniques to format based on a condition. In this chapter you will learn how to create, edit, and apply advanced formatting and filtering techniques. Model answers for this chapter's projects appear on the following pages.

Excel2010L2C1

Note: Before beginning the projects, copy to your storage medium the Excel2010L2C1 subfolder from the Excel2010L2 folder on the CD that accompanies this textbook and make Excel2010L2C1 the active folder. Steps on how to copy a folder are presented on the inside of the back cover of this textbook. Do this every time you start a chapter's projects.

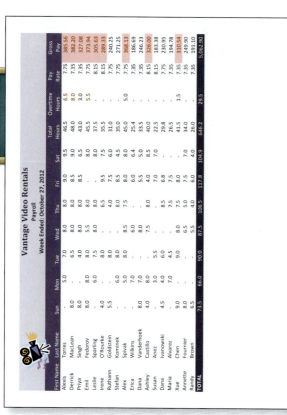

Project 1 Format Cells Based on Values
EL2-C1-P1-VantagePay-Oct27.xlsx

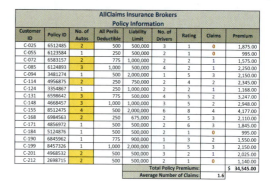

	AllClaims Insurance Brokers							
	Policy Information							
Customer ID	Policy ID	No. of Autos	All Perils Deductible	Liability Limit	No. of Drivers	Rating	Claims	Premium
C-025	6512485	2	500	500,000	3	1	0	1,875.00
C-055	6123584	1	250	500,000	2	1	0	995.00
C-072	6583157	2	775	1,000,000	2	2	1	1,575.00
C-085	6124893	3	1,000	500,000	4	2	1	2,250.00
C-094	3481274	1	500	2,000,000	1	5	3	2,150.00
C-114	4956875	2	250	750,000	2	4	2	2,345.00
C-124	3354867	1	250	1,000,000	2	2	1	1,168.00
C-131	6598642	3	775	500,000	4	5	2	3,247.00
C-148	4668457	3	1,000	1,000,000	3	5	2	2,948.00
C-155	8512475	4	500	2,000,000	6	8	4	4,177.00
C-168	6984563	2	250	675,000	2	5	3	2,110.00
C-171	4856972	1	500	500,000	2	6	3	1,845.00
C-184	5124876	1	500	500,000	2	1	0	995.00
C-190	6845962	1	775	900,000	1	3	2	1,550.00
C-199	8457326	1	1,000	2,000,000	1	5	3	2,150.00
C-201	4968532	2	500	500,000	3	2	1	2,025.00
C-212	2698715	2	500	500,000	2	1	0	1,140.00
						Total Policy Premiums:		$ 34,545.00
						Average Number of Claims:		1.6

Project 2 Apply Conditional Formatting to Insurance Policy Data
EL2-C1-P2-AllClaimsInsce-Autos2+.xlsx

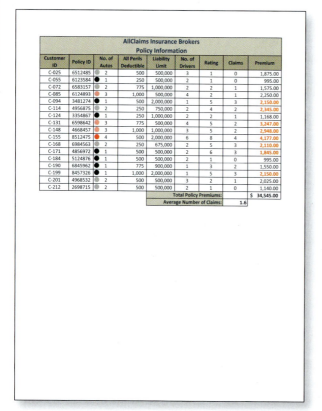

EL2-C1-P2-AllClaimsInsce.xlsx

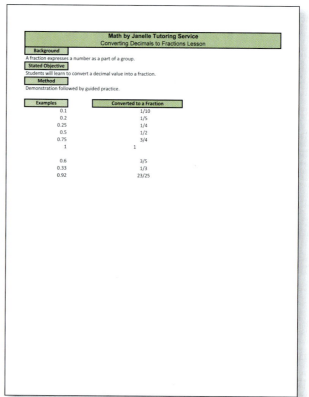

Project 3 Use Fraction and Scientific Formatting Options
EL2-C1-P3-JanelleTutorMathLsn.xlsx

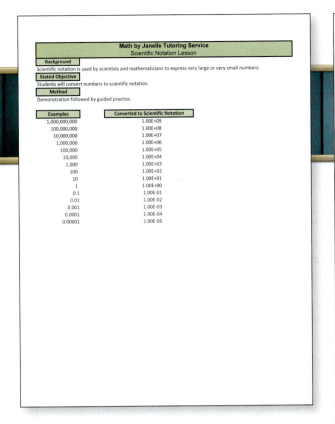

Math by Janelle Tutoring Service
Scientific Notation Lesson

Background
Scientific notation is used by scientists and mathematicians to express very large or very small numbers.

Stated Objective
Students will convert numbers to scientific notation.

Method
Demonstration followed by guided practice.

Examples	Converted to Scientific Notation
1,000,000,000	1.00E+09
100,000,000	1.00E+08
10,000,000	1.00E+07
1,000,000	1.00E+06
100,000	1.00E+05
10,000	1.00E+04
1,000	1.00E+03
100	1.00E+02
10	1.00E+01
1	1.00E+00
0.1	1.00E-01
0.01	1.00E-02
0.001	1.00E-03
0.0001	1.00E-04
0.00001	1.00E-05

EL2-C1-P3-JanelleTutorMathLsn.xlsx

Project 4 Apply Advanced Formatting Options

Precision Design and Packaging
Bulk Container Products
Custom imprinting available for all models

Model Number	Description	Dimensions L x W x D in inches	Test Weight in pounds	Recommended Weight in pounds
PD-1140	Gaylord with lid	48 x 40 x 36	200 lbs	100 lbs
PD-2185	Premium Gaylord with lid	48 x 40 x 36	200 lbs	125 lbs
PD-3695	Telescoping top and bottom	46 x 38 x 36	200 lbs	70 lbs
PD-4415	"EO" container	30 x 17 x 17	350 lbs	150 lbs
PD-5367	"EH" container	36 x 22 x 22	275 lbs	250 lbs
PD-6418	"E" container	40 x 28 x 24	275 lbs	500 lbs
PD-7459	Economy R.S.C.	36 x 36 x 36	200 lbs	65 lbs
PD-8854	Premium R.S.C.	36 x 36 x 36	200 lbs	100 lbs

Regional Sales Representatives		
North	Jordan Lavoie	(800) 555-3429
South	Pat Gallagher	(800) 555-3439
East	Alonso Rodriguez	(800) 555-3449
West	Karsten Das	(800) 555-3459
Canada	Kelli Olsen	(800) 555-3469
International	Bianca Santini	(800) 555-3479

Minimum order quantity of 25 applies.
Preferred carriers are UPS and DHL.

EL2-C1-P4-PrecisionProducts.xlsx

AllClaims Insurance Brokers
Policy Information

Customer ID	Policy ID	No. of Autos	All Perils Deductible	Liability Limit	No. of Drivers	Rating	Claims	Premium
C-114	4956875	2	250	750,000	2	4	2	2,345.00
C-131	6598642	3	775	500,000	4	5	2	3,247.00
C-148	4668457	3	1,000	1,000,000	3	5	2	2,948.00
C-168	6984563	2	250	675,000	2	5	3	2,110.00
C-171	4856972	1	500	500,000	2	6	3	1,845.00
C-190	6845962	1	775	900,000	1	3	2	1,550.00

Project 5 Filter and Sort Data Based on Values, Icon Set, and Font Color

EL2-C1-P5-AllClaimsInsce.xlsx

AllClaims Insurance Brokers
Policy Information

Customer ID	Policy ID	No. of Autos	All Perils Deductible	Liability Limit	No. of Drivers	Rating	Claims	Premium
C-055	6123584	1	250	500,000	2	1	0	995.00
C-094	3481274	1	500	2,000,000	1	5	3	2,150.00
C-124	3354867	1	250	1,000,000	2	2	1	1,168.00
C-171	4856972	1	500	500,000	2	6	3	1,845.00
C-184	5124876	1	500	500,000	2	1	0	995.00
C-190	6845962	1	775	900,000	1	3	2	1,550.00
C-199	8457326	1	1,000	2,000,000	1	5	3	2,150.00

EL2-C1-P5-AllClaimsInsce-1Auto.xlsx

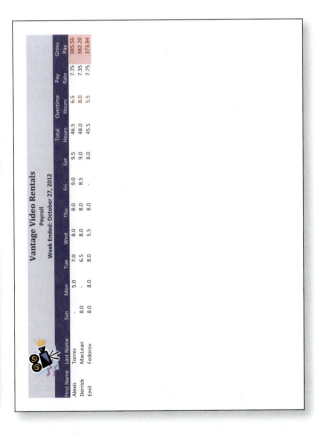

Vantage Video Rentals
Payroll
Week Ended: October 27, 2012

First Name	Last Name	Sun	Mon	Tue	Wed	Thu	Fri	Sat	Total Hours	Overtime Hours	Pay Rate	Gross Pay
Alexis	Torres	-	5.0	7.0	8.0	8.0	9.0	9.5	46.5	6.5	7.75	385.56
Derrick	MacLean	8.0	-	6.5	8.0	8.0	8.5	9.0	48.0	8.0	7.35	382.20
Emil	Fedorov	8.0	8.0	8.0	5.5	8.0	-	8.0	45.5	5.5	7.75	373.94

EL2-C1-P5-VantagePay-Oct27-HighOT.xlsx

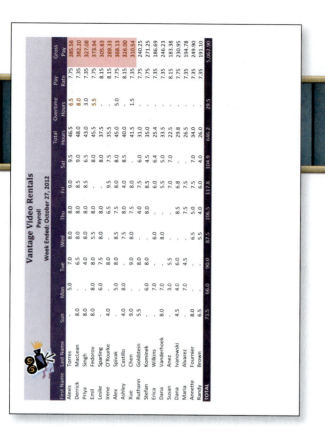

EL2-C1-P5-VantagePay-Oct27-Sorted.xlsx

Project 1 — Format Cells Based on Values

2 Parts

Working with a payroll worksheet, you will change the appearance of cells based on criteria related to overtime hours and gross pay.

Conditional
Formatting

Conditional Formatting

Conditional formatting applies format changes to a range of cells for those cells within the selection that meet a condition. Cells that do not meet the condition remain unformatted. Changing the appearance of a cell based on a condition allows you to quickly identify values that are high, low, or that represent a trend. Formatting can be applied based on a specific value, a value that falls within a range, or by using a comparison operator such as equals (=), greater than (>), or less than (<). Conditional formats can also be based on date, text entries, or duplicated values. Consider using conditional formatting to analyze a question such as *Which store locations earned sales above their target?* Using a different color and/or shading the cells that exceeded a sales target easily identifies the top performers. Excel 2010 provides predefined conditional formatting rules accessed from the Conditional Formatting button drop-down list shown in Figure 1.1. You can also create your own conditional formatting rules.

Figure 1.1 Conditional Formatting Button Drop-down List

Project 1a **Formatting Cells Based on a Value Comparison**

1. Start Excel.
2. Open **VantagePay-Oct27.xlsx**. (This workbook is located in the Excel2010L2C1 folder you copied to your storage medium.)
3. Save the workbook with Save As and name it **EL2-C1-P1-VantagePay-Oct27**.
4. Apply conditional formatting to highlight overtime hours that exceeded 5 for the week by completing the following steps:
   a. Select K6:K23.
   b. Click the Conditional Formatting button in the Styles group of the Home tab.
   c. Point to *Highlight Cells Rules* and then click *Greater Than* at the drop-down list.
   d. At the Greater Than dialog box, with the text already selected in the *Format cells that are GREATER THAN* text box, type 5.
   e. Click the down-pointing arrow next to the list box to the right of *with* (currently displays *Light Red Fill with Dark Red Text*) and then click *Red Text* at the drop-down list.

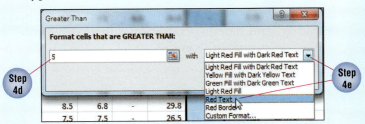

   f. Click OK to close the Greater Than dialog box and apply the conditional format.
   g. Click in any cell to deselect the range.
   h. Review the cells that have been conditionally formatted. Notice that cells with overtime hours greater than 5 are formatted with red text.
5. Save **EL2-C1-P1-VantagePay-Oct27.xlsx**.

Using the Top/Bottom Rules list you can elect to highlight cells based on a top ten or bottom ten value or percent, or by above average or below average values.

1. With **EL2-C1-P1-VantagePay-Oct27.xlsx** open, apply conditional formatting to the Gross Pay values to identify employees who earned above average wages for the week by completing the following steps:

   a. Select M6:M23.

   b. Click the Conditional Formatting button in the Styles group of the Home tab.

   c. Point to *Top/Bottom Rules* and then click *Above Average* at the drop-down list.

   d. At the Above Average dialog box, with *Light Red Fill with Dark Red Text* selected in the *Format cells that are ABOVE AVERAGE* list box, click OK.

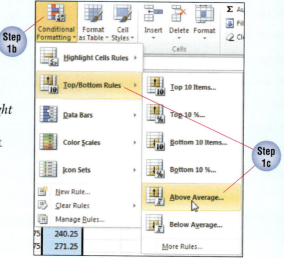

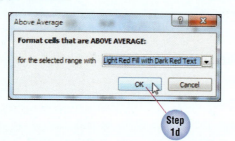

   e. Click in any cell to deselect the range.

   f. Review the cells that have been conditionally formatted.

2. Print the worksheet.

3. Save and then close **EL2-C1-P1-VantagePay-Oct27.xlsx**.

Project 2 **Apply Conditional Formatting to Insurance Policy Data** **4 Parts**

In an insurance claims worksheet you will format cells by creating, editing, clearing, and deleting conditional formatting rules and by classifying data into categories using an icon set.

Creating a New Formatting Rule

You can create a rule to format cells based on cell values, specific text, dates, blank, or error values.

Cells are conditionally formatted based on a rule. A rule defines the criterion by which the cell is selected for formatting and includes the formatting attributes that are applied to cells that meet the criterion. The predefined rules that you used in Project 1a and Project 1b allowed you to use the feature without having to specify each component in the rule's parameters. At the New Formatting Rule dialog box shown in Figure 1.2, you can create your own custom conditional formatting rule in which you define all parts of the criterion and the formatting. The *Edit the Rule Description* section of the dialog box varies depending on the active option in the *Select a Rule Type* section.

Figure 1.2 New Formatting Rule Dialog Box

Begin creating a new rule by choosing the type of condition you want Excel to check before formating

This section varies depending on the option selected in the *Select a Rule Type* section.

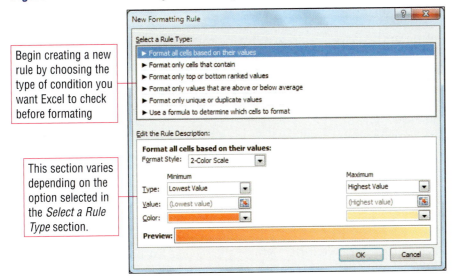

▼ **Quick Steps**

Create and Apply New Formatting Rule
1. Select desired range.
2. Click Conditional Formatting button.
3. Click *New Rule*.
4. Click desired rule type.
5. Add criteria as required.
6. Click Format button.
7. Select desired formatting attributes.
8. Click OK to close Format Cells dialog box.
9. Click OK to close New Formatting Rule dialog box.

Project 2a   **Creating and Applying New Formatting Rules**   Part 1 of 4

1. Open **AllClaimsInsce.xlsx**.
2. Save the workbook with Save As and name it **EL2-C1-P2-AllClaimsInsce**.
3. The owner of AllClaims Insurance Brokers is considering changing the discount plan for those customers with no claims or with only one claim. The owner would like to see the two claim criteria formatted in color to provide a reference for how many customers this discount would affect. Create a formatting rule that will change the appearance of cells in the claims columns for those values that equal 0 by completing the following steps:
   a. Select H4:H20.
   b. Click the Conditional Formatting button in the Styles group in the Home tab.
   c. Click *New Rule* at the drop-down list.
   d. At the New Formatting Rule dialog box, click *Format only cells that contain* in the *Select a Rule Type* section.
   e. Click the down-pointing arrow located at the right of the second list box from the left in the *Format only cells with* section (currently displays *between*) and then click *equal to* at the drop-down list.

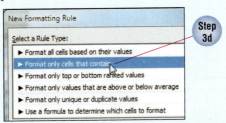

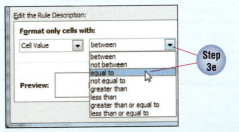

f. Click in the blank text box next to *equal to* and then type **0**.

g. Click the Format button in the *Preview* section.

h. At the Format Cells dialog box with the Font tab selected, change the *Color* to *Dark Red* (in the *Standard Colors* section), turn on bold, and then click OK.

i. Click OK at the New Formatting Rule dialog box.

4. Create a second formatting rule that will change the appearance of cells in the claims columns for those values that equal 1 by completing the following steps:

a. With H4:H20 still selected, click the Conditional Formatting button and then click *New Rule*.

b. At the New Formatting Rule dialog box, click *Format only cells that contain* in the *Select a Rule Type* section.

c. Click the down-pointing arrow located at the right of the second list box from the left in the *Format only cells with* section (currently displays *between*) and then click *equal to* at the drop-down list.

d. Click in the blank text box next to *equal to* and then type **1**.

e. Click the Format button.

f. At the Format Cells dialog box with the Font tab selected, change the *Color to Purple* (in the *Standard Colors* section), turn on bold, and then click OK.

g. Click OK at the New Formatting Rule dialog box.

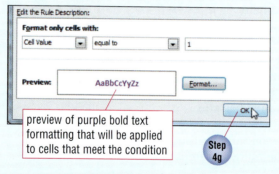

preview of purple bold text formatting that will be applied to cells that meet the condition

Step 4g

Rating	Claims
1	0
1	0
2	1
2	1
5	3
4	2
2	1
5	2
5	2
8	4
5	3
6	3
1	0
3	2
5	3
2	1
1	0

dark red bold formatting applied to cells containing 0 and purple bold formatting applied to cells containing 1

5. Click in any cell to deselect the range and review the conditionally formatted cells in column H.

6. Save **EL2-C1-P2-AllClaimsInsce.xlsx**.

▼ **Quick Steps**

Edit Formatting Rule

1. Select range.
2. Click Conditional Formatting button.
3. Click *Manage Rules.*
4. Click desired rule.
5. Click Edit Rule button.
6. Make desired changes to parameters and/or formatting options.
7. Click OK twice.

Editing and Deleting Conditional Formatting Rules

Edit the comparison rule criteria and/or formatting options for a conditional formatting rule by opening the Conditional Formatting Rules Manager dialog box. Click to select the rule that you want to change and then click the Edit Rule button. At the Edit Formatting Rule dialog box, make the desired changes and then click OK twice. By default, *Show formatting rules for* is set to *Current Selection* when you open the Conditional Formatting Rules Manager. If necessary, click the down-pointing arrow to the right of the list box and select *This Worksheet* to show all formatting rules in the current sheet.

To remove conditional formatting from a range, select the range, click the Conditional Formatting button, point to *Clear Rules* at the drop-down list, and then click either *Clear Rules from Selected Cells* or *Clear Rules from Entire Sheet*. You can also delete a custom rule at the Conditional Formatting Rules Manager dialog box. Formatting options applied to the cells by the rule that was deleted are removed.

▼ **Quick Steps**

Delete Formatting Rule
1. Click Conditional Formatting button.
2. Click *Manage Rules*.
3. Change *Show formatting rules for* to *This Worksheet*.
4. Click desired rule.
5. Click Delete Rule button.
6. Click OK.

Project 2b **Creating, Editing, and Deleting a Formatting Rule**

1. With **EL2-C1-P2-AllClaimsInsce.xlsx** open, create a new formatting rule to add a fill color to the cells in the *No. of Autos* column for those policies that have more than two cars by completing the following steps:
   a. Select C4:C20.
   b. Click the Conditional Formatting button and then click *New Rule* at the drop-down list.
   c. Click *Format only cells that contain* in the *Select a Rule Type* section of the New Formatting Rule dialog box.
   d. In the *Edit the Rule Description* section, change the rule's parameters to format only cells with a *Cell Value greater than 2*. (If necessary, refer to Project 2a, Steps 3e to 3f for assistance.)
   e. Click the Format button and then click the Fill tab at the Format Cells dialog box.
   f. Click the *Yellow* color square (fourth from left in last row) in the *Background Color* palette and then click OK.
   g. Click OK to close the New Formatting Rule dialog box and apply the rule to the selected cells.
   h. Deselect the range by clicking any cell.
2. After reviewing the formatted cells, you decide that cells should be formatted for all policies with 2 or more cars. Edit the formatting rule by completing the following steps:
   a. Select C4:C20.
   b. Click the Conditional Formatting button and then click *Manage Rules* at the drop-down list.

Customer ID	Policy ID	No. of Autos
C-025	6512485	2
C-055	6123584	1
C-072	6583157	2
C-085	6124893	3
C-094	3481274	1
C-114	4956875	2
C-124	3354867	1
C-131	6598642	3
C-148	4668457	3
C-155	8512475	4
C-168	6984563	2
C-171	4856972	1
C-184	5124876	1
C-190	6845962	1
C-199	8457326	1
C-201	4968532	2
C-212	2698715	2

formatting applied to cell values greater than 2

c. Click to select *Cell Value > 2* in the Conditional Formatting Rules Manager dialog box and then click the Edit Rule button.

d. Click the down-pointing arrow next to the second list box (currently displays *greater than*) and then click *greater than or equal to* at the drop-down list.

e. Click OK.

f. Click OK to close the Conditional Formatting Rules Manager dialog box and apply the revised rule to the selected cells.

g. Deselect the range by clicking any cell.

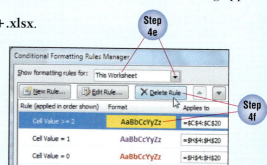

3. Save and print the worksheet.

4. After reviewing the printed copy of the formatted worksheet, you decide to experiment with another method of formatting the data that classifies the policies by the number of cars. You will do this in the next project. In preparation for the next project, save the revised worksheet under a new name and then delete the formatting rule in the original worksheet by completing the following steps:

a. Use Save As to name the workbook **EL2-C1-P2-AllClaimsInsce-Autos2+**. By saving the workbook under a new name you will have a copy of the conditional formatting applied in this project.

b. Close **EL2-C1-P2-AllClaimsInsce-Autos2+.xlsx**.

c. Open **EL2-C1-P2-AllClaimsInsce.xlsx**.

d. Click the Conditional Formatting button and then click *Manage Rules* at the drop-down list.

e. Click the down-pointing arrow next to the *Show formatting rules for* list box and then click *This Worksheet*.

f. Click to select *Cell Value >= 2* and then click the Delete Rule button.

g. Click OK to close the Conditional Formatting Rules Manager dialog box. Notice the formatting has been removed from the cells in column C.

5. Save **EL2-C1-P2-AllClaimsInsce.xlsx**.

Conditional Formatting Using Icon Sets

▼ Quick Steps

Apply Conditional Formatting Using Icon Set
1. Select desired range.
2. Click Conditional Formatting button.
3. Point to *Icon Sets*.
4. Click desired icon set.
5. Deselect range.

Format a range of values using an icon set to classify data into three to five categories. Excel places an icon in a cell to visually portray the cell's value relative to the other cell values within the selected range. Using an icon set, you can group similar data to easily spot high points, low points, or other trends. Icons are assigned to cells based on default threshold values for the selected range. For example, if you choose the *3 Arrows (Colored)* icon set, icons are assigned as follows:

• Green up arrow for values greater than or equal to 67 percent

• Red down arrow for values less than 33 percent

• Yellow sideways arrow for values between 33 and 67 percent

The available icon sets are shown in Figure 1.3 grouped into four sections: *Directional*, *Shapes*, *Indicators*, and *Ratings*. Choose the icon set that best represents the number of different categories within the range and the desired symbol type such as directional colored arrows, traffic light shapes, flag indicators, star ratings, and so on. You can modify the default threshold values or create your own icon set by opening the Manage Rules dialog box and editing an existing rule or creating a new rule.

Green Up Arrow

Red Down Arrow

Yellow Sideways Arrow

Figure 1.3 Conditional Formatting Icon Sets Gallery

| Project 2c | Applying Conditional Formatting Using an Icon Set | Part 3 of 4 |

1. With **EL2-C1-P2-AllClaimsInsce.xlsx** open, select C4:C20.
2. Classify the number of automobiles into categories using an icon set by completing the following steps:
   a. Click the Conditional Formatting button.
   b. Point to *Icon Sets*.
   c. Click *Red To Black* at the Icon Sets drop-down gallery (third icon set in the left column of the Shapes section).
   d. Click in any cell to deselect the range. Notice that Excel assigns an icon to each cell that correlates to the icon with the value group. For example, all cells containing the value 1 have the same icon, all cells containing the value 2 have the same icon, and so on.

3. Save **EL2-C1-P2-AllClaimsInsce.xlsx**.

Conditional Formatting Using Data Bars and Color Scales

Be careful not to overdo icon sets, color scales, and data bars. A reader can quickly lose focus with too many items competing for one's attention.

Excel 2010 also provides the ability to conditionally format cells using two-color scales, three-color scales, or data bars to provide visual guides to identify distributions or variations within a range. Use a data bar to easily see the higher and lower values within the range. A bar is added to the background of the cell with the length of the bar dependent on the value within the cell. A cell with a higher value within the range displays a longer bar than a cell with a lower value within the range. Excel offers six colors for bars, available in either a gradient fill or a solid fill.

Color scales format the range using either a two-color or three-color palette. Excel provides 12 color scale options, half of which are two-color combinations and half of which are three-color combinations. The gradation of color applied to a cell illustrates the cell's value in comparison to higher or lower values within the range. Color scales are useful to view the distribution of the data. In a two-color scale, the shade applied to a cell represents either a higher or lower value within the range. In a three-color scale, the shade of color applied to a cell represents a higher, middle, or lower value within the range. Figure 1.4 displays the payroll worksheet for Vantage Video Rentals with data bar and color scale conditional formatting applied. In column M, gross pay is shown with the Red Data Bar from the *Gradient Fill* section applied to the column. Notice the length of the colored bars in the background of the cells for various gross pay amounts. In column J, the *Red-White* two-color scale has been applied to show the distribution of total hours. Cells with higher values are displayed in gradations of red, while the lowest cell in the range is displayed in white and then white is mixed with red to achieve increasingly darker shades of pink in cells as the values increase.

Figure 1.4 Data Bar and Color Scale Conditional Formatting Applied to Payroll Worksheet

First Name	Last Name	Sun	Mon	Tue	Wed	Thu	Fri	Sat	Total Hours	Overtime Hours	Pay Rate	Gross Pay
Alexis	Torres	-	5.0	7.0	8.0	8.0	9.0	9.5	46.5	6.5	7.75	385.56
Derrick	MacLean	8.0	-	6.5	8.0	8.0	8.5	9.0	48.0	8.0	7.35	382.20
Priya	Singh	8.0	-	4.0	8.0	8.0	8.5	6.5	43.0	3.0	7.35	327.08
Emil	Fedorov	8.0	8.0	8.0	5.5	8.0	-	8.0	45.5	5.5	7.75	373.94
Leslie	Sparling	-	6.0	7.5	8.0	8.0	-	8.0	37.5	-	8.15	305.63
Irene	O'Rourke	4.0	-	8.0	-	6.5	9.5	7.5	35.5	-	8.15	289.33
Ruthann	Goldstein	5.5	-	8.0	-	4.0	7.5	6.0	31.0	-	7.75	240.25
Stefan	Kominek	-	6.0	8.0	-	8.0	8.5	4.5	35.0	-	7.75	271.25
Alex	Spivak	-	5.0	8.0	8.5	7.5	8.0	8.0	45.0	5.0	7.75	368.13
Erica	Wilkins	-	7.0	-	6.0	-	6.0	6.4	25.4	-	7.35	186.69
Dana	Vanderhoek	8.0	7.0	-	8.0	-	5.5	5.0	33.5	-	7.35	246.23
Ashley	Castillo	4.0	8.0	-	7.5	8.0	4.0	8.5	40.0	-	8.15	326.00
Susan	Anez	-	3.0	5.5	-	-	7.0	7.0	22.5	-	8.15	183.38
Dana	Ivanowski	4.5	4.0	6.0	-	8.5	6.8	-	29.8	-	7.75	230.95
Maria	Alvarez	-	7.0	4.5	-	7.5	7.5	-	26.5	-	7.35	194.78
Xue	Chen	9.0	-	9.0	8.0	7.5	8.0	-	41.5	1.5	7.35	310.54
Annette	Fournier	8.0	-	-	6.5	5.0	7.5	7.0	34.0	-	7.35	249.90
Randy	Brown	6.5	-	-	5.5	4.0	6.0	4.0	26.0	-	7.35	191.10
TOTAL		73.5	66.0	90.0	87.5	106.5	117.8	104.9	646.2	29.5		5,062.90

Vantage Video Rentals
Payroll
Week Ended: October 27, 2012

Gross Pay column with data bar conditional formatting applied

Total Hours column with *Red-White* color scale conditional formatting applied

Conditional Formatting Using a Formula

Sometimes you may want to format a cell based upon the value in another cell or by some other logical test. At the New Formatting Rule dialog box, choose *Use a formula to determine which cells to format* in the *Select a Rule Type* section. You can enter a formula, such as an IF statement, that is used to determine if a cell is formatted. For example, in Project 2d, you will format the premium values in the insurance worksheet in column I based on the rating value for each policy that is stored in column G. In this project, an IF statement allows you to conditionally format the premiums if the rating value for the policy is greater than 3. The IF function's logical test returns only a true or false result. The value in the rating cell is either greater than 3 (true), or it is not greater than 3 (false). Excel conditionally formats only those cells for which the conditional test returns a true result.

The formula that you will enter into the New Formatting Rule dialog box in Project 2d is: *=if(g4:g20>3,true,false)*. In the first cell in the selected range (I4), Excel will perform the following test: *is the value in G4 greater than 3?* In the first row, this test returns a false result so Excel will not conditionally format the value in I4. For those cells in which the test returns a true result, Excel will apply bold red font color to the cell.

<table>
<tr><td>Project 2d</td><td>**Applying Conditional Formatting Using a Formula**</td><td>Part 4 of 4</td></tr>
</table>

1. With **EL2-C1-P2-AllClaimsInsce.xlsx** open, clear the conditional formatting applied in the *Claims* column by completing the following steps:
   a. Select H4:H20.
   b. Click the Conditional Formatting button, point to *Clear Rules*, and then click *Clear Rules from Selected Cells*.
   c. Click in any cell to deselect the range.

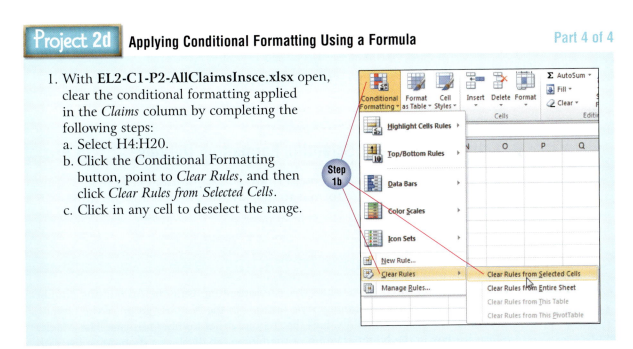

Step 1b

2. The owner of AllClaims Insurance Brokers would like the premiums for those clients who have a rating higher than 3 to stand out from the other cells. You decide to conditionally format the premiums using a formula that checks the value in the rating column by completing the following steps:

   a. Select I4:I20 and then click the Conditional Formatting button.

   b. Click *New Rule* at the drop-down list.

   c. At the New Formatting Rule dialog box, click *Use a formula to determine which cells to format* in the *Select a Rule Type* section.

   d. Click in the *Format values where this formula is true* text box in the *Edit the Rule Description* section of the New Formatting Rule dialog box and then type **=if(g4:g20>3,true,false)**.

   e. Click the Format button.

   f. At the Format Cells dialog box, click the Font tab and change the font color to *Red* (in the *Standard Colors* section), apply bold, and then click OK.

   g. Click OK to close the New Formatting Rule dialog box and apply the rule to the selected cells.

   h. Click in any cell to deselect the range. Notice that the cells that have bold red font color applied in column I are those for which the corresponding rating value in column G is greater than 3.

3. Save, print, and then close **EL2-C1-P2-AllClaimsInsce.xlsx**.

New Formatting Rule dialog box callouts:
Step 2c · Step 2d · Steps 2e-2f · Step 2g

Project 3 — Use Fraction and Scientific Formatting Options   1 Part

Using two lesson plan worksheets for a math tutor, you will format cells in a solution column to the appropriate format to display the answers for the tutor.

Fraction and Scientific Formatting

▼ Quick Steps

Apply Fraction Formatting
1. Select desired range.
2. Click *Number Format* list arrow.
3. Click *More Number Formats*.
4. Click *Fraction* in *Category* list box.
5. Click desired option in *Type* list box.
6. Click OK.
7. Deselect range.

While most worksheets have values that are formatted using the Accounting Number Format, Percent Style, or Comma Style buttons in the Number group of the Home tab, some worksheets contain values that require other number formats. The *Number Format* list box in the Number group of the Home tab displays a drop-down list with additional format options including date, time, fraction, scientific, and text options. Click *More Number Formats* at the Number Format drop-down list to open the Format Cells dialog box with the Number tab selected shown in Figure 1.5. At this dialog box you can specify additional parameters for the number format categories. For example, with the *Fraction* category you can choose the type of fraction you want displayed.

Scientific formatting converts a number to exponential notation. Part of the number is replaced with E + *n* where E means exponent and *n* represents the power. For example, the number *1,500,000.00* formatted in scientific number format displays as *1.50E+06*. In this example, *+06* means add 6 zeros to the right of the number left of E and then move the decimal point 6 positions to the right. Scientists, mathematicians, engineers, and statisticians often use exponential notation to write very large numbers or very small numbers in a more manageable way.

Figure 1.5 Format Cells Dialog Box with Number Tab Selected and Fraction
Category Active

▼ **Quick Steps**

**Apply Scientific
Notation Formatting**
1. Select desired range.
2. Click *Number Format*
   list box arrow.
3. Click *Scientific.*
4. Deselect range.

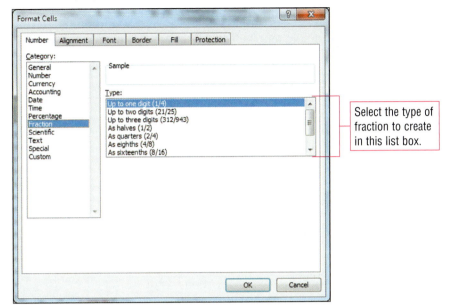

Select the type of
fraction to create
in this list box.

Project 3 **Applying Fraction and Scientific Formatting** Part 1 of 1

1. Open **JanelleTutorMathLsn.xlsx**.
2. Save the workbook with Save As and name it **EL2-C1-P3-JanelleTutorMathLsn**.
3. Make Fractions the active worksheet by clicking the Fractions sheet tab located at the
   bottom of the worksheet area just above the Status bar.
4. Apply fraction formatting to the values in column D in a fractions lesson to create the
   solution column for Janelle by completing the following steps:
   a. Select D11:D20.
   b. Click the down-pointing arrow at the right side of the
      Number Format list box (currently displays *General*) in the
      Number group of the Home tab.
   c. Click *More Number Formats* at the drop-down list.
   d. At the Format Cells dialog box with the Number tab
      selected, click *Fraction* in the *Category* list box.
   e. Click *Up to two digits (21/25)* in the *Type* list box.

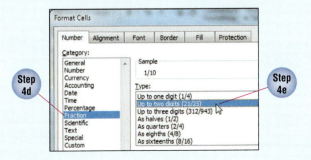

   f. Click OK.
   g. Click in any cell to deselect the range.

5. Save **EL2-C1-P3-JanelleTutorMathLsn**.
6. Print the worksheet.
7. Apply scientific notation formatting to the values in column D in a scientific notation lesson to create the solution column for Janelle by completing the following steps:
   a. Click the Exponents sheet tab located at the bottom of the worksheet area just above the Status bar.
   b. Select D11:D25.
   c. Click the down-pointing arrow at the right side of the *Number Format* list box (currently displays *Custom*) in the Number group of the Home tab and then click *Scientific* at the drop-down list.

10	Examples		Converted to Scientific Notation
11	1,000,000,000		1.00E+09
12	100,000,000		1.00E+08
13	10,000,000		1.00E+07
14	1,000,000		1.00E+06
15	100,000		1.00E+05
16	10,000		1.00E+04
17	1,000		1.00E+03
18	100		1.00E+02
19	10		1.00E+01
20	1		1.00E+00
21	0.1		1.00E-01
22	0.01		1.00E-02
23	0.001		1.00E-03
24	0.0001		1.00E-04
25	0.00001		1.00E-05

   scientific formatting applied to D11:D25 in Steps 7a-7d

   d. Click in any cell to deselect the range.
8. Print the worksheet.
9. Save and then close **EL2-C1-P3-JanelleTutorMathLsn.xlsx**.

Project 4 Apply Advanced Formatting Options   3 Parts

You will update a product worksheet by formatting telephone numbers, creating a custom number format to add descriptive characters before and after a value, and applying text alignment options for long labels.

Special Number Formats

At the Format Cells dialog box with the Number tab active, Excel provides special number formats that are specific to a country and language. For example, in a worksheet with social security numbers you can format the range that will contain the numbers and then type the data without the hyphens. Typing *000223456* converts the entry to *000-22-3456* in the cell with special formatting applied. As shown in Figure 1.6, four *Type* options are available for the *English (U.S.)* location: *Zip Code, Zip Code + 4, Phone Number,* and *Social Security Number*. Changing the location to *English (Canada)* displays two *Type* options: *Phone Number* and *Social Insurance Number*.

Figure 1.6 Format Cells Dialog Box with Number Tab Selected and Special Category Active

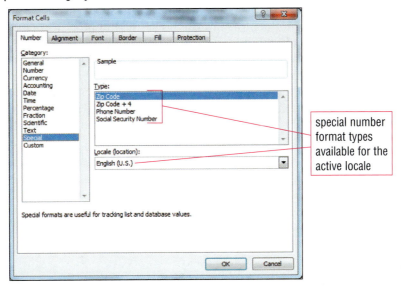

Applying Special Formatting   Part 1 of 3

1. Open **PrecisionProducts.xlsx**.
2. Save the workbook with Save As and name it **EL2-C1-P4-PrecisionProducts**.
3. Format the range that will contain telephone numbers to include brackets around the area code and a hyphen between the first three and last four digits of the number by completing the following steps:
   a. Select C15:C20.
   b. Click the Format Cells: Number dialog box launcher located at the bottom right of the Number group in the Home tab.
   c. At the Format Cells dialog box with the Number tab selected, click *Special* in the *Category* list box.
   d. Click *Phone Number* in the *Type* list box with *Locale (location)* set to *English (U.S.)*.
   e. Click OK.
   f. Click C15 to deselect the range and make the first cell to contain a telephone number active.

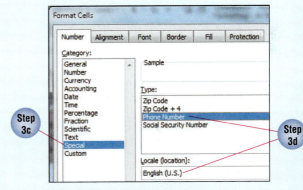

4. Type the telephone numbers for the sales representatives as follows:

C15	8005553429
C16	8005553439
C17	8005553449
C18	8005553459
C19	8005553469
C20	8005553479

14	Regional Sales Representatives		
15	North	Jordan Lavoie	(800) 555-3429
16	South	Pat Gallagher	(800) 555-3439
17	East	Alonso Rodriguez	(800) 555-3449
18	West	Karsten Das	(800) 555-3459
19	Canada	Kelli Olsen	(800) 555-3469
20	International	Bianca Santini	(800) 555-3479

5. Save **EL2-C1-P4-PrecisionProducts.xlsx**.

Quick Steps

**Create Custom
Number Format**
1. Select desired range.
2. Click Format Cells:
   Number dialog box
   launcher.
3. Click *Custom* in
   Category list box.
4. Select *General* in *Type*
   text box.
5. Press Delete.
6. Type desired custom
   format codes.
7. Click OK.
8. Deselect range.

Custom number
formats are stored in
the workbook in which
they are created.

Creating a Custom Number Format

You can create a custom number format for a worksheet in which you want to enter values that do not conform to the predefined number formats or values for which you want to add punctuation or text to the number. For example, in Project 4b you will create a custom number format to add a product category letter preceding all of the model numbers. By creating the custom number format, Excel adds the letter automatically. You can also specify a font color in a custom number format. Formatting codes are used in custom formats to specify the type of formatting to apply. You can type a custom number format code from scratch or select from a list of custom formats and modify the codes as necessary. Table 1.1 displays commonly used format codes along with examples of their usage.

Once the custom format is created you can apply the format elsewhere within the workbook by opening the Format Cells dialog box with the Number tab selected, selecting the *Custom* category, scrolling down to the bottom of the *Type* list box, clicking to select the custom format code, and then clicking OK.

Table 1.1 Custom Number Format Code Examples

Format Code	Description	Custom Number Format Example	Display Result
#	Represents a digit; type one for each digit. Excel will round if necessary to fit the number of decimals.	####.###	Typing *145.0068* displays *145.007*
0	Also used for digits. Excel rounds numbers to fit the number of decimals but also fills in leading zeros.	000.00	Typing *50.45* displays *050.45*
?	Rounds numbers to fit the number of decimals but also aligns the numbers vertically on the decimal point by adding spaces.	???.???	Typing *123.5, .8,* and *55.356* one below each other in a column aligns the numbers vertically on the decimal point.
"text"	Adds the characters between quotation symbols to the entry.	"Model No." ###	Typing *587* displays *Model No. 587*
[color]	Applies the font color specified in square brackets to the cell entry.	[Blue]##.##	Typing *55.346* displays **55.35**
;	Separates the positive value format from the negative value format.	[Blue];[Red]	Positive numbers are displayed in blue while negative numbers are displayed in red.

1. With **EL2-C1-P4-PrecisionProducts.xlsx** open, select A5:A12.
2. Create a custom number format to insert the characters *PD-* in front of each model number by completing the following steps:
   a. Click the Format Cells: Number dialog box launcher located at the bottom right of the Number group of the Home tab.
   b. Click *Custom* in the *Category* list box at the Format Cells dialog box with the Number tab selected.
   c. Scroll down the list of custom formats in the *Type* list box noting the various combinations of format codes for numbers, dates, and times.
   d. Select *General* in the *Type* text box, press Delete, and then type "PD-"####.
   e. Click OK.
   f. With the range A5:A12 still selected, click the Center button in the Alignment group of the Home tab.
   g. Deselect the range.

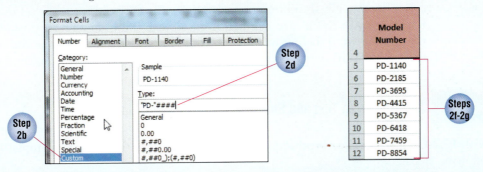

3. Create a custom number format to insert the characters *lbs* after the weights in columns D and E by completing the following steps:
   a. Select D5:E12.
   b. Click the Format Cells: Number dialog box launcher.
   c. Click *Custom* in the *Category* list box.
   d. Select *General* in the *Type* text box, press Delete, and then type ### "lbs". Make sure to include one space after ###.
   e. Click OK.
   f. Deselect the range.

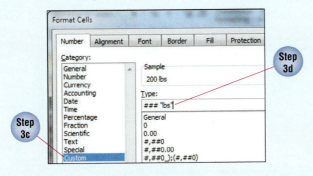

4. Save **EL2-C1-P4-PrecisionProducts.xlsx**.

Wrap Text

To delete a custom number format, open the workbook in which you created the custom format code, open the Format Cells dialog box with the Number tab selected, click *Custom* in the *Category* list box, scroll down the list of custom formats in the *Type* list box to the bottom of the list, click the custom format code that you created, and then click the Delete button. Cells within the workbook that had the format code applied have the custom formatting removed when the format is deleted.

Wrapping and Shrinking Text to Fit within a Cell ▪▪▪▪

Several options exist for formatting long labels that do not fit within the column width. The column width can be expanded, the font can be reduced to a smaller size, a group of cells can be merged, or you can allow the text to spill over into adjacent unused columns. Additional options available in the Format Cells dialog box with the Alignment tab selected include *Wrap text* and *Shrink to Fit* in the *Text control* section. Text wrapped within a cell causes the row height to automatically increase to accommodate the number of lines needed to display the text within the cell. Alternatively, shrinking the text to fit within the cell causes Excel to scale the font size down to the size required to fit all text within one line. Consider widening the column width before wrapping text or shrinking to fit to ensure the column is a reasonable width in which to display multiple lines of text or a smaller font size.

Project 4c Applying Wrap Text and Shrink to Fit Text Control Options   Part 3 of 3

1. With **EL2-C1-P4-PrecisionProducts.xlsx** open, wrap text within cells by completing the following steps:
   a. Select B22:B23.
   b. Click the Wrap Text button in the Alignment group of the Home tab.
   c. Print the worksheet.
2. You decide to try the Shrink to Fit option on the same cells to see if a better result is produced. Press Ctrl + Z or click the Undo button on the Quick Access toolbar to restore the cells back to their original state.
3. Shrink the text to fit within the cells by completing the following steps:
   a. With B22:B23 still selected, click the Format Cells: Alignment dialog box launcher button located at the bottom right of the Alignment group in the Home tab.
   b. At the Format Cells dialog box with the Alignment tab selected, click the *Shrink to fit* check box in the *Text control* section to insert a check mark.
   c. Click OK.
   d. Deselect the range.

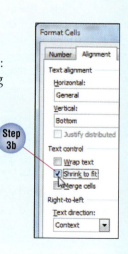

4. Save, print, and then close **EL2-C1-P4-PrecisionProducts.xlsx**.

 **Project 5** **Filter and Sort Data Based on Values, Icon Set, and Font Color** **4 Parts**

You will filter an insurance policy worksheet to show policies based on a range of liability limits and by number of claims, filter policies based on the number of automobiles, and filter and sort a payroll worksheet by font and cell colors.

Filtering a Worksheet Using a Custom AutoFilter ■■■■■

The AutoFilter feature is used to display only the rows that meet specified criteria defined using the filter arrow at the top of each column. Rows that do not meet the criteria are temporarily hidden from view. For each column in the selected range or table, the filter arrow button includes in the drop-down list each unique field value that exists within the column. Display the Custom AutoFilter dialog box shown in Figure 1.7 in a worksheet where you want to filter values by more than one criterion using a comparison operator. You can use the ? and * wildcard characters in a custom filter. For example, you could filter a list of products by a product number beginning with P using P* as the criteria.

Figure 1.7 Custom AutoFilter Dialog Box

Create a Custom AutoFilter to specify two criteria by which to filter that use either an *And* or *Or* statement.

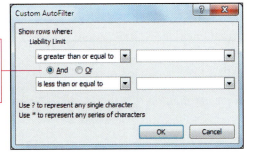

Quick Steps

Filter Using a Custom AutoFilter
1. Select range.
2. Click Sort & Filter button.
3. Click *Filter*.
4. Deselect range.
5. Click filter arrow button in desired column.
6. Point to *Number Filters*.
7. Click desired filter category.
8. Enter criteria at Custom AutoFilter dialog box.
9. Click OK.

Sort & Filter

Project 5a **Filtering Policy Information** **Part 1 of 4**

1. Open **AllClaimsInsce.xlsx**.
2. Save the workbook with Save As and name it **EL2-C1-P5-AllClaimsInsce**.
3. The owner of AllClaims Insurance Brokers wants to review policies with liability limits from $500,000 to $1 million and with claims greater than 1 to determine if customers should increase their coverage. Filter the policy information to produce the list of policies that meet the owner's request by completing the following steps:
   a. Select A3:I20.
   b. Click the Sort & Filter button in the Editing group of the Home tab.
   c. Click *Filter* at the drop-down list to display a filter arrow button at the top of each column.
   d. Deselect the range.

e. Click the filter arrow button next to *Liability Limit* in E3.

f. Point to *Number Filters* and then click *Between* at the drop-down list.

g. At the Custom AutoFilter dialog box with the insertion point positioned in the blank text box next to *is greater than or equal to*, type 500000.

h. Notice *And* is the option selected between criteria. This is correct since the owner wants a list of policies with the liability limit greater than or equal to 500,000 *and* less than or equal to 1,000,000.

i. Click in the blank text box next to *is less than or equal to* and type 1000000.

j. Click OK to close the Custom AutoFilter dialog box. The range is filtered to display the rows with liability limits from $500,000 to $1 million.

k. Click the filter arrow button next to *Claims* in H3.

l. Point to *Number Filters* and then click *Greater Than* at the drop-down list.

m. At the Custom AutoFilter dialog box with the insertion point positioned in the blank text box next to *is greater than*, type 1 and then click OK.

4. Print the filtered worksheet.

5. Save and then close **EL2-C1-P5-AllClaimsInsce.xlsx**.

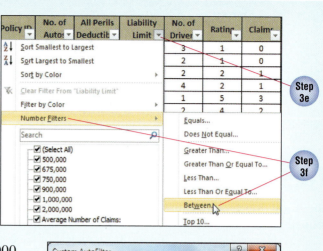

Step 3e

Step 3f

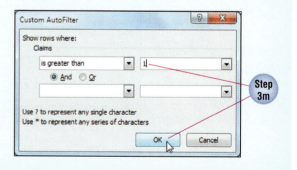

Step 3g

Step 3i

Step 3j

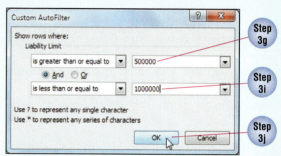

Step 3m

Filtering and Sorting Data Using Conditional Formatting or Cell Attributes

▼ **Quick Steps**

Filter by Icon Set
1. Select range.
2. Click Sort & Filter button.
3. Click *Filter*.
4. Deselect range.
5. Click filter arrow button in desired column.
6. Point to *Filter by Color*.
7. Click desired icon.

A worksheet with cells that have been formatted manually or by conditional formatting to change the cell or font color can be filtered by the colors. As well, a worksheet conditionally formatted by icon sets can be filtered by a cell icon. Click the filter arrow button in the column by which you want to filter and then point to *Filter by Color* at the drop-down list. Depending on the formatting that has been applied, the list contains the cell colors, font colors, or icon sets that have been applied to cells within the column. Click the desired color or icon option to filter the column.

The filter drop-down list also contains a *Sort by Color* option with which you can choose to sort rows within the range or table by a specified cell color, font color, or cell icon. Follow similar steps to sort by color as you would to filter by color. For example, to sort a column by a font color, point to *Sort by Color* from the column's filter drop-down list and then click the desired font color. Excel sorts the column placing cells with the specified font color at the top.

You can also sort or filter using the shortcut menu. For example, to filter by color or icon using the shortcut menu, right-click a cell that contains the color or icon you wish to filter by, point to *Filter*, and then click *Filter by Selected Cell's Color*, *Filter by Selected Cell's Font Color*, or *Filter by Selected Cell's Icon*.

▼ **Quick Steps**

Filter or Sort by Color
1. Select range.
2. Click Sort & Filter button.
3. Click *Filter*.
4. Deselect range.
5. Click filter arrow button in desired column.
6. Point to *Filter by Color* or *Sort by Color*.
7. Click desired color.
OR
1. Right-click a cell with desired color or icon.
2. Point to *Filter* or *Sort*.
3. Click desired filter or sort option.

Project 5b **Filtering by Icon Set**   Part 2 of 4

1. Open **EL2-C1-P2-AllClaimsInsce.xlsx**.
2. Save the workbook with Save As and name it **EL2-C1-P5-AllClaimsInsce-1Auto**.
3. Filter the worksheet to display the policies that have coverage for only one automobile by completing the following steps:
   a. Select A3:I20.
   b. Click the Sort & Filter button in the Editing group of the Home tab.
   c. Click *Filter* at the drop-down list to display a filter arrow button at the top of each column.
   d. Deselect the range. Note that the black circle icon in column C represents the *1* data set.
   e. Click the filter arrow button next to *No. of Autos* in C3.
   f. Point to *Filter by Color* at the drop-down list.
   g. Click the black circle icon in the *Filter by Cell Icon* list.
4. Print the filtered worksheet and then close **EL2-C1-P5-AllClaimsInsce-1Auto.xlsx**.

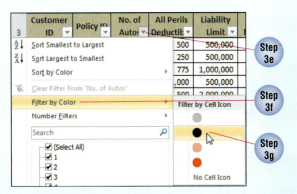

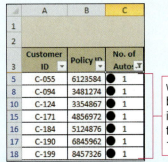

worksheet filtered by black circle icon representing the policies with 1 auto at Step 3

1. Open **EL2-C1-P1-VantagePay-Oct27.xlsx**.
2. Save the workbook with Save As and name it **EL2-C1-P5-VantagePay-Oct27-HighOT**.
3. The store manager wants a list of employees who worked more than five overtime hours during the pay period. You recall conditionally formatting the overtime hours by applying red font color to cells greater than 5. Filter the worksheet by the conditional formatting by completing the following steps:
   a. Select K6:K23.
   b. Right-click within the selected range.
   c. Point to *Filter* and then click *Filter by Selected Cell's Font Color* at the shortcut menu.

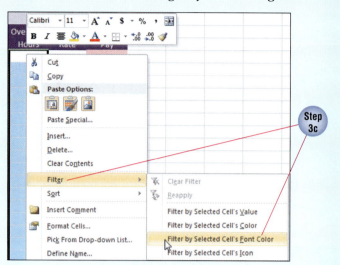

4. Print the filtered worksheet.
5. Save and then close **EL2-C1-P5-VantagePay-Oct27-HighOT.xlsx**.

1. Open **EL2-C1-P1-VantagePay-Oct27.xlsx**.
2. Save the workbook with Save As and name it **EL2-C1-P5-VantagePay-Oct27-Sorted**.
3. Sort the payroll worksheet in descending order by cell color by completing the following steps:
   a. Select A5:M23, click the Sort & Filter button in the Editing group of the Home tab, and then click *Filter* at the drop-down list.
   b. Deselect the range.
   c. Click the filter arrow button next to Gross Pay in M5.
   d. Point to *Sort by Color* and then click the pink fill color box in the *Sort by Cell Color* section.

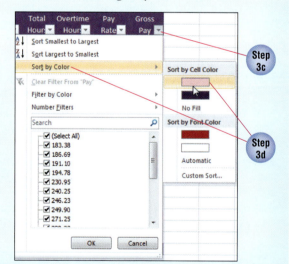

4. Print the sorted worksheet.
5. Save and then close **EL2-C1-P5-VantagePay-Oct27-Sorted.xlsx**.

In a worksheet with more than one cell or font color applied to a column, you would have to define a custom sort. Click the Sort & Filter button in the Editing group of the Home tab and then click *Custom Sort* at the drop-down list.

At the Sort dialog box, define the color to sort first and then add a level for each other color in the order in which you want sorting by color to occur. The *Sort On* drop-down list at the Sort dialog box allows you to sort by *Values, Cell Color, Font Color,* or *Cell Icon.* Figure 1.8 shows an example of a sort definition for a column in which four cell icons have been used.

Figure 1.8 Sort Dialog Box with Four-Color Sort Defined

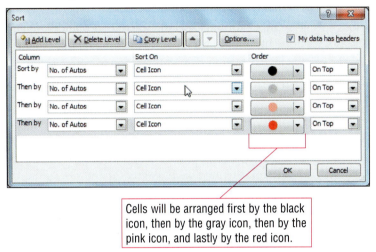

Cells will be arranged first by the black icon, then by the gray icon, then by the pink icon, and lastly by the red icon.

Chapter Summary

- Conditional formatting applies format changes to cells based on a condition; cells that meet the condition have the formatting applied whereas cells that do not meet the condition remain unformatted.
- Conditional formats can be based on values, dates, text entries, or duplicated values.
- Use the *Highlight Cells Rules* option at the Conditional Formatting button drop-down list to conditionally format based on a value comparison.
- Use the *Top/Bottom Rules* option at the Conditional Formatting button drop-down list to conditionally format based on the top ten or bottom ten percent values or on average values.
- Conditional formats are based on rules which specify the criterion by which the cells are tested and the formatting attributes to apply to cells that meet the condition.
- Create your own conditional formatting rules by selecting *New Rule* at the Conditional Formatting button drop-down list.
- Edit or delete a rule at the Conditional Formatting Rules Manager dialog box.
- Conditionally format using data bars, color scales, or icon sets to add small bar charts, gradations of color, or icons to cells to draw attention to data.
- Conditionally format using a formula to apply desired formatting to the selected range of cells based on values in other cells.

- An IF statement can be used to conditionally format those cells that calculate to a true result for the logical test.
- Fraction formatting converts decimal values to fractions.
- To choose the type of fraction you want to convert, open the Format Cells dialog box with the Number tab selected.
- Scientific formatting displays numbers in exponential notation where part of the number that is formatted is replaced with $E + n$ where E stands for exponent and n represents the power.
- Excel provides special number formats specific to countries and language to format entries such as telephone numbers, social security numbers, or postal codes.
- Custom number formats use formatting codes to create the format definition.
- A custom number format can be used to add text or punctuation to a value entered into a cell.
- Long labels can be formatted to fit within a cell by either wrapping the text within the cell or shrinking the font size to fit the cell.
- Display the Custom AutoFilter dialog box to filter values by more than one criterion using a comparison operator such as greater than or equal to.
- A worksheet that has been formatted manually or by conditional formatting can be filtered by the colors or icons.
- A worksheet that has been formatted manually or by conditional formatting can also be sorted by the colors.
- Define a custom sort if the worksheet contains more than one cell color, font color, or cell icon and you want to specify the order of the colors to sort.

Commands Review

FEATURE	RIBBON TAB, GROUP	BUTTON	KEYBOARD SHORTCUT
Conditional formatting	Home, Styles		
Custom AutoFilter	Home, Editing		Ctrl + Shift + L
Custom number format	Home, Number		Ctrl + 1
Fraction number format	Home, Number		Ctrl + 1
Scientific number format	Home, Number		Ctrl + 1
Shrink to Fit	Home, Alignment		
Special number format	Home, Number		Ctrl + 1
Wrap text	Home, Alignment		

Concepts Check Test Your Knowledge

Completion: In the space provided at the right, indicate the correct term, command, or number.

1. Point to this option from the Conditional Formatting button drop-down list to format cells based on a comparison operator such as *Greater Than*. _____

2. To conditionally format a range using the *Above Average* condition, click this option from the Conditional Formatting button drop-down list. _____

3. Open this dialog box to create, edit, or delete a conditional formatting rule. _____

4. Excel uses threshold values to classify data into three to five categories when conditionally formatting by this option. _____

5. Select this option in the *Select a Rule Type* section of the New Formatting Rule dialog box to create a rule that conditionally formats cells based on the value(s) in another cell. _____

6. Open this dialog box to format a selected range using a fraction and select the type of fraction to display. _____

7. Scientific formatting is used by scientists or others who need to write very large numbers using this notation. _____

8. The special number format options displayed in the *Type* list box are dependent on this other setting. _____

9. What would display in a cell in which you typed *156.3568* for which the custom number format code *###.##* is applied? _____

10. Use either of these two text control options to format a long label within the existing column width. _____

11. Open this dialog box to filter by more than one criterion using a comparison operator. _____

12. A worksheet can be filtered by a cell color that has been applied manually or by this feature. _____

13. Open this dialog box to arrange cells in a worksheet by more than one color. _____

Skills Check Assess Your Performance

1 USE CONDITIONAL AND FRACTION FORMATTING

1. Open **RSRServRpt.xlsx**.
2. Save the workbook with Save As and name it **EL2-C1-A1-RSRServRpt**.
3. Apply the following formatting changes to the worksheet:
   a. Format C6:C23 to fractions using the type *As quarters (2/4)*.
   b. Format the rate codes in D6:D22 with icon set *3 Traffic Lights (Rimmed)*. This is the first option in the right column of the Shapes section.
   c. Format the parts values in F6:F22 to color the cell with *Light Red Fill* for those cells that are equal to zero.
   d. Bold the values in G6:G22.
   e. Format the total invoice values in G6:G22 using the *Red Data Bar* option in the *Gradient Fill* section of the Data Bars side menu.
4. Save, print, and then close **EL2-C1-A1-RSRServRpt.xlsx**.

Assessment

2 APPLY CUSTOM NUMBER FORMATTING

1. Open **EL2-C1-A1-RSRServRpt.xlsx**.
2. Save the workbook with Save As and name it **EL2-C1-A2-RSRServRpt**.
3. Create and apply the following custom number formats:
   a. Create a custom number format that displays *hrs* one space after the values in C6:C23. **Hint: After selecting Custom in the Category list box, click after the existing format codes in the Type text box and then add the required entry after the existing codes (do not delete what is already in the Type text box).**
   b. Create a custom number format that displays *RSR-* in front of each work order number in B6:B22.
4. Save, print, and then close **EL2-C1-A2-RSRServRpt.xlsx**.

Assessment

3 USE CUSTOM AUTOFILTER; FILTER AND SORT BY COLOR

1. Open **EL2-C1-A2-RSRServRpt.xlsx**.
2. Save the workbook with Save As and name it **EL2-C1-A3-RSRServRpt**.
3. Select A5:G22 and turn on the Filter feature.
4. Filter the worksheet as follows:
   a. Using the filter arrow button in the *Hours Billed* column, display those invoices where the hours billed is between 1.75 and 3.75 hours.
   b. Print the filtered worksheet.
   c. Clear the filter from the *Hours Billed* column.
   d. Filter the *Parts* column by color to show only those invoices for which no parts were billed.
   e. Print the filtered worksheet.
   f. Clear the filter from the *Parts* column.
   g. Filter the worksheet by the icon associated with rate code 3.
   h. Print the filtered worksheet.

    i. Clear the filter from the *Rate Code* column.
5. Remove the filter arrow buttons from the worksheet.
6. Define a custom sort to sort the invoices by the rate code icon set as follows:
    a. Make any cell active within the invoice list.
    b. Open the Sort dialog box.
    c. Define three sort levels as follows:

Sort by	*Sort On*	*Order*
Rate Code	Cell Icon	Red Traffic Light (On Top)
Rate Code	Cell Icon	Yellow Traffic Light (On Top)
Rate Code	Cell Icon	Green Traffic Light (On Top)

7. Print the sorted worksheet.
8. Save and then close **EL2-C1-A3-RSRServRpt.xlsx**.

Assessment

4   CREATE, EDIT, AND DELETE FORMATTING RULES

1. Open **VantagePay-Oct27.xlsx**.
2. Save the workbook with Save As and name it **EL2-C1-A4-VantagePay-Oct27**.
3. Create and apply two formatting rules for the values in the *Pay Rate* column as follows:
    a. Apply a light purple fill color to the values from 7.50 to 8.00.
    b. Apply a light green fill color to the values greater than 8.00.
4. Create a formatting rule for the *Gross Pay* column that will format the values in red bold font color if the employee has worked overtime hours.
5. Print the worksheet.
6. Edit the formatting rule for *Cell Value > 8* by changing the fill color to orange and applying bold to the font.
7. Delete the formatting rule for *Cell Value between 7.50 and 8.00*.
8. Print the revised worksheet.
9. Save and then close **EL2-C1-A4-VantagePay-Oct27.xlsx**.

Visual Benchmark Demonstrate Your Proficiency

FORMAT A BILLING SUMMARY

1. Open **BillingsOct8to12.xlsx**.
2. Save the workbook with Save As and name it **EL2-C1-VB-BillingsOct8to12**.
3. Format the worksheet to match the one shown in Figure 1.9 using the following information:
   - The data in the *Billing Code* column is custom formatted to add the text *Amicus#-* in front of the code number in blue font color.
   - Icon sets are used in the *Attorney Code* column and the same icon set should be applied in the Attorney Code Table section of the worksheet.
   - The Data bars added to the values in the *Legal Fees* column have been edited to change the bar appearance to *Turquoise, Accent 3* gradient fill. **Hint: Select More Rules *in the Data Bars side menu*.**
   - Values below 1500.00 in the *Total Due* column have been conditionally formatted and then the worksheet is sorted by the font color used for the conditional format.
4. Save, print, and then close **EL2-C1-VB-BillingsOct8to12.xlsx**.

Figure 1.9 Visual Benchmark

	File	Client	Date	Billing Code	Attorney Code	Legal Fees	Disbursements	Total Due		Billing Code Table	
										Code	Area of Practice
5	EP-652	10106	10/8/2012	Amicus#-3	● 1	1,028.50	23.75	1,052.25		1	Corporate
6	EL-632	10225	10/9/2012	Amicus#-5	○ 3	1,211.00	37.85	1,248.85		2	Divorce & Separation
7	CL-501	10341	10/10/2012	Amicus#-1	● 2	1,143.75	55.24	1,198.99		3	Wills & Estates
8	IN-745	10210	10/11/2012	Amicus#-6	○ 3	1,450.00	24.25	1,474.25		4	Real Estate
9	CL-412	10125	10/12/2012	Amicus#-1	● 2	1,143.75	38.12	1,181.87		5	Employment Litigation
10	IN-801	10346	10/12/2012	Amicus#-6	○ 3	1,425.00	62.18	1,487.18		6	Insurance Personal Injury
11	RE-501	10384	10/12/2012	Amicus#-4	● 4	1,237.50	34.28	1,271.78		7	Other
12	FL-325	10104	10/8/2012	Amicus#-2	● 1	2,273.75	95.10	2,368.85			
13	CL-412	10125	10/8/2012	Amicus#-1	● 2	2,493.75	55.40	2,549.15			Attorney Code Table
14	IN-745	10210	10/9/2012	Amicus#-6	○ 3	2,425.00	65.20	2,490.20		Code	Attorney
15	RE-475	10285	10/9/2012	Amicus#-4	● 4	3,807.00	48.96	3,855.96		● 1	Marty O'Donovan
16	CL-521	10334	10/10/2012	Amicus#-1	● 2	1,518.75	27.85	1,546.60		● 2	Toni Sullivan
17	PL-348	10420	10/10/2012	Amicus#-7	○ 3	2,500.00	34.95	2,534.95		○ 3	Rosa Martinez
18	RE-492	10425	10/10/2012	Amicus#-4	● 4	2,043.00	38.75	2,081.75		● 4	Kyle Williams
19	EL-632	10225	10/11/2012	Amicus#-5	○ 3	2,300.00	42.15	2,342.15			
20	PL-512	10290	10/11/2012	Amicus#-7	○ 3	1,620.00	65.15	1,685.15			
21	FL-385	10278	10/11/2012	Amicus#-2	● 1	2,040.00	85.47	2,125.47			
22	CL-450	10358	10/12/2012	Amicus#-1	● 2	1,762.50	55.24	1,817.74			
23	EP-685	10495	10/12/2012	Amicus#-3	○ 3	2,375.00	94.55	2,469.55			

O'DONOVAN & SULLIVAN LAW ASSOCIATES
BILLING SUMMARY
OCTOBER 8 TO 12, 2012

Case Study   Apply Your Skills

Part 1

You work as a market research assistant at NuTrends Market Research. Yolanda Robertson has provided you with a workbook named **USIncomeStats.xlsx**. This workbook contains data she obtained from the U.S. Census Bureau with the two-year average median household income by state for 2008. Open the workbook and use Save As to name it **EL2-C1-CS-P1-USIncomeStats**. Yolanda wants you to format the data using color to differentiate income levels. She has proposed the following categories for which she would like you to apply color formatting.

> *Average Median Income Range*
>
> Less than 45,000
>
> Between 45,000 and 55,000
>
> Greater than 55,000

Apply color formatting using Conditional Formatting for this request since Yolanda may change these salary ranges later after she reviews the data, and you want the ability to edit the formatting rule if that happens. Choose color formats that will be easy to distinguish from each other. Create a reference table starting in E3 that provides Yolanda with a legend to read the colors. For example, in E3 type **Less than 45,000** and in H3 type a sample value (such as 35,000) and format the cell to the color that represents the formatting you applied to the rule category. Save and then print the worksheet. *Note: If you submit your work in hard copy and do not have access to a color printer, write on the printout the color format options you applied to each category.*

Part 2

Yolanda has reviewed the worksheet from Part 1 and has requested some further work. Before you begin modifying the file, you decide to keep the original file intact in case this data can be used for another purpose. Use Save As to save the workbook using the name **EL2-C1-CS-P2-USIncomeStats**. Yolanda would like the worksheet sorted in descending order from the highest income level to the lowest. Do not include the entries in row 3 for the United States average in the sort operation. After sorting the worksheet, filter the median incomes to display the top 20 states. *Hint: You can customize the value in the Top 10 AutoFilter.* Yolanda wants to add a contact telephone list next to the Top 20 state data. Create the list using the telephone numbers provided below in a suitable location. Apply the special number format for phone numbers to ensure the data is displayed consistently. Save and then print the worksheet.

Yolanda (cell)	800 555 3117
Yolanda (office)	800 555 4629
Yolanda (home)	800 555 2169
Yolanda (fax)	800 555 6744

Part 3

Continuing with the worksheet formatted in Part 2 of this Case Study, you decide to experiment with the filtered census data worksheet to see if formatting using color scales will highlight the spread between the highest and lowest median incomes more distinctly. Apply conditional formatting using either a two-color or a three-color scale to the filtered cells in column C (exclude the United States median income at the top of the column). Use Save As to name the workbook **EL2-C1-CS-P3-USIncomeStats**. Print the worksheet. *Note: If you submit your work in hard copy and do not have access to a color printer, write on the printout the two- or three-color scale conditional formatting option you applied to the filtered values in column C.*

Part 4

Yolanda is preparing a seminar for new market researchers hired at NuTrends Market Research. For background material for the training section on U.S. Census Bureau statistics, Yolanda has asked you to research the history of the bureau. Using the Internet, go to the URL www.census.gov/ and find the page that describes the history of the Census Bureau. *Hint: Explore the tabbed pages at the **About the Bureau** link from the home page*. In a new sheet in the same file as the median income data, type in column A five to seven interesting facts you learned about the bureau from their website. Adjust the width of column A and apply wrap text or shrink to fit formatting to improve the appearance. Save the revised workbook and name it **EL2-C1-CS-P4-USIncomeStats**. Print the worksheet and then close the workbook.

Advanced Functions and Formulas

PERFORMANCE OBJECTIVES

Upon successful completion of Chapter 2, you will be able to:

- Create and use named ranges in formulas
- Use functions COUNTA, COUNTIF, COUNTIFS
- Use functions AVERAGEIF, AVERAGEIFS
- Use functions SUMIF, SUMIFS
- Edit a named range
- Rename and delete a named range
- Look up data using the lookup functions VLOOKUP and HLOOKUP
- Analyze loan payments using PPMT
- Use conditional logic functions IF, AND, and OR
- Modify text using the text functions PROPER, UPPER, LOWER, and SUBSTITUTE

Tutorials

2.1 Creating and Managing Range Names

2.2 Using Statistical Functions: Count Functions

2.3 Using Statistical Functions: AVERAGEIF and AVERAGEIFS

2.4 Using Math and Trigonometry Functions

2.5 Using Lookup Functions

2.6 Using the PPMT Function

2.7 Using Logical Functions

2.8 Using Text Functions

Excel includes numerous built-in functions grouped by function category. Eleven categories contain preprogrammed formulas to facilitate complex calculations for worksheets containing statistical, financial, scientific, database, and other data. The Insert function dialog box assists with locating and building function formulas. The structure of a function formula begins with the equals sign (=), followed by the name of the function, and then the function argument. Argument is the term given to the values to be included in the calculation. The structure of the argument is dependent on the type of function being used and can include a single cell, a range, multiple ranges, or any combination of the preceding. Model answers for this chapter's projects appear on the following pages.

Excel2010L2C2

Note: Before beginning the projects, copy to your storage medium the Excel2010L2C2 subfolder from the Excel2010L2 folder on the CD that accompanies this textbook and then make Excel2010L2C2 the active folder.

Project 1 Calculate Statistics and Sums Using Conditional Formulas — EL2-C2-P1-AllClaimsOct12VehRpt.xlsx

AllClaims Insurance Brokers
VEHICLE CLAIMS REPORT FOR OCTOBER 2012

Date of Claim	Policy ID	Claim No.	Auto No.	Driver No.	Rating	Deductible	Claim Estimate	Repair Shop
10/2/2012	6388569	5410	2	2	2	500.00	15,241.00	JFI Auto
10/3/2012	4236512	5411	3	3	2	750.00	5,124.00	Logans Auto Body
10/5/2012	6974583	5412	1	1	4	1,000.00	12,451.00	Logans Auto Body
10/5/2012	2563845	5413	2	1	3	1,000.00	6,582.00	JFI Auto
10/8/2012	2215473	5414	1	2	2	250.00	3,475.00	JFI Auto
10/8/2012	6952384	5415	3	4	4	500.00	4,800.00	JFI Auto
10/10/2012	4668457	5416	3	3	5	1,000.00	15,653.00	Logans Auto Body
10/10/2012	8512475	5417	4	3	5	2,000.00	18,653.00	West Collision
10/12/2012	6984563	5418	2	2	5	1,000.00	10,475.00	JFI Auto
10/15/2012	4856972	5419	1	2	3	2,500.00	14,652.00	Logans Auto Body
10/15/2012	6845962	5420	1	1	3	500.00	4,110.00	Logans Auto Body
10/15/2012	8457326	5421	1	2	1	1,000.00	8,624.00	West Collision
10/19/2012	4968532	5422	2	1	2	250.00	2,510.00	West Collision
10/22/2012	5741356	5423	4	1	1	250.00	1,896.00	West Collision
10/22/2012	2486597	5424	1	2	3	750.00	3,841.00	JFI Auto
10/23/2012	7134586	5425	2	3	3	500.00	6,253.00	JFI Auto
10/24/2012	4234875	5426	2	3	4	1,000.00	5,486.00	A+ Paint & Body
10/26/2012	3894124	5427	4	1	1	2,000.00	12,986.00	JFI Auto
10/29/2012	6952384	5428	3	3	4	500.00	2,475.00	A+ Paint & Body
10/30/2012	6845216	5429	3	1	2	250.00	7,684.00	A+ Paint & Body
10/31/2012	8663418	5430	2	2	1	500.00	3,486.00	A+ Paint & Body

Claim Report Statistics Summary

By Repair Shop	No. of Claims	Total Estimates
A+ Paint & Body	3	16,656
JFI Auto	9	66,128
Logans Auto Body	5	51,990
West Collision	4	31,683

JFI claims exceeding $5 thousand — 5

JFI claims for ratings greater than 3 — 5

By Rating	Avg. Est.
1	2,691
2	6,987
3	9,014
4	7,830
5	14,564

By Rating and Driver	
Rating 2, Driver 1	6,273
Rating 3, Driver 1	8,281

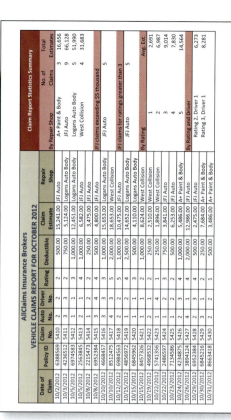

Project 2 Populate Cells by Looking Up Data — EL2-C2-P2-PrecisionPrices.xlsx

Precision Design and Packaging
Bulk Container Products Price List

Model Number	Description	Discount Category	List Price	Discount	Net Price
PD-1140	Gaylord with lid	A	18.67	10%	16.80
PD-2185	Premium Gaylord with lid	C	22.50	14%	19.35
PD-1150	Gaylord bottom	D	14.53	12%	12.79
PD-1155	Gaylord lid	A	5.25	16%	4.41
PD-3695	Telescoping top and bottom	A	18.54	10%	16.69
PD-3698	Telescoping bottom	A	17.65	10%	15.89
PD-3699	Telescoping top	A	17.65	10%	15.89
PD-4100	Additional lids for telescoping containers	D	9.88	16%	8.30
PD-4200	"D" 4 piece container	A	7.75	10%	6.98
PD-4415	"EO" container	A	8.25	10%	7.43
PD-5367	"EH" container	A	12.75	10%	11.48
PD-6418	"E" container	A	17.54	10%	15.79
PD-7459	Economy R.S.C.	C	8.56	20%	6.85
PD-8854	Premium R.S.C.	E	18.17	14%	15.63
PD-9101	Corrugated pads 15 x 15	E	1.10	20%	0.88
PD-9105	Corrugated pads 20 x 12	E	1.14	20%	0.91
PD-9110	Corrugated pads 24 x 18	E	1.17	20%	0.94
PD-9115	Corrugated pads 30 x 30	E	1.09	20%	0.87

Discount Table

Discount Category	Discount Percent
A	10%
B	12%
C	14%
D	16%
E	20%

NOTE: Use this price list for U.S. and Canadian orders only. Refer international customers to Bianca Santini for price quotations.

Project 3 Analyze an Expansion Project Loan — EL2-C2-P3-DeeringExpansion.xlsx

DEERING INDUSTRIES
BUILDING LOAN EXPANSION

	Victory Trust	Dominion Trust	
Interest Rate	8.15%	9.50%	annual rate
Amortization	20	15	years for repayment
Loan Amount	$ 775,000	775,000	principal amount borrowed
Monthly Payment	($6,554.95)	($8,092.74)	includes principal and interest
Monthly Principal Payment (1st payment)	($1,291.40)	($1,957.32)	payment on principal for the first month of the loan
Total Loan Payments	($1,573,187.00)	($1,456,693.43)	

NOTE: Both payments are calculated based on a constant interest rate and a constant payment.

Project 4 Calculate Benefit Costs Using Conditional Logic — EL2-C2-P4-VantageHOSalaryCosts.xlsx

Vantage Video Rentals
Head Office Salaried Employees
Salary and Benefit Costs

		Full-Time/ Part-Time	Health Plan	Dental Plan	Salary	Pension	Health	Dental	Total Benefits	Salary + Benefits
Terri	Burkowski	FT	Family	Declined	65,000.00	3,250.00	2,100.00		5,350.00	70,350.00
Beatriz	Santiago	FT	Single	Declined	51,500.00	2,575.00	1,380.00	1,500.00	5,455.00	56,955.00
Aram	Haji	PT	Declined	Declined	52,500.00	2,625.00	-		2,625.00	55,125.00
Gerri	Kinnear	FT	Family	Single	27,500.00	-	2,100.00	1,500.00	3,600.00	31,100.00
Sam	Quinn	PT	Single	Family	45,000.00	-	1,380.00	1,500.00	2,880.00	47,880.00
Andrea	Ruiz	PT	Family	Declined	22,500.00	-	2,100.00		2,100.00	24,600.00
Martina	Tisdale	PT	Declined	Declined	28,500.00	-	1,380.00		1,380.00	29,880.00
Carl	Wisenberg	FT	Declined	Declined	42,500.00					42,500.00
Chen	Zhao	FT	Declined	Single	40,500.00			1,500.00	1,500.00	42,000.00
TOTAL					375,500.00	8,450.00	10,440.00	6,000.00	24,890.00	400,390.00

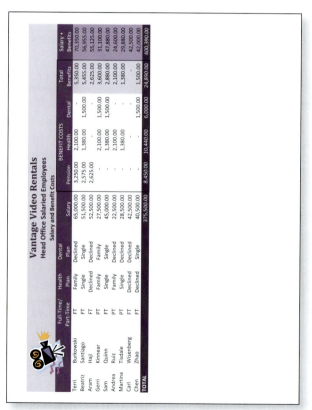

| Two-Year Average Median Household Income by State | | Two-Year Average Median Household Income by State | |
Median Income for 2008		Median Income for 2012	
United States	**51,233**	**UNITED STATES**	**54,973**
Alabama	44,155	ALABAMA	47,378
Alaska	64,701	ALASKA	69,424
Arizona	47,972	ARIZONA	51,474
Arkansas	40,974	ARKANSAS	43,965
California	57,445	CALIFORNIA	61,638
Colorado	62,217	COLORADO	66,759
Connecticut	65,644	CONNECTICUT	70,436
Delaware	53,695	DELAWARE	57,615
District of Columbia	54,162	DISTRICT OF COLUMBIA	58,116
Florida	46,206	FLORIDA	49,579
Georgia	48,369	GEORGIA	51,900
Hawaii	64,002	HAWAII	68,674
Idaho	49,247	IDAHO	52,842
Illinois	53,889	ILLINOIS	57,823
Indiana	47,898	INDIANA	51,395
Iowa	50,465	IOWA	54,149
Kansas	49,119	KANSAS	52,705
Kentucky	41,058	KENTUCKY	44,055
Louisiana	41,232	LOUISIANA	44,242
Maine	48,481	MAINE	52,020
Maryland	65,932	MARYLAND	70,745
Massachusetts	60,515	MASSACHUSETTS	64,933
Michigan	50,528	MICHIGAN	54,217
Minnesota	57,607	MINNESOTA	61,812
Mississippi	37,579	MISSISSIPPI	40,322
Missouri	46,906	MISSOURI	50,330
Montana	44,116	MONTANA	47,336
Nebraska	50,896	NEBRASKA	54,611
Nevada	55,440	NEVADA	59,487
New Hampshire	68,175	NEW HAMPSHIRE	73,152
New Jersey	64,070	NEW JERSEY	68,747
New Mexico	44,081	NEW MEXICO	47,299
New York	50,643	NEW YORK	54,340
North Carolina	44,058	NORTH CAROLINA	47,274
North Dakota	49,325	NORTH DAKOTA	52,926
Ohio	48,960	OHIO	52,534
Oklahoma	45,494	OKLAHOMA	48,815
Oregon	51,947	OREGON	55,739
Pennsylvania	50,850	PENNSYLVANIA	54,562
Rhode Island	54,767	RHODE ISLAND	58,765
South Carolina	44,034	SOUTH CAROLINA	47,248
South Dakota	49,901	SOUTH DAKOTA	53,544
Tennessee	41,240	TENNESSEE	44,251
Texas	47,157	TEXAS	50,599
Utah	59,062	UTAH	63,374
Vermont	49,959	VERMONT	53,606
Virginia	61,710	VIRGINIA	66,215
Washington	58,472	WASHINGTON	62,740
West Virginia	40,851	WEST VIRGINIA	43,833
Wisconsin	52,224	WISCONSIN	56,036
Wyoming	51,977	WYOMING	55,771

Data shown above is the two-year average median for 2007 to 2008. Two-year average median is the sum of two inflation-adjusted single-year medians divided by 2.

Source: U.S. Census Bureau
http://www.census.gov/hhes/www/income/statemedfaminc08.html

Project 5 Convert Text Using Text Functions

EL2-C2-P5-USIncomeStats.xlsx

Project 1   Calculate Statistics and Sums Using Conditional Formulas   7 Parts

You will create and manage range names in an insurance claims worksheet and use the range names in statistical formulas that count, find averages, and sum based on single and multiple criteria.

Naming Ranges

Assigning a name to a cell or a range of cells allows you to reference the source by a descriptive label rather than the cell address or range address when creating formulas, printing, or navigating a worksheet. Referencing by name makes the task of managing a complex formula easier. Another person editing the worksheet experiences clarity more quickly as to the formula's purpose. To demonstrate the use of names for clarity, read the formula examples in Table 2.1. Each row provides two formulas that reference the same source cells; however, the formula on the right is meaningful to you more quickly than the formula on the left. The formulas in the left column might require that you locate the source cell in the worksheet to figure out the calculation steps while the formula on the right provides comprehension almost immediately.

By default, the range to which a range name applies is referenced using absolute references. Later in this chapter when you create a lookup formula, you

▼ **Quick Steps**

Create Range Name
1. Select cell(s).
2. Click in Name box.
3. Type desired range name.
4. Press Enter.

Table 2.1 Standard Formulas and Formulas with Named Ranges

Standard Formula	Same Formula Using Named Ranges
=D3-D13	=Sales-Expenses
=J5*K5	=Hours*PayRate
=G10/J10	=ThisYear/LastYear
=IF(E4-B2>0,E4*D2,0)	=IF(Sales-Target>0,Sales*Bonus,0)

The Formulas tab contains a Create from Selection button in the Defined Names group that can be used to automatically create range names for a list or table. Select the list or table and click the button. Excel uses the names in the top row or leftmost column as the range names.

will take advantage of a range name's absolute referencing when you need to include a group of cells in the formula that stay fixed when the formula is copied.

Create a range name by selecting a single cell or range, clicking in the Name box located at the left end of the Formula bar, typing the name, and then pressing Enter. The Name box displays the active cell address or the cell name when one has been defined. When creating a name for a cell or a range of cells, the following naming rules apply:

- Names can be a combination of letters, numbers, underscore characters, or periods up to 255 characters.
- The first character must be a letter, an underscore, or a backslash (\).
- Spaces are not valid within a range name. Use underscore characters or periods to separate words.
- A valid cell address cannot become a range name.
- Range names are not case sensitive.

Project 1a Creating Range Names

Part 1 of 7

1. Open **AllClaimsOct12VehRpt.xlsx**.
2. Save the workbook with Save As and name it **EL2-C2-P1-AllClaimsOct12VehRpt**.
3. Assign names to ranges by completing the following steps:
   a. Select D4:D24.
   b. Click in the Name box located at the left end of the Formula bar, type **AutoNo**, and then press Enter.
   c. Select E4:E24, click in the Name box, type **DriverNo**, and then press Enter.
   d. Select F4:F24, click in the Name box, type **Rating**, and then press Enter.
   e. Select H4:H24, click in the Name box, type **ClaimEst**, and then press Enter.
   f. Select I4:I24, click in the Name box, type **RepShop**, and then press Enter.

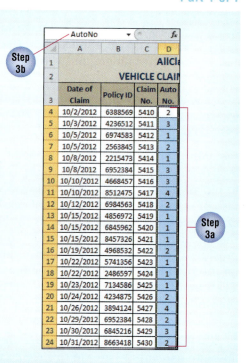

4. View the range names by clicking the down-pointing arrow to the right of the Name box.
5. Click *AutoNo* at the drop-down list to move the selected range to column D. One reason for creating a range name is to quickly move the active cell to navigate a large worksheet.
6. Deselect the range.
7. Save **EL2-C2-P1-AllClaimsOct12VehRpt.xlsx**.

Statistical Functions ■■■■■■■■ ■■■■■■■■■■ ■■■■■■

Commonly used statistical functions include AVERAGE, MAX, and MIN, where AVERAGE returns the arithmetic mean, MAX returns the largest value, and MIN returns the smallest value in the range. Another function used often is COUNT, which returns the number of cells that contain numbers or dates. Empty cells, text labels, or error values in the range are ignored. Excel provides additional AVERAGE and COUNT functions that are used to count text entries and count and find averages for a range based on a criterion.

COUNTA

In a worksheet that requires cells containing text, or cells containing a combination of text and numbers (such as *Model-2146*) to be counted, Excel provides the COUNTA function. COUNTA returns the number of cells that are not empty; therefore, this formula can be used to count a range of cells other than values. As shown in the worksheet in Figure 2.1, when the regular COUNT function is used in E8 to count parts in the range A2:A6, Excel returns a value of 0. However, in E9, when the same range is counted using COUNTA, Excel returns the value of 5.

COUNTIF and COUNTIFS

Use the COUNTIF function to count cells within a range that meet a single criterion. For example, in a grades worksheet you might use a COUNTIF function to count the number of students who achieved greater than 75 percent. This

Figure 2.1 COUNTA Example

	A	B	C	D	E
1	Part Number	Qty	Price		
2	Part#-134A	55	2.10		
3	Part#-1125	21	3.15		
4	Part#-874T	47	4.58		
5	Part#-784U	65	3.68		
6	Part#-546C	85	4.85		
7					
8	Count of column A using COUNT function:				0
9	Count of column A using COUNTA function:				5

Formula =*COUNT(A2:A6)* returns zero.

Formula =*COUNTA(A2:A6)* returns the correct result.

Create COUNTIF Formula
1. Make desired cell active.
2. Click Insert Function button.
3. Change category to *Statistical*.
4. Select *COUNTIF*.
5. Click OK.
6. Enter range address or range name to select by in *Range* text box.
7. Enter condition expression or text in *Criteria* text box.
8. Click OK.

Create COUNTIFS Formula
1. Make desired cell active.
2. Click Insert Function button.
3. Change category to *Statistical*.
4. Select *COUNTIFS*.
5. Click OK.
6. Enter range address or range name to select by in *Criteria_range1* text box.
7. Enter condition expression or text in *Criteria1* text box.
8. Enter range address or range name to select by in *Criteria_range2* text box.
9. Enter condition expression or text in *Criteria2* text box.
10. Continue adding criteria range expressions and criteria as needed.
11. Click OK.

Insert Function

function uses conditional logic where the criterion defines a conditional test so that only those cells that meet the test are selected for action. The structure of a COUNTIF function is *=COUNTIF(range,criteria)*. For the grades worksheet example, the function to count the cells of students who achieved greater than 75 percent would be *=COUNTIF(grades,">75")* assuming the range name *grades* has been defined. Notice the syntax of the argument requires criteria to be enclosed in quotation symbols. If you use the Insert Function dialog box to create formulas, Excel adds the required syntax automatically.

COUNTIFS is used to count cells that meet multiple criteria. The formula uses the same structure as COUNTIF with additional ranges and criteria within the argument. The structure of a COUNTIFS function is *=COUNTIFS(range1, criteria1,range2,criteria2. . .)*. Figure 2.2 illustrates a nursing education worksheet with a single criterion COUNTIF to count the number of RNs and a multiple criteria COUNTIFS to count the number of RNs who are current with their Professional Development activities. The formulas shown in Figure 2.2 include range names where *Title* references the entries in column D and *PDCurrent* references the entries in column H.

Figure 2.2 COUNTIF and COUNTIFS Formulas

	A	B	C	D	E	F	G	H	I	J	K
1	Department of Human Resources, Professional Development										
2	Full-Time Nursing Education Worksheet										
3	Employee Number	Employee LastName	Employee FirstName	Title	Unit	Extension	Years Experience	PD Current?		Nursing Education Statistical Summary	
4	FT02001	Santos	Susan	RN	Med/Surg	36415	30	Yes		Number of RNs	12
5	FT02002	Daniels	Jasmine	RN	Med/Surg	36415	27	No		Number of LPNs	7
6	FT02003	Walden	Virgina	RN	ICU	34211	22	No			
7	FT02004	Jaffe	Paul	LPN	CSRU	36418	24	Yes		RNs who are current with PD	7
8	FT02005	Salvatore	Terry	LPN	ICU	34211	22	Yes		LPNs who are current with PD	4
9	FT02006	Mander	Kaitlynn	RN	ICU	34211	24	Yes			
10	FT02007	Lavigne	Gisele	RN	CSRU	36418	20	No			
11	FT02008	Williamson	Forman	RN	CSRU	36418	19	Yes			
12	FT02009	Orlowski	William	RN	Ortho	31198	22	No			
13	FT02010	El-Hamid	Lianna	LPN	Med/Surg	36415	20	No			
14	FT02011	Vezina	Ursula	LPN	Ortho	31198	20	No			
15	FT02012	Jorgensen	Macy	RN	Med/Surg	36415	10	Yes			
16	FT02013	Pieterson	Eric	RN	ICU	34211	8	Yes			
17	FT02014	Costa	Michael	RN	Ortho	31198	10	No			
18	FT02015	Besterd	Mary	RN	PreOp	32881	7	Yes			
19	FT02016	Oste	Frank	LPN	Med/Surg	36415	7	Yes			
20	FT02017	Hillman	John	LPN	PreOp	32881	5	No			
21	FT02018	Cano	Rodney	RN	ICU	34211	4	Yes			
22	FT02019	Rivere	Waylan	LPN	CSRU	36418	2	Yes			

Formula
=COUNTIF(Title,"RN")

Formula
=COUNTIFS(Title,"RN",PDCurrent,"Yes")

1. With **EL2-C2-P1-AllClaimsOct12VehRpt.xlsx** open, make L4 the active cell.
2. Create a COUNTIF function to count the number of claims where A+ Paint & Body is the repair shop by completing the following steps:

   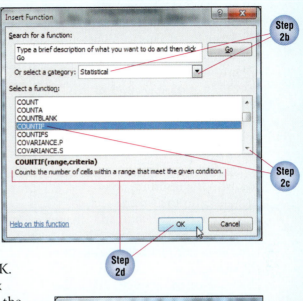

   a. Click the Insert Function button in the Formula bar.
   b. At the Insert Function dialog box, click the down-pointing arrow to the right of the *Or select a category* list box and then click *Statistical* at the drop-down list. **Note: Skip this step if Statistical is already selected as the category**.
   c. Scroll down the *Select a function* list box and then click *COUNTIF*.
   d. Read the formula description below the function list box and then click OK.
   e. At the Function Arguments dialog box with the insertion point positioned in the *Range* text box, type **RepShop** and then press Tab. Recall from Project 1a that you defined a range name for the entries in column I. **Note: If necessary, drag the Function Arguments dialog box title bar left or right if the dialog box is obscuring your view of the worksheet.**

   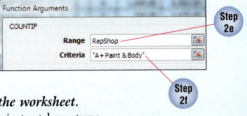

   f. With the insertion point positioned in the *Criteria* text box, type **A+ Paint & Body** and then press Tab. When you press Tab, Excel adds the quotation symbols to the criteria text.
   g. Click OK. Excel returns the value *3* in L4.
   h. Look at the formula in the Formula bar created by the Function Arguments dialog box: *=COUNTIF(RepShop,"A+ Paint & Body")*.
3. Make L5 the active cell, type the formula **=countif(repshop,"JFJ Auto")**, and then press Enter.

   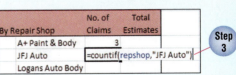

4. Enter the following COUNTIF formulas in the cells indicated using either the Insert Function dialog box or by typing the formula directly into the cell.

   L6   **=COUNTIF(RepShop,"Logans Auto Body")**
   L7   **=COUNTIF(RepShop,"West Collision")**

   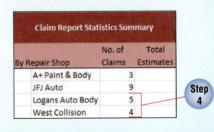

5. Save **EL2-C2-P1-AllClaimsOct12VehRpt.xlsx**.

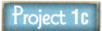

1. With **EL2-C2-P1-AllClaimsOct12VehRpt.xlsx** open, make L10 the active cell.
2. Create a COUNTIFS function to count the number of claims where the repair shop is JFJ Auto and the claims estimate is greater than $5,000 by completing the following steps:
   a. Click the Insert Function button in the Formula bar.
   b. With *Statistical* the category in the *Or select a category* list box, scroll down the *Select a function* list box and then click *COUNTIFS*.

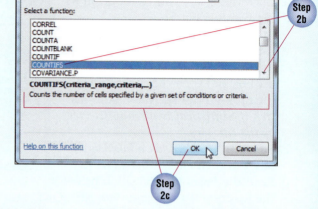

   c. Read the formula description below the function list box and then click OK.
   d. At the Function Arguments dialog box with the insertion point positioned in the *Criteria_range1* text box, type **RepShop** and then press Tab. After you press Tab, a *Criteria_range2* text box is added to the dialog box.
   e. With the insertion point positioned in the *Criteria1* text box, type **JFJ Auto** and then press Tab.
   f. With the insertion point positioned in the *Criteria_range2* text box, type **ClaimEst** and then press Tab.
   g. With the insertion point positioned in the *Criteria2* text box, type **>5000** and then press Tab.
   h. Click OK. Excel returns the value *5* in L10.

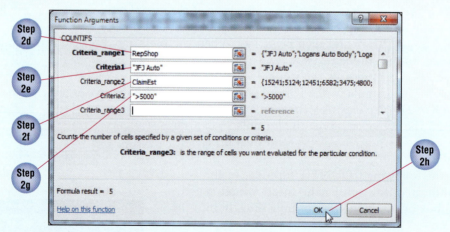

3. Look at the formula in the Formula bar created by the Function Arguments dialog box: =COUNTIFS(RepShop,"JFJ Auto",ClaimEst,">5000").
4. Enter the following COUNTIFS formula in L13 using either the Insert Function dialog box or by typing the formula directly into the cell:

   =COUNTIFS(RepShop,"JFJ Auto",Rating,">3")

5. Save **EL2-C2-P1-AllClaimsOct12VehRpt.xlsx**.

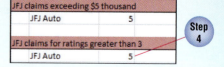

JFJ claims exceeding $5 thousand	
JFJ Auto	5
JFJ claims for ratings greater than 3	
JFJ Auto	5

AVERAGEIF and AVERAGEIFS

The AVERAGEIF function is used to find the arithmetic mean of the cells within the specified range that meet a single criterion. The structure of an AVERAGEIF function is =AVERAGEIF(range,criteria,average_range) where *range* is the cells to be tested for the criterion, *criteria* is the conditional statement used to select cells, and *average_range* is the range containing the values you want to average.

AVERAGEIFS is used to average cells that meet multiple criteria using the formula =AVERAGEIFS(average_range,criteria_range1,criteria1,criteria_range2,criteria2. . .). Figure 2.3 illustrates an executive management salary report for a hospital. Below the salary data, average salary statistics are shown. In the first two rows of salary statistics, the average total salary is calculated for each of two hospital campuses. In the second two rows of salary statistics, average total salary is calculated for each campus for those executives hired before 2010. The formulas shown in Figure 2.3 include range names where *Year* references the values in column E, *Campus* references the entries in column F, and *Total* references the values in column I.

Figure 2.3 AVERAGEIF and AVERAGEIFS Formulas

	A	B	C	D	E	F	G	H	I
1				**Columbia River General Hospital**					
2				Executive Management Salary Report					
3				For the fiscal year 2012 to 2013					
4				Job Title	Year Hired	Campus	Salary	Benefits	Total
5	Ms.	Michelle	Tan	Chief Executive Officer	2001	Sunnyside	$ 155,000	$ 18,400	$ 173,400
6	Mr.	Douglas	Brown	Legal Counsel	2011	Sunnyside	90,500	17,500	108,000
7	Mrs.	Lauren	Quandt	Chief Financial Officer	2011	Portland	110,750	18,400	129,150
8	Dr.	Dana	Pembroke	Medical Director	2005	Portland	101,500	14,650	116,150
9	Mrs.	Gina	Wright	Director of Nursing	2010	Portland	95,475	14,650	110,125
10	Mr.	Fernando	Ortega	Director of Patient Care Services	2011	Sunnyside	87,750	12,675	100,425
11	Mr.	Joshua	Vitello	Director of Facilities	2008	Sunnyside	85,000	9,275	94,275
12	Miss	Carin	Ledicke	Director of Human Resources	2006	Portland	85,000	9,275	94,275
13	Mr.	William	Formet	Director of Planning	2004	Portland	85,000	9,275	94,275
14	Mr.	Paul	Kosovic	Director, Community Relations	1998	Sunnyside	72,500	8,975	81,475
15									
16							$ 968,475	$133,075	$1,101,550
17									
18		**Salary Statistics**							
19				Average executive total salary at Portland campus			$ 108,795		
20				Average executive total salary at Sunnyside campus			$ 111,515		
21									
22				Average executive total salary at Portland campus hired before 2010			$ 101,567		
23				Average executive total salary at Sunnyside campus hired before 2010			$ 116,383		

Formula
=AVERAGEIF(Campus,"Portland",Total)

Formula
=AVERAGEIFS(Total,Campus,"Sunnyside",Year,"<2010")

Create AVERAGEIF Formula
1. Make desired cell active.
2. Click Insert Function button.
3. Change category to *Statistical*.
4. Select *AVERAGEIF*.
5. Click OK.
6. Enter range address or range name to select by in *Range* text box.
7. Enter condition expression or text in *Criteria* text box.
8. Enter range address or range name to average in *Average_range* text box.
9. Click OK.

Create AVERAGEIFS Formula
1. Make desired cell active.
2. Click Insert Function button.
3. Change category to *Statistical*.
4. Select *AVERAGEIFS*.
5. Click OK.
6. Enter range address or range name to average in *Average_range* text box.
7. Enter range address or range name to select by in *Criteria_range1* text box.
8. Enter condition expression or text in *Criteria1* text box.
9. Enter range address or range name to select by in *Criteria_range2* text box.
10. Enter condition expression or text in *Criteria2* text box.
11. Continue adding criteria range expressions and criteria as needed.
12. Click OK.

1. With **EL2-C2-P1-AllClaimsOct12VehRpt.xlsx** open, make M16 the active cell.
2. Create an AVERAGEIF function to calculate the average claim estimate for those claims with a rating of 1 by completing the following steps:
   a. Click the Insert Function button in the Formula bar.
   b. With *Statistical* the category in the *Or select a category* list box, click *AVERAGEIF* in the *Select a function* list box.
   c. Read the formula description below the function list box and then click OK.
   d. At the Function Arguments dialog box with the insertion point positioned in the *Range* text box, type **Rating** and then press Tab.
   e. With the insertion point positioned in the *Criteria* text box, type **1** and then press Tab.

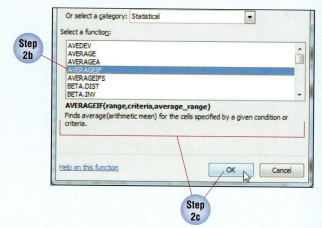

   f. With the insertion point positioned in the *Average_range* text box, type **ClaimEst** and then press Tab.
   g. Click OK. Excel returns the value *2691* in M16.

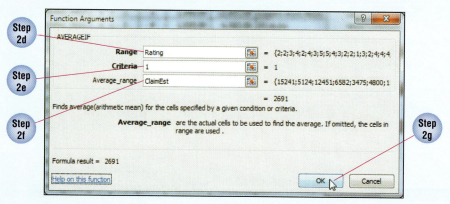

   h. Look at the formula in the Formula bar created by the Function Arguments dialog box: *=AVERAGEIF(Rating,1,ClaimEst)*.
3. Format M16 to Comma Style number format with zero decimals.
4. Make M17 the active cell, type the formula **=averageif(rating,2,claimest)**, and then press Enter.
5. Format M17 to Comma Style number format with zero decimals.
6. Make M17 the active cell and then drag the fill handle down to M18:M20.
7. Edit the formulas in M18, M19, and M20 by changing the rating criterion value from *2* to *3*, *4*, and *5*, respectively. When completed, the AVERAGEIF formulas will be as follows:

   M18   *=AVERAGEIF(Rating,3,ClaimEst)*
   M19   *=AVERAGEIF(Rating,4,ClaimEst)*
   M20   *=AVERAGEIF(Rating,5,ClaimEst)*

By Rating	Avg. Est.
1	2,691
2	6,987
3	9,014
4	7,830
5	14,564

Step 7

8. Save **EL2-C2-P1-AllClaimsOct12VehRpt.xlsx**.

1. With **EL2-C2-P1-AllClaimsOct12VehRpt.xlsx** open, make M22 the active cell.
2. Create an AVERAGEIFS function to calculate the average claim estimate for those claims with a rating of 2 and driver number 1 by completing the following steps:
   a. Click the Insert Function button in the Formula bar.
   b. With *Statistical* the category in the *Or select a category* list box, click *AVERAGEIFS* in the *Select a function* list box.
   c. Read the formula description below the function list box and then click OK.
   d. At the Function Arguments dialog box with the insertion point positioned in the *Average_range* text box, type **ClaimEst** and then press Tab.
   e. Type **Rating** in the *Criteria_range1* text box and then press Tab.
   f. Type **2** in the *Criteria1* text box and then press Tab.
   g. Type **DriverNo** in the *Criteria_range2* text box and then press Tab.
   h. Type **1** in the *Criteria2* text box and then click OK. Excel returns the value *6272.666667* in the cell.

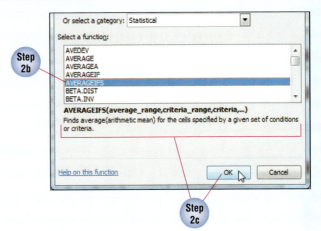

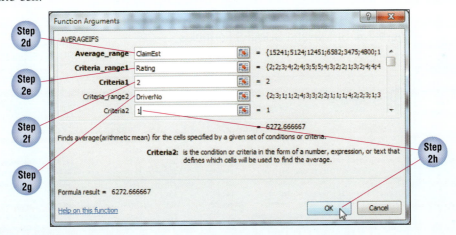

   i. Format M22 to Comma Style number format with zero decimals.
3. Copy the AVERAGEIFS formula in M22 and paste to M23.
4. Edit the formula in M23 to change the rating criterion from *2* to *3*. When completed, the AVERAGEIFS formula will be: *=AVERAGEIFS(ClaimEst,Rating,3,DriverNo,1)*.
5. If necessary, format M23 to Comma Style number format with zero decimals.
6. Save **EL2-C2-P1-AllClaimsOct12VehRpt.xlsx**.

▼ **Quick Steps**

**Create SUMIF
Formula**
1. Make desired cell
   active.
2. Click Formulas tab.
3. Click Math & Trig
   button.
4. Scroll down and click
   SUMIF.
5. Enter range address
   or range name to
   select by in *Range*
   text box.
6. Enter condition
   expression or text in
   Criteria text box.
7. Enter range address
   or range name to add
   in *Sum_range* text
   box.
8. Click OK.

Math & Trig
Functions

Math and Trigonometry Functions ▪▪▪▪▪▪▪▪▪▪▪▪▪▪▪

Excel includes several math and trigonometry functions such as ABS to return the absolute value of a number, SQRT to find the square root of a number, and RAND to return a random number between 0 and 1, to name a few. At the Insert Function dialog box change the *Or select a category* option to *Math & Trig* to scroll the list of available functions in the category.

SUMIF and SUMIFS

Within the math and trigonometry function category, Excel includes SUMIF to add the cells within a range that meet a single criterion and SUMIFS to add the cells within a range that meet multiple criteria. The structure of the SUMIF formula is *=SUMIF(range,criteria,sum_range)* where *range* is the cells to be tested for the criterion, *criteria* is the conditional statement used to select cells, and *sum_range* is the range containing the values to add.

SUMIFS is used to add cells that meet multiple criteria using the formula *=SUMIFS(sum_range,criteria_range1,criteria1,criteria_range2,criteria2. . .)*. Figure 2.4 provides an example of SUMIF and SUMIFS formulas used in a medical clinic's standard cost worksheet for examination room supplies. At the right of the clinic supplies inventory, a SUMIF formula sums the cost for items by supplier number. A SUMIFS formula sums the cost for items by supplier number for items that require a minimum stock quantity over 4 items. The formulas shown in Figure 2.4 include range names where *Supplier* references the entries in column C, *MinQty* references the values in column E, and *StdCost* references the values in column F.

Figure 2.4 SUMIF and SUMIFS Formulas

> Formula
> =SUMIF(Supplier,"101",StdCost)

Item	Unit	Supplier Number	Price	Minimum Stock Qty	Standard Cost	Exam Room Cost Analysis	
						North Shore Medical Clinic	
						Clinic Supplies Inventory Units and Price	
Sterile powder-free synthetic gloves, size Small	per 100	101	35.95	4	143.80	**Cost by Supplier**	
Sterile powder-free synthetic gloves, size Medium	per 100	101	35.95	8	287.60	Supplier Number 101	1,401.40
Sterile powder-free synthetic gloves, size Large	per 100	101	35.95	10	359.50	Supplier Number 155	364.33
Sterile powder-free latex gloves, size Small	per 100	101	16.25	4	65.00	Supplier Number 201	1,918.00
Sterile powder-free latex gloves, size Medium	per 100	101	16.25	8	130.00	Supplier Number 350	790.80
Sterile powder-free latex gloves, size Large	per 100	101	16.25	10	162.50		
Sterile powder-free vinyl gloves, size Small	per 100	101	11.50	4	46.00		
Sterile powder-free vinyl gloves, size Medium	per 100	101	11.50	8	92.00	**Cost by Supplier with**	
Sterile powder-free vinyl gloves, size Large	per 100	101	11.50	10	115.00	**Minimum Qty over 4**	
Disposable earloop mask	per 50	155	5.61	8	44.88	Supplier Number 101	1,146.60
Disposable patient gown	per dozen	155	7.90	16	126.40	Supplier Number 155	310.80
Disposable patient slippers	per dozen	155	4.27	16	68.32	Supplier Number 201	1,330.00
Cotton patient gown	per dozen	201	133.00	10	1,330.00	Supplier Number 350	659.00
Cotton patient robe	per dozen	201	147.00	4	588.00		
Disposable examination table paper	per roll	155	8.90	8	71.20		
Lab coat, size Small	each	350	32.95	4	131.80		
Lab coat, size Medium	each	350	32.95	8	263.60		
Lab coat, size Large	each	350	32.95	12	395.40		
Disposable shoe cover	per 300	155	37.75	1	37.75		
Disposable bouffant cap	per 100	155	7.89	2	15.78		
TOTAL STANDARD EXAM ROOM SUPPLIES COST:					4,474.53		

> Formula
> =SUMIFS(StdCost,Supplier,"350",MinQty,">4")

Note: At Step 5 you will print the worksheet. Check with your instructor before printing to see if you need to print two copies of the worksheets for all projects in this chapter: one as displayed and another displaying cell formulas. Save the worksheet before displaying formulas (Ctrl + ~) so that you can adjust column widths as necessary and then close without saving the changes.

1. With **EL2-C2-P1-AllClaimsOct12VehRpt.xlsx** open, make M4 the active cell.
2. Create a SUMIF function to sum the claim estimates for those claims being repaired at A+ Paint & Body by completing the following steps:
   a. Click the Formulas tab.
   b. Click the Math & Trig button in the Function Library group.
   c. Scroll down the drop-down list and click *SUMIF*.
   d. At the Function Arguments dialog box with the insertion point positioned in the *Range* text box, type **RepShop** and then press Tab.
   e. Type **A+ Paint & Body** in the *Criteria* text box and then press Tab.
   f. Type **ClaimEst** in the *Sum_range* text box and then click OK. Excel returns the value *16656* in M4.

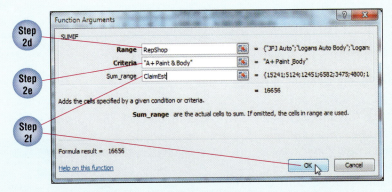

   g. Format M4 to Comma Style number format with zero decimals.
3. Enter the following SUMIF formulas in the cells indicated using either the Function Arguments dialog box or by typing the formula directly into the cell.

   M5 =SUMIF(RepShop,"JFJ Auto",ClaimEst)
   M6 =SUMIF(RepShop,"Logans Auto Body",ClaimEst)
   M7 =SUMIF(RepShop,"West Collision",ClaimEst)

4. Format M5:M7 to Comma Style number format with zero decimals.
5. Save and then print **EL2-C2-P1-AllClaimsOct12VehRpt.xlsx**.

Claim Report Statistics Summary		
By Repair Shop	No. of Claims	Total Estimates
A+ Paint & Body	3	16,656
JFJ Auto	9	66,128
Logans Auto Body	5	51,990
West Collision	4	31,683

Steps 3-4

Managing Range Names ▪▪▪▪▪▪▪▪▪▪▪▪▪▪▪▪▪▪▪▪▪▪▪▪▪

The Name Manager dialog box can be used to create, edit, or delete range names. A range name can be edited by changing the name or modifying the range address associated with the name. A range name can also be deleted if the name is not being used. Exercise caution when deleting a range name. If a range name used in a formula is deleted, cells that used the range name display the error #NAME? New range names can also be added to the workbook using the Name Manager dialog box shown in Figure 2.5.

Figure 2.5 Name Manager Dialog Box

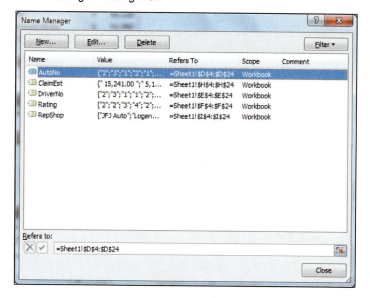

Project 1g — **Editing and Deleting a Range Name** Part 7 of 7

1. With **EL2-C2-P1-AllClaimsOct12VehRpt.xlsx** open, click the Formulas tab if it is not currently active.
2. Delete the range name *AutoNo* by completing the following steps:
   a. Click the Name Manager button in the Defined Names group.
   b. At the Name Manager dialog box, with *AutoNo* already selected in the *Name* list box, click the Delete button.
   c. At the Microsoft Excel message box asking you to confirm the deletion of the name *AutoNo*, click OK.

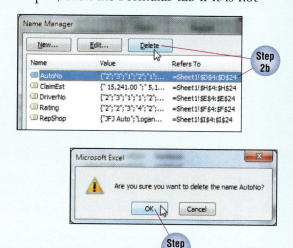

3. Edit the range name for the range named *ClaimEst* by completing the following steps:
   a. Click *ClaimEst* in the *Name* list box and then click the Edit button.
   b. At the Edit Name dialog box with *ClaimEst* already selected in the *Name* text box, type **ClaimEstimate** and then click OK. Notice the new range name is now displayed in the *Name* list box.
   c. Click the Close button located at the bottom right of the Name Manager dialog box.
4. Click in cell M4 and look at the formula in the Formula bar. Notice Excel automatically changed the range name in the formula from *ClaimEst* to *ClaimEstimate*.
5. Save and then close **EL2-C2-P1-AllClaimsOct12VehRpt.xlsx**.

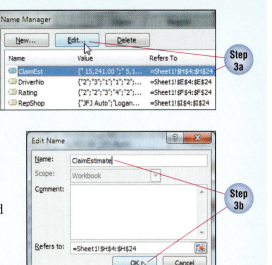

Step 3a

Step 3b

---

roject **2** **Populate Cells by Looking Up Data**   **1 Part**

You will use a lookup formula to automatically enter discounts for containers and then calculate net prices.

Lookup Functions ▪▪▪▪▪ ▪▪▪▪▪ ▪▪▪▪▪ ▪▪▪▪▪

The Lookup & Reference category of functions provides formulas that can be used to look up values in a range. For example, in a grades worksheet, the final numerical score for a student can be looked up in a range of cells that contain the letter grades with corresponding numerical scores for each grade. The letter grade can be returned in the formula cell by looking up the student's score. The ability to look up a value automates data entry in large worksheets and when used properly can avoid inaccuracies from data entry errors. Excel provides two lookup functions: VLOOKUP and HLOOKUP, which refer to a vertical or horizontal lookup, respectively. The layout of the lookup range (referred to as a lookup table) determines whether to use VLOOKUP or HLOOKUP. VLOOKUP is more commonly used since most lookup tables are arranged with comparison data in columns, which means Excel searches for the lookup value in a vertical order. HLOOKUP is used when the lookup range has placed comparison data in rows and Excel searches for the lookup value in a horizontal pattern.

VLOOKUP

The structure of a VLOOKUP formula is =*VLOOKUP(lookup_value,table_array,col_index_num,range_lookup)*. Table 2.2 explains each section of the VLOOKUP argument.

VLOOKUP is easier to understand using an example. In the worksheet shown in Figure 2.6, VLOOKUP is used to return the starting salary for new hires at a

▼ **Quick Steps**

Create VLOOKUP Formula
1. Make desired cell active.
2. Click Formulas tab.
3. Click Lookup & Reference button.
4. Click *VLOOKUP*.
5. Enter cell address, range name, or value in *Lookup_value* text box.
6. Enter range or range name in *Table_array* text box.
7. Type column number to return values from in *Col_index_num* text box.
8. Type **FALSE** or leave blank for *TRUE* in *Range_lookup* text box.
9. Click OK.

Lookup & Reference

medical center. Each new hire is assigned a salary grid number that places his or her starting salary depending on their education and years of work experience. The lookup table contains the grid numbers with the corresponding starting salary. VLOOKUP formulas in column E automatically insert the starting salary for each new employee based on the employee's grid number in column D. In the formula shown in Figure 2.6 range names have been included where *Rating* references the values in column D and *grid* represents the lookup table in G2:H8.

Table 2.2 VLOOKUP Argument Parameters

Argument Parameter	Description
Lookup_value	The value that you want Excel to search for in the lookup table. You can enter a value or a cell reference to a value.
Table_array	The range address or range name for the lookup table that you want Excel to search.
Col_index_num	The column number from the lookup table that contains the data you want placed in the formula cell.
Range_lookup	Enter TRUE or FALSE to instruct Excel to find an exact match for the lookup value or an approximate match. If this parameter is left out of the formula, Excel assumes TRUE, which means if an exact match is not found, Excel returns the value for the next largest number that is less than the lookup value. For the formula to work properly, the first column of the lookup table must be sorted in ascending order.

Enter FALSE to instruct Excel to return only exact matches to the lookup value. |

Figure 2.6 VLOOKUP Example

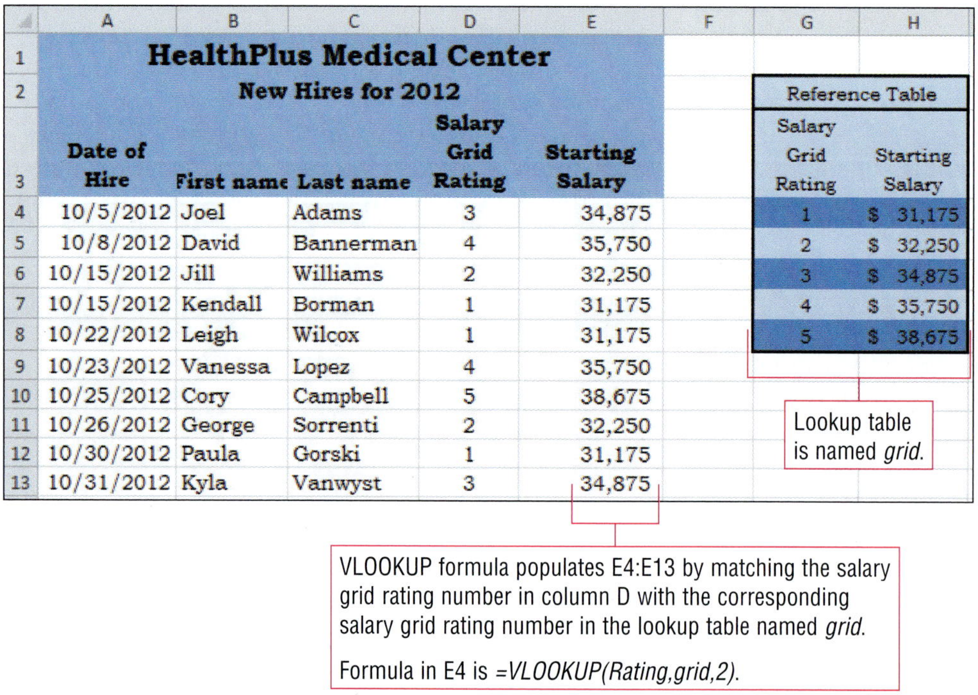

	A	B	C	D	E	F	G	H
1	**HealthPlus Medical Center**							
2	**New Hires for 2012**						Reference Table	
3	Date of Hire	First name	Last name	Salary Grid Rating	Starting Salary		Salary Grid Rating	Starting Salary
4	10/5/2012	Joel	Adams	3	34,875		1	$ 31,175
5	10/8/2012	David	Bannerman	4	35,750		2	$ 32,250
6	10/15/2012	Jill	Williams	2	32,250		3	$ 34,875
7	10/15/2012	Kendall	Borman	1	31,175		4	$ 35,750
8	10/22/2012	Leigh	Wilcox	1	31,175		5	$ 38,675
9	10/23/2012	Vanessa	Lopez	4	35,750			
10	10/25/2012	Cory	Campbell	5	38,675			
11	10/26/2012	George	Sorrenti	2	32,250		Lookup table is named *grid*.	
12	10/30/2012	Paula	Gorski	1	31,175			
13	10/31/2012	Kyla	Vanwyst	3	34,875			

VLOOKUP formula populates E4:E13 by matching the salary grid rating number in column D with the corresponding salary grid rating number in the lookup table named *grid*.

Formula in E4 is *=VLOOKUP(Rating,grid,2)*.

1. Open **PrecisionPrices.xlsx**.
2. Save the workbook with Save As and name it **EL2-C2-P2-PrecisionPrices**.
3. Create a VLOOKUP formula to find the correct discount values for each product by completing the following steps:

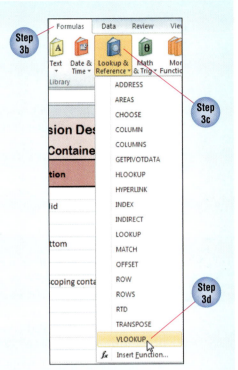

   a. Select H4:I8 and name the range *DiscTable*.
   b. Make E4 the active cell and then click the Formulas tab.
   c. Click the Lookup & Reference button in the Function Library group.
   d. Click *VLOOKUP* at the drop-down list.
   e. If necessary, drag the Function Arguments dialog box out of the way so that you can see the first few rows of the products price list and the Discount Table data.
   f. With the insertion point positioned in the *Lookup_value* text box, type **c4** and then press Tab. Product discounts are categorized by letter codes. To find the correct discount, you need Excel to look for the matching category letter code for the product within the first column of the Discount Table. Notice the letter codes in the Discount Table are listed in ascending order.
   g. Type **DiscTable** in the *Table_array* text box and then press Tab. Using a range name for a reference table is a good idea since the formula will be copied and absolute references are needed for the cells in the lookup table.
   h. Type **2** in the *Col_index_num* text box and then press Tab.
   i. Type **false** in the *Range_lookup* text box and then click OK. By typing *false*, you are instructing Excel to return a value for exact matches only. Should a discount category be typed into a cell in column C for which no entry exists in the Discount Table, Excel will return *#N/A* in the formula cell, which will alert you that an error has occurred in the data entry.

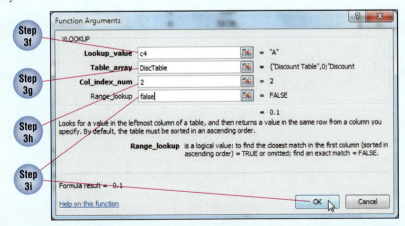

4. Look at the formula in the Formula bar =*VLOOKUP(C4,DiscTable,2,FALSE)*.
5. Format E4 to Percent Style.

6. Make F4 the active cell, type the formula **=d4-(d4*e4)**, and then press Enter.
7. Select E4:F4 and then drag the fill handle down to row 21.
8. Deselect the range.
9. Print the worksheet.
10. Save and then close **EL2-C2-P2-PrecisionPrices.xlsx**.

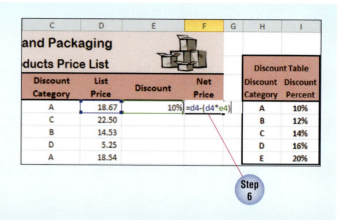

Step 6

HLOOKUP

The HLOOKUP function uses the same argument parameters as VLOOKUP. Use HLOOKUP when the table in which you want to search for a comparison value is arranged in a horizontal arrangement similar to the one shown in Figure 2.7. Excel searches across the table in the first row for a matching value and then returns to the formula cell the value from the same column. The structure of an HLOOKUP formula is *=HLOOKUP(lookup_value,table_array,row_index_num,range_lookup)*. The argument parameters are similar to VLOOKUP's parameters described in Table 2.2. Excel searches the first row of the table for the lookup value. When a match is found, Excel returns the value from the same column in the row number specified in the *row_index_num* argument.

Figure 2.7 HLOOKUP Example

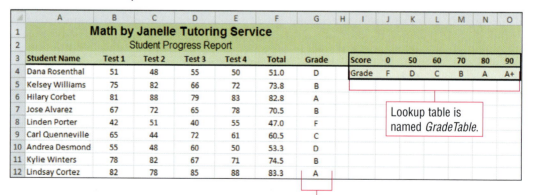

HLOOKUP formula populates G4:G12 by looking up the total value in column F with the first row in GradeTable. Excel stops at the largest value in the table that does not go over the lookup value. Looking for *62.3* would cause Excel to stop at *60* because moving to the next value, *70*, would be over the lookup value. Formula in G4 is *=HLOOKUP(F4,GradeTable,2)*.

roject **3** **Analyze an Expansion Project Loan** **1 Part**

You will use a financial function to calculate the principal portion of an expansion loan payment for two lenders.

Financial Functions ■■■■■■■■■■■■■■■■■■■■■■■■■■■■■

Financial functions can be used for a variety of financial analyses including loan amortizations, annuity payments, investment planning, depreciation, and so on. The PMT function is used to calculate a payment for a loan based on a constant interest rate and constant payments for a set period of time. Excel provides two related financial functions: PPMT, to calculate the principal portion of the loan payment; and IPMT, to calculate the interest portion.

PPMT

Knowing the principal portion of a loan payment is useful to determine the amount of the payment that is being used to reduce the principal balance owing. The difference between the loan payment and the PPMT value represents the interest cost. The function returns the principal portion of a specific payment for a loan. For example, you can calculate the principal on the first payment, the last payment, or any payment in between. The structure of a PPMT function is *=PPMT(rate,per,nper,pv,fv,type)* where:

* *rate* is the interest rate per period,
* *per* is the period for which you want to find the principal portion of the payment,
* *nper* is the number of payment periods,
* *pv* is the amount of money borrowed,
* *fv* is the balance at the end of the loan (if left blank, zero is assumed), and
* *type* is either 0 (payment at end of period) or 1 (payment at beginning of period).

   Be careful to be consistent with the units for the interest rate and payment periods. If you divide the interest rate by 12 for a monthly rate, make sure the payment periods are also expressed monthly—for example, multiply the term by 12 if the amortization is entered in the worksheet in years.

▼ **Quick Steps**

Create PPMT Formula
1. Make desired cell active.
2. Click Formulas tab.
3. Click Financial button.
4. Click *PPMT*.
5. Enter value, cell address, or range name for interest rate in *Rate* text box.
6. Enter number representing payment to find principal for in *Per* text box.
7. Enter value, cell address, or range name for total number of payments in *Nper* text box.
8. Enter value, cell address, or range name for amount borrowed in *Pv* text box.
9. Click OK.

Financial Functions

Project 3 **Calculating Principal Portion of Loan Payments** **Part 1 of 1**

1. Open **DeeringExpansion.xlsx**.
2. Save the workbook with Save As and name it **EL2-C2-P3-DeeringExpansion.xlsx**.
3. Calculate the principal portion of loan payments for two loan proposals to fund a building loan expansion project by completing the following steps:
   a. Make C10 the active cell.

b. If necessary, click the Formulas tab.

c. Click the Financial button in the Function Library group.

d. Scroll down the Financial functions drop-down list and then click *PPMT*.

e. If necessary, move the Function Arguments dialog box to the right side of the screen so that you can see all of the values in column C.

f. With the insertion point positioned in the *Rate* text box, type **c4/12** and then press Tab. Since the interest rate is stated per annum, dividing the rate by 12 calculates the monthly rate.

g. Type **1** in the *Per* text box to calculate principal for the first loan payment and then press Tab.

h. Type **c5*12** in the *Nper* text box and then press Tab. Since loan payments are made each month, the number of payments is 12 times the amortization period.

i. Type **c6** in the *Pv* text box and then click OK. Pv refers to present value and in this example means the loan amount for which the payments are being calculated. Excel returns the value *-1,291.40* in C10. Payments are shown as negative numbers since they represent cash that would be paid out. In this worksheet, negative numbers have been formatted to display in red and enclosed in brackets.

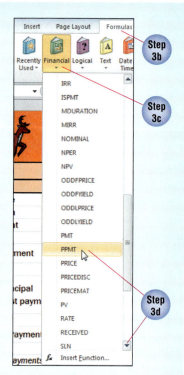

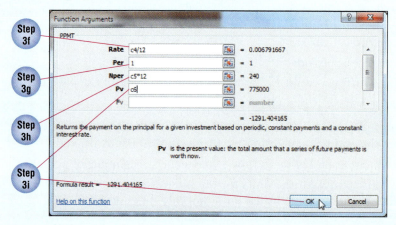

4. Copy and paste the formula from C10 to E10 and then press Esc to remove the moving marquee from C10.

5. Make C12 the active cell, type **=c8*12*c5**, and then press Enter.

6. Copy and paste the formula from C12 to E12. Press Esc to remove the moving marquee from C12 and then AutoFit the width of column E. Notice the loan from Dominion Trust is a better choice for Deering Industries provided the company can afford the higher monthly payments. Although the interest rate is higher than Victory Trust's loan, the shorter term means the loan is repaid faster at a lesser total cost.

7. Print the worksheet.

8. Save **EL2-C2-P3-DeeringExpansion.xlsx**.

3		Victory Trust
4	Interest Rate	8.15%
5	Amortization	20
6	Loan Amount	$ 775,000
7		
8	Monthly Payment	($6,554.95)
9		
10	Monthly Principal Payment (1st payment)	($1,291.40)
11		
12	Total Loan Payments	=c8*12*c5

Project **4** **Calculate Benefit Costs Using Conditional Logic** **2 Parts**

You will create formulas to calculate the employee benefit costs for Vantage Video Rentals using logical functions to test multiple conditions.

Logical Functions ■■■■■■■■ ■ ■■■■■■■■■■ ■■■■■■■ ■■

Conditional logic in formulas requires Excel to perform a calculation based on the outcome of a conditional test where one calculation is performed if the test proves true and another calculation is performed if the test proves false. For example, an IF statement to calculate a sales bonus if sales exceed a target could be created similar to the following: *=IF(Sales>Target,Bonus,0)*. Excel first tests the value in the cell named Sales to see if the value is greater than the value in the cell named Target. If the condition proves true, Excel returns the value in the cell named *Bonus;* if Sales are not greater than Target, the condition proves false and Excel places a *0* in the cell. The structure of the IF statement is *=IF(condition,value_if_true,value_if false)*.

Nested Functions

If you need Excel to perform more than two actions, create a nested IF function. A nested IF function is an IF function inside of another IF function. For example, assume that a company has three sales commission rates based on the level of sales achieved by the salesperson. If sales are less than $40 thousand, the salesperson earns 5% commission; if sales are over $40 thousand but less than $80 thousand, the salesperson earns 7% commission; for sales over $80 thousand, the salesperson earns 9% commission. Since there are three possible sales commission rates, a single IF function will not work. To correctly calculate the sales commission rate, one would need to do two conditional tests.

Consider the following formula: *=IF(Sales<40000,Sales*5%,IF(Sales< 80000,Sales*7%,Sales*9%))*. This formula includes two IF functions. In the first IF function, the conditional test is to determine if the sales value is less than $40 thousand (*Sales<40000*). If the test proves true (for example, sales are $25,000), then Excel calculates the sales times 5% and returns the result in the active cell. If the test proves false, then Excel reads the next section of the argument which is the next IF function that includes the conditional test to determine if sales are less than $80 thousand (*Sales<80000*). If this second conditional test proves true, then Excel calculates the sales times 7%. If the test proves false, Excel calculates the sales times 9%. Since these are the only three possible actions, the formula ends.

You can nest any function inside of another function. For example, in the PPMT formula you learned in the previous section, Excel returns a negative value for the principal portion of the payment. You can nest the PPMT formula inside of the ABS formula to have the principal payment displayed without a negative symbol. ABS is the function used to return the absolute value of a number (the number without its sign). For example, *=ABS(PPMT(C4/12,1,C5*12,C6))* would display the payment calculated in Project 3 as $1,291.40 instead of -$1,291.40.

▼ **Quick Steps**
Create IF Formula
1. Make desired cell active.
2. Click Formulas tab.
3. Click Logical button.
4. Click *IF.*
5. Type conditional test argument in *Logical_test* text box.
6. Press Tab.
7. Type argument in *Value_if_true* text box.
8. Press Tab.
9. Type argument in *Value_if_false* text box.
10. Click OK.

H I N T

If you type a nested IF function directly into a cell, Excel color-codes the brackets for each IF function so that you can keep track of each IF function separately.

H I N T

The number of right brackets needed to end a nested IF statement equals the number of times IF appears in the formula.

Logical Functions

Create AND Formula
1. Make desired cell active OR nest formula in IF statement *Logical_test* text box.
2. Type **=AND(** or **AND(** if nesting in IF statement.
3. Type first conditional test argument.
4. Type **,**.
5. Type second conditional test argument.
6. Repeat Steps 4–5 for remaining conditions.
7. Type **)**.

Create OR Formula
1. Make desired cell active OR nest formula in IF statement *Logical_test* text box.
2. Type **=OR(** or **OR(** if nesting in IF statement.
3. Type first conditional test argument.
4. Type **,**.
5. Type second conditional test argument.
6. Repeat Steps 4–5 for remaining conditions.
7. Type **)**.

H I N T

You can nest an AND or OR function with an IF function to test multiple conditions.

AND and OR

Other logic functions offered in Excel include AND and OR. These functions use Boolean logic to construct a conditional test in a formula. Table 2.3 describes how the functions work to test a statement and provides an example for each.

Table 2.3 AND and OR Logical Functions

Logical Function	Description	Example
AND	Excel returns *True* if all conditions test true. Excel returns *False* if any one of the conditions tests false.	=AND(Sales>Target,NewClients>5) Returns *True* if both test true. If Sales>Target but NewClients<5, returns *False*. If Sales<Target but NewClients>5, returns *False*.
OR	Excel returns *True* if any condition tests true. Excel returns *False* if all conditions test false.	=OR(Sales>Target,NewClients>5) Returns *True* if either Sales>Target or NewClients>5. Returns *False* only if both Sales is not greater than Target and NewClients is not greater than 5.

Project 4a **Calculating Pension Cost Using Nested IF and AND Functions** Part 1 of 2

1. Open **VantageHOSalaryCosts.xlsx**.
2. Save the workbook with Save As and name it **EL2-C2-P4-VantageHOSalaryCosts**.
3. Vantage Video Rentals contributes 5% of an employee's salary into a privately managed company retirement account if the employee is full-time and earns more than $45 thousand in salary. Calculate the pension benefit cost for eligible employees by completing the following steps:
   a. Make H6 the active cell.
   b. Click the Formulas tab.

c. Click the Logical button in the Function Library group and then click *IF* at the drop-down list.

d. If necessary, drag the Function Arguments dialog box down until you can see all of row 6 in the worksheet.

e. With the insertion point positioned in the *Logical_test* text box, type **and(c6="FT",g6>45000)** and then press Tab. An AND function is required since both conditions must be true for the company to contribute to the pension plan. ***Note: Excel requires quotation symbols around text when used in a conditional test formula***.

f. Type **g6*5%** in the *Value_if_true* text box and then press Tab.

g. Type **0** in the *Value_if_false* text box and then click OK.

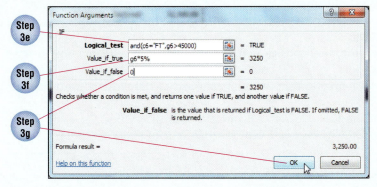

h. Look at the formula *=IF(AND(C6="FT",G6>45000),G6*5%,0)* in the Formula bar. Notice the AND function is nested within the IF function. Since both conditions for the first employee tested true, the pension cost is calculated.

i. Copy the formula in H6 to H7:H14. Notice that only the first three employees have a pension benefit value. The first three employees are the only ones who are both full-time and earn over $45 thousand.

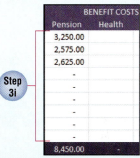

4. Save **EL2-C2-P4-VantageHOSalaryCosts.xlsx**.

Project 4b **Calculating Health and Dental Costs Using Nested IF and OR Functions**   Part 2 of 2

1. With **EL2-C2-P4-VantageHOSalaryCosts.xlsx** open, make I6 the active cell.

2. Vantage Video Rentals offers to pay the annual health premiums for employees who are not covered by any other medical plan. The company pays $2,100 per year per employee for family coverage and $1,380 per year for single coverage. Calculate the cost of the health benefit for those employees who opted into the plan by completing the following steps:

a. This formula requires a nested IF statement since the result will be either *$2,180* or *$1,380* depending on the contents in cell D6. (An OR statement will not work for this formula since two different values are used.) Type the formula shown below in I6 and then press Enter. ***Note: Recall that Excel requires quotation symbols around text entries within an IF function***.

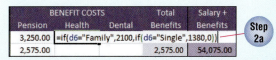

=if(d6="Family",2100,if(d6="Single",1380,0))

b. Copy the formula in I6 to I7:I14. Notice the cells for which no value is entered. In column D, these employees show the text *Declined*. Excel returned zero since both conditions *D6 ="Family"* and *D6 ="Single"* proved false.

3. Vantage Video Rentals negotiated a flat fee with their dental benefit service provider. The company pays the same rate of $1,500 per year for all employees regardless of the type of coverage. The service provider requires Vantage to report each person's coverage as *Family* or *Single* for audit purposes. The dental plan is optional and some employees have declined the coverage. Calculate the dental plan cost by completing the following steps:

a. Make J6 the active cell.

b. If necessary, click the Formulas tab.

c. Click the Logical button and then click *IF* at the drop-down list.

d. If necessary, drag the Function Arguments dialog box down until you can see all of row 6 in the worksheet.

e. With the insertion point positioned in the *Logical_test* text box, type **or(e6="Family",e6="Single")** and then press Tab. An OR function is suited to this benefit since either condition can be true for the company to contribute to the dental plan.

f. Type **1500** in the *Value_if_true* text box and then press Tab.

g. Type **0** in the *Value_if_false* text box and then click OK.

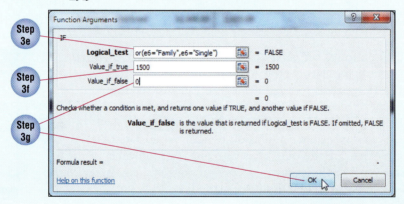

h. Look at the formula *=IF(OR(E6 ="Family",E6 ="Single"),1500,0)* in the Formula bar. Notice the OR function is nested within the IF function. Since E6 contained neither *Family* nor *Single*, the OR statement tested false and the result of *0* is returned in J6.

i. Copy the formula in J6 to J7:J14.

4. Save **EL2-C2-P4-VantageHOSalaryCosts.xlsx**.

5. Print and then close **EL2-C2-P4-VantageHOSalaryCosts.xlsx**.

| BENEFIT COSTS | | | Total | Salary + |
Pension	Health	Dental	Benefits	Benefits
3,250.00	2,100.00	-	5,350.00	70,350.00
2,575.00	1,380.00	1,500.00	5,455.00	56,955.00
2,625.00	-	-	2,625.00	55,125.00
-	2,100.00	1,500.00	3,600.00	31,100.00
-	1,380.00	1,500.00	2,880.00	47,880.00
-	2,100.00	-	2,100.00	24,600.00
-	1,380.00	-	1,380.00	29,880.00
-	-	-	-	42,500.00
-	-	1,500.00	1,500.00	42,000.00
8,450.00	10,440.00	6,000.00	24,890.00	400,390.00

> You will open a worksheet with data downloaded from the U.S. Census Bureau
> and use text functions to modify a heading and convert state names to uppercase.

Text Functions ■■■■■■■■■■■■■■■■■■■■■■■■■■

Text can be formatted or modified using a text function formula. For example, text can be converted from uppercase to lowercase or vice versa using the LOWER and UPPER functions. Text that has incorrect capitalization can be changed to initial case using the PROPER function. Substitute existing text with new text using the SUBSTITUTE function. Table 2.4 provides the structure of each of these functions, with a description and examples.

Table 2.4 Text Function Examples

Text Function	Description	Example
=PROPER(text)	Capitalizes the first letter of each word.	=PROPER("annual budget") returns *Annual Budget* in formula cell OR A3 holds the text *annual budget*; =PROPER(A3) entered in C3 causes C3 to display *Annual Budget*
=UPPER(text)	Converts text to uppercase.	=UPPER("annual budget") returns *ANNUAL BUDGET* in formula cell OR A3 holds the text *annual budget*; =UPPER(A3) entered in C3 causes C3 to display *ANNUAL BUDGET*
=LOWER(text)	Converts text to lowercase.	=LOWER("ANNUAL BUDGET") returns *annual budget* in formula cell OR A3 holds the text *ANNUAL BUDGET*; =LOWER(A3) entered in C3 causes C3 to display *annual budget*
=SUBSTITUTE(text)	New text is inserted in place of old text.	A3 holds the text *Annual Budget*; =SUBSTITUTE(A3,"Annual","2010") entered in C3 causes C3 to display *2010 Budget*

▼ **Quick Steps**

Substitute Text Formula
1. Make desired cell active.
2. Type **=SUBSTITUTE(**.
3. Type source text cell address.
4. Type **,**.
5. Type text to be changed in quotation symbols.
6. Type **,**.
7. Type replacement text in quotation symbols.
8. Type **)**.
9. Press Enter.

Convert Text to Uppercase
1. Make desired cell active.
2. Type **=UPPER(**.
3. Type source cell address. OR Type text to convert in quotation symbols.
4. Type **)**.
5. Press Enter.

Text Functions

1. Open **USIncomeStats.xlsx**.
2. Save the workbook with Save As and name it **EL2-C2-P5-USIncomeStats**.
3. The worksheet contains 2008 median income data downloaded from the U.S. Census Bureau. You want to estimate 2012 median income using a formula based on 2008 statistics. To begin, copy and substitute text at the top of the worksheet to create the layout for 2012 data by completing the following steps:
   a. Copy A1 and paste to F1. Click the Paste Options button and then click the *Keep Source Column Widths* button in the *Paste* section of the drop-down gallery.

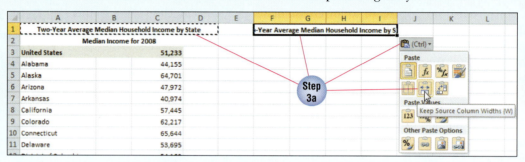

   b. Press the ESC key to remove the moving marquee from A1.
   c. Make F2 the active cell, type **=substitute(a2,"2008","2012")** and then press Enter.

   d. Merge and center F2 across F2:I2.
4. Copy A3 and the state names below A3 from column A to column F and convert the text to uppercase by completing the following steps:
   a. Make F3 the active cell.
   b. Type **=upper(a3)** and then press Enter. Excel returns the text *UNITED STATES* in F3.
   c. Press the Up Arrow key to move the active cell back to F3 and then drag the fill handle down to F54.

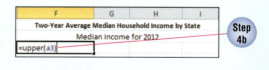

5. Enter the formula to estimate 2012 median income based on 2008 data plus 7.3 percent by completing the following steps:
   a. Make H3 the active cell.
   b. Type **=(c3*7.3%)+c3** and then press Enter.
   c. Press the Up Arrow key to move the active cell back to H3 and then format the cell to Comma Style number format with no decimals.

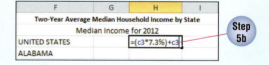

   d. Drag the fill handle in H3 down to H54.
   e. Deselect the range.

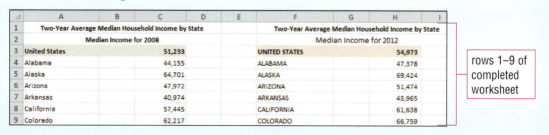

rows 1–9 of completed worksheet

6. Select F3:H54 and change the font size to 10.
7. Select F3:H3, apply Bold, and change the Fill Color to *Orange, Accent 6, Lighter 80%* (last option in second row of *Theme Colors* section).
8. Save, print, and then close **EL2-C2-P5-USIncomeStats.xlsx**.

In this chapter you learned how to use a small sampling of functions from the statistical, math and trigonometry, lookup, financial, logical, and text function lists. Excel includes over 300 functions in eleven categories. When you need to enter a complex formula and are not sure if Excel includes a preprogrammed function, open the Insert Function dialog box, type a description of the function in the *Search for a function* text box, and then click the Go button.

Chapter Summary

- Assign names to cells or ranges to reference by name in formulas or navigation.
- Using range names in formulas make formulas easier to comprehend.
- Create range names by selecting the source range and then typing a name in the Name box.
- COUNTA is a statistical function that counts nonblank cells. Use the function to count cells containing text and a combination of text and numbers.
- The COUNTIF statistical function counts cells within a range based on a single criterion.
- Use COUNTIFS to count cells within a range based on multiple criteria.
- Find the arithmetic mean of a range of cells based on a single criterion using the statistical AVERAGEIF function.
- AVERAGEIFS finds the arithmetic mean for a range based on multiple criteria.
- The math function SUMIF adds cells within a range based on a single criterion.
- To add cells within a range based on multiple criteria, use the SUMIFS function.
- Open the Name Manager dialog box to create, edit, or delete a range name, or edit the cells a range name references.
- Lookup & Reference functions VLOOKUP and HLOOKUP look up data in a reference table and return in the formula cell a value from a column or row in the lookup table.
- The PPMT financial function returns the principal portion of a specified loan payment within the term based on an interest rate, total number of payments, and loan amount.
- Conditional logic in a formula performs a calculation based on the outcome of a conditional test where one action is performed if the test proves true, or another action is performed if the test proves false.
- A nested function is a function inside of another function.

- Use the AND logical function to test multiple conditions. Excel returns *TRUE* if all conditions test true and returns *FALSE* if any one of the conditions tests false.
- The OR logical function also tests multiple conditions. The function returns *TRUE* if any one of the conditions tests true and *FALSE* only if all of the conditions test false.
- The text function =PROPER capitalizes the first letter of each word in the text source.
- Convert the case of text from lowercase to uppercase, or uppercase to lowercase, using the =UPPER and =LOWER text functions.
- Replace a text string with new text using the SUBSTITUTE text function.

Commands Review

FEATURE	RIBBON TAB, GROUP	BUTTON	KEYBOARD SHORTCUT
Financial functions	Formulas, Function Library		
Insert Function dialog box	Formulas, Function Library		Shift + 3
Logical functions	Formulas, Function Library		
Lookup & Reference functions	Formulas, Function Library		
Math & Trigonometry functions	Formulas, Function Library		
Name Manager dialog box	Formulas, Defined Names		Ctrl + 3
Statistical functions accessed from More Functions button	Formulas, Function Library		
Text functions	Formulas, Function Library		

Concepts Check Test Your Knowledge

Completion: In the space provided at the right, indicate the correct term, command, or number.

1. Assign a name to a selected range by typing the desired name in this text box. _____

2. A range name can be a combination of letters, numbers, underscore characters, and this punctuation character. _____

3. This COUNTIF function would count the number of cells in a range named *sales* where the values are greater than $50 thousand. _____

4. Use this statistical function to find the mean of a range based on two criteria. _____

5. SUMIF is found in this function category. _____

6. Open this dialog box to delete a range name. _____

7. Use this lookup function to look up a value in a reference table where the comparison data in the table is arranged in rows. _____

8. This financial function returns the principal portion of a specified loan payment. _____

9. The IF function is accessed from this button in the Function Library group of the Formulas tab. _____

10. This term refers to a formula where one function is created inside of another function. _____

11. Excel's AND and OR functions use this type of logic to construct a conditional test. _____

12. When would Excel return False for an OR function? _____

13. This text function can be used to capitalize the first letter of each word in a cell. _____

14. This formula converts text typed in lowercase within a cell to all uppercase characters. _____

15. Use this text function to change a text string in the source cell to new text in the formula cell. _____

Skills Check Assess Your Performance

Assessment

1 CREATE RANGE NAMES AND USE THE LOOKUP FUNCTION

Note: If you submit your work in hard copy, check with your instructor before printing assessments to see if you need to print two copies of each assessment—one as displayed and another with cell formulas displayed.

1. Open **RSROctLaborCost.xlsx**.
2. Save the workbook with Save As and name it **EL2-C2-A1-RSROctLaborCost**.
3. Create the following range names:
C7:C22	*Hours*
D7:D22	*TechCode*
F7:F22	*LaborCost*
I3:J5	*RateChart*
4. In E7 create the VLOOKUP formula to return the correct hourly rate based on the technician code in D7. Use the range name *RateChart* within the formula to reference the hourly rate chart. Make sure Excel will return values for exact matches only.
5. Copy the VLOOKUP formula in E7 and paste to E8:E22.
6. In F7 create the formula to extend the labor cost by multiplying the hours in C7 times the hourly rate in E7.
7. Copy the formula in F7 and paste to F8:F22.
8. Create the formula in F23 to sum the column.
9. Preview and then print the worksheet.
10. Save and then close **EL2-C2-A1-RSROctLaborCost.xlsx**.

Assessment

2 USE CONDITIONAL STATISTICAL AND MATH FUNCTIONS

Note: For all functions in Assessment 2 with the exception of Step 3, use range names in the formulas to reference sources.

1. Open **EL2-C2-A1-RSROctLaborCost.xlsx**.
2. Save the workbook with Save As and name it **EL2-C2-A2-RSROctLaborCost**.
3. In I23 create a COUNTA formula to count the number of calls made in October using the dates in column A as the source range.
4. Create the COUNTIF formulas in the cells indicated below.
I9	Count the number of calls made by Technician 1
I10	Count the number of calls made by Technician 2
I11	Count the number of calls made by Technician 3
5. In I14 create a COUNTIFS formula to count the number of calls made by Technician 3 where the hours logged were greater than 3.
6. Create the SUMIF formulas in the cells indicated below.
J9	Add the labor cost for calls made by Technician 1
J10	Add the labor cost for calls made by Technician 2
J11	Add the labor cost for calls made by Technician 3

7. Format J9:J11 to Comma Style number format.
8. In J14 create a SUMIFS formula to add the labor cost for calls made by Technician 3 where the hours logged were greater than 3.
9. Format J14 to Comma Style number format.
10. Create the AVERAGEIF formulas in the cells indicated below.

      J18   Average the labor cost for calls made by Technician 1
      J19   Average the labor cost for calls made by Technician 2
      J20   Average the labor cost for calls made by Technician 3

11. Format J18:J20 to Comma Style number format.
12. Save, print, and then close **EL2-C2-A2-RSROctLaborCost.xlsx**.

Assessment

3 USE FINANCIAL FUNCTIONS PMT AND PPMT

1. Open **PrecisionWarehouse.xlsx**.
2. Save the workbook with Save As and name it **EL2-C2-A3-PrecisionWarehouse.xlsx**.
3. Create the PMT formula in D8 to calculate the monthly loan payment for the proposed loan from NewVentures Capital Inc. *Note: The PMT payment uses the same arguments as PPMT with the exception that there is no Per criterion.*
4. Find the principal portion of the loan payment for the first loan payment in D10 and the last loan payment in D11 using PPMT formulas.
5. In D13 create the formula to calculate the total cost of the loan by multiplying the monthly loan payment times 12 times the amortization period in years.
6. In D14 create the formula to calculate the interest cost of the loan by entering the formula **=d13+d6**. *Note: Normally, you would calculate interest cost on a loan by subtracting the amount borrowed from the total payments made; however, in this worksheet you have to add the two cells because the total cost of the loan is a negative number. Subtracting D6 from D13 would cause Excel to add the two values because two negative values create a positive.*
7. Print the worksheet.
8. Save and then close **EL2-C2-A3-PrecisionWarehouse.xlsx**.

Assessment

4 USE LOGICAL FUNCTIONS

1. Open **AllClaimsPremiumReview.xlsx**.
2. Save the workbook with Save As and name it **EL2-C2-A4-AllClaimsPremiumReview.xlsx**.
3. Create the following range names:

      B4:B23   *Claims*
      C4:C23   *AtFault*
      D4:D23   *Rating*
      E4:E23   *Deductible*

4. Create the formula in G4 to display the text *Yes* if the number of At Fault Claims is greater than 1 and the Current Rating is greater than 2. Both conditions must test true to display *Yes*; otherwise display *No* in the cell. *Hint: Use a nested IF and AND formula.*
5. Center the result in G4 and then copy the formula to G5:G23.

6. Create the formula in H4 to display the text *Yes* in the cell if either the number of claims is greater than 2 or the current deductible is less than $1,000.00; otherwise display *No* in the cell. **Hint: Use a nested IF and OR formula**.
7. Center the result in H4 and then copy the formula to H5:H23. Deselect the range after copying.
8. Save, print, and then close **EL2-C2-A4-AllClaimsPremiumReview.xlsx**.

Assessment

5 USE THE HLOOKUP FUNCTION

1. Open **JanelleTutoringProgressRpt.xlsx**.
2. Save the workbook with Save As and name it **EL2-C2-A5-JanelleTutoringProgressRpt**.
3. Click the sheet tab labeled ProgressComments and review the layout of the lookup table. Notice that the data is organized in rows with the score in row 1 and the grade comment in row 2.
4. Select A1:G2 and create the range name *GradeTable*.
5. Deselect the range and then make StudentProgress the active sheet.
6. Create a formula in G4 that will look up the student's total score in the range named *GradeTable* and return the appropriate progress comment.
7. Copy the formula in G4 and paste it to G5:G12.
8. Save, print, and then close **EL2-C2-A5-JanelleTutoringProgressRpt.xlsx**.

Visual Benchmark Demonstrate Your Proficiency

1 USE LOOKUP, STATISTICAL, AND MATH FUNCTIONS IN A BILLING SUMMARY

1. Open **BillableHrsOct8to12.xlsx**.
2. Save the workbook with Save As and name it **EL2-C2-VB1-BillableHrsOct8to12**.
3. Review the worksheet shown in Figure 2.8. The gray shaded cells require formulas to complete the worksheet. Use the following information to create the required formulas. Create range names to use in all of the formulas so that the reader can easily interpret the formula.

   - In column F, create a formula to look up the attorney's hourly rate from the table located at the bottom right of the worksheet.
   - In column G, calculate the legal fees billed by multiplying the billable hours times the hourly rate.
   - In J6:J9 calculate the total legal fees billed by attorney.
   - In J13:J16 calculate the average hours billed by attorney.

4. Save, print, and then close **EL2-C2-VB1-BillableHrsOct8to12.xlsx**.

Figure 2.8 Visual Benchmark 1

	A	B	C	D	E	F	G	H	I	J
1					O'DONOVAN & SULLIVAN LAW ASSOCIATES					
2					BILLING SUMMARY					
3					OCTOBER 8 TO 12, 2012					
4	File	Client	Date	Attorney Code	Billable Hours	Hourly Rate	Legal Fees		Billing Statistics	
5	FL-325	10104	10/8/2012	1	26.75			**Total Legal Fees Billed by Attorney**		
6	EP-652	10106	10/8/2012	1	12.10			1	Marty O'Donovan	
7	CL-412	10125	10/8/2012	2	33.25			2	Toni Sullivan	
8	IN-745	10210	10/9/2012	3	24.25			3	Rosa Martinez	
9	EL-632	10225	10/9/2012	3	12.11			4	Kyle Williams	
10	RE-475	10285	10/9/2012	4	42.30				TOTAL $	-
11	CL-501	10341	10/10/2012	2	15.25					
12	CL-521	10334	10/10/2012	2	20.25			**Average Billable Hours by Attorney**		
13	PL-348	10420	10/10/2012	3	25.00			1	Marty O'Donovan	
14	RE-492	10425	10/10/2012	4	22.70			2	Toni Sullivan	
15	EL-632	10225	10/11/2012	3	23.00			3	Rosa Martinez	
16	PL-512	10290	10/11/2012	3	16.20			4	Kyle Williams	
17	IN-745	10210	10/11/2012	3	14.50					
18	FL-385	10278	10/11/2012	1	24.00				**Attorney Code Table**	
19	CL-412	10125	10/12/2012	2	15.25			Code	Attorney	Hourly Rate
20	CL-450	10358	10/12/2012	2	23.50			1	Marty O'Donovan	85.00
21	IN-801	10346	10/12/2012	3	14.25			2	Toni Sullivan	75.00
22	EP-685	10495	10/12/2012	3	23.75			3	Rosa Martinez	100.00
23	RE-501	10384	10/12/2012	4	13.75			4	Kyle Williams	90.00
24				TOTAL	402.16	TOTAL $	-			

2 USE LOOKUP AND LOGICAL FUNCTIONS TO CALCULATE CARDIOLOGY COSTS

1. Open **WPMCCardiologyCosts.xlsx**.
2. Save the workbook with Save As and name it
   EL2-C2-VB2-WPMCCardiologyCosts.
3. This worksheet already has range names created for you. Spend a few
   moments reviewing the range names and the cells each name references to
   become familiar with the worksheet.
4. Review the worksheet shown in Figure 2.9 and complete the worksheet to
   match the one shown by creating formulas using the following information:

   • In column G, create a formula to look up the surgery fee in the table
     located at the bottom of the worksheet. Specify in the formula to return a
     result for exact matches only.

   • In column H insert the aortic or mitral valve cost if the cardiac surgery
     required a replacement valve; otherwise place a zero into the cell. *Hint: The
     surgery codes for surgeries that include a replacement valve are **ART** and
     MRT*.

   • In column I, calculate the postoperative hospital cost by multiplying the
     number of days the patient was in hospital by the postoperative cost per day.

   • In column J, calculate the total cost as the sum of the surgery fee, valve
     cost, and postoperative hospital cost.

   • Calculate the total cost for each column in row 22.

5. Save, print, and then close **EL2-C2-VB2-WPMCCardiologyCosts.xlsx**.

Figure 2.9 Visual Benchmark 2

	A	B	C	D	E	F	G	H	I	J
1					Wellington Park Medical Center					
2					Division of Cardiology					
3					Adult Cardiac Surgery Costs					
4	Month:	October	Surgeon:	Novak						
5	Patient No	Patient Last Name	Patient First Name	Surgery Code	Days in hospital		Surgery Fee	Valve Cost	Postoperative Hospital Cost	Total Cost
6	60334124	Wagner	Sara	MRP	7		$ 5,325.00	$ -	$ 6,317.50	$ 11,642.50
7	60334567	Gonzalez	Hector	ARP	10		$ 4,876.00	$ -	$ 9,025.00	$ 13,901.00
8	60398754	Vezina	Paula	ABP	5		$ 4,820.00	$ -	$ 4,512.50	$ 9,332.50
9	60347821	Dowling	Jager	MRT	11		$ 6,240.00	$ 775.00	$ 9,927.50	$ 16,942.50
10	60328192	Ashman	Carl	ARP	4		$ 4,876.00	$ -	$ 3,610.00	$ 8,486.00
11	60321349	Kaiser	Lana	ART	12		$ 6,190.00	$ 775.00	$ 10,830.00	$ 17,795.00
12	60398545	Van Bomm	Emile	ABP	7		$ 4,820.00	$ -	$ 6,317.50	$ 11,137.50
13	60342548	Youngblood	Frank	ABP	6		$ 4,820.00	$ -	$ 5,415.00	$ 10,235.00
14	60331569	Lorimar	Hannah	MRT	8		$ 6,240.00	$ 775.00	$ 7,220.00	$ 14,235.00
15	60247859	Peterson	Mark	ART	9		$ 6,190.00	$ 775.00	$ 8,122.50	$ 15,087.50
16	60158642	O'Connor	Terry	ABP	7		$ 4,820.00	$ -	$ 6,317.50	$ 11,137.50
17	60458962	Jenkins	Esther	MRP	9		$ 5,325.00	$ -	$ 8,122.50	$ 13,447.50
18	68521245	Norfolk	Leslie	ABP	8		$ 4,820.00	$ -	$ 7,220.00	$ 12,040.00
19	63552158	Adams-Wiley	Susan	MRT	6		$ 6,240.00	$ 775.00	$ 5,415.00	$ 12,430.00
20	68451278	Estevez	Stefan	ARP	6		$ 4,876.00	$ -	$ 5,415.00	$ 10,291.00
21										
22	Postoperative hosptial cost per day:		$ 902.50		Total Cost:		$ 80,478.00	$ 3,875.00	$ 103,787.50	$ 188,140.50
23	Aortic or Mitral valve cost:		$ 775.00							
24										
25		Surgery Code	Surgery Fee	Surgery Procedure						
26		ABP	4,820	Artery Bypass						
27		ARP	4,876	Aortic Valve Repair						
28		ART	6,190	Aortic Valve Replacement						
29		MRP	5,325	Mitral Valve Repair						
30		MRT	6,240	Mitral Valve Replacement						

Case Study   Apply Your Skills

Yolanda Robertson of NuTrends Market Research was pleased with your previous work and has requested that you be assigned to assist her with a new client. Yolanda is preparing a marketing plan for a franchise expansion for the owners of Pizza By Mario. The franchise was started in Michigan and has stores in Ohio, Wisconsin, and Iowa. The owners plan to double their locations within the next two years by expanding into neighboring states. The owners have provided a confidential franchise sales report to Yolanda in an Excel file named **PizzaByMarioSales.xlsx**. Yolanda needs your help with Excel to extract some statistics and calculate franchise royalty payments. With this information, Yolanda can develop a franchise communication package for prospective franchisees. Open the workbook and name it **EL2-C2-CS-P1-PizzaByMarioSales**. Yolanda has asked for the following statistics:

- A count of the number of stores with gross sales greater than $500 thousand
- A count of the number of stores located in Michigan with sales greater than $500 thousand
- Average sales for the Detroit, Michigan stores
- Average sales for the Michigan stores established prior to 2004
- Total sales for stores established prior to 2010
- Total sales for the Michigan stores established prior to 2010

Create the formulas for Yolanda in rows 3 to 16 of columns H and I. Create range names for the data so that Yolanda will be able to easily understand the formula when she reviews the worksheet. You determine the layout, labels, and other formats for the statistics section. Save and print the worksheet.

In the marketing package for new prospects, Yolanda plans to include sample sales figures and related franchise royalty payments. Pizza By Mario charges stores a royalty percentage based on the store's annual sales. As sales increase, the royalty percentage increases. For example, a store that earns gross sales of $430 thousand pays a royalty of 2% on sales, while a store that earns gross sales of $765 thousand pays a royalty of 5% of gross sales. A royalty rate table is included in the worksheet. Create a range name for the table and then create a lookup formula to insert the correct royalty percentage for each store in column F. Next, create a formula to calculate the dollar amount of the royalty payment based on the store's sales times the percent value in column F. Format the royalty percent and royalty fee columns appropriately. Save the revised workbook and name it **EL2-C2-CS-P2-PizzaByMarioSales**. Print the worksheet.

Use the Help feature to learn about the MEDIAN and STDEV functions. Yolanda would like to calculate further statistics in a separate worksheet. Copy A2:E29 to Sheet2 keeping the source column widths. Using the sales data in column E, calculate the following statistics. You determine the layout, labels, and other formats.

- Average sales
- Maximum store sales
- Minimum store sales
- Median store sales
- Standard deviation of the sales data

Create a text box below the statistics and write an explanation in each box to explain to the reader what the median and standard deviation numbers mean based on what you learned in Help. Print the worksheet making sure the printout fits on one page. Save the revised workbook and name it **EL2-C2-CS-P3-PizzaByMarioSales**.

Choose two states that are in close proximity to Michigan, Ohio, Wisconsin, and Iowa and research statistics on the Internet that Yolanda can use to prepare a marketing plan. Within each state find population and income statistics for two cities. In a new worksheet within the Pizza By Mario franchise workbook, prepare a summary of your research findings. Include the URLs of the sites from which you obtained your data in the worksheet in case Yolanda wants to explore the links for further details. Print the worksheet making sure the printout fits on one page. Save the revised workbook and name it **EL2-C2-CS-P4-PizzaByMarioSales**. Close the workbook.

Working with Tables and Data Features

PERFORMANCE OBJECTIVES

Upon successful completion of Chapter 3, you will be able to:

- Create a table in a worksheet
- Expand a table to include new rows and columns
- Add a calculated column in a table
- Format a table by applying table styles and table style options
- Add a total row to a table and add formulas to total cells
- Sort and filter a table
- Split contents of a cell into separate columns
- Remove duplicate records
- Restrict data entry by creating validation criteria
- Convert a table to a normal range
- Create subtotals in groups of related data
- Group and ungroup data

Tutorials

3.1 Creating and Modifying Tables
3.2 Adding Rows to a Table
3.3 Formatting Data as a Table
3.4 Using the Sort Feature in Tables
3.5 Filtering a Table
3.6 Using Data Tools
3.7 Removing Duplicate Records
3.8 Validating and Restricting Data Entry
3.9 Converting a Table to a Normal Range; Subtotalling Related Data
3.10 Grouping and Ungrouping Data

A *table* is a range that can be managed separately from other rows and columns in the worksheet. Data in a table can be sorted, filtered, and totaled as a separate unit. A worksheet can contain more than one table so that multiple groups of data can be managed separately within the same workbook. In this chapter you will learn how to use the table feature to manage a range. You will use data tools such as validation, duplicate records, and converting text to a table. You will also convert a table back to a normal range and use data tools such as grouping related records and calculating subtotals. Model answers for this chapter's projects appear on the following pages.

Excel2010L2C3

Note: Before beginning the projects, copy to your storage medium the Excel2010L2C3 subfolder from the Excel2010L2 folder on the CD that accompanies this textbook and then make Excel2010L2C3 the active folder.

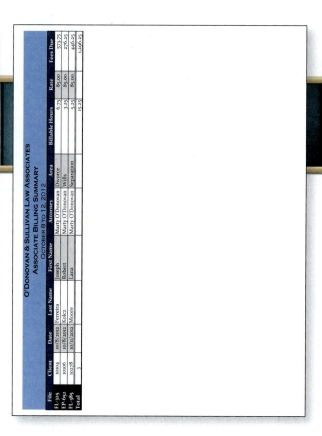

O'DONOVAN & SULLIVAN LAW ASSOCIATES
ASSOCIATE BILLING SUMMARY
OCTOBER 8 TO 12, 2012

File	Client	Date	Last Name	First Name	Attorney	Area	Billable Hours	Rate	Fees Due
FL-335	10104	10/8/2012	Ferreira	Joseph	Marty O'Donovan	Divorce	6.75	85.00	573.75
EP-652	10106	10/8/2012	Kolcz	Robert	Marty O'Donovan	Wills	3.25	85.00	276.25
FL-385	10278	10/11/2012	Moore	Lana	Marty O'Donovan	Separation	5.25	85.00	446.25
Total	3						15.25		1,296.25

Project 1 Create and Modify a Table
Project 1c, EL2-C3-P1-BillingSummaryOctWk1.xlsx

Project 1d, EL2-C3-P1-BillingSummaryOctWk1.xlsx

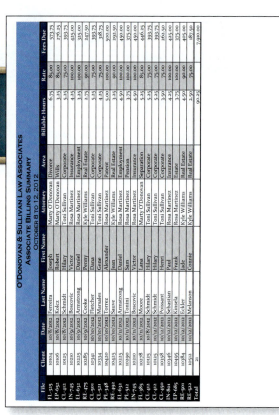

Project 1d, EL2-C3-P1-BillingSummaryOctWk1.xlsx

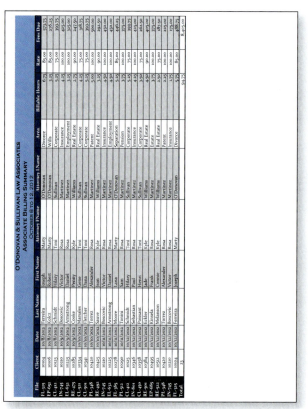

Project 2 Use Data Tools to Split Data and Ensure Data Integrity
Project 2e, EL2-C3-P2-BillingSummaryOctWk1.xlsx

Model Answers

Project 3a, EL2-C3-P3-BillingSummaryOctWk1.xlsx

O'DONOVAN & SULLIVAN LAW ASSOCIATES
ASSOCIATE BILLING SUMMARY
OCTOBER 8 TO 12, 2012

File	Client	Date	Last Name	First Name	Attorney FName	Attorney LName	Area	Billable Hours	Rate	Fees Due
IN-745	10210	10/9/2012	Boscovic	Victor	Rosa	Martinez	Insurance	4.25	100.00	425.00
IN-745	10210	10/11/2012	Boscovic	Victor	Rosa	Martinez	Insurance	4.50	100.00	450.00
IN-745	10210	10/12/2012	Boscovic	Victor	Rosa	Martinez	Insurance	1.75	100.00	175.00
EL-632	10225	10/9/2012	Armstrong	Daniel	Rosa	Martinez	Employment	3.25	100.00	325.00
EL-632	10225	10/11/2012	Armstrong	Daniel	Rosa	Martinez	Employment	4.50	100.00	450.00
PL-512	10290	10/11/2012	Tonini	Sam	Rosa	Martinez	Pension	3.75	100.00	375.00
IN-801	10346	10/12/2012	Sebastian	Paul	Rosa	Martinez	Insurance	4.25	100.00	425.00
PL-348	10420	10/10/2012	Torrez	Alexander	Rosa	Martinez	Patent	5.00	100.00	500.00
PL-348	10420	10/12/2012	Torrez	Alexander	Rosa	Martinez	Patent	2.25	100.00	225.00
EP-685	10495	10/12/2012	Kinsela	Frank	Rosa	Martinez	Estate	3.75	100.00	375.00
Martinez Total										3,725.00
FL-335	10104	10/8/2012	Ferreira	Joseph	Marty	O'Donovan	Divorce	6.75	85.00	573.75
FL-335	10104	10/12/2012	Ferreira	Joseph	Marty	O'Donovan	Divorce	5.75	85.00	488.75
EP-652	10106	10/8/2012	Kolcz	Robert	Marty	O'Donovan	Wills	3.25	85.00	276.25
FL-385	10278	10/11/2012	Moore	Lana	Marty	O'Donovan	Separation	5.25	85.00	446.25
O'Donovan Total										1,785.00
CL-412	10125	10/8/2012	Schmidt	Hilary	Toni	Sullivan	Corporate	5.25	75.00	393.75
CL-412	10125	10/12/2012	Schmidt	Hilary	Toni	Sullivan	Corporate	5.25	75.00	393.75
CL-521	10334	10/10/2012	Marsales	Gene	Toni	Sullivan	Corporate	4.25	75.00	318.75
CL-501	10341	10/10/2012	Fletcher	Dana	Toni	Sullivan	Corporate	5.25	75.00	393.75
CL-450	10358	10/12/2012	Poissant	Henri	Toni	Sullivan	Corporate	3.50	75.00	262.50
Sullivan Total										1,762.50
RE-475	10285	10/9/2012	Cooke	Penny	Kyle	Williams	Real Estate	2.75	90.00	247.50
RE-501	10384	10/12/2012	Eckler	Jade	Kyle	Williams	Real Estate	4.50	90.00	405.00
RE-492	10425	10/10/2012	Sauve	Jean	Kyle	Williams	Real Estate	3.25	90.00	292.50
RE-522	10512	10/12/2012	Melanson	Connie	Kyle	Williams	Real Estate	2.50	75.00	187.50
Williams Total										1,132.50
Grand Total										8,405.00

Project 3 Group and Subtotal Related Records

Project 3b, EL2-C3-P3-BillingSummaryOctWk1-Prj3b.xlsx

O'DONOVAN & SULLIVAN LAW ASSOCIATES
ASSOCIATE BILLING SUMMARY
OCTOBER 8 TO 12, 2012

File	Client	Date	Last Name	First Name	Attorney FName	Attorney LName	Area	Billable Hours	Rate	Fees Due
IN-745	10210	10/9/2012	Boscovic	Victor	Rosa	Martinez	Insurance	4.25	100.00	425.00
IN-745	10210	10/11/2012	Boscovic	Victor	Rosa	Martinez	Insurance	4.50	100.00	450.00
IN-745	10210	10/12/2012	Boscovic	Victor	Rosa	Martinez	Insurance	1.75	100.00	175.00
EL-632	10225	10/9/2012	Armstrong	Daniel	Rosa	Martinez	Employment	3.25	100.00	325.00
EL-632	10225	10/11/2012	Armstrong	Daniel	Rosa	Martinez	Employment	4.50	100.00	450.00
PL-512	10290	10/11/2012	Tonini	Sam	Rosa	Martinez	Pension	3.75	100.00	375.00
IN-801	10346	10/12/2012	Sebastian	Paul	Rosa	Martinez	Insurance	4.25	100.00	425.00
PL-348	10420	10/10/2012	Torrez	Alexander	Rosa	Martinez	Patent	5.00	100.00	500.00
PL-348	10420	10/12/2012	Torrez	Alexander	Rosa	Martinez	Patent	2.25	100.00	225.00
EP-685	10495	10/12/2012	Kinsela	Frank	Rosa	Martinez	Estate	3.75	100.00	375.00
Martinez Average								3.73		372.50
Martinez Count								10		
Martinez Total										3,725.00
FL-335	10104	10/8/2012	Ferreira	Joseph	Marty	O'Donovan	Divorce	6.75	85.00	573.75
FL-335	10104	10/12/2012	Ferreira	Joseph	Marty	O'Donovan	Divorce	5.75	85.00	488.75
EP-652	10106	10/8/2012	Kolcz	Robert	Marty	O'Donovan	Wills	3.25	85.00	276.25
FL-385	10278	10/11/2012	Moore	Lana	Marty	O'Donovan	Separation	5.25	85.00	446.25
O'Donovan Average								5.25		446.25
O'Donovan Count								4		
O'Donovan Total										1,785.00
CL-412	10125	10/8/2012	Schmidt	Hilary	Toni	Sullivan	Corporate	5.25	75.00	393.75
CL-412	10125	10/12/2012	Schmidt	Hilary	Toni	Sullivan	Corporate	5.25	75.00	393.75
CL-521	10334	10/10/2012	Marsales	Gene	Toni	Sullivan	Corporate	4.25	75.00	318.75
CL-501	10341	10/10/2012	Fletcher	Dana	Toni	Sullivan	Corporate	5.25	75.00	393.75
CL-450	10358	10/12/2012	Poissant	Henri	Toni	Sullivan	Corporate	3.50	75.00	262.50
Sullivan Average								4.70		352.50
Sullivan Count								5		
Sullivan Total										1,762.50
RE-475	10285	10/9/2012	Cooke	Penny	Kyle	Williams	Real Estate	2.75	90.00	247.50
RE-501	10384	10/12/2012	Eckler	Jade	Kyle	Williams	Real Estate	4.50	90.00	405.00
RE-492	10425	10/10/2012	Sauve	Jean	Kyle	Williams	Real Estate	3.25	90.00	292.50
RE-522	10512	10/12/2012	Melanson	Connie	Kyle	Williams	Real Estate	2.50	75.00	187.50
Williams Average								3.25		283.13
Williams Count								4		
Williams Total										1,132.50
Grand Average								4.12		395.43
Grand Count								23		
Grand Total										8,405.00

Project 3c, EL2-C3-P3-BillingSummaryOctWk1-Prj3c.xlsx

O'DONOVAN & SULLIVAN LAW ASSOCIATES
ASSOCIATE BILLING SUMMARY
OCTOBER 8 TO 12, 2012

File	Client	Date	Last Name	First Name	Attorney FName	Attorney LName	Area	Billable Hours	Rate	Fees Due
IN-745	10210	10/9/2012	Boscovic	Victor	Rosa	Martinez	Insurance	4.25	100.00	425.00
IN-745	10210	10/11/2012	Boscovic	Victor	Rosa	Martinez	Insurance	4.50	100.00	450.00
IN-745	10210	10/12/2012	Boscovic	Victor	Rosa	Martinez	Insurance	1.75	100.00	175.00
EL-632	10225	10/9/2012	Armstrong	Daniel	Rosa	Martinez	Employment	3.25	100.00	325.00
EL-632	10225	10/11/2012	Armstrong	Daniel	Rosa	Martinez	Employment	4.50	100.00	450.00
PL-512	10290	10/11/2012	Tonini	Sam	Rosa	Martinez	Pension	3.75	100.00	375.00
IN-801	10346	10/12/2012	Sebastian	Paul	Rosa	Martinez	Insurance	4.25	100.00	425.00
PL-348	10420	10/10/2012	Torrez	Alexander	Rosa	Martinez	Patent	5.00	100.00	500.00
PL-348	10420	10/12/2012	Torrez	Alexander	Rosa	Martinez	Patent	2.25	100.00	225.00
EP-685	10495	10/12/2012	Kinsela	Frank	Rosa	Martinez	Estate	3.75	100.00	375.00
Martinez Total										3,725.00
O'Donovan Total										1,785.00
Sullivan Total										1,762.50
Williams Total										1,132.50
Grand Total										8,405.00

Project 1 Create and Modify a Table

4 Parts

You will convert data in a billing summary worksheet to a table and then modify the table by applying Table Style options and sorting and filtering the data.

Creating Tables

▼ Quick Steps

Create Table
1. Select range.
2. Click Insert tab.
3. Click Table button.
4. Click OK.
5. Deselect range.

Table

A table in Excel is similar in structure to a database. Columns are called *fields* and are used to store a single unit of information about a person, place, or object. The first row of the table contains column headings and is called the *field names row* or *header row*. Each column heading in the table should be unique. Below the field names, data entered in rows are called *records*. A record contains all of the field values related to one person, place, or object that is the topic of the table. No blank rows exist within the table as shown in Figure 3.1. To create a table in Excel, enter the data in the worksheet and then define the range as a table using the Table button in the Tables group of the Insert tab or using the Format as Table button in the Styles group of the Home tab. Before converting a range to a table, delete any blank rows between column headings and data or within the data range.

Figure 3.1 Worksheet with Range Formatted as a Table

The first row of a table contains field names and is called a header row.

Vantage Video Rentals
Classic Video Collection

Stock No.	Title	Year	Genre	Stock Date	Director	Copies	VHS	DVD	Blu-ray	Category	Cost Price
CV-1001	Abbott & Costello Go to Mars	1953	Comedy	9/5/2006	Charles Lamont	2	Yes	No	No	7-day rental	5.87
CV-1002	Miracle on 34th Street	1947	Family	9/15/2006	George Seaton	8	Yes	No	Yes	2-day rental	7.55
CV-1003	Moby Dick	1956	Action	10/4/2006	John Huston	3	No	Yes	No	7-day rental	8.10
CV-1004	Dial M for Murder	1954	Thriller	10/12/2006	Alfred Hitchcock	5	No	Yes	No	7-day rental	6.54
CV-1005	Breakfast at Tiffany's	1961	Comedy	11/1/2006	Blake Edwards	1	Yes	No	Yes	7-day rental	4.88
CV-1006	Gone with the Wind	1939	Drama	11/29/2006	Victor Fleming	4	Yes	No	Yes	7-day rental	8.22
CV-1007	Doctor Zhivago	1965	Drama	12/8/2006	David Lean	4	Yes	No	Yes	7-day rental	5.63
CV-1008	The Great Escape	1963	War	1/15/2007	John Sturges	3	Yes	No	No	2-day rental	6.15
CV-1009	The Odd Couple	1968	Comedy	2/15/2007	Gene Saks	4	Yes	Yes	No	2-day rental	4.95
CV-1010	The Sound of Music	1965	Musical	3/9/2007	Robert Wise	5	Yes	Yes	Yes	2-day rental	5.12
CV-1011	A Christmas Carol	1951	Family	7/18/2007	Brian Hurst	4	Yes	Yes	Yes	2-day rental	5.88
CV-1012	The Bridge on the River Kwai	1957	War	8/15/2007	David Lean	2	Yes	No	No	2-day rental	6.32
CV-1013	Cool Hand Luke	1967	Drama	10/23/2007	Stuart Rosenberg	5	Yes	Yes	Yes	2-day rental	5.42
CV-1014	Patton	1970	War	12/18/2007	Franklin Schaffner	3	Yes	Yes	Yes	7-day rental	6.84
CV-1015	Blue Hawaii	1961	Musical	1/25/2008	Norman Taurog	1	Yes	No	No	7-day rental	4.52
CV-1016	Psycho	1960	Horror	1/31/2008	Alfred Hitchcock	2	Yes	No	Yes	2-day rental	7.54
CV-1017	The Longest Day	1962	War	2/5/2008	Ken Annakin	5	Yes	Yes	No	7-day rental	6.51
CV-1018	To Kill a Mockingbird	1962	Drama	2/12/2008	Robert Mulligan	2	Yes	No	Yes	2-day rental	8.40
CV-1019	Bonnie and Clyde	1967	Drama	3/15/2009	Arthur Penn	3	Yes	Yes	Yes	2-day rental	8.95
CV-1020	The Maltese Falcon	1941	Drama	11/10/2009	John Huston	1	No	No	Yes	2-day rental	12.15
CV-1021	Doctor Zhivago	1965	Drama	12/8/2006	David Lean	4	Yes	No	Yes	7-day rental	5.63
CV-1022	The Wizard of Oz	1939	Musical	5/3/2010	Victor Fleming	5	Yes	Yes	Yes	7-day rental	9.56
CV-1023	Rear Window	1954	Thriller	8/15/2010	Alfred Hitchcock	3	Yes	Yes	Yes	7-day rental	8.55
CV-1004	Dial M for Murder	1954	Thriller	10/12/2006	Alfred Hitchcock	5	No	Yes	No	7-day rental	6.54
CV-1024	Citizen Kane	1941	Drama	6/10/2011	Orson Welles	2	No	Yes	Yes	2-day rental	9.85
CV-1025	Ben-Hur	1959	History	10/15/2011	William Wyler	1	No	No	Yes	7-day rental	9.85

A row in a table is called a record.

A column in a table contains a single unit of information and is called a field.

1. Open **BillingSummaryOctWk1.xlsx**.
2. Save the workbook with Save As and name it **EL2-C3-P1-BillingSummaryOctWk1**.
3. Convert the billing summary data to a table by completing the following steps:
   a. Select A4:I24.
   b. Click the Insert tab.
   c. Click the Table button in the Tables group.
   d. At the Create Table dialog box with =$A$4:$I$24 selected in the *Where is the data for your table?* text box and the *My table has headers* check box selected, click OK.
   e. Deselect the range.
4. Double-click each column boundary to AutoFit each column's width.
5. Save **EL2-C3-P1-BillingSummaryOctWk1.xlsx**.

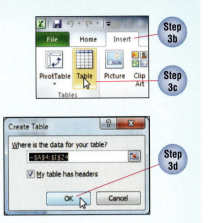

Modifying a Table

Once a table has been defined, typing new data in the row immediately below the last row of the table or in the column immediately right of the last column causes the table to automatically expand to include the new entries. Excel displays the AutoCorrect Options button when the table is expanded. Click the button to display a drop-down list with the options *Undo Table AutoExpansion* and *Stop Automatically Expanding Tables*. If you need to add data near a table without having the table expand, leave a blank column or row between the table and the new data.

Typing a formula in the first row of a new table column automatically creates a calculated column. In a calculated column, Excel copies the formula from the first cell to the remaining cells in the column as soon as you enter the formula. The AutoCorrect Options button appears when Excel converts a column to a calculated column with the options *Undo Calculated Column* and *Stop Automatically Creating Calculated Columns* available in the drop-down list.

▼ **Quick Steps**

Add Rows or Columns to Table
Type data in first row below table or first column to right of table.

Add Calculated Column
1. Type formula in first record in column.
2. Press Enter.

1. With **EL2-C3-P1-BillingSummaryOctWk1.xlsx** open, add a new record to the table by completing the following steps:
   a. Make A25 the active cell, type **RE-522**, and then press Enter. Excel automatically expands the table to include the new row and displays the AutoCorrect Options button.
   b. Make B25 the active cell and then type the remainder of the record as follows:

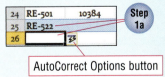

AutoCorrect Options button

Client	**10512**
Date	**10/12/2012**
Last Name	**Melanson**
First Name	**Connie**
Attorney	**Kyle Williams**

	Rate ▼	Fees D▼
Area	85.00	573.75
Billable Hours	85.00	276.25
Rate	75.00	393.75
	100.00	425.00
	100.00	325.00
	90.00	247.50
	75.00	393.75
	75.00	318.75
	100.00	500.00
	90.00	292.50
	100.00	450.00
	100.00	375.00
	100.00	450.00
	85.00	446.25
	75.00	393.75
	75.00	393.75
	75.00	262.50
	100.00	425.00
	100.00	375.00
	90.00	405.00
	75.00	187.50

Area **Real Estate**
Billable Hours **2.5**
Rate **75.00**

Steps 2a & 2b

Step 2c

2. Add a calculated column to multiply Billable Hours times Rate by completing the following steps:
   a. Make J4 the active cell.
   b. Type **Fees Due** and then press Enter. Excel automatically expands the table to include the new column.
   c. With J5 the active cell, type **=h5*i5** and then press Enter. Excel creates a calculated column and copies the formula to the rest of the rows in the table.
   d. Double-click the column J boundary to AutoFit the column.
3. Adjust the centering and fill color of the titles across the top of the table by completing the following steps:
   a. Make A1 the active cell.
   b. Click the Merge & Center button in the Alignment group in the Home tab to unmerge A1:I1.
   c. Select A1:J1 and then click the Merge & Center button.
   d. Make A2 the active cell and then repeat Steps 3b and 3c to merge and center row 2 across columns A through J.
   e. Make A3 the active cell and then repeat Steps 3b and 3c to merge and center row 3 across columns A through J.
4. Save **EL2-C3-P1-BillingSummaryOctWk1.xlsx**.

Table Styles and Table Style Options

▼ Quick Steps

Change Table Style
1. Make cell active within table.
2. If necessary, click Table Tools Design tab.
3. Click desired style in Table Styles gallery. OR Click More button in Table Styles gallery and click desired style at drop-down gallery.

Add Total Row
1. Make cell active within table.
2. If necessary, click Table Tools Design tab.
3. Click *Total Row* check box.
4. Click in total row in column to add function.
5. Click down-pointing arrow.
6. Click desired function.

The contextual Table Tools Design tab shown in Figure 3.2 contains options for formatting the table. Apply a different visual style to the table using the Table Styles gallery. Excel provides several table styles categorized by Light, Medium, and Dark color themes. By default, Excel bands the rows within the table, which means that even rows are formatted differently from odd rows. *Banding* rows or columns makes the task of reading data across a row or down a column in a large table easier. You can remove the banding from the rows and/or add banding to the columns. Use the *First Column* and *Last Column* check boxes in the Table Style Options group to add emphasis to the first or last column in the table by formatting the column separately from the rest of the table. The *Header Row* check box is used to show or hide the column headings row in the table.

Adding a total row to the table causes Excel to add the word *Total* in a new row at the bottom of the table in the leftmost cell. A Sum function is added automatically to the last numeric column in the table. Click in a cell in the total row to display a down-pointing arrow from which you can select a function formula in a pop-up list.

More

Figure 3.2 Table Tools Design Tab

Add a total row to the table in which you can choose the function to apply to numeric columns.

Click this check box to show or hide the column headings in the table.

Add emphasis to the first or last column with these check boxes. Generally the column is formatted with a darker fill color and the font color is reversed, or bold is added. Formatting is dependent on the Table Style in effect.

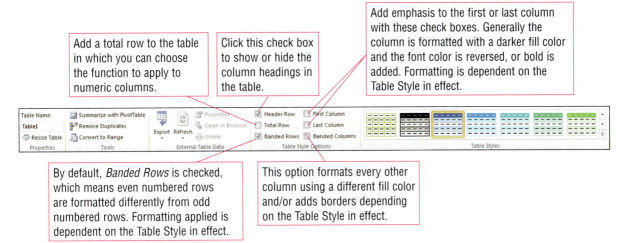

By default, *Banded Rows* is checked, which means even numbered rows are formatted differently from odd numbered rows. Formatting applied is dependent on the Table Style in effect.

This option formats every other column using a different fill color and/or adds borders depending on the Table Style in effect.

 **Project 1c**   **Formatting a Table and Adding a Total Row**   Part 3 of 4

1. With **EL2-C3-P1-BillingSummaryOctWk1.xlsx** open, change the table style by completing the following steps:
   a. Click any cell within the table to activate the table and the contextual Table Tools Design tab.
   b. Click the Table Tools Design tab.
   c. Click the More button located at the bottom of the vertical scroll bar in the Table Styles gallery.
   d. Click *Table Style Medium 15* at the drop-down gallery (first option in third row in *Medium* section).

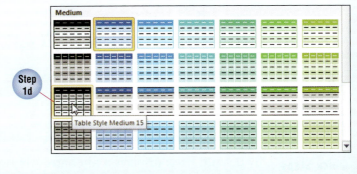

Step 1d

2. Change the Table Style options to remove the row banding, insert column banding, and emphasize the first column in the table by completing the following steps:
   a. Click the *Banded Rows* check box in the Table Style Options group in the Table Tools Design tab to clear the box. All of the rows in the table are now formatted the same.
   b. Click the *Banded Columns* check box in the Table Style Options group to insert a check mark. Every other column in the table is now formatted differently.
   c. Click the *First Column* check box in the Table Style Options group. Notice the first column has a darker fill color and reverse font color applied.

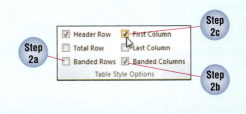

Step 2c

Step 2a

Step 2b

d. Click the *Header Row* check box in the Table Style Options group to clear the box. Notice the first row of the table containing the column headings disappears and is replaced with empty cells. The row is also removed from the table range definition.

e. Click the *Header Row* check box to insert a check mark and redisplay the column headings.

3. Add a total row and add function formulas to numeric columns by completing the following steps:

a. Click the *Total Row* check box in the Table Style Options group to add a total row to the bottom of the table. Excel formats row 26 as a total row, adds the label *Total* in A26, and automatically creates a Sum function in J26.

b. Make H26 the active cell.

c. Click the down-pointing arrow that appears in H26 and then click *Sum* at the pop-up list.

None	75.00	393.75
Average	75.00	393.75
Count		
Count Numbers	75.00	262.50
Max	100.00	425.00
Min	100.00	375.00
Sum		
StdDev	90.00	405.00
Var		
More Functions...	75.00	187.50
		7,910.00

Step 3c

Fees Due automatically summed when Total row added in Step 3a

d. Make B26 the active cell, click the down-pointing arrow that appears, and then click *Count* at the pop-up list.

25	RE-522	10512	10/12/2012	Melanson	Connie	Kyle Williams	Real Estate		2.50	75.00	187.50
26	Total	21							90.25		7,910.00

Step 3d

4. Click the Page Layout tab and change *Width* to *1 page* in the Scale to Fit group.

5. Preview and then print the worksheet.

6. Save **EL2-C3-P1-BillingSummaryOctWk1.xlsx**.

Sorting and Filtering a Table ▪■■■■■■■ ■■■■■■■ ■

▼ **Quick Steps**

Filter Table
1. Click desired filter arrow button.
2. Click desired filter options.
3. Click OK.

Sort Table
1. Click desired filter arrow button.
2. Click desired sort order.
OR
1. Click Sort & Filter button.
2. Click *Custom Sort*.
3. Define sort levels.
4. Click OK.

By default, Excel displays a filter arrow button next to each label in the table header row. Click the filter arrow button to display a drop-down list with the same sort and filter options you used in Chapter 1.

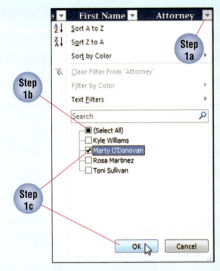

1. With **EL2-C3-P1-BillingSummaryOctWk1.xlsx** open, filter the table by attorney name to print a list of billable hours for Marty O'Donovan by completing the following steps:
   a. Click the filter arrow button located next to *Attorney* in F4.
   b. Click the *(Select All)* check box to clear the check mark from the check box.
   c. Click the *Marty O'Donovan* check box to insert a check mark and then click OK. The table is filtered to display only those records with *Marty O'Donovan* in the *Attorney* field. The Sum functions in columns H and J reflect the totals for the filtered records only.
   d. Print the filtered worksheet.
2. Redisplay all records by clicking the Attorney filter arrow button and then clicking *Clear Filter From "Attorney"* at the drop-down list.
3. Sort the table first by the attorney name, then by the area of law, and then by the client last name using the Sort dialog box by completing the following steps:

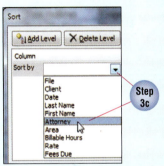

   a. With the active cell positioned anywhere within the table, click the Home tab.
   b. Click the Sort & Filter button in the Editing group and then click *Custom Sort* at the drop-down list.
   c. At the Sort dialog box, click the down-pointing arrow next to the *Sort by* list box in the *Column* section and then click *Attorney* at the drop-down list. The default options for *Sort On* and *Order* are correct since you want to sort by the column values in ascending order.
   d. Click the Add Level button.
   e. Click the down-pointing arrow next to the *Then by* list box and then click *Area* at the drop-down list.
   f. Click the Add Level button.
   g. Click the down-pointing arrow next to the second *Then by* list box and then click *Last Name* at the drop-down list.
   h. Click OK.

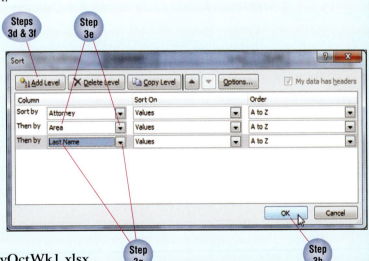

4. Print the sorted table.
5. Save and then close **EL2-C3-P1-BillingSummaryOctWk1.xlsx**.

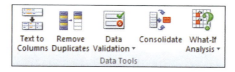

Project **2** | **Use Data Tools to Split Data and Ensure Data Integrity** | **5 Parts**

You will use Excel's data tools to split the attorney first and last names into two separate columns, remove duplicate records, and restrict the type of data that can be entered into a field.

▼ **Quick Steps**

Split Text into Multiple Columns
1. Insert blank column(s) next to source data.
2. Select data to be split.
3. Click Data tab.
4. Click Text to Columns button.
5. Click Next at first dialog box.
6. Select delimiter check box for character that separates data.
7. Click Next.
8. Click Finish.
9. Deselect range.

Data Tools ■■■■■■■■■ ■■■■■■■■ ■■■■■■■ ■■■■ ■

The Data Tools group in the Data tab shown in Figure 3.3 includes features useful for working with data in tables. A worksheet in which more than one field has been entered into the same column can be separated into multiple columns using the Text to Columns feature. For example, a worksheet with a column that has first and last names entered into the same cell can have the first name split into one column and the last name split into a separate column. Breaking up the data into separate columns facilitates sorting and other data management functions. Before using the Text to Columns feature, insert the number of blank columns you will need to separate the data immediately right of the column to be split. Next, select the column containing multiple data and then click the Text to Columns button to start the Convert Text to Columns Wizard. The wizard contains three dialog boxes to guide you through the steps of separating the data.

Figure 3.3 Data Tools Group in Data Tab

Text to Columns

Project 2a | **Separating Attorney Names into Two Columns** | Part 1 of 5

1. Open **EL2-C3-P1-BillingSummaryOctWk1.xlsx**.
2. Save the workbook with Save As and name it **EL2-C3-P2-BillingSummaryOctWk1**.
3. Position the active cell anywhere within the table, click the Sort & Filter button in the Editing group of the Home tab, and then click *Clear* at the drop-down list to clear the existing sort criteria.
4. Create a custom sort to sort the table first by *Date* (Oldest to Newest) and then by *Client* (Smallest to Largest). Refer to Project 1d, Step 3 if you need assistance with this step.
5. Split the attorney first and last names in column F into two columns by completing the following steps:
   a. Right-click column letter G at the top of the worksheet area and then click *Insert* at the shortcut menu to insert a blank column between the *Attorney* and *Area* columns in the table.
   b. Select F5:F25.
   c. Click the Data tab.
   d. Click the Text to Columns button in the Data Tools group.

Step 3

e. At the Convert Text to Columns Wizard - Step 1 of 3 dialog box, with *Delimited* selected in the *Choose the file type that best describes your data* section, click Next.

f. At the Convert Text to Columns Wizard - Step 2 of 3 dialog box, click the *Space* check box in the *Delimiters* section and then click Next. The *Data preview* section of the dialog box updates after you click the *Space* check box to show the names split into two columns.

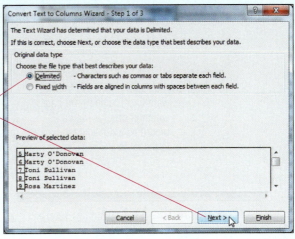

Step 5e

Step 5f

Step 6   **Step 7**

Attorney FName	Attorney LName
Marty	O'Donovan
Marty	O'Donovan
Toni	Sullivan
Toni	Sullivan
Rosa	Martinez
Rosa	Martinez
Kyle	Williams
Toni	Sullivan
Toni	Sullivan
Rosa	Martinez
Kyle	Williams
Rosa	Martinez
Rosa	Martinez
Marty	O'Donovan
Rosa	Martinez
Toni	Sullivan
Rosa	Martinez
Toni	Sullivan
Kyle	Williams
Rosa	Martinez
Kyle	Williams

Attorney first and last names split into two columns at Steps 5a–5g.

g. Click Finish at the last Convert Text to Columns Wizard dialog box to accept the default *General* data format for both columns.

h. Deselect the range.

6. Make F4 the active cell, edit the label to *Attorney FName*, and then AutoFit the column width.

7. Make G4 the active cell, edit the label to *Attorney LName*, and then AutoFit the column width.

8. Save **EL2-C3-P2-BillingSummaryOctWk1.xlsx**.

Removing Duplicate Records

Excel can compare records within a worksheet and automatically delete duplicate rows based on the columns you select that might contain duplicate values. At the Remove Duplicates dialog box shown in Figure 3.4, by default all columns are selected when the dialog box is opened. Click the Unselect All button to remove the check marks from each column and then click the individual columns you want to compare if you do not want Excel to check for duplicates in every column. When you click OK, Excel performs an automatic deletion of rows containing duplicate values and displays a message box when the operation is completed informing you of the number of rows that were removed from the worksheet or table and the number of unique values that remain. Consider conditionally formatting duplicate values first to view the records that will be deleted. Use the *Duplicate Values* option in *Highlight Cells Rules* from the

▼ **Quick Steps**

Remove Duplicate Rows
1. Select range or make cell active in table.
2. Click Data tab.
3. Click Remove Duplicates button.
4. Select columns to compare.
5. Click OK.
6. Click OK.

Remove Duplicates

Figure 3.4 Remove Duplicates Dialog Box

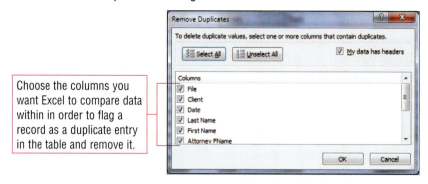

Choose the columns you want Excel to compare data within in order to flag a record as a duplicate entry in the table and remove it.

Conditional Formatting drop-down list. (Recall from Chapter 1 that you can display the Conditional Formatting drop-down list by clicking the Conditional Formatting button in the Styles group in the Home tab.)

Excel includes the Remove Duplicates button in the Data Tools group in the Data tab and in the Tools group in the Table Tools Design tab. Click Undo if you remove duplicate rows by mistake.

Project 2b **Removing Duplicate Rows** Part 2 of 5

1. With **EL2-C3-P2-BillingSummaryOctWk1.xlsx** open, remove duplicate rows in the billing summary table by completing the following steps:
   a. With the active cell positioned anywhere within the table, click the Remove Duplicates button in the Data Tools group in the Data tab.
   b. At the Remove Duplicates dialog box with all columns selected in the *Columns* list box, click the Unselect All button.
   c. The billing summary table should have only one record per file per client per date since attorneys record once per day the total hours spent on each file. A record is a duplicate if the same values exist in the three columns that store the file number, client number, and date. Click the *File* check box to insert a check mark.

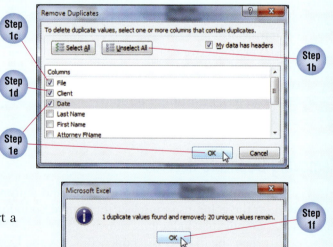

   d. Click the *Client* check box to insert a check mark.
   e. Click the *Date* check box to insert a check mark and then click OK.
   f. Click OK at the Microsoft Excel message box that says 1 duplicate value was found and removed and 20 unique values remain.
2. Scroll the worksheet to view the total in K25. Compare the total with your printout from Project 1d, Step 4. Notice the total in *Fees Due* is now *7,516.25* compared to *7,910.00* in the printout.
3. Save **EL2-C3-P2-BillingSummaryOctWk1.xlsx**.

Validating and Restricting Data Entry

Excel's data validation feature allows you to control the type of data that is accepted for entry in a cell. You can specify the type of data that is allowed as well as parameters that validate whether the entry is within a certain range of acceptable values, dates, times, or text length. You can also set up a list of values that display in a drop-down list when the cell is made active. At the Data Validation dialog box shown in Figure 3.5, begin by choosing the type of data you want to validate in the *Allow* list box in the Settings tab. Additional list or text boxes appear in the dialog box depending on the option chosen in the *Allow* list.

As well as defining acceptable data entry parameters, you have the option of adding an input message and an error alert message to the range. You define the text that appears in these messages. The input message displays when the cell is made active for which data validation rules apply. These messages are informational in nature. Error alerts are messages that appear if incorrect data is entered in the cell. Three styles of error alerts are available. A description and example for each type of alert are described in Table 3.1.

If an error alert message has not been defined, Excel displays the Stop error alert with a default error message of *The value you entered is not valid. A user has restricted values that can be entered into this cell.*

▼ Quick Steps

Create Data Validation Rule
1. Select desired range.
2. Click Data tab.
3. Click Data Validation button.
4. Specify validation criteria in Settings tab.
5. Click Input Message tab.
6. Type input message title and text.
7. Click Error Alert tab.
8. Select error style.
9. Type error alert title and message text.
10. Click OK.

Data Validation

Figure 3.5 Data Validation Dialog Box with Settings Tab Selected

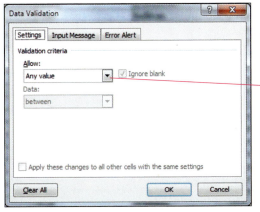

Specify the type of data you will allow to be entered into the cells within the range by specifying one of the following options: *Whole number, Decimal, List, Date, Time, Text length, Custom.* Other parameter boxes appear depending on the selection made in *Allow.*

Table 3.1 Data Validation Error Alert Message Styles

Error Alert Icon	Error Alert Style	Description	
❌	Stop	Prevent the data from being entered into the cell. The error alert message box provides three buttons to ensure new data is entered.	Date is outside accepted range — ❌ Please enter a date from October 8 to October 12, 2012 — Retry Cancel Help — Was this information helpful?
⚠️	Warning	Do not prevent the data from being entered into the cell. The error alert message box provides four buttons displayed below the prompt *Continue?*	Check number of hours — ⚠️ The hours you have entered are greater than 8 — Continue? — Yes No Cancel Help — Was this information helpful?
ℹ️	Information	Do not prevent the data from being entered into the cell. The error alert message box provides three buttons displayed below the error message.	Verify hours entered — ℹ️ The hours you have entered are outside the normal range — OK Cancel Help — Was this information helpful?

Project 2c   **Restricting Data Entry to Dates Within a Range**   Part 3 of 5

1. With **EL2-C3-P2-BillingSummaryOctWk1.xlsx** open, create a validation rule, input message, and error alert for dates in the billing summary worksheet by completing the following steps:
   a. Select C5:C24.
   b. Click the Data Validation button in the Data Tools group in the Data tab.
   c. With Settings the active tab at the Data Validation dialog box, click the down-pointing arrow next to the *Allow* list box (currently displays *Any value*) and then click *Date* at the drop-down list. Validation options are dependent on the *Allow* setting. When you choose *Date*, Excel adds *Start date* and *End date* text boxes to the *Validation criteria* section.
   d. With *between* automatically selected in the *Data* list box, click in the *Start date* text box and then type **10/08/2012**.
   e. Click in the *End date* text box and then type **10/12/2012**. Since the billing summary worksheet is for the week of October 8 to 12, 2012, entering this validation criteria will ensure that only dates between the start date and end date are accepted.
   f. Click the Input Message tab.

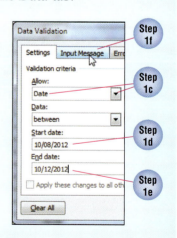

Step 1f
Step 1c
Step 1d
Step 1e

g. Click in the *Title* text box and then type **Billing Date**.

h. Click in the *Input message* text box and then type **This worksheet is for the week of October 8 to October 12 only**.

i. Click the Error Alert tab.

j. With *Stop* selected in the *Style* list box, click in the *Title* text box and then type **Date is outside accepted range**.

k. Click in the *Error message* text box and then type **Please enter a date from October 8 to October 12, 2012**.

l. Click OK. Since the range is active for which the data validation rules apply, the input message box appears.

m. Deselect the range.

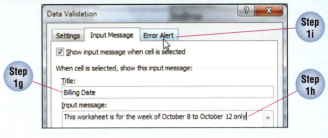

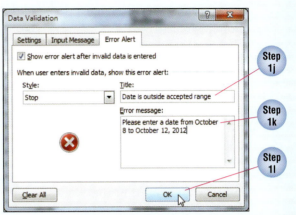

2. Add a new record to the table to test the date validation rule by completing the following steps:

a. Right-click row number 25 and then click *Insert* at the shortcut menu to insert a new row into the table.

b. Make A25 the active cell, type **PL-348**, and then press Tab.

c. Type **10420** in the *Client* column and then press Tab. The input message title and text appear when the *Date* column is made active.

d. Type **10/15/2012** and then press Enter. Since the date entered is invalid, the error alert message box appears.

e. Click the Retry button.

f. Type **10/12/2012** and then press Tab.

g. Enter the data in the remaining fields as follows. Press Tab to move from column to column in the table.

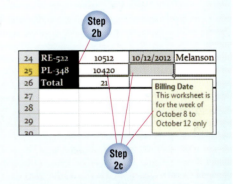

Last Name	**Torrez**
First Name	**Alexander**
Attorney FName	**Rosa**
Attorney LName	**Martinez**
Area	**Patent**
Billable Hours	**2.25**
Rate	**100.00**

3. Save **EL2-C3-P2-BillingSummaryOctWk1.xlsx**.

1. With **EL2-C3-P2-BillingSummaryOctWk1.xlsx** open, create a list of values that are allowed in a cell by completing the following steps:
   a. Select J5:J25.
   b. Click the Data Validation button in the Data Tools group.
   c. If necessary, click the Settings tab.
   d. Click the down-pointing arrow next to the *Allow* list box and then click *List* at the drop-down list.
   e. Click in the *Source* text box and then type **75.00,85.00,90.00,100.00**.
   f. Click OK.
   g. Deselect the range.

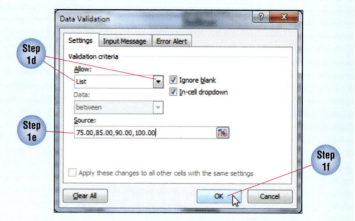

2. Add a new record to the table to test the rate validation list by completing the following steps:
   a. Right-click row number 26 and then click *Insert* at the shortcut menu to insert a new row into the table.
   b. Make A26 the active cell and then type data in the fields as follows. Press Tab to move from column to column in the table.

File	**IN-745**
Client	**10210**
Date	**10/12/2012**
Last Name	**Boscovic**
First Name	**Victor**
Attorney FName	**Rosa**
Attorney LName	**Martinez**
Area	**Insurance**
Billable Hours	**1.75**

   c. At the *Rate* field, the validation list becomes active and a down-pointing arrow appears at the field. Type **125.00** and then press Tab to test the validation rule. Since no error alert message was entered, the default message appears.

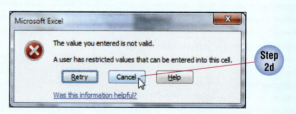

   d. Click the Cancel button. The value is cleared from the field.
   e. Click the down-pointing arrow at the end of the field, click *100.00* at the drop-down list, and then press Tab.

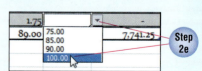

3. Save **EL2-C3-P2-BillingSummaryOctWk1.xlsx**.

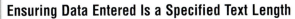

1. With **EL2-C3-P2-BillingSummaryOctWk1.xlsx** open, create a validation rule to ensure that all client identification numbers are five characters in length to coincide with the firm's accounting system by completing the following steps:

   a. Select B5:B26 and click the Data Validation button in the Data Tools group in the Data tab.

   b. Click the down-pointing arrow next to the *Allow* list box and then click *Text length* at the drop-down list.

   c. Click the down-pointing arrow next to *Data* and then click *equal to* at the drop-down list.

   d. Click in the *Length* text box, type **5**, and then click OK.

   e. Deselect the range.

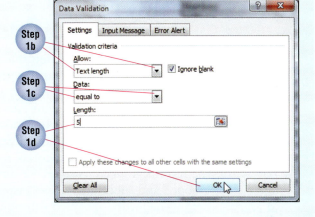

2. Add a new record to the table to test the client identification validation rule by completing the following steps:

   a. Right-click row number 27 and then click *Insert* at the shortcut menu.

   b. Make A27 the active cell, type **FL-325**, and then press Tab.

   c. Type **1010411** in B27 and then press Tab. Since this value is greater than the specified number of characters allowed in the cell, the default error message appears.

   d. Click the Retry button.

   e. Delete the selected text, type **1010**, and then press Tab. Since this value is less than the specified text length, the default error message appears again. Using a Text Length validation rule ensures that all entries in the range have the same number of characters. This rule is useful to validate customer numbers, employee numbers, inventory numbers, or any other data that requires a consistent number of characters.

   f. Click the Cancel button, type **10104**, and then press Tab. Since this entry is five characters in length, Excel moves to the next field.

   g. Enter the remaining fields as follows:

Date	**10/12/2012**
Last Name	**Ferreira**
First Name	**Joseph**
Attorney FName	**Marty**
Attorney LName	**O'Donovan**
Area	**Divorce**
Billable Hours	**5.75**
Rate	**85.00**

3. Save, print, and then close **EL2-C3-P2-BillingSummaryOctWk1.xlsx**.

roject **3** **Group and Subtotal Related Records** **3 Parts**

You will convert the billing summary table to a normal range, sort the rows by the attorney names, and then add subtotals to display total fees due, a count of fees, and the average billable hours and fees due for each attorney.

Convert Table to Range
1. Make cell active within the table.
2. Click Table Tools Design tab.
3. Click Convert to Range button.
4. Click Yes.

Create Subtotals
1. Select range.
2. Click Data tab.
3. Click Subtotals button.
4. Select field to group by in *At each change in* list box.
5. Select desired function in *Use function* list box.
6. Select field(s) to subtotal in *Add subtotal to* list box.
7. Click OK.
8. Deselect range.

Convert to Range

Converting a Table to a Normal Range ■■■■■■■■■■■■■

A table can be converted to a normal range using the Convert to Range button in the Tools group of the Table Tools Design tab. Convert a table to a range in order to use the Subtotal feature or if you no longer need to treat the table data as a range independent of data in the rest of the worksheet.

Subtotaling Related Data ■■■■■■■■■■■■■■■■■■■■■■■

A range of data with a column that has multiple rows with the same field value can be grouped and subtotals created for each group automatically. For example, a worksheet with multiple records with the same department name in a field can be grouped by the department names and a subtotal of a numeric field calculated for each department. You can choose from a list of functions for the subtotal such as Average or Sum and you can also create multiple subtotal values for each group. Prior to creating subtotals, sort the data by the fields in which you want the records grouped. Also, make sure no blank rows exist within the range to be grouped and subtotaled. Excel displays a new row with a summary total when the field value for the specified subtotal column changes content. A grand total is also automatically included at the bottom of the range. Excel displays the subtotals with buttons along the left side of the worksheet area used to show or hide the details for each group using Excel's Outline feature. Excel can create an outline with up to eight levels. Figure 3.6 illustrates the data you will group and subtotal in Project 3a displayed with the worksheet at level 2 of the outline. In Figure 3.7, the same worksheet is shown with two attorney groups expanded to show the detail records.

Figure 3.6 Worksheet with Subtotals by Attorney Last Name Displaying Level 2 of the Outline

Outline level buttons

		A	B	C	D	E	F	G	H	I	J	K
	1					O'DONOVAN & SULLIVAN LAW ASSOCIATES						
	2					ASSOCIATE BILLING SUMMARY						
	3					OCTOBER 8 TO 12, 2012						
	4	File	Client	Date	Last Name	First Name	Attorney FName	Attorney LName	Area	Billable Hours	Rate	Fees Due
+	15							Martinez Total				3,725.00
+	20							O'Donovan Total				1,785.00
+	26							Sullivan Total				1,762.50
+	31							Williams Total				1,132.50
−	32							Grand Total				8,405.00

Hide Detail button   Show Detail button

Figure 3.7 Worksheet with Subtotals by Attorney Last Name with Martinez and Sullivan Groups Expanded

	File	Client	Date	Last Name	First Name	Attorney FName	Attorney LName	Area	Billable Hours	Rate	Fees Due
					O'DONOVAN & SULLIVAN LAW ASSOCIATES						
					ASSOCIATE BILLING SUMMARY						
					OCTOBER 8 TO 12, 2012						
5	IN-745	10210	10/9/2012	Boscovic	Victor	Rosa	Martinez	Insurance	4.25	100.00	425.00
6	IN-745	10210	10/11/2012	Boscovic	Victor	Rosa	Martinez	Insurance	4.50	100.00	450.00
7	IN-745	10210	10/12/2012	Boscovic	Victor	Rosa	Martinez	Insurance	1.75	100.00	175.00
8	EL-632	10225	10/9/2012	Armstrong	Daniel	Rosa	Martinez	Employment	3.25	100.00	325.00
9	EL-632	10225	10/11/2012	Armstrong	Daniel	Rosa	Martinez	Employment	4.50	100.00	450.00
10	PL-512	10290	10/11/2012	Tonini	Sam	Rosa	Martinez	Pension	3.75	100.00	375.00
11	IN-801	10346	10/12/2012	Sebastian	Paul	Rosa	Martinez	Insurance	4.25	100.00	425.00
12	PL-348	10420	10/10/2012	Torrez	Alexander	Rosa	Martinez	Patent	5.00	100.00	500.00
13	PL-348	10420	10/12/2012	Torrez	Alexander	Rosa	Martinez	Patent	2.25	100.00	225.00
14	EP-685	10495	10/12/2012	Kinsela	Frank	Rosa	Martinez	Estate	3.75	100.00	375.00
15							Martinez Total				3,725.00
20							O'Donovan Total				1,785.00
21	CL-412	10125	10/8/2012	Schmidt	Hilary	Toni	Sullivan	Corporate	5.25	75.00	393.75
22	CL-412	10125	10/12/2012	Schmidt	Hilary	Toni	Sullivan	Corporate	5.25	75.00	393.75
23	CL-521	10334	10/10/2012	Marsales	Gene	Toni	Sullivan	Corporate	4.25	75.00	318.75
24	CL-501	10341	10/10/2012	Fletcher	Dana	Toni	Sullivan	Corporate	5.25	75.00	393.75
25	CL-450	10358	10/12/2012	Poissant	Henri	Toni	Sullivan	Corporate	3.50	75.00	262.50
26							Sullivan Total				1,762.50
31							Williams Total				1,132.50
32							Grand Total				8,405.00

Project 3a   **Converting a Table to a Range and Creating Subtotals**   Part 1 of 3

1. Open **EL2-C3-P2-BillingSummaryOctWk1.xlsx**.
2. Save the workbook with Save As and name it **EL2-C3-P3-BillingSummaryOctWk1.xlsx**.
3. Convert the table to a normal range in order to group and subtotal the records by completing the following steps:
   a. Position the active cell anywhere within the table and click the Table Tools Design tab.
   b. Click the *Total Row* check box in the Table Style Options group to remove the total row from the table. The Subtotal feature includes a grand total automatically so the total row is no longer needed.
   c. Click the *Banded Columns* check box in the Table Style Options to remove the banded formatting.
   d. Click the Convert to Range button in the Tools group.
   e. Click Yes at the Microsoft Excel message box asking if you want to convert the table to a normal range.

   f. Select columns A–K and adjust the column width to AutoFit.
   g. Deselect the columns.
4. Sort the data by the fields you want to subtotal and group by completing the following steps:
   a. Select A4:K27.
   b. Click the Sort & Filter button in the Editing group in the Home tab and then click *Custom Sort* at the drop-down list.

c. At the Sort dialog box, define three levels to group and sort records as follows:

Column	Sort On	Order
Attorney LName	Values	A to Z
Client	Values	Smallest to Largest
Date	Values	Oldest to Newest

  d. Click OK.

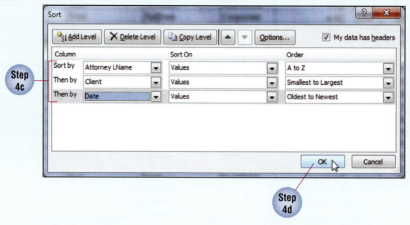

5. Create subtotals at each change in attorney last name by completing the following steps:
   a. With A4:K27 still selected, click the Data tab.
   b. Click the Subtotal button in the Outline group.
   c. At the Subtotal dialog box, click the down-pointing arrow to the right of the *At each change in* list box (current displays *File*), scroll down the list, and then click *Attorney LName*.

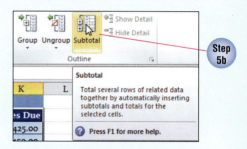

  d. With *Use function* set to *Sum* and *Fees Due* selected in the *Add subtotal to* list box, click OK.
  e. Deselect the range.
6. Print the worksheet.

7. Show and hide levels in the outlined worksheet by completing the following steps:

   a. Click the level 1 button located at the top left of the worksheet area below the Name text box. Excel collapses the worksheet to display only the grand total of the *Fees Due* column.

   b. Click the level 2 button to display the subtotals by attorney last name. Notice a button with a plus symbol displays next to each subtotal in the Outline section at the left side of the worksheet area. The button with the plus symbol is the Show Detail button and the button with the minus symbol is the Hide Detail button. Compare your worksheet with the one shown in Figure 3.6 on page 88.

   c. Click the Show Detail button (displays as a plus symbol) next to the row with the Martinez subtotal. The detail rows for the group of records for Martinez are displayed.

   d. Click the Show Detail button next to the row with the Sullivan subtotal.

   e. Compare your worksheet with the one shown in Figure 3.7 on page 89.

   f. Click the level 3 button to display all detail rows.

8. Save **EL2-C3-P3-BillingSummaryOctWk1.xlsx**.

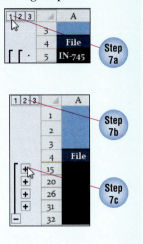

Step 7a

Step 7b

Step 7c

Project 3b **Modifying Subtotals**   Part 2 of 3

1. With **EL2-C3-P3-BillingSummaryOctWk1.xlsx** open, add a subtotal to count the number of billable records for each attorney for the week by completing the following steps:

   a. Select A4:K32 and click the Subtotal button in the Outline group in the Data tab. The Subtotal dialog box opens with the settings used for the subtotals created in Project 3a.

   b. Click the *Replace current subtotals* check box to clear the check mark. By clearing the check box you are instructing Excel to add another subtotal row to each group.

   c. Click the down-pointing arrow next to the *Use function* list box and then click *Count* at the drop-down list.

   d. With *Fees Due* still selected in the *Add subtotal to* list box, click OK. Excel adds a new subtotal row to each group with the count of records displayed.

2. Add a subtotal to calculate the average billable hours and average fees due for each attorney by completing the following steps:

   a. With the data range still selected, click the Subtotal button.

   b. Click the down-pointing arrow next to the *Use function* list box and then click *Average* at the drop-down list.

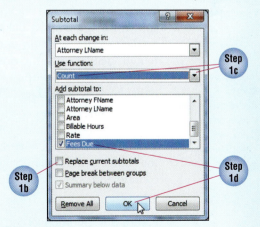

Step 1b

Step 1c

Step 1d

c. Click the *Billable Hours* check box in the *Add subtotal to* list box and then click OK. Excel adds a new subtotal row to each group with the average billable hours and average fees due for each attorney.

Attorney LName	Area	Billable Hours	Rate	Fees Due
Martinez	Insurance	4.25	100.00	425.00
Martinez	Insurance	4.50	100.00	450.00
Martinez	Insurance	1.75	100.00	175.00
Martinez	Employment	3.25	100.00	325.00
Martinez	Employment	4.50	100.00	450.00
Martinez	Pension	3.75	100.00	375.00
Martinez	Insurance	4.25	100.00	425.00
Martinez	Patent	5.00	100.00	500.00
Martinez	Patent	2.25	100.00	225.00
Martinez	Estate	3.75	100.00	375.00
Martinez Average		3.73		372.50
Martinez Count				10
Martinez Total				3,725.00

average row shown for Martinez group; average of *Billable Hours* and *Fees Due* columns added to subtotals for all attorneys in Steps 2a–2d

d. Deselect the range.
3. Use Save As to save the revised workbook and name it **EL2-C3-P3-BillingSummaryOctWk1-Prj3b**.
4. Click the Page Layout tab and scale the height of the worksheet to 1 page.
5. Print the worksheet.
6. Save and then close **EL2-C3-P3-BillingSummaryOctWk1-Prj3b.xlsx**.

Grouping and Ungrouping Data ■■■■■■■■■ ■ ■■■■■■

▼ **Quick Steps**

Group Data by Rows
1. Select range to be grouped within outlined worksheet.
2. Click Group button.
3. Click OK.

Ungroup Data by Rows
1. Select grouped range within outlined worksheet.
2. Click Ungroup button.
3. Click OK.

Use the Group and Ungroup buttons when a worksheet is outlined to individually manage collapsing and expanding groups of records at the various levels. For example, in an outlined worksheet with detailed rows displayed, selecting a group of records and clicking the Ungroup button opens the Ungroup dialog box shown in Figure 3.8. Clicking OK with *Rows* selected removes the group feature applied to the selection and the Hide Detail button is removed so the records remain displayed at the outline level. Selecting records that have been ungrouped and clicking the Group button reattaches the group feature to the selection and redisplays the Hide Detail button.

Columns can also be grouped and ungrouped. The outline section with the level numbers and Show and Hide Detail buttons displays across the top of the worksheet area. For example, in a worksheet where two columns are used to arrive at a formula, the source columns can be grouped and the details hidden so that only the formula column with the calculated results is displayed in an outlined worksheet.

Figure 3.8 Ungroup Dialog Box

1. Open **EL2-C3-P3-BillingSummaryOctWk1.xlsx.** Group client data within the Martinez attorney group by completing the following steps:

a. Select A5:K7. These three rows contain billing information for Client 10210.

b. Click the Group button in the Outline group in the Data tab. (Do not click the down-pointing arrow on the button.)

c. At the Group dialog box with *Rows* selected, click OK. Excel adds a fourth outline level to the worksheet and a Hide Detail button is added below the last row of the grouped records in the Outline section.

d. Select A12:K13, click the Group button, and then click OK at the Group dialog box.

e. Deselect the range.

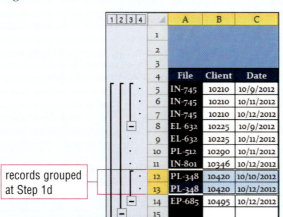

records grouped at Step 1d

2. Experiment with the Hide Detail buttons in the Martinez group by hiding the detail for Client 10210 and then hiding the detail for Client 10420.

3. Redisplay the detail rows by clicking the Show Detail button for each client.

4. Select A5:K7, click the Ungroup button (do not click the down-pointing arrow on the button), and then click OK at the Ungroup dialog box.

5. Select A12:K13, click the Ungroup button, and then click OK at the Ungroup dialog box.

6. Select A5:K14, click the Ungroup button, and then click OK at the Ungroup dialog box. Notice the Hide Detail button is removed for the entire Martinez group.

7. Deselect the range and then click the level 2 button at the top of the outline section. Notice the Martinez records do not collapse like the others since they are no longer grouped.

8. Use Save As to save the revised workbook and name it **EL2-C3-P3-BillingSummaryOctWk1-Prj3c.**

9. Print and then close **EL2-C3-P3-BillingSummaryOctWk1-Prj3c.xlsx.**

Chapter Summary

- A table in Excel is a range of cells similar in structure to a database in which no blank rows exist and the first row of the range contains column headings.

- Define a range as a table using the Table button in the Tables group of the Insert tab.

- Columns in a table are called fields and rows are called records.

- The first row of a table contains column headings and is called the field names row or header row.

- A table automatically expands to include data typed in a row or column immediately adjacent to a range that has been defined as a table.

- Typing a formula in the first row of a new column causes Excel to define the column as a calculated column and automatically copy the formula to the remaining rows in the table.

- The contextual Table Tools Design tab contains options for formatting tables.

- The Table Styles gallery contains several options with which you can change the visual appearance of a table.

- Banding rows or columns formats every other row or column differently to make reading a large table easier.

- You can add emphasis to the first column or the last column in a table. Excel generally formats the column with a darker fill color and reverse font or bold font and borders depending on the Table Style in effect.

- The row containing field names in a table can be shown or hidden using the *Header Row* option in the Table Style Options group.

- Adding a Total row to a table causes Excel to add the word *Total* in the leftmost column and create a Sum function in the last numeric column in the table. You can add additional functions by clicking in the desired column in the Total row and selecting a function from the pop-up list.

- Excel includes a filter arrow button automatically at the top of each column in a table with which you can filter and sort the table.

- A column containing text that you want to split can be separated into multiple columns using the Text to Columns button in the Data Tools group of the Data tab. The Convert Text to Columns wizard contains three dialog boxes to define how to split the data.

- Using the Remove Duplicates dialog box, you can instruct Excel to compare records within a worksheet and automatically delete rows that are duplicated.

- Data can be validated as it is being entered into a worksheet and either invalid data can be prevented from being stored or a warning can be issued to inform that data has been entered that does not conform to the restrictions.

- At the Settings tab in the Data Validation dialog box you define the validation criteria for the cell entry. You can allow data based on values, dates, times, text length, or restrict the entries to values within a drop-down list.

- At the Input Message tab in the Data Validation dialog box you can define a message that pops up when a cell for which data is restricted becomes active.

- At the Error Alert tab in the Data Validation dialog box you define the type of error alert to display and the content of the error message.
- Convert a table to a normal range to use the Subtotal feature or when you no longer need to treat a range of cells independently from the rest of the worksheet.
- Sort a worksheet by the column(s) for which you want to group data for subtotals before opening the Subtotals dialog box.
- The Subtotals button is located in the Outline group of the Data tab.
- Excel adds a subtotal automatically at each change in content for the column you specify as the subtotal field. A grand total is also automatically added to the bottom of the range.
- You can display more than one subtotal row for a group to calculate multiple functions such as Sum and Average.
- A subtotaled range is outlined and detail records can be collapsed or expanded using level number, Hide Detail, and Show Detail buttons.
- Use the Group and Ungroup buttons when a worksheet is outlined to manage the display of individual groups.

Commands Review

FEATURE	RIBBON TAB, GROUP	BUTTON	KEYBOARD SHORTCUT
Convert Text to Columns	Data, Data Tools		
Convert to Range	Table Tools Design, Tools		
Create Table	Insert, Tables		Ctrl + T
Data Validation	Data, Data Tools		
Group Data	Data, Outline		Shift + Alt + Right arrow key
Remove Duplicates	Data, Data Tools OR Table Tools Design, Tools		
Table Styles	Table Tools Design, Table Styles		
Sort & Filter table	Home, Editing		
Subtotals	Data, Outline		
Total row	Table Tools Design, Table Style Options		Ctrl + Shift + T
Ungroup	Data, Outline		Shift + Alt + Left arrow key

Concepts Check Test Your Knowledge

Completion: In the space provided at the right, indicate the correct term, command, or number.

1. The first row of a table that contains the column headings is called the field names row or this row.

_____

2. Typing a formula in the first row of a column in a table causes Excel to define the field as this type of column.

_____

3. This is the term that describes the formatting feature in a table in which even rows are formatted differently than odd rows.

_____

4. Change the visual appearance of a table using this gallery in the Table Tools Design tab.

_____

5. Clicking this button causes the Convert Text to Columns wizard to appear.

_____

6. Open this dialog box to instruct Excel to compare the entries in the columns you specify and automatically delete rows that contain repeated data.

_____

7. Open this dialog box to restrict entries in a cell to those that you set up in a drop-down list.

_____

8. This option in the *Allow* list box is used to force data entered into a cell to be a specific number of characters.

_____

9. This is the default error alert style that prevents invalid data from being entered into a cell.

_____

10. The Convert to Range button is found in this tab.

_____

11. Prior to creating subtotals using the Subtotal button in the Outline group of the Data tab, arrange the data in this order.

_____

12. In a worksheet with subtotal rows only displayed, click this button next to a subtotal row in order to view the grouped rows.

_____

13. Click this button in an outlined worksheet to collapse the rows for a group.

_____

14. In an outlined worksheet, this button collapses all records and displays only the Grand Total row.

_____

15. Clicking this button in an outlined worksheet will cause the Hide Detail button for the selected rows to be removed.

_____

Skills Check Assess Your Performance

Assessment

1 CREATE AND FORMAT A TABLE

1. Open **VantageClassics.xlsx**.
2. Save the workbook with Save As and name it **EL2-C3-A1-VantageClassics**.
3. Select A4:L30 and create a table using *Table Style Medium 12* (fifth option in second row in *Medium* section).
4. Add a calculated column to the table in column M. Type the label **Total Cost** as the column heading and create a formula in the first record that multiplies the number of copies in column G times the cost price in column L.
5. Adjust the three rows above the table to merge and center across columns A through M.
6. Adjust all column widths to AutoFit.
7. Band the columns instead of the rows and emphasize the last column in the table.
8. Add a Total row to the table. Add Average functions that calculate the average number of copies and the average cost price of a classic video.
9. Format the average value in the *Copies* column of the Total row to zero decimals.
10. The video *Blue Hawaii* cannot be located and the manager of Vantage Videos would like to remove the record from the table. Delete the row in the table for the record with Stock No. CV-1015.
11. Format the *Total Cost* column to display two decimals.
12. Save, print, and then close **EL2-C3-A1-VantageClassics.xlsx**.

Assessment

2 USE DATA TOOLS

1. Open **EL2-C3-A1-VantageClassics.xlsx**.
2. Save the workbook with Save As and name it **EL2-C3-A2-VantageClassics**.
3. Remove the banding on the columns and band the rows.
4. Insert a new blank column to the right of the column containing the director names.
5. Split the director names into two columns. Edit the column headings to **Director FName** and **Director LName**, respectively.
6. Use the Remove Duplicates feature to find and remove any duplicate rows using *Title* as the comparison column.
7. Create the following validation rules:
   a. Create a validation rule for the *Stock No.* column that ensures all new entries are seven characters in length. Add an input message to the column to advise the user that stock numbers need to be seven characters. You determine the title and message text. Use the default error alert options.
   b. The manager would like to ensure that five copies is the maximum inventory of any individual classic video in the collection. Create a validation rule that restricts entries in the copies column to a number less than six. Add an appropriate input and error message. Use the default Stop error alert.

c. Create a drop-down list for the *Genre* column with the entries provided. Do not enter an input message and use the default error alert settings.
Action,Comedy,Drama,Family,History,Horror,Musical,Thriller,War

8. Add the following record to the table to test the data validation rules. Initially enter incorrect values in the *Stock No.*, *Genre*, and *Copies* columns to make sure the rule and the messages work correctly.

Stock No.	**CV-1026**
Title	**The Philadelphia Story**
Year	**1940**
Genre	**Comedy**
Stock Date	**12/12/2011**
Director FName	**George**
Director LName	**Cukor**
Copies	**3**
VHS	**No**
DVD	**Yes**
Blu-ray	**Yes**
Category	**7-day rental**
Cost Price	**10.15**

9. Save, print, and then close **EL2-C3-A2-VantageClassics.xlsx**.

Assessment

3 SUBTOTAL RECORDS

1. Open **EL2-C3-A2-VantageClassics.xlsx**.
2. Save the workbook with Save As and name it **EL2-C3-A3-VantageClassics**.
3. Remove the Total row, remove the row banding, and remove the emphasis from the last column in the table.
4. Convert the table to a normal range.
5. Adjust all column widths to AutoFit.
6. Sort the list first by the genre, then by the director's last name, and then by the title of the video. Use the default sort values and sort order for each level.
7. Add subtotals using the Subtotal button in the Outline group of the Data tab to the *Total Cost* column to calculate the sum and average total costs of videos by genre.
8. Display the worksheet at Level 2 of the outline.
9. Show the details for the Comedy, Drama, and Family genres.
10. Print the worksheet.
11. Save and then close **EL2-C3-A3-VantageClassics.xlsx**.

Visual Benchmark · Demonstrate Your Proficiency

1 USING TABLE AND DATA TOOLS IN A CALL LIST

1. Open **WPMCNurseCallList.xlsx**.
2. Save the workbook with Save As and name it **EL2-C3-VB1-WPMCNurseCallList**.
3. Format and apply data tools as required to duplicate the worksheet in Figure 3.9 using the following information:
   - The worksheet has *Table Style Medium 5* applied to the table range.
   - Look closely at the sorted order. The table is sorted by three levels using the fields *Designation, Hourly Rate*, and *Hire Date*.
   - Shift cost multiplies the hourly rate times 8 hours.
   - Split the names into two columns.
   - Include the Total row and apply the appropriate banded options.
4. Save, print, and then close **EL2-C3-VB1-WPMCNurseCallList.xlsx**.

Figure 3.9 Visual Benchmark 1

Wellington Park Medical Center
Nursing Division Casual Relief Call List

Payroll No	First Name	Last Name	Designation	Hire Date	Telephone	OR Exp?	Day Shift Only?	Night Shift Only?	Either Shift?	Hourly Rate	Shift Cost
78452	Terry	Mason	RN	5/3/1998	555-1279	Yes	No	Yes	No	38.50	308.00
19658	Paula	Sanderson	RN	4/28/2000	555-3485	No	No	No	Yes	38.50	308.00
38642	Tania	Ravi	RN	6/22/2002	555-6969	Yes	Yes	No	Weekends only	38.50	308.00
96523	Lynn	Pietre	RN	10/22/1998	555-2548	Yes	Yes	No	Weekends only	35.00	280.00
45968	David	Featherstone	RN	9/9/2001	555-5961	No	No	No	Yes	35.00	280.00
46956	Orlando	Zambian	RN	11/10/2001	555-1186	No	Yes	No	No	35.00	280.00
56983	Amanda	Sanchez	RN	4/27/1999	555-4896	Yes	No	Yes	No	33.00	264.00
68429	Rene	Quenneville	RN	8/15/2003	555-4663	Yes	Yes	No	Weekends only	22.50	180.00
69417	Denis	LaPierre	RN	8/23/2003	555-8643	No	No	Yes	No	22.50	180.00
37944	Fernando	Este	RN	7/18/2005	555-4545	No	No	No	Yes	22.50	180.00
78647	Jay	Bjorg	RN	5/14/2007	555-6598	No	No	No	Yes	22.50	180.00
95558	Sam	Vargas	RN	3/2/2009	555-4571	No	No	No	Yes	22.50	180.00
98731	Zail	Singh	RN	5/6/2011	555-3561	Yes	Yes	No	No	22.50	180.00
58612	Savana	Ruiz	RN	4/15/2012	555-8457	Yes	No	Yes	Weekends only	22.50	180.00
96721	Noreen	Kalir	RN	4/3/2009	555-1876	Yes	Yes	No	No	21.50	172.00
89367	Xiu	Zheng	LPN	4/23/2006	555-7383	Yes	Yes	No	No	18.75	150.00
14586	Alma	Fernandez	LPN	8/3/1997	555-7412	Yes	No	No	Yes	16.75	134.00
48652	Dana	Casselman	LPN	10/15/1997	555-6325	Yes	No	No	Yes	16.75	134.00
85412	Kelly	Lund	LPN	11/19/1998	555-3684	No	Yes	No	Weekends only	15.75	126.00
98364	Lana	Bourne	LPN	7/15/2008	555-9012	Yes	Yes	No	No	15.50	124.00
90467	Nadir	Abouzeen	LPN	8/12/2008	555-9023	No	No	No	Yes	14.50	116.00
68475	Kelly	O'Brien	LPN	1/20/2012	555-6344	No	Yes	No	Weekends only	13.75	110.00
									Average Hourly Rate and Shift Cost:	24.74	197.91

2 USING SUBTOTALS IN A CALL LIST

1. Open **EL2-C3-VB1-WPMCNurseCallList.xlsx**.
2. Save the workbook with Save As and name it **EL2-C3-VB2-WPMCNurseCallList**.
3. Create subtotals and view the revised worksheet at the appropriate level to display as shown in Figure 3.10
4. Save, print, and then close **EL2-C3-VB2-WPMCNurseCallList.xlsx**.

Figure 3.10 Visual Benchmark 2

	A	B	C	D	E	F	G	H	I	J	K	L
1						Wellington Park Medical Center						
2						Nursing Division Casual Relief Call List						
3	Payroll No	Firstname	Lastname	Designation	Hire Date	Telephone	OR Exp?	Day Shift Only?	Night Shift Only?	Either Shift?	Hourly Rate	Shift Cost
19				RN Average							28.83	230.67
27				LPN Average							15.96	127.71
28				Grand Average							24.74	197.91

Case Study   Apply Your Skills

Part 1

Rajiv Patel, Vice-President of NuTrends Market Research, has sent you a file named **NuTrendsMktPlans.xlsx**. The workbook contains client information for the company's first quarter marketing plans for three marketing consultants. Rajiv would like you to improve the reporting in the file by completing the following tasks:

- Set up the data as a table sorted first by the consultant's last name and then by the marketing campaign's start date, both in ascending order. Rajiv would prefer that the consultant names be split into two columns.
- Improve the formatting of the dollar values.
- Add a Total row to sum the columns containing dollar amounts.
- Add formatting to the titles above the table that are suited to the colors in the table style you selected.
- Make any other formatting changes you think would improve the worksheet's appearance.

Save the revised workbook and name it **EL2-C3-CS-P1-NuTrendsMktPlans**. Print the worksheet in landscape orientation with the width scaled to 1 page.

Part 2

Rajiv would like statistics for each consultant added to the workbook. Specifically, Rajiv would like to see the following information:

- The total marketing plan budget values being managed by each consultant as well as the total planned expenditures by month.
- The average marketing plan budget being managed by each consultant as well as the average planned expenditures by month.

Rajiv would like a printout that displays only the total and average values for each consultant as well as the grand average and grand total. Save the revised workbook and name it **EL2-C3-CS-P2-NuTrendsMktPlans**. Print and then close the worksheet.

Rajiv has asked that you provide another report from the file named **NuTrendsMktPlans.xlsx**. Specifically, Rajiv would like a printout of the worksheet that shows the original data at the top of the worksheet and a few blank rows below the worksheet, Rajiv would like to see the marketing plan details for Yolanda Robertson's clients that have a campaign starting after January 31, 2012.

Research in Help how to filter a range of cells using the Advanced Filter button in the Sort & Filter group of the Data tab. Make sure you read how to copy rows that meet your filter criteria to another area of the worksheet. Using the information you learned in Help, open **NuTrendsMktPlans.xlsx**, insert three new rows above the worksheet and use these rows to create the criteria range. Filter the list as per Rajiv's specifications. Rows that meet the criteria should be copied below the worksheet starting in A22. Add an appropriate title to describe the copied data in A21. Make any formatting changes you think would improve the appearance of the worksheet. Save the revised workbook and name it **EL2-C3-CS-P3-NutrendsMktPlans**. Print the worksheet and then close the workbook.

Rajiv is looking for information on current salary ranges for a market researcher in the United States. Use the Internet to find the information for Rajiv. If possible, find salary information that is regional to your state for a minimum of three cities. Find a low salary and a high salary for a market researcher in each city. Create a workbook that summarizes the results of your research. Include in the workbook the Web site addresses as hyperlinked cells next to the salary range information. Organize the data in the workbook as a table. Apply table formatting options so that the data is attractively presented and easy to read. Add a Total row to the table and include an Average function to find the average salary from the three cities. Find a minimum of three resources and a maximum of five. Save the workbook and name it **EL2-C3-CS-P4-NuTrendsSalaryAnalysis**. Print the worksheet and then close the workbook.

Summarizing and Consolidating Data

PERFORMANCE OBJECTIVES

Upon successful completion of Chapter 4, you will be able to:

- Summarize data by creating formulas with range names that reference other worksheets
- Modify the range assigned to a range name
- Summarize data by creating 3-D formulas
- Create formulas that link to cells in other worksheets or workbooks
- Edit a link to a source workbook
- Break a link to an external reference
- Use the Consolidate feature to summarize data in multiple worksheets
- Create, edit, and format a PivotTable
- Filter a PivotTable using Slicers
- Create and format a PivotChart
- Create and format Sparklines

Tutorials

4.1 Summarizing Data in Multiple Worksheets Using Range Names and 3-D References

4.2 Summarizing Data by Linking Ranges in Other Worksheets or Workbooks

4.3 Summarizing Data Using the Consolidate Feature

4.4 Creating a PivotTable Report

4.5 Filtering a PivotTable Using Slicers

4.6 Creating a PivotChart

4.7 Summarizing Data with Sparklines

You can summarize data by creating formulas that reference cells in other areas of the active worksheet, in other worksheets within the same workbook, or by linking to cells in other worksheets or workbooks. The Consolidate feature can also be used to summarize data from other worksheets or other workbooks into a master worksheet. Once the data has been summarized, consider presenting or analyzing the data by creating and formatting a PivotTable or a PivotChart. Sparklines are miniature charts inserted into a cell that allow you to see at a glance a trend or other pattern in the data. In this chapter you will learn how to summarize data using a variety of methods and present visually summarized data for analysis. Model answers for this chapter's projects appear on the following pages.

Excel2010L2C4

Note: Before beginning the projects, copy to your storage medium the Excel2010L2C4 subfolder from the Excel2010L2 folder on the CD that accompanies this textbook and then make Excel2010L2C4 the active folder.

National Park Service
U.S. Department of the Interior
May 2012
Attendance Summary
Southwest Region, Zone C

Private Vehicle and Individual Entrances Only	10,460
Commercial Tour Vehicles Only	15,069
Total Attendance	25,529

National Park Service
U.S. Department of the Interior
May 2012
Attendance Summary
Southwest Region, Zone C

Private Vehicle and Individual Entrances Only	10,460
Commercial Tour Vehicles Only	15,434
Total Attendance	25,894

Project 1 Calculate Park Attendance Totals

Project 1c, EL2-C4-P1-MayParkEntries.xlsx

Project 1d, EL2-C4-P1-MayParkEntries.xlsx

NewAge Dental Services
Fee Revenue Summary

	January	February	March	Total
General Examination	3,374.47	3,386.41	3,510.45	10,271.33
Cleanings and Fillings	9,634.98	9,016.37	7,107.42	25,758.77
Teeth Whitening	2,743.90	5,993.69	4,431.19	13,168.78
Bonding	5,835.61	7,262.00	7,420.33	20,517.94
Porcelain Veneers	5,674.21	3,685.67	3,671.52	13,031.40
Crowns and Bridges	4,977.27	10,636.33	7,119.07	22,732.67
Full and Partial Dentures	7,608.05	8,926.64	11,886.13	28,420.82
Emergency Extractions	1,301.24	1,291.32	1,515.69	4,108.25
Root Canals	3,157.20	2,488.20	6,034.21	11,679.61
Total	44,306.93	52,686.63	52,696.01	149,689.57

Project 2 Calculate Total Fees Billed by Three Dentists

EL2-C4-P2-NewAgeDentalQ1Fees.xlsx

Model	(Multiple Items)			
Sum of Sale Price	**Column Labels**			
Row Labels	Clarke	Fernandez	Kazmarek	Grand Total
Central	4,470		5,224	9,694
North	1,150		8,099	9,249
South	2,499	1,150		3,649
West			1,575	1,575
Grand Total	**8,119**	**1,150**	**14,898**	**24,167**

Project 3 Analyze Fitness Equipment Sales Data in a PivotTable and PivotChart

Project 3b, EL2-C4-P3-PremiumFitnessJanSales.xlsx

Model	(All)				
Sum of Sale Price	**Column Labels**				
Row Labels	Adams	Clarke	Fernandez	Kazmarek	Grand Total
Central	5,520	4,470		8,474	18,464
East	7,682	1,199	4,090	3,540	16,511
North	2,250	7,120	4,545	8,099	22,014
South		4,744	6,295		11,039
West	3,974	4,838	2,944	2,574	14,330
Grand Total	**19,426**	**22,371**	**17,874**	**22,687**	**82,358**

Model	VS2200		
Sum of Sale Price	**Column Labels**		
Row Labels	Fernandez	Grand Total	
East	1,745	1,745	
West	1,745	1,745	
Grand Total	**3,490**	**3,490**	

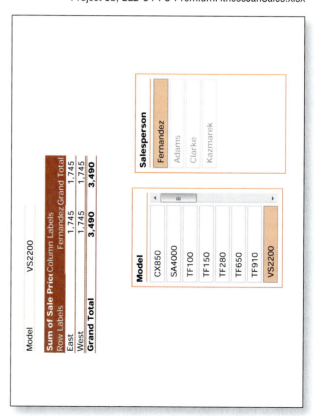

Project 3b, EL2-C4-P3-PremiumFitnessJanSales.xlsx

Project 3c, EL2-C4-P3-PremiumFitnessJanSales.xlsx

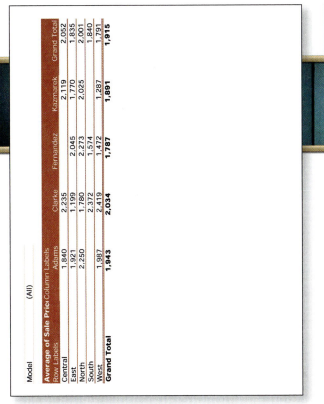

Model	(All)				
Average of Sale Price	Column Labels				
Row Labels	Adams	Clarke	Fernandez	Kazmarek	Grand Total
Central	1,840	2,235	2,045	2,119	2,052
East	1,921	1,199	2,273	1,770	1,835
North	2,250	1,780	1,574	2,025	2,001
South		2,372	1,472	1,287	1,840
West	1,987	2,419			1,791
Grand Total	**1,943**	**2,034**	**1,787**	**1,891**	**1,915**

Project 3d, EL2-C4-P3-PremiumFitnessAvgJanSales.xlsx

Project 3e, EL2-C4-P3-PremiumFitnessJanSales.xlsx

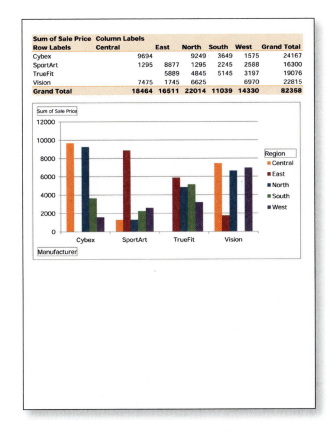

Sum of Sale Price	Column Labels					
Row Labels	Central	East	North	South	West	Grand Total
Cybex	9694		9249	3649	1575	24167
SportArt	1295	8877	1295	2245	2588	16300
TrueFit		5889	4845	5145	3197	19076
Vision	7475	1745	6625		6970	22815
Grand Total	**18464**	**16511**	**22014**	**11039**	**14330**	**82358**

Project 3f, EL2-C4-P3-PremiumFitnessJanSales.xlsx

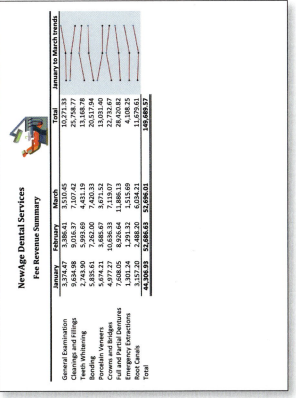

NewAge Dental Services
Fee Revenue Summary

	January	February	March	Total	January to March trends
General Examination	3,374.47	3,386.41	3,510.45	10,271.33	
Cleanings and Fillings	9,634.98	9,016.37	7,107.42	25,758.77	
Teeth Whitening	2,743.90	5,993.69	4,431.19	13,168.78	
Bonding	5,835.61	7,262.00	7,420.33	20,517.94	
Porcelain Veneers	5,674.21	3,685.67	3,671.52	13,031.40	
Crowns and Bridges	4,977.27	10,636.33	7,119.07	22,732.67	
Full and Partial Dentures	7,608.05	8,926.64	11,886.13	28,420.82	
Emergency Extractions	1,301.24	1,291.32	1,515.69	4,108.25	
Root Canals	3,157.20	2,488.20	6,034.21	11,679.61	
Total	44,306.93	52,686.63	52,696.01	149,689.57	

Project 4 Add Sparklines in a Worksheet to Show Trends
EL2-C4-P4-NewAgeDentalQ1Fees.xlsx

Project 3f, EL2-C4-P3-PremiumFitnessJanSales.xlsx

You will create and modify range names and calculate total park attendance at three national parks from data stored in separate worksheets and by linking to a cell in another workbook. You will also edit a linked workbook and update the link in the destination file.

Quick Steps

Sum Multiple Worksheets Using Range Names
1. Make formula cell active.
2. Type =sum(.
3. Type first range name.
4. Type comma ,.
5. Type second range name.
6. Type comma ,.
7. Continue typing range names separated by commas until finished.
8. Type).
9. Press Enter.

Modify a Named Range Reference
1. Click Formulas tab.
2. Click Name Manager button.
3. Click range name to be modified.
4. Click Edit button.
5. Click in *Refers to* text box or click collapse button.
6. Modify range address(es) as required.
7. Click OK.
8. Click Close.

Name Manager

Expand Dialog

Summarizing Data in Multiple Worksheets Using Range Names and 3-D References

A workbook that has been organized with data in separate worksheets can be summarized by creating formulas that reference cells in other worksheets. When you create a formula that references a cell in the same worksheet, you do not need to include the sheet name in the reference. For example, the formula =*A3+A4* causes Excel to add the value in A3 in the active worksheet to the value in A4 in the active worksheet. Assume you want Excel to add the value in A3 that resides in Sheet2 to the value in A3 that resides in Sheet3 in the workbook. To do this you need to include the worksheet name in the formula by typing =*Sheet2!A3+Sheet3!A3* into the formula cell. This formula contains worksheet references as well as cell references. A worksheet reference precedes the cell reference and is separated from the cell reference with an exclamation point. Absent a worksheet reference, Excel assumes the active worksheet. A formula that references the same cell in a range that extends over two or more worksheets is often called a ***3-D reference***. 3-D formulas can be typed directly in the cell or entered using a point and click approach.

As an alternative, consider using range names to simplify formulas that summarize data in multiple worksheets. A range name includes the worksheet reference by default; therefore typing the range name in the formula automatically references the correct worksheet. For example, assume A3 in Sheet2 has been named *ProductA* and A3 in Sheet3 has been named *ProductB*. To add the two values you would type the formula =*ProductA+ProductB* in the formula cell. Notice you do not need to remember worksheet references. Another advantage to using range names is that the name can describe the worksheet with the source data. By using range names you also do not have to make each worksheet identical in organizational structure. Recall from your work with range names in Chapter 2 that cell references in range names are absolute references.

1. Open **MayParkEntries.xlsx**.
2. Save the workbook with Save As and name it **EL2-C4-P1-MayParkEntries**.
3. Click each sheet tab and review the data. Each park has attendance data entered as a separate worksheet. In the workbook, range names have already been created for two of the three parks. Create the third range name needed for the data in the MesaVerde sheet by completing the following steps:

   a. Click the MesaVerde sheet tab to activate the worksheet.

   b. Select B7:B22.

   c. Hold down the Ctrl key and then select E7:E21.

   d. Click in the Name text box, type **Mesa**, and then press Enter.

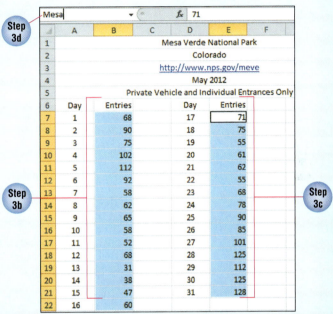

4. Check each range name to make sure the cell references are correct before creating the summary formula by completing the following steps:

   a. Click the down-pointing arrow next to the Name text box and then click *Bryce* at the drop-down list. Notice the BryceCanyon sheet is active and the ranges B7:B22 and E7:E21 are selected.

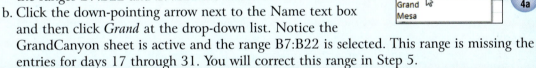

   b. Click the down-pointing arrow next to the Name text box and then click *Grand* at the drop-down list. Notice the GrandCanyon sheet is active and the range B7:B22 is selected. This range is missing the entries for days 17 through 31. You will correct this range in Step 5.

   c. Click the down-pointing arrow next to the Name text box and then click *Mesa* at the drop-down list. The MesaVerde sheet is active and the ranges B7:B22 and E7:E21 are selected.

5. Modify the references in a range name by adding the data in column E of the GrandCanyon worksheet to the range named *Grand* by completing the following steps:

   a. Click in any cell to deselect the *Mesa* range.

   b. Click the Formulas tab.

   c. Click the Name Manager button in the Defined Names group.

   d. Click *Grand* in the *Name* list at the Name Manager dialog box.

   e. Click the Edit button.

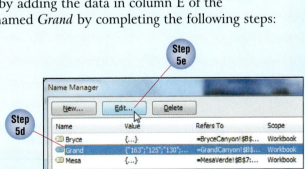

f. At the Edit Name dialog box, click the Collapse Dialog button located at the end of the *Refers to* text box (currently displays =GrandCanyon!$B$7:$B$22).

Step 5f

g. With GrandCanyon the active worksheet and with the range B7:B22 selected, hold down the Ctrl key and then select E7:E21.

h. Click the Expand Dialog button to restore the Edit Name dialog box. Notice that a comma separates nonadjacent ranges in the range name and that the cell addresses are absolute references.

6	Day	Entries	Day	Entries
7	1	163	17	175
8	2	125	18	201
9	3	130	19	212
10	4	145	20	288
11	5	118	21	196
12	6	122	22	250
13	7	124	23	230
14	8	150	24	242
15	9	170	25	250
16	10	186	26	290
17	11	180	27	310
18	12	166	28	325
19	13	170	29	388
20	14	185	30	341
21	15	155	31	401
22	16	196		

Edit Name - Refers to:

$B$7:$B$22,GrandCanyon!$E$7:$E$21

Step 5h

Step 5g

This range is automatically selected when you collapse the Edit Name dialog box.

i. Click OK to close the Edit Name dialog box.

j. Click Close to close the Name Manager dialog box.

k. Click the down-pointing arrow next to the Name text box and then click *Grand* at the drop-down list to make sure the revised range name is referencing B7:B22 and E7:E21 in the GrandCanyon worksheet.

6. Create the formula to add the attendance for May at all three parks by completing the following steps:

a. Click the AttendanceSummary tab to activate the worksheet.

b. If necessary, make F7 the active cell.

c. Type **=sum(bryce,grand,mesa)** and press Enter. Notice that in a Sum formula, multiple range names are separated with commas. Excel returns the result *10460* in F7 of the AttendanceSummary worksheet.

d. Format F7 to Comma Style with zero decimals.

5	Southwest Region, Zone C	
6		
7	Private Vehicle and Individual Entrances Only	=sum(bryce,grand,mesa)

Step 6c

7. Save and then close **EL2-C4-P1-MayParkEntries.xlsx**.

A disadvantage to using range names applies when several worksheets need to be summarized, since you have to create the range name reference in each individual worksheet. If several worksheets need to be summed, a more efficient method is to use a 3-D reference. Generally, when using a 3-D reference, setting up the data in each worksheet in identical cells is a good idea. In Project 1b, you will calculate the same attendance total for the three parks using a 3-D reference instead of range names.

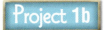
1. Open **MayParkEntries.xlsx**.
2. Save the workbook with Save As and name it **EL2-C4-P1-3D-MayParkEntries**.
3. Calculate the attendance total for the three parks using a point-and-click approach to creating a 3-D reference by completing the following steps:
   a. Make F7 in the AttendanceSummary worksheet the active cell, and then type =**sum(**.
   b. Click the BryceCanyon sheet tab.
   c. Hold down the Shift key and then click the MesaVerde sheet tab. Using the Shift key while clicking a sheet tab selects all worksheets from the first sheet tab through to the last sheet tab clicked. Notice in the Formula bar the formula reads =*sum('BryceCanyon:MesaVerde'!*

   d. With BryceCanyon the active worksheet, select B7:B22, hold down the Ctrl key, and select E7:E21.
   e. Type **)** and press Enter. Excel returns the value *10460* in F7 in the AttendanceSummary worksheet.
   f. Format F7 to Comma Style with zero decimals.

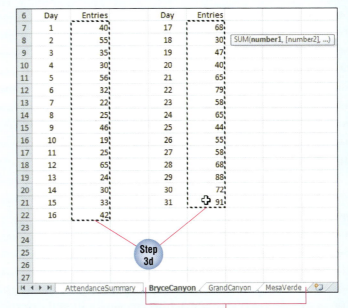

the three worksheets grouped in the 3-D reference at Steps 3b and 3c

4. Press the Up Arrow key to move the active cell back to F7 and compare your formula with the one shown in Figure 4.1.
5. Save and then close **EL2-C4-P1-3D-MayParkEntries.xlsx**.

Figure 4.1 3-D Formula Created in Project 1b

3-D formula created in Project 1b, Step 3 using point-and-click approach

	F7			f_x	=SUM(BryceCanyon:MesaVerde!B7:B22,BryceCanyon:MesaVerde!E7:E21)					
	A	B	C	D	E	F	G	H	I	J	K
1			National Park Service								
2			U.S. Department of the Interior								
3			May 2012								
4			Attendance Summary								
5			Southwest Region, Zone C								
6											
7	Private Vehicle and Individual Entrances Only					10,460					

Summarizing Data by Linking to Ranges in Other Worksheets or Workbooks ▪▪▪▪▪▪▪▪▪▪ ▪▪▪▪▪▪▪ ▪▪

▼ **Quick Steps**

Create Link to External Reference
1. Open source workbook.
2. Open destination workbook.
3. Arrange windows as desired.
4. Make formula cell active in destination workbook.
5. Type =.
6. Click to activate source workbook.
7. Click source cell.
8. Press Enter.

Using a similar method as that used in Project 1a or Project 1b, you can summarize data in one workbook by linking to a cell, range, or range name in another worksheet or workbook. When data is linked, a change made in the source cell (the cell in which the original data is stored) is updated in any other cell to which the source cell has been linked. A link is established by creating a formula that references the source data. For example, the formula *=Sheet1!B10* entered into a cell in Sheet2 creates a link. The cell in Sheet2 displays the value in the source cell. If the data in B10 in Sheet1 is changed, the value in the linked cell in Sheet2 is also changed.

As an alternative to creating a formula yourself, copy the source cell to the Clipboard. Make the destination cell active, click the Paste button arrow in the Clipboard group, and then click the Paste Link button in the *Other Paste Options* section of the drop-down gallery. Excel creates the link formula for you using an absolute reference to the source cell.

Linking to a cell in another workbook incorporates external references and requires that a workbook name reference be added to a formula. For example, linking to cell A3 in a sheet named ProductA in a workbook named Sales would require that you enter *=[Sales.xlsx]ProductA!A3* in the formula cell. Notice the workbook reference is entered first in square brackets. The workbook in which the external reference is added becomes the destination workbook. The workbook containing the data that is linked to the destination workbook is called the source workbook. In Project 1c you will create a link to an external cell containing the attendance total for the tour group entrances for the three parks. The point-and-click approach to creating a linked external reference creates an absolute reference to the source cell. Delete the dollar symbols in the cell reference if you plan to copy the formula and need the source cell to be relative. Note that workbook and worksheet references remain absolute regardless.

Project 1c Summarizing Data by Linking to Another Workbook   Part 3 of 5

1. Open **EL2-C4-P1-MayParkEntries.xlsx**.
2. Open **MayParkGroupSales.xlsx**. This workbook contains tour group attendance data for the three national parks. Tour groups are charged a flat rate entrance fee and their attendance values represent bus capacity and not actual counts of patrons on each bus.
3. Click the View tab, click the Arrange All button in the Window group, click *Vertical* in the *Arrange* section of the Arrange Windows dialog box, and then click OK.
4. Create a linked external reference in the worksheet you created in Project 1a to the total attendance in the worksheet with the commercial tour vehicle attendance data by completing the following steps:
   a. Click in the **EL2-C4-P1-MayParkEntries.xlsx** worksheet to make the worksheet active. Make sure the active worksheet is AttendanceSummary.
   b. Make A9 the active cell, type **Commercial Tour Vehicles Only**, and then press Enter.
   c. Make F9 the active cell.
   d. Type =.

e. Click the **MayParkGroupSales.xlsx** title bar to activate the worksheet and then click F7. Notice the formula that is being entered into the formula cell contains a workbook reference and a worksheet reference in front of the cell reference.

f. Press Enter.

g. Format F9 to Comma Style with zero decimals.

h. With F9 the active cell, compare your worksheet with the one shown below.

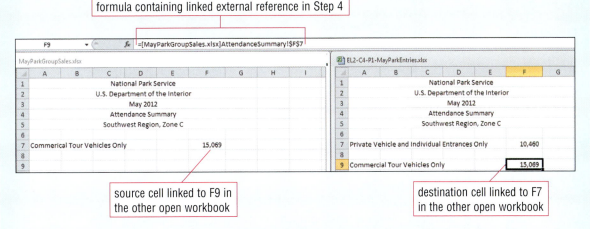

formula containing linked external reference in Step 4

source cell linked to F9 in the other open workbook

destination cell linked to F7 in the other open workbook

5. Click the Maximize button in the **EL2-C4-P1-MayParkEntries.xlsx** title bar.

6. Make A11 the active cell, type **Total Attendance**, and then press Enter.

7. Make F11 the active cell and then create a formula to add the values in F7 and F9.

8. Print the AttendanceSummary worksheet in **EL2-C4-P1-MayParkEntries.xlsx**. *Note: Check with your instructor if you submit your work in hard copy and need to print two copies of the worksheet with one copy displaying cell formulas*.

9. Save and then close **EL2-C4-P1-MayParkEntries.xlsx**.

10. Close **MayParkGroupSales.xlsx**. Click Don't Save when prompted to save changes.

Maintaining External References

When you link to an external reference, Excel includes the drive and folder names in the path to the source workbook. If you move the source workbook or change the workbook name, the link will no longer work. By default, when you open a workbook with a linked external reference, automatic updates is disabled and Excel displays a security warning message in the Message bar area located above the worksheet. From the message bar you can enable the content so that links can be updated. Links can be edited or broken at the Edit Links dialog box shown in Figure 4.2. If more than one link is present in the workbook, begin by clicking the link to be changed in the Source list. Click the Change Source button to open the Change Source dialog box in which you can navigate to the drive and/or folder in which the source workbook was moved or renamed. Click the Break Link button to permanently remove the linked reference and convert the linked cells to their existing values. The Undo feature does not operate to restore a link. If you break a link that you decide you want to restore, you will have to recreate the linked formula.

▼ **Quick Steps**

Edit Link to External Reference

1. Open destination workbook.
2. Click Data tab.
3. Click Edit Links button.
4. Click link.
5. Click Change Source button.
6. Navigate to drive and/or folder.
7. Double-click source workbook file name.
8. Click Close button.
9. Save and close destination workbook.

Edit Links

Figure 4.2 Edit Links Dialog Box

Break Link to External Reference
1. Open destination workbook.
2. Click Data tab.
3. Click Edit Links button.
4. Click link.
5. Click Break Link button.
6. Click Break Links button.
7. Click Close button.
8. Save and close destination workbook.

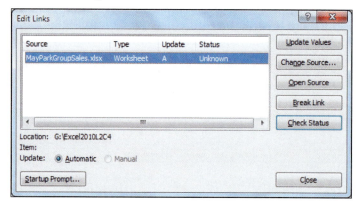

Project 1d   **Editing Source Data and Updating an External Link**   Part 4 of 5

1. Open **MayParkGroupSales.xlsx**.
2. Save the workbook with Save As and name it **EL2-C4-P1-Source**.
3. Edit the attendance data values at each park by completing the following steps:
   a. Click the BryceCanyon tab.
   b. Make B8 the active cell and then change the value from *55* to *361*.
   c. Click the GrandCanyon tab.
   d. Make B20 the active cell and then change the value from *275* to *240*.
   e. Click the MesaVerde tab.
   f. Make E21 the active cell and then change the value from *312* to *406*.
4. Click the AttendanceSummary tab. Note the updated value in F7 is *15,434*.
5. Save and then close **EL2-C4-P1-Source.xlsx**.
6. Open **EL2-C4-P1-MayParkEntries.xlsx**. Notice the security warning that appears in the Message bar above the worksheet area with the message that automatic update of links has been disabled. Instruct Excel to allow automatic updates for this workbook since you are sure the content is from a trusted source by clicking the Enable Content button in the Message bar located between the ribbon and the worksheet area. *Note: If a Security Warning dialog box appears asking if you want to make the file a Trusted Document, click No.*

7. Edit the link to retrieve the data from the workbook revised in Steps 2–5 by completing the following steps:
   a. Click the Data tab.
   b. Click the Edit Links button in the Connections group.

c. At the Edit Links dialog box click the Change Source button.
d. At the Change Source: MayParkGroupSales.xlsx dialog box, double-click *EL2-C4-P1-Source.xlsx* in the file list box. Excel returns to the Edit Links dialog box and updates the source workbook file name and path.
e. Click the Close button.

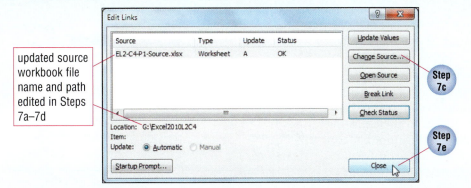

updated source workbook file name and path edited in Steps 7a–7d

Step 7c

Step 7e

8. Click F9 in the AttendanceSummary worksheet to view the updated linked formula. Notice the workbook reference in the formula is [EL2-C4-P1-Source.xlsx] and the drive and path are included in the formula. (Your drive and/or path may vary from the one shown.)

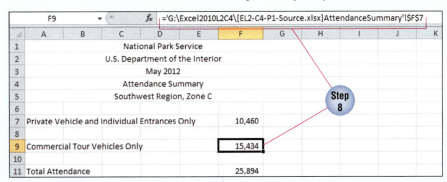

9. Print the AttendanceSummary worksheet.
10. Save and then close **EL2-C4-P1-MayParkEntries.xlsx**.

Project 1e Removing a Linked External Reference

Part 5 of 5

1. Open **EL2-C4-P1-MayParkEntries.xlsx**.
2. At the Microsoft Excel message box that appears stating that the workbook contains links to other sources, read the message text and then click the Update button to update the links. *Note: Depending on the system settings on the computer you are using, this message may not appear. Proceed to Step 3.*

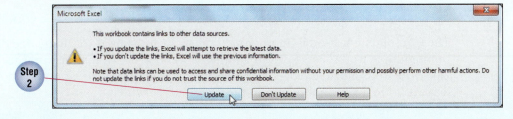

Step 2

3. Remove the linked external reference to attendance values for commercial tour vehicles by completing the following steps:
   a. With Data the active tab, click the Edit Links button in the Connections group.
   b. Click the Break Link button at the Edit Links dialog box.
   c. Click the Break Links button at the Microsoft Excel message box that says breaking links permanently converts formulas and external references to their existing values and cannot be undone and asks if you are sure you want to break the links.

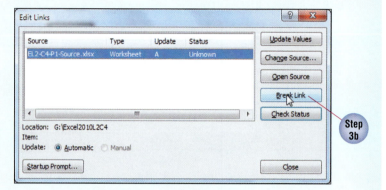

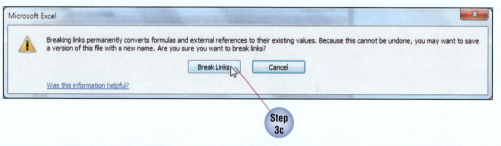

   d. Click the Close button at the Edit Links dialog box with no links displayed.
4. With F9 in the AttendanceSummary worksheet the active cell, look in the Formula bar. Notice the linked formula has been replaced with the latest cell value, *15434*.
5. Save and then close **EL2-C4-P1-MayParkEntries.xlsx**.
6. Reopen **EL2-C4-P1-MayParkEntries.xlsx**. Notice that since the workbook no longer contains a link to an external reference, the security warning message no longer appears in the Message bar.
7. Close **EL2-C4-P1-MayParkEntries.xlsx**. Click Don't Save if prompted to save changes.

Project 2 Calculate Total Fees Billed by Three Dentists   1 Part

You will use the Consolidate feature to summarize the total dental fees billed by treatment category for three dentists.

Summarizing Data Using the Consolidate Feature ■■■■■

The Consolidate feature is another method that can be used to summarize data from multiple worksheets or from another workbook into a master worksheet. Open the Consolidate dialog box shown in Figure 4.3 from the Consolidate button located in the Data Tools group in the Data tab.

Figure 4.3 Consolidate Dialog Box

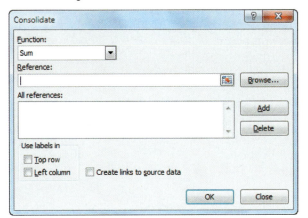

▼ **Quick Steps**
Consolidate Data
1. Make starting cell active.
2. Click Data tab.
3. Click Consolidate button.
4. If necessary, change *Function*.
5. Enter first range in *Reference* text box.
6. Click Add button.
7. Enter next range in *Reference* text box.
8. Click Add button.
9. Repeat Steps 7–8 until all ranges have been added.
10. If necessary, select *Top row* and/or *Left column* check boxes.
11. If necessary, click *Create links to source data* check box.
12. Click OK.

By default, the Sum function is active. Change to a different function such as Count or Average using the *Function* drop-down list. In the *Reference* text box, type the range name or use the Collapse Dialog button to navigate to the cells to be consolidated. If the cells are located in another workbook, use the Browse button to navigate to the drive and/or folder and locate the file name. Once the correct reference is inserted in the *Reference* text box, click the Add button. Continue adding references for each unit of data to be summarized. Click *Top row* or *Left column* in the *Use labels in* section to indicate where the labels are located in the source ranges. Click the *Create links to source data* to instruct Excel to update the data automatically when the source ranges change. Make sure enough empty cells are available to the right and below the active cell when you open the Consolidate dialog box since Excel populates the rows and columns based on the size of the source data.

Consolidate

Project 2 **Summarizing Data Using Consolidate Feature**   Part 1 of 1

1. Open **NewAgeDentalQ1Fees.xlsx**.
2. Save the workbook using Save As and name it **EL2-C4-P2-NewAgeDentalQ1Fees**.
3. The workbook is organized with the first quarter's fees for each of three dentists entered in a separate worksheet. Range names have been defined for each dentist's first quarter earnings. Review the workbook structure by completing the following steps:
   a. Click the down-pointing arrow in the Name text box and then click *Popovich* at the drop-down list. Excel makes the Popovich worksheet active and selects the range A2:F13. Deselect the range.
   b. Display the defined range for the range name *Vanket* and then deselect the range.
   c. Display the defined range for the range name *Jovanovic* and then deselect the range.
4. Use the Consolidate feature to total the fees billed by treatment category for each month by completing the following steps:
   a. Make FeeSummary the active worksheet.
   b. With A5 the active cell, click the Data tab.
   c. Click the Consolidate button in the Data Tools group.

d. With *Sum* already selected in the *Function* list box at the Consolidate dialog box and with the insertion point positioned in the *Reference* text box, type **Popovich** and then click the Add button.

e. With the text *Popovich* selected in the *Reference* text box, type **Vanket** and then click the Add button.

f. With the text *Vanket* selected in the *Reference* text box, type **Jovanovic** and then click the Add button.

g. Click the *Top row* and *Left column* check boxes in the *Use labels in* section to insert a check mark in each check box.

h. Click OK.

5. Deselect the consolidated range in the FeeSummary worksheet.

6. Adjust the width of each column in the FeeSummary worksheet to AutoFit.

7. Move the data in E5:E15 to F5:F15 and then AutoFit the column width.

8. Use Format Painter to apply the formatting options for the column headings and the total row from any of the three dentist worksheets to the FeeSummary worksheet.

9. Print the FeeSummary worksheet.

10. Save and then close **EL2-C4-P2-NewAgeDentalQ1Fees.xlsx**.

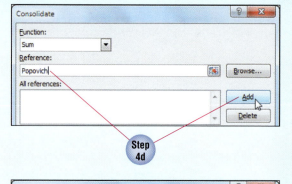

Step 4d

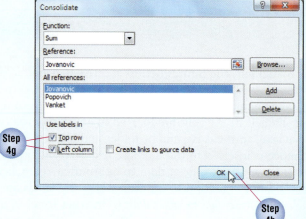

Step 4g

Step 4h

Project 3 — Analyze Fitness Equipment Sales Data in a PivotTable and PivotChart — 6 Parts

You will create and edit a PivotTable and a PivotChart to analyze fitness equipment sales by region and by salesperson.

Creating a PivotTable Report

A *PivotTable* is an interactive table that organizes and summarizes data based on category labels you designate from row headings and column headings. A numeric column you select is then grouped by the row and column category and the data summarized using a function such as Sum, Average, or Count. PivotTables are useful management tools since you can analyze data in a variety of scenarios by filtering a row or column category and instantly seeing the change in results. The interactivity of a PivotTable allows one to examine a variety of scenarios with just a few mouse clicks.

Before creating a PivotTable, examine the source data and determine the following elements before you begin:

- Which row and column headings will define how to group the data?
- Which numeric field contains the values that should be grouped?
- Which summary function will be applied to the values? For example, do you want to sum, average, or count?
- How do you want the layout of the table to be structured? For example, which label do you want used as a row heading and which do you want to use as a column heading?
- Do you want the ability to filter the report as a whole as well as by columns or rows?
- Do you want the PivotTable to be beside the source data or in a new sheet?
- How many reports do you want to extract from the PivotTable by filtering fields?

To begin a PivotTable, select the source range or make sure the active cell is positioned within the list range, click the Insert tab, and then click the PivotTable button in the Tables group. At the Create PivotTable dialog box, confirm the source range is correct and select whether to place the PivotTable in the existing worksheet or in a new worksheet. Figure 4.4 presents the initial PivotTable report and PivotTable Field List pane in which you define the report layout. Each column or row heading in the source range becomes a field in the PivotTable Field List.

Build a PivotTable by selecting fields in the PivotTable Field List pane. Click the check box next to a field to add it to the PivotTable. By default, non-numeric fields are added to the *Row Labels* box and numeric fields are added to the *Values* box in the layout section of the pane. You can move a field to a different box by dragging the field header or by clicking the field header to display a pop-up menu. As you add each field, the PivotTable report updates to show the results. If you do not like the results, uncheck the field's check box to remove it from the report. Figure 4.5 displays the PivotTable you will build in Project 3a.

▼ Quick Steps
Create PivotTable
1. Select source range.
2. Click Insert tab.
3. Click PivotTable button.
4. Click OK.
5. Add fields as needed using PivotTable Field List pane.
6. Modify and/or format as required.

H I N T
Make sure the source data contains no blank rows or columns and that the data is structured in such a way that repeated data in columns or rows can be grouped.

PivotTable

Figure 4.4 PivotTable Report and PivotTable Field List Pane Used to Define Report Layout

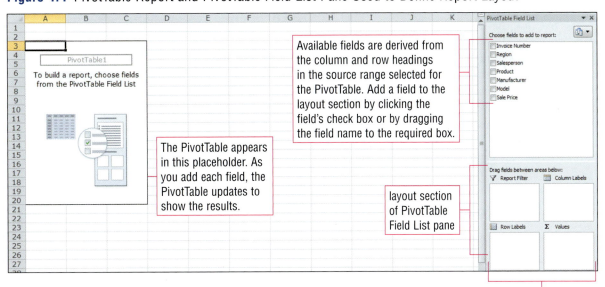

Available fields are derived from the column and row headings in the source range selected for the PivotTable. Add a field to the layout section by clicking the field's check box or by dragging the field name to the required box.

The PivotTable appears in this placeholder. As you add each field, the PivotTable updates to show the results.

layout section of PivotTable Field List pane

When you add a field to the report, Excel adds the field's header to the corresponding list box in the *Layout* section.

Figure 4.5 PivotTable for Project 3a

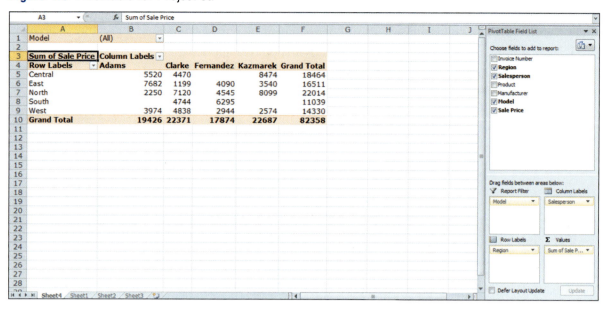

Creating a PivotTable Report Part 1 of 6

1. Open **PremiumFitnessJanSales.xlsx**.
2. Save the workbook with Save As and name it **EL2-C4-P3-PremiumFitnessJanSales**.
3. Create a PivotTable report to summarize the fitness equipment sales by region and by salesperson as shown in Figure 4.5 by completing the following steps:
   a. A range name has been defined to select the list data. Click the down-pointing arrow in the Name text box and then click *JanSales* at the drop-down list.
   b. Click the Insert tab.
   c. Click the PivotTable button in the Tables group. (Do not click the down-pointing arrow on the button.)
   d. At the Create PivotTable dialog box, with *Sheet1!$A$4:$G$47* entered in the *Table/Range* text box and *New Worksheet* selected for *Choose where you want the PivotTable report to be placed*, click OK.

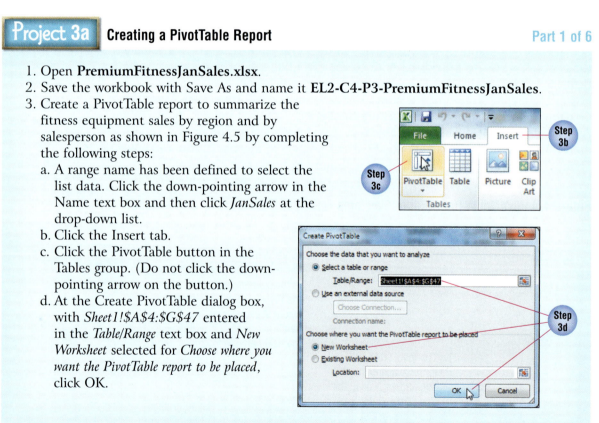

e. Click the *Region* check box in the PivotTable Field List pane. *Region* is added to the *Row Labels* list box in the layout section of the pane and the report updates to show one row per region with a filter arrow button at the top of the column and a *Grand Total* row automatically added to the bottom of the table. Since *Region* is a non-numeric field, Excel automatically placed it as a row label.

f. Click the *Salesperson* check box in the PivotTable Field List pane. Excel automatically adds *Salesperson* to the *Row Labels* list box in the layout section. In the next step you will correct the placement of the field to move it to the *Column Labels* list box.

g. Click the *Salesperson* field header in the *Row Labels* list box in the layout section and then click *Move to Column Labels* at the pop-up list. Notice the layout of the report now displays one row per region and one column per salesperson. In the next step you will drag a field from the PivotTable Field List to the desired list box in the layout section.

h. Position the mouse pointer over *Model* in the PivotTable Field List, hold down the left mouse button, drag the field to the *Report Filter* list box in the layout section, and then release the mouse. Notice *Model* is added as a filter at the top left of the PivotTable report in A1:B1.

i. Click the *Sale Price* check box in the PivotTable Field List pane. Since the field is a numeric field, Excel adds it automatically to the *Values* list box in the layout section and the report updates to show the Sum function applied to the grouped values in the PivotTable report. Compare your results with the PivotTable shown in Figure 4.5.

4. Save **EL2-C4-P3-PremiumFitnessJanSales.xlsx**.

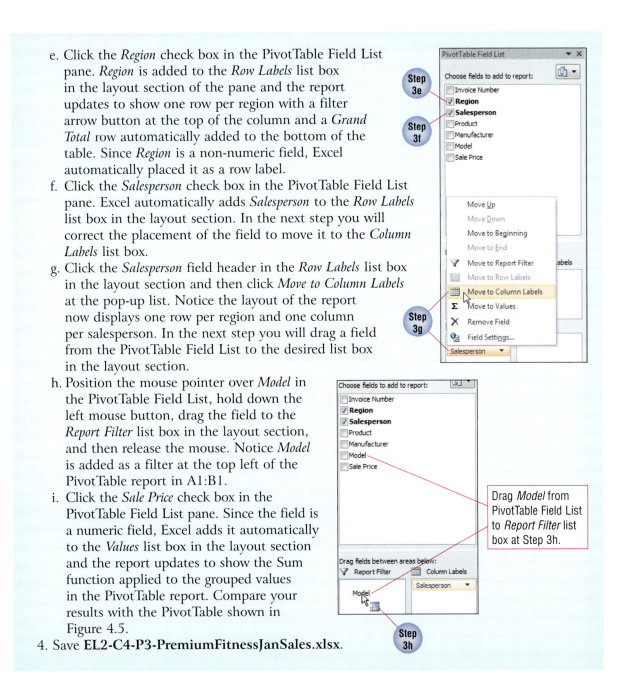

When the active cell is positioned inside a PivotTable, the contextual PivotTable Tools Options tab and PivotTable Tools Design tab become available. Features in the PivotTable Tools Design tab shown in Figure 4.6 are similar to those learned in Chapter 3 for tables.

Figure 4.6 Contextual PivotTable Tools Design Tab

1. With **EL2-C4-P3-PremiumFitnessJanSales.xlsx** open, apply formatting options to the PivotTable to improve the report's appearance by completing the following steps:
   a. With the active cell positioned in the PivotTable report, click the PivotTable Tools Design tab.
   b. Click the More button located at the bottom of the vertical scroll bar in the PivotTable Styles gallery.
   c. Click *Pivot Style Medium 2* at the drop-down gallery (second option in first row of *Medium* section).
   d. Click the *Banded Rows* check box in the PivotTable Style Options group. Excel adds border lines between rows in the PivotTable. Recall from Chapter 3 that banded rows or banded columns add a fill color or border style depending on the style in effect when the option is added.
   e. Select B5:F10, click the Home tab, and then click the Comma Style button in the Number group.
   f. Click the Decrease Decimal button in the Number group twice to remove the zeros to the right of the decimal.
   g. Deselect the range.
   h. Select columns B through F and change the column width to 12.
   i. Right-align the labels in B4:F4.

	A	B	C	D	E	F
1	Model	(All)				
2						
3	**Sum of Sale Price**	Column Labels				
4	**Row Labels**	Adams	Clarke	Fernandez	Kazmarek	Grand Total
5	Central	5,520	4,470		8,474	18,464
6	East	7,682	1,199	4,090	3,540	16,511
7	North	2,250	7,120	4,545	8,099	22,014
8	South		4,744	6,295		11,039
9	West	3,974	4,838	2,944	2,574	14,330
10	**Grand Total**	**19,426**	**22,371**	**17,874**	**22,687**	**82,358**

Steps 1a-1i

2. Filter the PivotTable report to view sales for a group of model numbers by completing the following steps:
   a. Click the filter arrow button next to *(All)* in B1.
   b. Click the *Select Multiple Items* check box to turn on the display of check boxes next to each model number in the drop-down list.
   c. Click the *(All)* check box to clear the check marks for all of the model numbers.
   d. Click the six check boxes for those model numbers that begin with *CX* to select all of the models from Cybex.
   e. Click OK.
   f. Select columns B through E and change the column width to 12.
   g. Print the filtered PivotTable.
   h. Click the filter arrow button next to *(Multiple Items)* in B1, click the *(All)* check box to select all model numbers in the drop-down list, and then click OK.
   i. Experiment with the Column Labels and Row Labels filter arrow buttons to filter the PivotTable by region or by salesperson.
   j. Make sure all filters are cleared.

3. Select columns B through F and change the column width to 12.
4. Print the PivotTable in landscape orientation.
5. Save **EL2-C4-P3-PremiumFitnessJanSales.xlsx**.

Filtering a PivotTable Using Slicers

Slicers are a new feature added to Excel 2010 that allow you to filter a PivotTable report or PivotChart without opening the Filter drop-down list. When Slicers are added to a PivotTable or PivotChart, a Slicer pane containing all of the unique values for the specified field is added to the window. Click the desired option in the Slicer pane to immediately filter the PivotTable or PivotChart. You can add several Slicer panes to the PivotTable or PivotChart to filter by more than one field as needed.

To insert a Slicer pane, make any cell within the PivotTable report active, click the PivotTable Tools Options tab, and then click the Insert Slicer button in the Sort & Filter group. Excel opens the Insert Slicers dialog box, which contains a list of the fields in the PivotTable with a check box next to each field. Click the check box for each field for which you wish to add a Slicer pane and then click OK.

▼ **Quick Steps**

Add Slicer to PivotTable Report
1. Make any cell within PivotTable active.
2. Click PivotTable Tools Options tab.
3. Click Insert Slicer button.
4. Click check box for desired field.
5. Click OK.

Insert Slicer

Project 3c   **Using a Slicer to Filter a PivotTable**   Part 3 of 6

1. With **EL2-C4-P3-PremiumFitnessJanSales.xlsx** open, display a Slicer pane for the Model field by completing the following steps:
   a. Make any cell active within the PivotTable.
   b. Click the PivotTable Tools Options tab.
   c. Click the Insert Slicer button in the Sort & Filter group.
   d. At the Insert Slicers dialog box, click the *Model* check box to insert a check mark and then click OK. Excel inserts a Slicer pane in the worksheet with all of the model numbers.
2. If necessary, position the mouse pointer at the top of the Model Slicer pane until the pointer changes to the four-headed arrow move icon and then drag the pane to an empty location below the PivotTable.

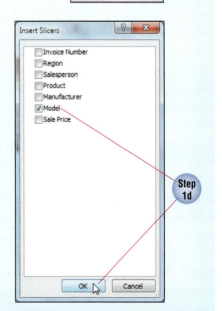

3. Click *CX700* in the Model Slicer pane to filter the PivotTable. Excel filters the PivotTable by the CX700 model number. Notice that the *Model* filter arrow button in B1 displays *CX700*.

4. Click the Clear Filter button at the top right of Model Slicer pane to redisplay all data.

5. Add a second Slicer pane and filter by two fields by completing the following steps:

   a. Make any cell active within the PivotTable.

   b. Click the PivotTable Tools Options tab and then click the Insert Slicer button.

   c. Click the *Salesperson* check box in the Insert Slicers dialog box and then click OK.

   d. Drag the Salesperson Slicer pane below the PivotTable next to the Model Slicer pane.

   e. Click *Fernandez* in the Salesperson Slicer pane to filter the PivotTable.

   f. Click *VS2200* in the Model Slicer pane to filter Fernandez's sales by the VS2200 model number.

6. Print the filtered PivotTable.

7. Redisplay all data and remove the two Slicer panes by completing the following steps:

   a. Click the Clear Filter button at the top right of the Salesperson Slicer pane.

   b. Click the Clear Filter button at the top right of the Model Slicer pane.

   c. Right-click the top of the Model Slicer pane and then click *Remove "Model"* at the shortcut menu.

   d. Right-click the top of the Salesperson Slicer pane and then click *Remove "Salesperson"* at the shortcut menu.

8. Select columns B through F and change the column width to 12.

9. Save **EL2-C4-P3-PremiumFitnessJanSales.xlsx**.

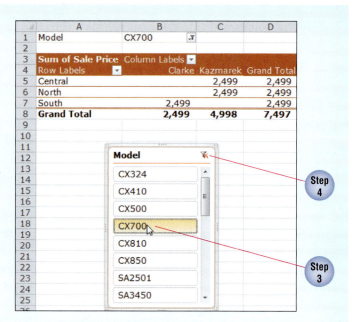

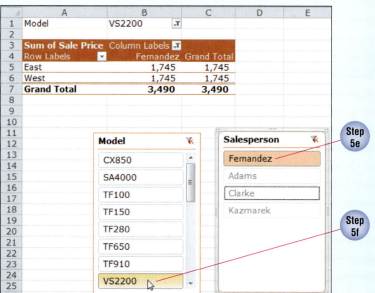

A Slicer pane can be customized with buttons in the Slicer Tools Options tab. Click a Slicer pane to activate the Slicer Tools Options tab. Click the tab to display customization options such as Slicer Styles. You can also change the height and width of the buttons in the Slicer pane and/or the height and width of the pane.

Changing the Summary Function

By default Excel uses the Sum function to summarize the numeric value added to a PivotTable. To change Sum to another function, click any numeric value within the PivotTable or click the cell containing *Sum of [Fieldname]* at the top left of the PivotTable. Click the PivotTable Tools Options tab and then click the Field Settings button in the Active Field group. This opens the Value Field Settings dialog box in which you can choose a function other than Sum. Alternatively, you can right-click any numeric value within the PivotTable, point to *Summarize Values By* at the shortcut menu, and then click the desired function name.

▼ **Quick Steps**

Change PivotTable Summary Function
1. Make values field cell active.
2. Click PivotTable Tools Options tab.
3. Click Field Settings button.
4. Click desired function.
5. Click OK.

Field Settings

Project 3d　**Changing the Values Function in a PivotTable**　　Part 4 of 6

1. With **EL2-C4-P3-PremiumFitnessJanSales.xlsx** open, use Save As and name the workbook **EL2-C4-P3-PremiumFitnessAvgJanSales**.
2. Change the function for the *SalePrice* field from Sum to Average by completing the following steps:
   a. Make A3 the active cell in the PivotTable. This cell contains the label *Sum of Sale Price*.
   b. Click the PivotTable Tools Options tab.
   c. Click the Field Settings button in the Active Field group.
   d. At the Value Field Settings dialog box with the Summarize Values By tab active, click *Average* in the *Summarize value field by* list box and then click OK.
3. Select columns B through F, change the column width to 12 and then print the revised PivotTable.
4. Save and then close **EL2-C4-P3-PremiumFitnessAvgJanSales.xlsx**.

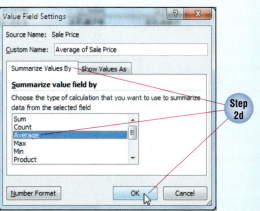

Creating a PivotChart ■■■■■■■■■■■■■■■■■■■■■■■■■■

A *PivotChart* visually displays the data from a PivotTable in chart form. As with a PivotTable, you can filter the data to examine various scenarios between categories. Excel displays the PivotChart Filter pane when a PivotChart is active so that you can filter the data as needed. As you make changes to the PivotChart, the PivotTable that is associated with the PivotChart is also updated. Figure 4.7 displays the PivotChart you will create in Project 3e.

In a worksheet that already contains a PivotTable, position the active cell anywhere within the PivotTable, click the PivotTable Tools Options tab, and then

PivotChart

Figure 4.7 PivotChart for Project 3e

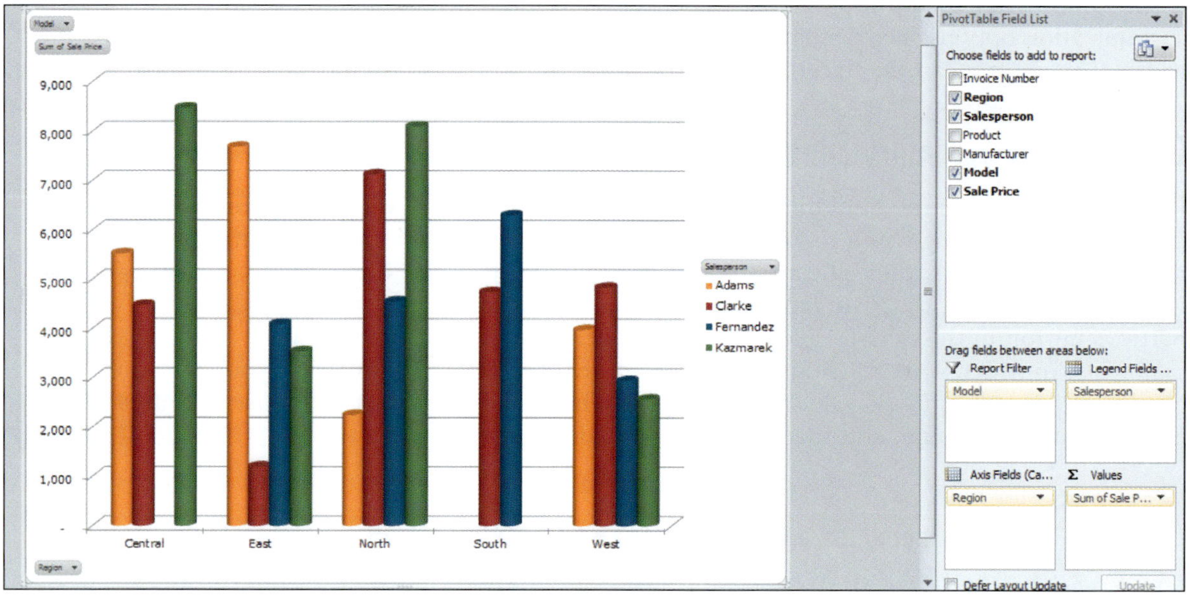

The chart shows Sum of Sale Price by Region (Central, East, North, South, West) with Salesperson legend (Adams, Clarke, Fernandez, Kazmarek). The PivotTable Field List pane shows fields: Invoice Number, Region, Salesperson, Product, Manufacturer, Model, Sale Price. Report Filter: Model; Legend Fields: Salesperson; Axis Fields: Region; Values: Sum of Sale Price.

Quick Steps

Create PivotChart from PivotTable
1. Make cell active within PivotTable.
2. Click PivotTable Tools Options tab.
3. Click PivotChart button.
4. Select desired chart type.
5. Click OK.

Create PivotChart without Existing PivotTable
1. Select range containing data for chart.
2. Click Insert tab.
3. Click down-pointing arrow on PivotTable button.
4. Click *PivotChart*.
5. Click OK.
6. Add fields as needed in PivotTable Field List pane to build chart.
7. Modify and/or format as required.

Move Chart

click the PivotChart button in the Tools group to create a chart from the existing summary data. Excel displays the Insert Chart dialog box in which you choose the type of chart to create. Once the PivotChart has been generated, the PivotTable and PivotChart become connected. Changes made to the data by filtering in one object cause the other object to update with the same filter. For example, filtering the chart by an individual salesperson name causes the PivotTable to also filter by the same salesperson name.

If you open a worksheet that does not contain a pre-existing PivotTable and create a PivotChart, Excel displays a blank chart window with the PivotTable Field List pane and a PivotChart Filter pane. Build the chart using the same techniques you used to build a PivotTable. Before you begin creating a PivotChart from scratch, examine the source data and determine the following elements:

- Which row or column heading contains the labels that you want to display along the *x* axis? In other words, how do you want to compare data when viewing the chart—by time period such as months or years, by salesperson names, by department name, or by some other category?

- Which row or column heading contains the labels that you want to display as legend fields? In other words, how many data series (bars in a column chart) do you want to view in the chart—one for each region, product, salesperson, department, or some other category?

- Which numeric field contains the values you want to graph in the chart?

As you build a PivotChart from scratch, Excel will also build a PivotTable in the background that is connected to the PivotChart.

1. Open **EL2-C4-P3-PremiumFitnessJanSales.xlsx**.
2. Create a PivotChart to visually present the data in the PivotTable by completing the following steps:
    a. If necessary, click any cell within the PivotTable to activate the PivotTable contextual tabs.
    b. Click the PivotTable Tools Options tab.
    c. Click the PivotChart button in the Tools group.
    d. At the Insert Chart dialog box, with *Column* selected in the left pane, click *Clustered Cylinder* (first option in second row in *Column* section) and then click OK.
3. Filter the PivotChart to display sales for only one salesperson by completing the following steps:
    a. Click the Salesperson field button in the PivotChart. This is the button above the salesperson names in the PivotChart legend.
    b. Click the *(Select All)* check box to clear all of the check boxes.
    c. Click the *Kazmarek* check box and then click OK.
    d. Notice the PivotTable behind the chart is also filtered to reflect the chart's display. ***Note: If necessary, drag the PivotChart border to move the chart out of the way if the chart is obscuring your view of the PivotTable.***
    e. Click the Salesperson field button in the PivotChart and then click *Clear Filter From "Salesperson"*.

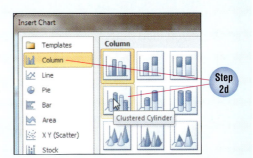

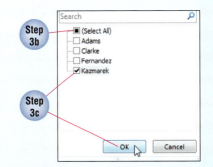

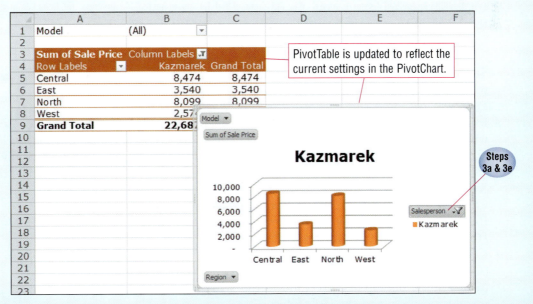

PivotTable is updated to reflect the current settings in the PivotChart.

4. Move the PivotChart to a separate worksheet by completing the following steps:

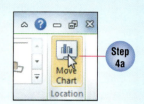

Step 4a

a. Click the Move Chart button in the Location group of the PivotChart Tools Design tab.

b. At the Move Chart dialog box, click *New sheet*, type **PivotChart** in the *New sheet* text box, and then click OK. Excel moves the PivotChart to a separate worksheet. Compare your PivotChart with the one shown in Figure 4.7 on page 124.

Step 4b

5. Print the PivotChart.

6. Rename the sheet tab for the worksheet containing the PivotTable (Sheet4) to *PivotTable*.

7. Save and then close **EL2-C4-P3-PremiumFitnessJanSales.xlsx**.

Project 3f Creating a PivotChart from Scratch

Part 6 of 6

1. Open **PremiumFitnessJanSales.xlsx**.

2. Save the workbook with Save As and name it **EL2-C4-P3-PremiumFitnessChart**.

3. Create a PivotChart to chart the sales by manufacturer by region by completing the following steps:

a. Select the *JanSales* named range and then click the Insert tab.

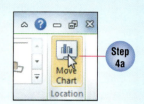

Step 3a

b. Click the down-pointing arrow on the PivotTable button in the Tables group and then click *PivotChart* at the drop-down list.

Step 3b

c. At the Create PivotTable with PivotChart dialog box, with *Sheet1!$A$4:$G$47* entered in the *Table/Range* text box and with *New Worksheet* selected in the *Choose where you want the PivotTable and PivotChart to be placed* section, click OK.

d. Excel displays a blank sheet with the PivotTable Field List pane at the right side of the window. A PivotTable placeholder and a PivotChart placeholder appear in the worksheet area. As you build the PivotChart, notice that a PivotTable is created automatically.

e. Click the *Manufacturer* check box in the PivotTable Field List. Excel adds the field to the *Axis Fields (Categories)* list box in the layout section.

f. Click the *Region* check box in the PivotTable Field List. Excel adds the field below *Manufacturer* in the *Axis Fields (Categories)* list box in the layout section.

Step 3g

g. Click the *Region* field header in the *Axis Fields (Categories)* list box and then click *Move to Legend Fields (Series)* at the pop-up list. Excel moves the field and updates the chart and the PivotTable.

h. Click the *Sale Price* check box in the PivotTable Field List. Excel graphs the sum of the Sale Price values in the PivotChart and updates the PivotTable.

4. Point to the border of the PivotChart and then drag the PivotChart below the PivotTable.
5. Resize the chart to the approximate height and width shown.

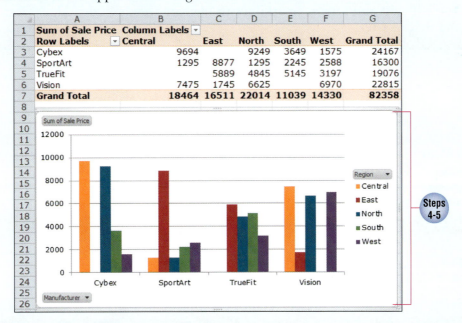

6. Select A1:G7 and then change the font size to 10.
7. Print the PivotTable and PivotChart worksheet.
8. Rename the sheet containing the PivotTable and PivotChart (Sheet4) to *SummaryData*.
9. Save and then close **EL2-C4-P3-PremiumFitnessJanSales.xlsx**.

Table 4.1 provides a summary of the functions of a PivotTable and PivotChart for reporting and summarizing large amounts of data.

Table 4.1 Functions of a PivotTable and PivotChart

Type of Report	Description
PivotTable Report	Summarizes large amounts of data by grouping the data on a column or row label. The report presents the results in a tabular format. By default Excel uses a Sum function to aggregate the values. Once tabulated, the PivotTable report can be filtered or sliced by a field to show various results.
PivotChart Report	Graphically presents data from a PivotTable report. A PivotChart is like any other Excel chart with data series and axes. A PivotChart can also be filtered or sliced to present various comparisons.

Project 4 Add Sparklines in a Worksheet to Show Trends   2 Parts

You will add and format Sparklines to identify trends in dental services fees over the first quarter.

Summarizing Data with Sparklines ■■■■■■■■■■■■■■■■■

▼ Quick Steps

Create Sparklines
1. Select empty range in which to insert Sparklines.
2. Click Insert tab.
3. Click Line, Column, or Win/Loss in Sparklines group.
4. Type data range address or drag to select data range in *Data Range* text box.
5. Click OK.

Sparklines are a new feature added to Excel 2010. *Sparklines* are miniature charts that are embedded into the background of a cell. The entire chart exists in a single cell. Since Sparklines can be placed directly next to the data which is being represented, the reader can quickly determine visually if a trend or pattern exists within the data set. Consider using Sparklines to show high or low values within a range, trends, or other patterns. Figure 4.8 illustrates each of the three Sparklines charts: Line, Column, and Win/Loss.

Creating a Sparkline

To create a Sparkline, select the empty cell range in which to insert Sparklines, click the Insert tab, and then click the desired Sparkline type in the Sparklines group shown in Figure 4.9. At the Create Sparklines dialog box, type or click the range for the cells that contain the data that you wish to graph in the *Data Range* text box and then click OK.

Figure 4.8 Line, Column, and Win/Loss Sparklines Added to a Worksheet

NewAge Dental Services
Fee Revenue Summary

	Q1 Fees	Q2 Fees	Q3 Fees	Q4 Fees	Fees Summary
Popovich	72,148.09	90,435.25	95,123.45	104,356.82	
Vanket	35,070.13	33,188.97	31,876.45	37,908.22	
Jovanovic	42,471.35	47,845.21	32,158.42	38,452.12	
Total	149,689.57	171,469.43	159,158.32	180,717.16	Q4 set new record!

Use Line or Column Sparklines to show trends or patterns over a time period.

Since Sparklines are the background of a cell you can add text to the Sparklines cell.

Increase or Decrease in Fees Compared to Last Year

Popovich	-3.0%	2.5%	4.5%	6.0%	
Vanket	5.5%	-8.0%	-10.0%	3.8%	
Jovanovic	4.5%	6.4%	-12.0%	1.2%	

Use Win/Loss Sparklines to show positive and negative values using bars. Notice the bars are all the same height but those quarters in which fees are lower than last year (negative percentages) show as red bars below the baseline.

Figure 4.9 Sparklines Group

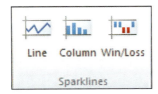

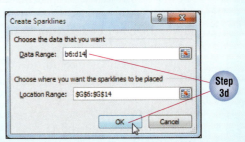

Project 4a   **Creating Sparklines**   Part 1 of 2

1. Open **EL2-C4-P2-NewAgeDentalQ1Fees.xlsx**.
2. Save the workbook with Save As and name it **EL2-C4-P4-NewAgeDentalQ1Fees**.
3. Create a Sparkline to illustrate the trends in each dental service fee category during the first quarter by completing the following steps:
   a. Select G6:G14.
   b. Click the Insert tab.
   c. Click the Line button in the Sparklines group.
   d. At the Create Sparklines dialog box, with the insertion point positioned in the *Data Range* text box, type **b6:d14** and then click OK. Excel inserts miniature line charts within the cells.
4. Spend a few moments reviewing the Sparklines to determine what the charts are indicating. Notice that the lines in G7 (Cleanings and Fillings) and G10 (Porcelain Veneers) have a downward slope. The lines in G8 (Teeth Whitening) and G11 (Crowns and Bridges) have a similar shape that shows these dental services peaked in February and are on a decline.
5. Save **EL2-C4-P4-NewAgeDentalQ1Fees.xlsx**.

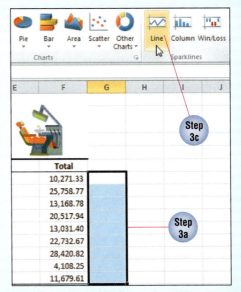

Customizing Sparklines

Activate any Sparkline cell and the Sparkline Tools Design tab shown in Figure 4.10 becomes visible. Click the Edit Data button to edit a range used to generate the Sparklines or instruct Excel how to graph hidden or empty cells in the data range. Use buttons in the Type group to change the chart type from line to column or win/loss. Click the check boxes in the Show group to show or hide data points in the chart or show markers. With options in the Style group you can change the line and/or marker appearance. Click the Axis button in the last group to customize the horizontal or vertical axis in the charts. Sparklines can be grouped, ungrouped, or cleared with the last three buttons in the tab.

▼ **Quick Steps**

Customize Sparklines
1. Click in any Sparklines cell.
2. Click Sparkline Tools Design tab.
3. Change chart type, show/hide points or markers, change chart style, color, or marker color.

Figure 4.10 Sparkline Tools Design Tab

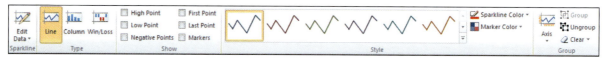

Project 4b **Customizing Sparklines** Part 2 of 2

1. With **EL2-C4-P4-NewAgeDentalQ1Fees.xlsx** open, customize the Sparklines by completing the following steps:

   a. If necessary, click any Sparkline cell to activate the Sparkline Tools Design tab.

   b. Click the Sparkline Tools Design tab.

   c. Click the Sparkline Color button in the Style group and then click *Dark Red* (first option in the *Standard Colors* section) at the drop-down color palette.

   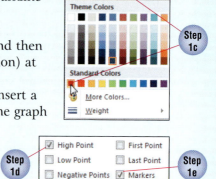

   d. Click the *High Point* check box in the Show group to insert a check mark in the box. Excel adds a marker to each line graph at the highest point.

   e. Click the *Markers* check box in the Show group to insert a check mark. Excel adds a marker to each of the other data points on each line. Note that the color of the High Point marker is different from the color of the other markers.

   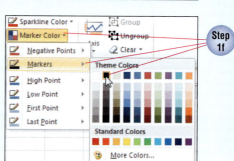

   f. Click the Marker Color button in the Style group, point to *Markers*, and then click *Black, Text 1* (second option in first row of *Theme Colors* section) at the drop-down color palette.

2. Improve the appearance of the Sparklines by widening the column and adding fill color by completing the following steps:

   a. Change the width of column G to 22.

   b. Select G6:G14, click the Home tab, and then apply *Blue, Accent 1, Lighter 80%* (fifth option in second row of *Theme Colors* section) fill color to the selected cells.

   c. Click in any cell to deselect the range.

3. Select G1:G4 and apply *White, Background 1* fill color (first option in *Theme Colors* section) at the drop-down color palette.

4. Make G5 the active cell, type **January to March trends**, and then format the cell so that it has the same formatting as the other titles in row 5.

5. Make G4 the active cell and apply a *Thick Bottom Border*.

6. Change the page orientation to landscape and then print the FeeSummary worksheet.

7. Save and then close **EL2-C4-P4-NewAgeDentalQ1Fees.xlsx**.

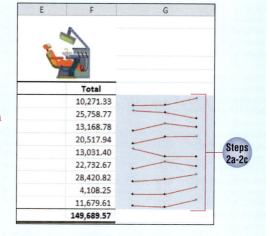

Chapter Summary

- A formula that references a cell in another worksheet within the same workbook contains a worksheet reference as well as a cell reference separated by an exclamation point.

- Range names can be used to simplify references to cells in another worksheet since the worksheet reference is automatically included in the range name definition.

- A disadvantage to using range names to reference other worksheets exists if there are several worksheets to be summarized since each name has to be defined before you can create the formula.

- A 3-D reference is used to summarize the same cell in a range that extends over two or more worksheets.

- A 3-D reference includes the starting worksheet name and the ending worksheet name separated by a colon similar to the method used to define a range of cells.

- A formula that references another worksheet is linked so that a change made in the source cell is automatically changed in the other worksheet to which the source cell has been linked.

- Formulas that reference a cell in another workbook must include a workbook reference in front of the worksheet and cell reference. Workbook references are enclosed in square brackets.

- When you create a formula that links to an external reference, Excel includes the drive and folder name in the path to the source workbook. If you move the location of the source workbook or change the source workbook file name, you have to edit the linked reference.

- Open the Edit Links dialog box to edit or remove a linked external reference.

- The Consolidate feature is another method that can be used to summarize data in multiple worksheets or workbooks.

- The Consolidate button is located in the Data Tools group in the Data tab.

- At the Consolidate dialog box, choose the summary function you want to use for the data that will be aggregated, add the references containing the data you want to summarize, specify the location of the labels to duplicate, and indicate whether to create a link to the source data.

- PivotTables are interactive tables that organize and summarize data based on categories in rows or columns.

- Create a PivotTable using the PivotTable button in the Tables group in the Insert tab.

- Add fields to the PivotTable using the field name check boxes in the PivotTable Field List pane.

- Once created, a PivotTable can be used to view a variety of scenarios by filtering the row, column, or report headings.

- Use buttons in the contextual PivotTable Tools Options and Design tabs to format the PivotTable and/or edit the features used in the table.

- Slicers are used to filter data in a PivotTable without having to open a filter drop-down list.

- A Slicer pane contains all of the items in the designated field so that the report can be filtered with one mouse click.
- Click the Insert Slicer button in the Sort & Filter group of the PivotTable Tools Options tab to add a Slicer pane to a PivotTable.
- A PivotChart displays the data in a PivotTable in a specified chart type.
- Filter a PivotChart using buttons in the PivotChart Filter pane.
- Sparklines are miniature charts inserted into a cell.
- Add Sparklines to a worksheet to show trends or high or low values in a range next to the source data.
- To add Sparklines, select an empty range next to the source data, click the Insert tab and then click the desired chart type in the Sparklines group. At the Create Sparklines dialog box, type the range containing the values you want to graph, or drag to select the range and then click OK.
- Sparklines can be customized using options in the Sparkline Tools Design tab.

Commands Review

FEATURE	RIBBON TAB, GROUP	BUTTON	KEYBOARD SHORTCUT
Consolidate	Data, Data Tools		
Edit Links	Data, Connections		
Manage range names	Formulas, Defined Names		Ctrl + F3
PivotChart	Insert, Tables OR PivotTable Tools Options, Tools		
PivotTable	Insert, Tables		
Sparklines	Insert, Sparklines		

Concepts Check Test Your Knowledge

Completion: In the space provided at the right, indicate the correct term, command, or number.

1. This symbol separates a worksheet reference from a cell reference.

   _____

2. This term describes a formula that references the same cell in a range that spans two or more worksheets.

   _____

3. Assume a workbook contains the following defined range names that reference cells in four worksheets: Qtr1, Qtr2, Qtr3, and Qtr4. Provide the Sum formula to add the data in the four ranges.

   _____

4. This would be the formula entry to link to an external reference C12 in a worksheet named Summary in a workbook named QtrlySales.

   _____

5. Open this dialog box to change the source of a linked external reference if you moved the source workbook to another folder.

   _____

6. Click this button to permanently remove a linked external reference and convert the linked cells to their existing values.

   _____

7. This is the default function active when you open the Consolidate dialog box.

   _____

8. Add fields to a PivotTable report by clicking the field check box in this pane.

   _____

9. The PivotTable Styles gallery is accessible from this tab.

   _____

10. Insert this type of pane to filter a PivotTable with one mouse click.

    _____

11. Change the summary function for a PivotTable numeric field by clicking this button in the PivotTable Tools Options tab.

    _____

12. A PivotChart visually displays the data from this source.

    _____

13. Buttons to filter a PivotChart are found here.

    _____

14. This is the first step to complete to add Sparklines in a worksheet.

    _____

15. Click this tab to customize Sparklines.

    _____

Skills Check   Assess Your Performance

Note: Check with your instructor before completing these Assessments if you submit your work in hard copy to see if you need to print two copies of worksheets in which you have created formulas with one copy showing the cell formulas.

Assessment

1 SUMMARIZE DATA IN MULTIPLE WORKSHEETS USING RANGE NAMES

1. Open **NewAgeDentalQ1Fees.xlsx**.
2. Save the workbook with Save As and name it **EL2-C4-A1-NewAgeDentalQ1Fees**.
3. The workbook contains three worksheets with dental fees earned in January, February, and March for three dentists at the dental clinic. Create a range name in F13 of each worksheet to reference the total fees earned by the dentist for the quarter as follows:
   a. Name F13 in the Popovich worksheet *PopovichTotal*.
   b. Name F13 in the Vanket worksheet *VanketTotal*.
   c. Name F13 in the Jovanovic worksheet *JovanovicTotal*.
4. Make FeeSummary the active worksheet and then type the following label in A6:

   Quarter 1 fees for Popovich, Vanket, and Jovanovic
5. Make F6 the active cell and create the Sum formula to add the total fees earned by each dentist using the range names created in Step 3.
6. Format F6 to the Accounting Number Format style and then adjust the column width to AutoFit.
7. Print the FeeSummary worksheet.
8. Save and then close **EL2-C4-A1-NewAgeDentalQ1Fees.xlsx**.

Assessment

2 SUMMARIZE DATA USING LINKED EXTERNAL REFERENCES

1. Open **PremiumFitnessSalesSummary.xlsx**.
2. Save the workbook with Save As and name it **EL2-C4-A2-PremiumFitnessSalesSummary**.
3. Open **PremiumFitnessQ1.xlsx**, **PremiumFitnessQ2.xlsx**, **PremiumFitnessQ3.xlsx**, and **PremiumFitnessQ4.xlsx**.
4. Tile all of the open workbooks.
5. Starting in cell B5 in **EL2-C4-A2-PremiumFitnessSalesSummary.xlsx**, create formulas to populate the cells in column B by linking to the appropriate source cell in **PremiumFitnessQ1.xlsx**. *Hint: After creating the first formula, edit the entry in B5 to use a relative reference to the source cell (instead of an absolute) so you can copy and paste the formula in B5 to B6:B9.*
6. Create formulas to link to the appropriate source cells for the second, third, and fourth quarter sales.
7. Close the four quarterly sales workbooks. Click Don't Save when prompted to save changes.

8. Maximize **EL2-C4-A2-PremiumFitnessSalesSummary.xlsx**.
9. Print the worksheet.
10. Save and then close **EL2-C4-A2-PremiumFitnessSalesSummary.xlsx**.

Assessment

3 BREAK LINKED REFERENCES

1. Open **EL2-C4-A2-PremiumFitnessSalesSummary.xlsx**. Click the Enable Content button in the Message bar if the Security Warning appears saying that Automatic update of links has been disabled.
2. Convert the formulas to their existing values by breaking the links to the external references in the four quarterly sales workbooks.
3. Save, print, and then close **EL2-C4-A2-PremiumFitnessSalesSummary.xlsx**.

Assessment

4 SUMMARIZE DATA USING 3-D REFERENCES

1. Open **MayParkEntries.xlsx**.
2. Save the workbook with Save As and name it **EL2-C4-A4-MayParkEntries**.
3. With AttendanceSummary the active worksheet, summarize the data in the three park worksheets using 3-D references as follows:
   a. Delete the label in A7.
   b. Copy A6:A22 from any of the park worksheets and paste to A6:A22 in the AttendanceSummary worksheet.
   c. Copy D6:D21 from any of the park worksheets and paste to D6:D21 in the AttendanceSummary worksheet.
   d. Type the label **Entries** right-aligned in B6 and E6.
   e. Make B7 the active cell and then create a 3-D formula to sum the attendance values in the three park worksheets for Day 1. Copy and paste the formula to the remaining cells in column B to complete the summary to Day 16.
   f. Make E7 the active cell and then create a 3-D formula to sum the attendance values in the three park worksheets for Day 17. Copy and paste the formula to the remaining cells in column E to complete the summary to Day 31.
   g. Type the label **Total Vehicle and Individual Entrances** in A24.
   h. Create a Sum formula in E24 to compute the grand total.
   i. Apply formatting options to the grand total as desired to make the total stand out.
4. Print the AttendanceSummary worksheet.
5. Save and then close **EL2-C4-A4-MayParkEntries.xlsx**.

Assessment

5 SUMMARIZE DATA IN A PIVOTTABLE AND PIVOTCHART

1. Open **NewAgeDental2012Fees.xlsx**.
2. Save the workbook with Save As and name it **EL2-C4-A5-NewAgeDental2012Fees**.
3. Create a PivotTable report in a new worksheet as follows:
   a. Display the range named *FeeSummary* and then insert a PivotTable in a new worksheet.
   b. Add the *Service Provided* field as row labels.

c. Add the *Dentist* field as column labels.

d. Sum the *FeesBilled* field.

4. Apply *Pivot Style Medium 20* to the PivotTable (sixth option in third row in *Medium* section).

5. Format the values to the Comma Style number format with zero decimals and right-align the dentist names.

6. Name the worksheet *PivotTable*. In rows 1 and 2 above the table enter an appropriate title and subtitle merged and centered across the PivotTable report and then print the PivotTable report.

7. Create a PivotChart from the PivotTable using the Clustered Column chart type and move the chart to its own sheet named *PivotChart*.

8. Filter the PivotChart by the dentist named *Jovanovic*.

9. Print the PivotChart.

10. Save and then close **EL2-C4-A5-NewAgeDental2012Fees.xlsx**.

Assessment

 6 FILTERING A PIVOTTABLE USING SLICERS

1. Open **EL2-C4-A5-NewAgeDental2012Fees.xlsx**.

2. Save the workbook with Save As and name it **EL2-C4-A6-DentalFeesFiltered**.

3. Click the PivotTable sheet to view the PivotTable report.

4. Insert Slicer panes for the *Dentist* and *Service Provided* fields.

5. Move the Slicer panes below the PivotTable report.

6. Using the Dentist Slicer pane, filter the PivotTable by *Popovich*. Hold down the Shift key and then click the button for *Vanket* in the Dentist Slicer pane. Use the Shift key to filter by multiple fields in a Slicer pane when the two fields are adjacent in the pane.

7. Using the Service Provided Slicer pane, filter the PivotTable report by *Crowns and Bridges*. Hold down the Ctrl key and then click the button for *Root Canals*. Use the Ctrl key to filter by multiple fields in a Slicer pane when the fields are not adjacent in the pane.

8. Print the PivotTable report.

9. Save and then close **EL2-C4-A6-DentalFeesFiltered.xlsx**.

Assessment

7 CREATING AND CUSTOMIZING SPARKLINES

1. Open **EL2-C4-A2-PremiumFitnessSalesSummary.xlsx**.

2. Save the workbook with Save As and name it **EL2-C4-A7-PremiumFitnessSalesSummary**.

3. Select H5:H9 and insert Line Sparklines referencing the data range B5:E9.

4. Show the high point and markers on each line.

5. Change the Sparkline color to *Dark Blue* (in *Standard Colors* section).

6. Change the width of column H to 19.

7. Type the label Region Sales by Quarter in H4.

8. Change the page orientation to landscape and then print the worksheet.

9. Save and then close **EL2-C4-A7-PremiumFitnessSalesSummary.xlsx**.

Visual Benchmark Demonstrate Your Proficiency

SUMMARIZING REAL ESTATE SALES AND COMMISSION DATA

1. Open **HillsdaleOctSales.xlsx**.
2. Save the workbook with Save As and name it **EL2-C4-VB-HillsdaleOctSales**.
3. Create the PivotTable report shown in Figure 4.11 in a new worksheet named *PivotTable*. Use *Pivot Style Medium 11* and column widths set to 18.
4. Create the PivotChart report shown in Figure 4.12 in a new worksheet named *PivotChart*. Use the 3-D Clustered Column chart type and *Style 26*.
5. Print the PivotTable and PivotChart sheets.
6. Save and then close **EL2-C4-VB-HillsdaleOctSales.xlsx**.

Figure 4.11 Visual Benchmark PivotTable

	A	B	C	D	E
1		Hillsdale Realtors			
2		October Sales			
3	Sum of Sale Price	Column Labels			
4	Row Labels	Condominium	Single family home	Townhome	Grand Total
5	Chandler	$ 610,900	$ 325,500	$ 952,100	$ 1,888,500
6	Glendale	640,400	881,375		1,521,775
7	Mesa	275,800	846,750	165,800	1,288,350
8	Phoenix	695,000	2,148,100	174,900	3,018,000
9	**Grand Total**	$ 2,222,100	$ 4,201,725	$ 1,292,800	$ 7,716,625

Figure 4.12 Visual Benchmark PivotChart

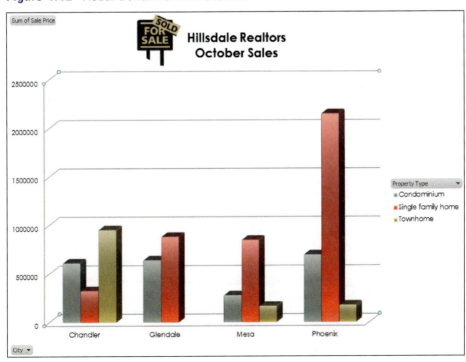

Case Study   Apply Your Skills

Part 1

Yolanda Robertson of NuTrends Market Research is continuing to work on the franchise expansion plan for the owners of Pizza By Mario. Yolanda has received a new workbook from the owners with profit information by store. Yolanda would like the data summarized. Open the workbook named **PizzaByMarioSales&Profits.xlsx** and review the structure of the data. Yolanda would like a PivotTable report that provides the average gross sales and the average net income by city by state. You determine how to organize the layout of the report. *Hint: You can add more than one numeric field to the* **Values** *list box*. Remove the grand totals at the right of the report so that a grand total row appears only at the bottom of the PivotTable. *Hint: Use the Grand Totals button in the Layout group of the PivotTable Tools Design tab*. Apply formatting options to improve the report's appearance and make sure the report prints on one page in landscape orientation. Rename the worksheet containing the report *PivotTable*. Save the revised workbook and name it **EL2-C4-CS-P1-PizzaByMarioRpt**.

Part 2

Yolanda would like a chart that graphs the average net income data for the state of Michigan only. Create a PivotChart in a new sheet named *PivotChart* and filter the chart appropriately to meet Yolanda's request. You determine an appropriate chart style and elements to include in the chart. Yolanda will be using this chart at an upcoming meeting with the franchise owners and wants the chart to be of professional quality. Print the chart. Save the revised workbook and name it **EL2-C4-CS-P2-PizzaByMarioRpt** and then close the workbook.

Part 3

Help

Open **EL2-C4-CS-P1-PizzaByMarioRpt.xlsx**. Use the Help feature to find out how to modify a numeric field setting to show values as ranked numbers from largest to smallest. For example, instead of seeing the average value next to a city, you will see the city's ranking as it compares to other cities in the same state. Ranking from largest to smallest means the highest value in the state is ranked as 1. Using the information you learned in Help, change the display of the average sales to show the values ranked from largest to smallest using *City* as the base field. Remove the *Net Income* field from the PivotTable. Remove the grand total row at the bottom of the PivotTable. Make any other formatting changes to the report you think will improve the appearance. Print the PivotTable. Save the revised workbook and name it **EL2-C4-CS-P3-PizzaByMarioRpt**.

Part 4

Yolanda would like you to do some comparison research of another pizza franchise. Use the Internet to research the sales and net income information of a pizza franchise with which you are familiar. Create a new workbook that compares the total annual sales and net income values of the pizza franchise you researched with the Pizza By Mario information in **EL2-C4-CS-P1-PizzaByMarioRpt.xlsx**. Provide the URL of the website from which you obtained the competitive data. Create a chart that visually presents the comparison data. Save the workbook and name it **EL2-C4-CS-P4-PizzaFranchiseComparison**. Print the comparison data and the chart. Close **EL2-C4-CS-P4-PizzaFranchiseComparison.xlsx**.

Performance Assessment

Access
Excel2010L2U1

Note: Before beginning assessments, copy to your storage medium the Excel2010L2U1 subfolder from the Excel2010L2 folder on the CD that accompanies this textbook and then make Excel2010L2U1 the active folder.

Assessing Proficiency ■■■■■■■■■■■■■■■■

In this unit, you have learned to apply advanced formatting options such as conditional formatting and custom number formats; perform advanced sort and filtering techniques; create functions that incorporate conditional logic, look up data, convert text, and calculate financial results; define a table and apply data management features to a table or list range; consolidate and summarize data and present summary information in PivotTables, PivotCharts, or Sparklines.

Assessment 1 Conditionally Format and Filter a Help Desk Worksheet

1. Open **RSRHelpDeskRpt.xlsx**.
2. Save the workbook using the name **EL2-U1-A1-RSRHelpDeskRpt**.
3. Apply conditional formatting to display the *3 Flags* icon set to the values in the *Priority* column. Calls with a priority code of 1 should display a red flag, priority 2 calls should display a yellow flag and priority 3 calls should display a green flag.
4. Create a custom format for the values in the *Time Spent* column. The format should display leading zeros, two decimal places, and the text *hrs* at the end of the entry separated by one space from the number.
5. Create two conditional formatting rules for the values in the *Time Spent* column as follows:
   a. For all entries where the time spent is less than 1 hour, apply bold and a pale green fill color.
   b. For all entries where the time spent is more than 2 hours, apply a bright yellow fill color.
6. Filter the worksheet by the bright yellow fill color applied in the *Time Spent* column. If necessary, delete the clip art image if the image overlaps the data.
7. Print the filtered worksheet.
8. Clear the filter and the filter arrow buttons and then print the worksheet.
9. Save and then close **EL2-U1-A1-RSRHelpDeskRpt.xlsx**.

Assessment 2 Use Conditional Logic Formulas in a Help Desk Worksheet

1. Open **EL2-U1-A1-RSRHelpDeskRpt.xlsx**.
2. Save the workbook using the name **EL2-U1-A2-RSRHelpDeskRpt.xlsx**.
3. Create range names for the following ranges. You determine appropriate names.
   a. Name the cells in A4:E6, which will be used in a lookup formula.
   b. Name the entries in the *Operator ID* column.
   c. Name the values in the *Time Spent* column.
   d. Name the cells in the *Status* column.
4. In I4, create a COUNTA formula to count the number of help desk calls in March using column A as the source range.
5. In I5 and I6, create COUNTIF formulas to count the number of active calls (I5) and the number of closed calls (I6). Use range names in the formulas.
6. Create COUNTIF formulas in K3 through K6 to count the calls assigned to Operator ID 1, 2, 3, and 4, respectively. Use range names in the formulas.
7. Create SUMIF formulas in L3 through L6 to calculate the total time spent on calls assigned to Operator ID 1, 2, 3, and 4, respectively. Use range names in the formulas. Format the results to display two decimal places.
8. Create AVERAGEIF formulas in M3 through M6 to find the average time spent on calls assigned to Operator ID 1, 2, 3, and 4, respectively. Use range names in the formulas. Format the results to display two decimal places.
9. Create the HLOOKUP formula with an exact match in F8 to return the last name for the operator assigned to the call. Use the range name for the lookup table in the formula.
10. Create the HLOOKUP formula with an exact match in G8 to return the first name for the operator assigned to the call. Use the range name for the lookup table in the formula.
11. Copy the HLOOKUP formulas in F8:G8 and paste to the remaining rows in the list.
12. Save, print, and then close **EL2-U1-A2-RSRHelpDeskRpt.xlsx**.

Assessment 3 Use Table and Data Management Features in a Help Desk Worksheet

1. Open **EL2-U1-A2-RSRHelpDeskRpt.xlsx**.
2. Save the workbook using the name **EL2-U1-A3-RSRHelpDeskRpt.xlsx**.
3. Format A7:I30 as a table using *Table Style Medium 20*.
4. Add a calculated column to the table in column J that multiplies the time spent times 15.00. Use the column heading *Cost* in J7. Format the results to display Comma Style number format.
5. Add a total row to the table. Display a sum total in columns H and J.
6. Add emphasis to the last column in the table and band the columns instead of the rows.
7. Create a drop-down list for the *Operator ID* column that displays the entries 1, 2, 3, 4.

8. RSR has a policy that help desk operators cannot spend more than three hours on a call. Calls that require more than three hours must be routed to the Help Desk manager and assigned to another group. Create a validation rule in the *Time Spent* column that ensures no value greater than 3 is entered. Create appropriate input and error messages.

9. Add the following two records to the table:

Date	3/30/2012	3/30/2012
Ticket No	14424	14425
Priority	2	2
Type of Call	Email	Password
Operator ID	3	4
Time Spent	.75	.25
Status	Active	Closed

10. Filter the table to display only those calls with a *Closed* status.
11. Print the filtered list.
12. Filter the worksheet to display only those calls with a *Closed* status where the type of call was *Password*.
13. Print the filtered list.
14. Clear both filters.
15. Save, print, and then close **EL2-U1-A3-RSRHelpDeskRpt.xlsx**.

Assessment 4 Add Subtotals and Outline a Help Desk Worksheet

1. Open **EL2-U1-A3-RSRHelpDeskRpt.xlsx**.
2. Save the workbook using the name **EL2-U1-A4-RSRHelpDeskRpt**.
3. Remove the Total row from the table.
4. Convert the table to a normal range.
5. Sort the list first by the operator's last name, then by the operator's first name, then by the call priority, and finally by the type of call, all in ascending order.
6. Add a subtotal to the list at each change in the operator last name to calculate the total cost of calls by operator.
7. Display the outlined worksheet at level 2 and then print the worksheet.
8. Display the outlined worksheet at level 3 and then print the worksheet.
9. Save and then close **EL2-U1-A4-RSRHelpDeskRpt.xlsx**.

Assessment 5 Use Financial and Text Functions to Analyze Data for a Project

1. Open **AllClaimsLoan.xlsx**.
2. Save the workbook using the name **EL2-U1-A5-AllClaimsLoan**.
3. Create formulas to analyze the cost of the loan from NEWFUNDS TRUST and DELTA CAPITAL as follows:
   a. In C10 and E10, calculate the monthly loan payments from each lender.
   b. In C12 and E12, calculate the principal portion of each payment for the first loan payment.
   c. In C14 and E14, calculate the total loan payments that will be made over the life of the loan from each lender.
4. In E20, use the text function =*PROPER* to return the loan company name for the loan that represents the lowest total cost to AllClaims Insurance Brokers. ***Hint: The argument for the function will reference either C4 or E4***.
5. In E21, use the text function =*LOWER* to return the loan application number for the loan company name you displayed in E20.
6. Save, print, and then close **EL2-U1-A5-AllClaimsLoan.xlsx**.

Assessment 6 Analyze Sales Using a PivotTable, a PivotChart, and Sparklines

1. Open **PrecisionBulkSales.xlsx**.
2. Save the workbook using the name **EL2-U1-A6-PrecisionBulkSales**.
3. Select A4:I22 and create a PivotTable in a new worksheet named *PivotTable* as follows:
   a. Add the *Category* field as the report filter field.
   b. Add the *Distributor* field as the row labels.
   c. Sum the North, South, East, and West sales values.
4. Apply formatting options to the PivotTable to make the data easier to read and interpret.
5. Print the PivotTable.
6. Create a PivotChart in a separate sheet named *PivotChart* that graphs the data from the PivotTable in a Clustered Cylinder chart.
7. Edit the chart fields to display only the sum of the North and the South values.
8. Move the legend to the bottom of the chart.
9. Print the chart.
10. Make Sheet1 the active sheet and then create Sparklines in J5:J22 that show the North, South, East, and West sales in a line chart. Set the width of column J to 18. Customize the Sparklines by changing the Sparkline color and adding data points. You determine which data point to show and the color of the points. Type an appropriate label in J4 and add other formatting you think would improve the appearance.
11. Save, print, and then close **EL2-U1-A6-PrecisionBulkSales.xlsx**.

Assessment 7 Link to an External Data Source and Calculate Distributor Payments

1. Open **PrecisionDistPymnt.xlsx**.
2. Save the workbook using the name **EL2-U1-A7-PrecisionDistPymnt**.
3. Open **EL2-U1-A6-PrecisionBulkSales.xlsx**.
4. Save the workbook using the name **EL2-U1-A7-PrecisionSource**.
5. Make the PivotTable worksheet active and then edit the PivotTable Field List so that *Sum of Total* is the only numeric field displayed in the table.
6. Save **EL2-U1-A7-PrecisionSource.xlsx**.
7. Arrange the display of the two workbooks vertically.
8. Create linked external references starting in D6 in **EL2-U1-A7-PrecisionDistPymnt.xlsx** to the appropriate source cells in the PivotTable in **EL2-U1-A7-PrecisionSource.xlsx** so that the distributor payment worksheet displays the total sales for each distributor. *Note: Since you are linking to a PivotTable, Excel automatically generates a GETPIVOTDATA function formula in each linked cell.*
9. Close **EL2-U1-A7-PrecisionSource.xlsx**.
10. Maximize **EL2-U1-A7-PrecisionDistPymnt.xlsx**.
11. Format D6:D8 to the Accounting Number format style with zero decimals.

12. Precision Design and Packaging pays each distributor a percentage of sales depending on the total sales achieved. In the chart below is the percentage for each sales level.

Sales	Percentage
$600,000 or less	1%
Over $600,000 and up to $900,000	2%
Over $900,000	4%

Calculate the payment owed for the distributors in H6:H8. Perform the calculation using either one of the following two methods—choose the method that you find easier to understand.

- Create a nested IF statement; OR

- Create a lookup table in the worksheet that contains the sale ranges and the three percentage values. Next, add a column next to each distributor with a lookup formula to return the correct percentage and then calculate the payment using total sales times the percent value.

13. Format H6:H8 to the Comma Style number format.
14. Add the label *TOTALS* in B10 and then create formulas in D10 and H10 to calculate the total sales and total payments respectively. Format the totals and adjust column widths as necessary.
15. Print the worksheet. Write the GETPIVOTDATA formula for D6 at the bottom of the printout.
16. Break the link to the external references and convert the formulas to their existing values.
17. Save, print, and then close **EL2-U1-A7-PrecisionDistPymnt.xlsx**.

Writing Activities ■■■■■■■■■■ ■■■■■ ■■ ■■■

The following activities give you the opportunity to practice your writing skills along with demonstrating an understanding of some of the important Excel features you have mastered in this unit. Use appropriate word choices and correct grammar, capitalization, and punctuation when setting up new worksheets. Labels should clearly describe the data that are presented.

Activity 1 Create a Worksheet to Track Video Rental Memberships

Vantage Video Rentals is offering a new membership program for their frequent customers. Customers will pay an annual membership fee that then entitles them to a discount on video rentals based on their membership category. Table U1.1 provides the three membership levels and discounts. The manager of Vantage

Table U1.1 Activity 1

Membership Category	Annual Fee	Discount on Video Rentals
Gold	$45.00	15%
Silver	$30.00	12%
Classic	$20.00	10%

Video Rentals has asked you to create a worksheet that will be used to provide a master list of customers who are participating in the membership program, the membership level for which they have paid, and the discount on video rentals they are entitled to receive. The worksheet will need to provide in list format the following information:

- Date annual membership needs to be renewed
- Customer name
- Customer telephone number
- Membership level
- Annual membership fee
- Discount on video rentals

Create a worksheet for the membership list. Use a lookup table to populate the cells containing the membership fee and the discount level. Create a drop-down list for the cell containing the membership level that restricts the data entered to the three membership categories. Use a special number format for the telephone number column so that all telephone numbers include the area code and are displayed in a consistent format. Enter a minimum of five sample records to test the worksheet with your settings. The manager anticipates approximately 35 regular customers will subscribe to the membership program. Format enough rows with the data features to include at least 35 memberships. Save the completed worksheet and name it **EL2-U1-Act01-VantageMemberships**. Print and then close the worksheet.

Activity 2 Create a Worksheet to Log Hours Walked in a Company Fitness Contest

The company at which you work is sponsoring a contest this year to encourage employees to participate in a walking fitness program during lunch hours. The company is offering to pay for a spa weekend at an exclusive luxury resort for participating employees in the department that logs the most miles or kilometers walked during the year. You work in Human Resources and are in charge of keeping track of each department's walking records. Create a worksheet that can be used to enter each department's totals by month and summarize the data to show the total distance walked for the entire company at the end of the year as follows:

- Four departments have signed up for the contest: Accounting, Human Resources, Purchasing, and Marketing. Create a separate worksheet for each department.

- Each department will send you a paper copy of their walking log each month. You will use this source document to enter the miles or kilometers walked by day. At the end of each month you want to calculate statistics by department to show the total distance walked, the average distance walked, and the number of days in the month in which employees walked during their lunch hour. When calculating the average and the number of days, include only those days in which employees logged a distance. In other words, exclude from the statistics those days in which employees did not log any distance. *Hint: Consider adding a column that contains Yes or No to record whether or not employees participated in the walking program each day to use as the criteria range.*

- Create a summary worksheet that calculates the total of all miles or kilometers walked for all four departments.

Enter at least five days of sample data in each worksheet to test your settings. Save the completed workbook and name it **EL2-U1-Act02-FitnessProgram**. Print the entire workbook and then close the workbook.

Optional: Using the Internet or other sources, find information on the health benefits of walking. Prepare a summary of the information and include it in a memo announcing the contest. The memo is to be sent from Human Resources to all departments. Save the memo and name it **EL2-U2-Act02-FitnessMemo**. Print the memo and close the file.

Internet Research ■■■■■■■■■■■■■■■■■■■■■■■■

Create a Worksheet to Compare Online Auction Listing Fees

You are assisting a friend who is interested in selling a few items by auction on the Internet. Research a minimum of two Internet auction sites for all selling and payment fees associated with selling online. For example, be sure to find out costs for the following activities involved in an auction sale:

- Listing fees (sometimes called insertion fees)
- Optional features that can be attached to an ad such as reserve bid fees, picture fees, listing upgrades, and so on
- Fees paid when the item is sold based on the sale value
- Fees paid to a third party to accept credit card payments (such as PayPal)

Create a worksheet in which you compare the fees for each auction site you researched. Include for each auction site two sample transactions and calculate the total fees that would be paid.

        Sample transaction 1   Item sold at $24.99
        Sample transaction 2   Item sold at $49.99

- Add optional features to the listing such as a picture and/or a reserve bid
- Assume in both sample transactions the buyer pays by credit card using a third party service

Based on your analysis, decide which auction site is the better choice from a cost perspective. Apply formatting options to make the worksheet easy to read and explain your recommendation for the lower cost auction site. Save the completed worksheet and name it **EL2-U1-Act03-AuctionAnalysis**. Print and then close the worksheet.

Level 2

Unit 2 ■ Managing and Integrating Data and the Excel Environment

Using Data Analysis Features

PERFORMANCE OBJECTIVES

Upon successful completion of Chapter 5, you will be able to:

- Switch data arranged in columns to rows and vice versa
- Perform a mathematical operation during a paste routine
- Populate a cell using Goal Seek
- Save and display various worksheet models using Scenario Manager
- Create a scenario summary report
- Create a one-variable data table to analyze various outcomes
- Create a two-variable data table to analyze various outcomes
- View relationships between cells in formulas
- Identify Excel error codes and troubleshoot a formula using formula auditing tools
- Circle invalid data
- Use the Watch Window to track a value

Tutorials

5.1 Pasting Data Using Paste Special Options

5.2 Using Goal Seek to Populate a Cell

5.3 Using Scenario Manager

5.4 Performing What-If Analysis Using Data Tables

5.5 Using Auditing Tools

5.6 Circling Invalid Data and Watching Formulas

Excel's Paste Special dialog box includes several options for pasting copied data. You can choose to paste attributes of a copied cell or alter the paste routine to perform a more complex operation. A variety of *what-if* analysis tools allow you to manage data to assist with decision-making or management tasks. Formula auditing tools can be used to troubleshoot a formula or view dependencies between cells. By working through the projects in this chapter, you will learn about these tools and features available in Excel to assist with accurate data analysis. Model answers for this chapter's projects appear on the following pages.

Excel2010L2C5

Note: Before beginning the projects, copy to your storage medium the Excel2010L2C5 subfolder from the Excel2010L2 folder on the CD that accompanies this textbook and then make Excel2010L2C5 the active folder.

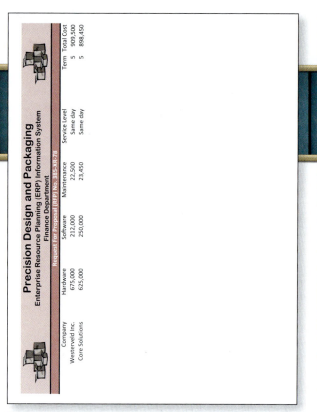

Precision Design and Packaging
Enterprise Resource Planning (ERP) Information System
Finance Department
Request For Proposal (RFP) No. 385-KR-78

Company	Hardware	Software	Maintenance	Service Level	Term	Total Cost
Westerveld Inc.	675,000	212,000	22,500	Same day	5	909,500
Core Solutions	625,000	250,000	23,450	Same day	5	898,450

Project 1 Analyze Data from a Request for Proposal

Project 1a, EL2-C5-P1-PrecisionERP.xlsx

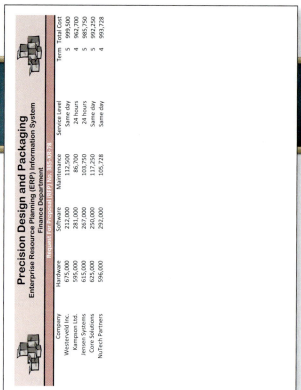

Precision Design and Packaging
Enterprise Resource Planning (ERP) Information System
Finance Department
Request For Proposal (RFP) No. 385-KR-78

Company	Hardware	Software	Maintenance	Service Level	Term	Total Cost
Westerveld Inc.	675,000	212,000	112,500	Same day	5	999,500
Kampson Ltd.	595,000	281,000	86,700	24 hours	4	962,700
Jensen Systems	615,000	267,000	103,750	24 hours	5	985,750
Core Solutions	625,000	250,000	117,250	Same day	5	992,250
NuTech Partners	596,000	292,000	105,728	Same day	4	993,728

Project 1b, EL2-C5-P1-PrecisionERP.xlsx

Math by Janelle Tutoring Service		
Student Assessment Report		
Whitney Orlowicz		
Assessments	**100**	**Session**
Objective test	64.5	1
Performance test	72.0	6
Problem-solving test	83.5	10
Comprehensive test	78.5	15
Final test	81.5	20
Average grade	76.0	

Project 2 Calculate a Target Test Score

EL2-C5-P2-JanelleTutorOrlowiczRpt.xlsx

Precision Design and Packaging
Cost Price Analysis
"E" Container Bulk Cargo Box

Factory costs per shift	Variable unit production impact on cost
Direct materials	3.21
	425,000	3.78
Direct labor	450,000	3.57
Overhead	475,000	3.38
Total cost	500,000	3.21
	525,000	3.06
	550,000	2.92
Standard production	575,000	2.79
Cost per unit	

Scenario Summary				
	Current Values:	LowInflation	HighInflation	OriginalForecast
Changing Cells:				
WageInc	13,016	12,010	15,224	13,016
SuppliesInc	2,255	2,150	2,765	2,255
TrainingInc	6,385	5,276	7,236	6,385
AdminIncrease	2,479	1,998	3,195	2,479
Result Cells:				
TotalNewCosts	659,786	657,085	664,071	659,786

Notes: Current Values column represents values of changing cells at
time Scenario Summary Report was created. Changing cells for each
scenario are highlighted in gray.

Project 3 Forecast a Budget Based on Various Inflation Rates

EL2-C5-P3-NationalCSDeptBdgt.xlsx

Project 4 Compare Impact of Various Inputs Related to Cost and Sales Pricing

EL2-C5-P4-PrecisionEBoxCost.xlsx

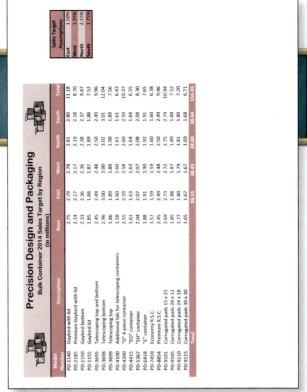

EL2-C5-P4-PrecisionEBoxSell.xlsx

Project 5 Audit a Worksheet to View and Troubleshoot Formulas

EL2-C5-P5-PrecisionSalesTrgt.xlsx

Project **1** | # Analyze Data from a Request for Proposal | **2 Parts**

You will manipulate a worksheet containing vendor quotations for an enterprise resource planning information system by copying and pasting using Paste Special options.

Pasting Data Using Paste Special Options ▪▪▪▪▪▪▪▪

The Paste drop-down gallery contains many options for pasting copied data grouped into three sections: *Paste*, *Paste Values*, and *Other Paste Options*. In Excel 2010, the Paste gallery includes a live preview of how the data will be pasted to assist you with choosing the correct paste option. Click *Paste Special* at the bottom of the Paste gallery to open the Paste Special dialog box shown in Figure 5.1. Use options in this dialog box to paste specific attributes of the source data, perform a mathematical operation in the destination range based on values in the source range, or carry out a more complex paste sequence.

Several options in the Paste Special dialog box are also available by clicking a button at the Paste drop-down gallery. For example, if you copied a range of cells that has border formatting applied and you want to paste the range without the borders, click the Paste button arrow and then click the No Borders button (first button in second row of the *Paste* section) at the drop-down gallery. This produces the same result as clicking the Paste button arrow, clicking *Paste Special* at the drop-down gallery, clicking *All except borders* in the *Paste* section of the Paste Special dialog box, and then clicking OK.

Figure 5.1 Paste Special Dialog Box

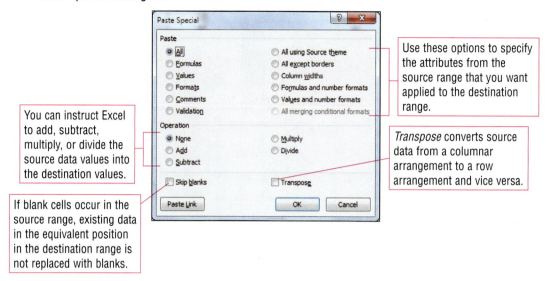

You can instruct Excel to add, subtract, multiply, or divide the source data values into the destination values.

Use these options to specify the attributes from the source range that you want applied to the destination range.

Transpose converts source data from a columnar arrangement to a row arrangement and vice versa.

If blank cells occur in the source range, existing data in the equivalent position in the destination range is not replaced with blanks.

Transposing Data

▼ Quick Steps

Transpose a Range
1. Select source range.
2. Click Copy button.
3. Click starting cell in destination range.
4. Click Paste button arrow.
5. Click *Transpose*.

A worksheet may have data arranged in a way that is not suitable for the analysis you want to perform. For example, examine the worksheet shown in Figure 5.2. This is the worksheet you will be working with in Project 1. Notice the layout of the information shows each company that submitted a proposal arranged in a separate column with the criteria for analysis, such as the cost of the hardware, arranged in rows. While at first glance this layout may seem appropriate, consider how you would analyze this data if you wanted to examine only those vendors that offer a five-year contract. To use the filter feature on this data, you need the contract term in a columnar format. Rearranging the data in this worksheet manually would be time-consuming and risky due to the possibility of errors made during the conversion process. The *Transpose* option in the Paste drop-down gallery or the Paste Special dialog box will convert columns to rows and rows to columns.

Figure 5.2 Project 1 Worksheet

	A	B	C	D	E	F
1		**Precision Design and Packaging**				
2		Enterprise Resource Planning (ERP) Information System				
3		Finance Department				
4		Request For Proposal (RFP) No. 385-XR-78				
5	Company	Westerveld Inc.	Kampson Ltd.	Jensen Systems	Core Solutions	NuTech Partners
6	Hardware	675,000	595,000	615,000	625,000	596,000
7	Software	212,000	281,000	267,000	250,000	292,000
8	Maintenance	22,500	21,675	20,750	23,450	26,432
9	Service Level	Same day	24 hours	24 hours	Same day	Same day
10	Term	5	4	5	5	4
11	Total Cost	909,500	897,675	902,750	898,450	914,432

1. Open **PrecisionERP.xlsx**.
2. Save the workbook with Save As and name it **EL2-C5-P1-PrecisionERP**.
3. Convert the worksheet to arrange the company names in rows and the criteria data in columns by completing the following steps:
   a. Select A5:F11.
   b. Click the Copy button.
   c. Click in cell A13.
   d. Click the Paste button arrow and then click *Transpose* (last button in *Paste* section) at the drop-down gallery.

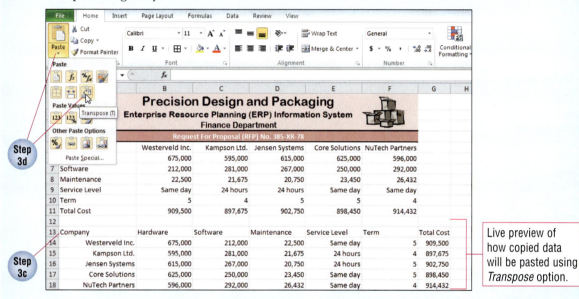

Step 3d

Step 3c

Live preview of how copied data will be pasted using *Transpose* option.

    e. Press the Esc key to remove the moving marquee from the source range and then click in any cell to deselect the range.
4. Delete rows 5–12.
5. Correct the merge and centering in rows 1–4 to extend the titles across columns A–G. If necessary, move or otherwise adjust the position of the clip art at the right side of the worksheet after merging and centering to column G.
6. Add a thick bottom border to A3 and A4.
7. Right-align the labels in A5:G5.
8. Select A5:G10, turn on the Filter feature, and then click in any cell to deselect the range.
9. Click the filter arrow button in F5 and then filter the worksheet to display only those vendors offering a 5-year contract.

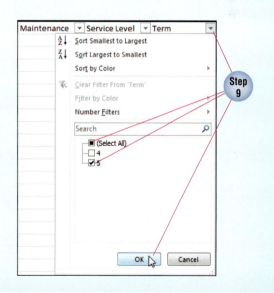

Step 9

10. Click the filter arrow button in E5 and then filter the remaining rows to display only those vendors offering same day service.

Request For Proposal (RFP) No. 385-XR-78						
Company	Hardware	Software	Maintenance	Service Level	Term	Total C
Westerveld Inc.	675,000	212,000	22,500	Same day	5	909,500
Core Solutions	625,000	250,000	23,450	Same day	5	898,450

Step 10

11. Print the filtered worksheet.
12. Turn off the Filter feature and then save **EL2-C5-P1-PrecisionERP.xlsx**.

▼ **Quick Steps**

Perform Mathematical Operation during Paste
1. Select source range values.
2. Click Copy button.
3. Click starting cell in destination range.
4. Click Paste button arrow.
5. Click *Paste Special*.
6. Click desired mathematical operation.
7. Click OK.

Performing a Mathematical Operation while Pasting

A range of cells in a copied source range can be added to, subtracted from, multiplied by, or divided by the cells in the destination range by opening the Paste Special dialog box and selecting the mathematical operation you want to perform. For example, in the worksheet for Project 1a, the values in the *Maintenance* column relate to annual maintenance fees charged by each vendor. To compare the total cost of the system from all of the vendors, you want to see the maintenance value for the life cycle of the contract. In Project 1b, you will copy and paste using a multiply operation to perform the calculation for you. This method means you will not have to add a new column to the worksheet to show the maintenance fees for the entire term of the contract.

Project 1b   **Multiplying the Source Cells by the Destination Cells**   Part 2 of 2

1. With **EL2-C5-P1-PrecisionERP.xlsx** open, select F6:F10. These are the cells that contain the term for each company's contract.
2. Click the Copy button.
3. Paste the source range and instruct Excel to multiply the values when pasting by completing the following steps:
   a. Click D6.
   b. Click the Paste button arrow and then click *Paste Special* at the drop-down gallery.

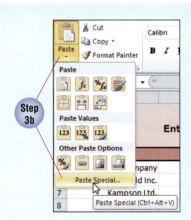

Step 3b

c. Click *Multiply* in the *Operation* section of the Paste Special dialog box and then click OK.

d. Press the *Esc* key to remove the moving marquee from the source range and then click in any cell to deselect the range.

4. Print the worksheet.

5. Save and then close **EL2-C5-P1-PrecisionERP.xlsx**.

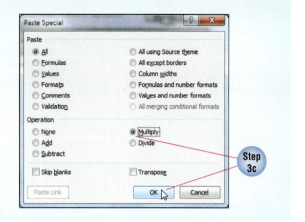

Selecting Other Paste Special Options

Other options at the Paste Special dialog box include *Formulas* or *Values* to paste the source formulas or displayed values only, *Formats* to paste only formatting options from the source, *Validation* to paste a validation rule, *All using Source theme* to apply the theme from the source, *All except borders* to paste everything except borders from the source, and *Column widths* to adjust the destination cells to the same column width as the source. To paste formulas or values including the number formats from the source click the *Formulas and number formats* or the *Values and number formats* option.

Project **2** **Calculate a Target Test Score**   **1 Part**

Using a grades worksheet for a student, you will determine the score a student needs to earn on a final test in order to achieve a specified final average grade.

Using Goal Seek to Populate a Cell

Goal Seek calculates a value using a target that you want to achieve in another cell that is dependent on the cell you want Goal Seek to populate. For example, the worksheet shown in Figure 5.3 shows Whitney's grades on the first four tutoring assessments. The value in B11 (average grade) is calculated as the average of the five values in B5:B9. Note that the final test is showing a grade of zero although the test has not yet occurred. Once the final test grade is entered, the value in B11 will update to reflect the average of all five scores. Suppose Whitney wants to achieve a final average grade of 76% in her tutoring assessments. Using Goal Seek, you can determine the score she needs to earn on the final test in order to achieve the 76% average.

In Project 2 you will return a value in B9 that the Goal Seek feature will calculate based on the target value you will set in B11. Goal Seek causes Excel to calculate in reverse—you specify the ending value and Excel figures out the input numbers that will achieve the end result you want. Note that the cell in which you want Excel to calculate the target value must be referenced by a formula in the *Set cell* box. Goal Seek is useful for any situation where you know the result you want to achieve but are not sure what value will get you there.

Quick Steps

Use Goal Seek to Return a Value
1. Make desired cell active.
2. Click Data tab.
3. Click What-If Analysis button.
4. Click *Goal Seek*.
5. Enter desired cell address in *Set cell* text box.
6. Enter desired target value in *To value* text box.
7. Enter dependent cell address in *By changing cell* text box.
8. Click OK.
9. Click OK or Cancel to accept or reject results.

Figure 5.3 Project 2 Worksheet

	A	B	C
1	**Math by Janelle Tutoring Service**		
2	**Student Assessment Report**		
3	Whitney Orlowicz		
4	**Assessments**	**100**	**Session**
5	Objective test	64.5	1
6	Performance test	72.0	6
7	Problem-solving test	83.5	10
8	Comprehensive test	78.5	15
9	Final test	0.0	20
10			
11	Average grade	59.7	

Goal Seek

Goal Seek can determine the value that needs to be entered for the final test in order to achieve an average grade that you specify in B11.

Project 2   **Using Goal Seek to Return a Target Value**   Part 1 of 1

1. Open **JanelleTutorOrlowiczRpt.xlsx**.
2. Save the workbook with Save As and name it **EL2-C5-P2-JanelleTutorOrlowiczRpt**.
3. Use Goal Seek to find the score Whitney needs to earn on the final test to achieve a 76% average grade by completing the following steps:
   a. Make B11 the active cell.
   b. Click the Data tab.
   c. Click the What-If Analysis button in the Data Tools group and then click *Goal Seek* at the drop-down list.
   d. If necessary, drag the Goal Seek dialog box to the right of the worksheet so that you can see all of the values in column B.
   e. With *B11* already entered in the *Set cell* text box, click in the *To value* text box and then type 76.
   f. Press Tab and then type b9 in the *By changing cell* text box.
   g. Click OK.
   h. Click OK at the Goal Seek Status dialog box that shows Excel found a solution.
4. Notice that Excel entered the value *81.5* in B9. This is the score Whitney must earn in order to achieve a final average grade of 76%.
5. Assume that Whitney wants to achieve a final average grade of 80%. Use Goal Seek to find the value that she will need to earn on the final test to accomplish the new target by completing the following steps:
   a. Click the What-If Analysis button in the Data Tools group and then click *Goal Seek* at the drop-down list.
   b. Click in the *To value* text box, type 80, and then press Tab.
   c. Type b9 in the *By changing cell* text box.
   d. Click OK.

Step 3c

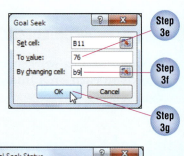

Step 3e

Step 3f

Step 3g

Step 3h

e. Notice that the value returned in B9 is 101.5. This is the new value Excel has calculated Whitney needs on the final test in order to earn an 80% final average grade.

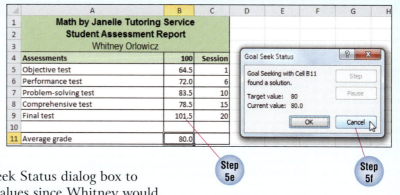

Step 5e

Step 5f

f. Click the Cancel button at the Goal Seek Status dialog box to restore the previous values since Whitney would not be able to score over 100 on the final test.

6. Save, print, and then close **EL2-C5-P2-JanelleTutorOrlowiczRpt.xlsx**.

$\mathcal{P}$roject  **Forecast a Budget Based on Various Inflation Rates**　　　　**3 Parts**

You will determine the impact on a department's budget of various inflation rates to determine the funding request to present to management to maintain service.

Creating Assumptions for What-If Analysis Using Scenario Manager

The *Scenario Manager* allows you to store multiple sets of assumptions about data and then view the impact of those assumptions on your worksheet. You can switch the display between scenarios to test the various inputs on your worksheet model. You can save each scenario using a descriptive name such as *Best Case* or *Worst Case* to indicate the type of data assumptions you have stored. Examine the worksheet shown in Figure 5.4. In this worksheet, the Computing Services department budget for the next year has been calculated based on projected increases for various expense items. Assume that the department manager has more than one estimate for the percentages based on different inflation rates or vendor rate increases for

Quick Steps

Add a Scenario
1. Click Data tab.
2. Click What-If Analysis button.
3. Click *Scenario Manager*.
4. Click Add button.
5. Type name in *Scenario name* text box.
6. Type or select variable cells in *Changing cells* text box.
7. Click OK.
8. Enter values for each changing cell.
9. Click OK.
10. Click Close button.

Scenario Manager

Figure 5.4 Project 3 Worksheet

	A	B	C	D
1	**National Online Marketing Inc.**			
2	**Computing Services Department**			
3		Current budget	Projected increase	New budget
4	Wages and benefits	371,875	13,016	384,891
5	Computer supplies	150,350	2,255	152,605
6	Training and development	63,850	6,385	70,235
7	Other administrative costs	49,576	2,479	52,055
8	Total costs:	635,651		659,786

next year. The manager can create and save various scenarios in order to view the impact on total costs for a combination of different forecasts.

Using the Scenario Manager dialog box shown in Figure 5.5 you can create as many models as you want to save in order to test various what-if conditions. For example, two scenarios have been saved in the example shown in Figure 5.5, *LowInflation* and *HighInflation*. When you add a scenario, you define which cells will change and then enter the data to be stored under the scenario name.

Figure 5.5 Scenario Manager Dialog Box and Scenario Values Dialog Box

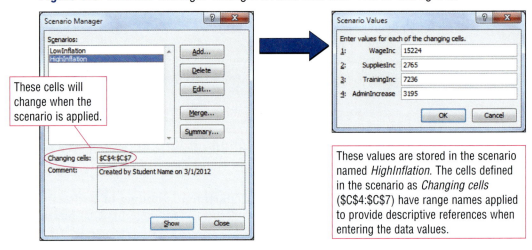

These cells will change when the scenario is applied.

These values are stored in the scenario named *HighInflation*. The cells defined in the scenario as *Changing cells* ($C$4:$C$7) have range names applied to provide descriptive references when entering the data values.

Project 3a   **Adding Scenarios to a Worksheet Model**   Part 1 of 3

1. Open **NationalCSDeptBdgt.xlsx**.
2. Save the workbook with Save As and name it **EL2-C5-P3-NationalCSDeptBdgt**.
3. View the range names already created in the worksheet by clicking the down-pointing arrow at the right of the *Name* text box and then clicking *WageInc* at the drop-down list. The active cell moves to C4. A range name has been created for each data cell in column C to allow a descriptive label to show when you add scenarios in Steps 4 and 5.
4. Add a scenario with values assuming a low inflation rate for next year by completing the following steps:
   a. Click the Data tab.
   b. Click the What-If Analysis button in the Data Tools group and then click *Scenario Manager* at the drop-down list.
   c. Click the Add button at the Scenario Manager dialog box.
   d. At the Add Scenario dialog box with the insertion point positioned in the *Scenario name* text box, type **LowInflation** and then press Tab.
   e. Type **c4:c7** in the *Changing cells* text box and then press Enter or click OK. (As an alternative, you can move the dialog box out of the way and select the cells that will change in the worksheet.)

By default, Excel stores the user name and the date the scenario was created

Step 4d

Step 4e

f. With the insertion point positioned in the first text box labeled *1: WageInc*, type **12010** and press Tab.

g. Type **2150** and press Tab.

h. Type **5276** and press Tab.

i. Type **1998** and then press Enter or click OK.

5. Add a second scenario to the worksheet assuming a high inflation rate by completing the following steps:

a. Click the Add button at the Scenario Manager dialog box.

b. Type **HighInflation** in the *Scenario name* text box and then click OK. Notice the *Changing cells* text box already contains the range C4:C7.

c. At the Scenario Values dialog box, add the following values in the text boxes indicated:

1: WageInc   15224
2: SuppliesInc   2765
3: TrainingInc   7236
4: AdminIncrease 3195

d. Click OK.

6. Add a third scenario named *OriginalForecast* that contains the original worksheet's values by completing the following steps:

a. Click the Add button at the Scenario Manager dialog box.

b. Type **OriginalForecast** in the *Scenario name* text box and then click OK.

c. At the Scenario Values dialog box, notice the original values are already entered in each text box. Click OK.

7. Click the Close button to close the Scenario Manager dialog box.

8. Save **EL2-C5-P3-NationalCSDeptBdgt.xlsx**.

Applying a Scenario

After you have created the various scenarios you want to save with the worksheet, you can apply the values stored in a scenario to the variable cells to view the effects on your worksheet model. To do this, open the Scenario Manager dialog box, click the name of the scenario that contains the values you want to apply to the worksheet, and then click the Show button. Generally, you should create a scenario with the original values in the worksheet since Excel replaces the changing cell's contents when you show a scenario.

Editing a Scenario

Change the values associated with a scenario by opening the Scenario Manager dialog box, clicking the name of the scenario that contains the values you want to change, and then clicking the Edit button. At the Edit Scenario dialog box, make any desired changes to the scenario name and/or changing cells and click OK to open the Scenario Values dialog box to edit the individual values associated with each changing cell. Click OK and then click Close when finished editing.

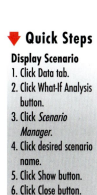

▼ **Quick Steps**

Display Scenario
1. Click Data tab.
2. Click What-If Analysis button.
3. Click *Scenario Manager*.
4. Click desired scenario name.
5. Click Show button.
6. Click Close button.

Deleting a Scenario

To delete a scenario, open the Scenario Manager dialog box, click the scenario you want to remove, click the Delete button, and then click the Close button.

Project 3b **Applying a Scenario's Values to the Worksheet** Part 2 of 3

1. With **EL2-C5-P3-NationalCSDeptBdgt.xlsx** open, apply the scenario containing the values for the low inflation rate assumptions by completing the following steps:
   a. With Data the active tab, click the What-If Analysis button and then click *Scenario Manager* at the drop-down list.
   b. Click *LowInflation* in the *Scenarios* list box and then click the Show button. Excel changes the values in the range C4:C7 to the values stored within the scenario. Notice the total cost of the new budget under a low inflation assumption is $657,085.
2. With the Scenario Manager dialog box still open, change the worksheet to display the high inflation rate assumptions by clicking *HighInflation* in the *Scenarios* list box and then clicking the Show button. Notice the total cost of the new budget under the high inflation assumption is $664,071.
3. Show the worksheet with the *OriginalForecast* scenario's data values.
4. Click the Close button.
5. Save **EL2-C5-P3-NationalCSDeptBdgt.xlsx**.

Step 1b

⬜	A	B	C	D
1	**National Online Marketing Inc.**			
2	**Computing Services Department**			
3		Current budget	Projected increase	New budget
4	Wages and benefits	371,875	15,224	387,099
5	Computer supplies	150,350	2,765	153,115
6	Training and development	63,850	7,236	71,086
7	Other administrative costs	49,576	3,195	52,771
8	Total costs:	635,651		664,071

worksheet with *HighInflation* values shown at Step 2

Quick Steps

Create Scenario Summary Report
1. Click Data tab.
2. Click What-If Analysis button.
3. Click *Scenario Manager*.
4. Click Summary button.
5. If necessary, change cell address in *Result cells* text box.
6. Click OK.

Compiling a Scenario Summary Report

You can create a scenario summary report to compare scenarios side-by-side in a worksheet or a PivotTable. At the Scenario Summary dialog box shown in Figure 5.6 in the *Result cells* text box, enter the formula cell or cells that change by applying the data in the various scenarios. Enter multiple cell addresses in this text box separated by commas.

Figure 5.6 Scenario Summary Dialog Box

Enter the cell address of the cell containing the total or other formula results that is impacted by the changing cells in each scenario. Enter multiple results cell addresses separated by commas.

Project 3c   **Generating a Scenario Summary Report**   Part 3 of 3

1. With **EL2-C5-P3-NationalCSDeptBdgt.xlsx** open, display a scenario summary report by completing the following steps:
   a. With Data the active tab, click the What-If Analysis button and then click *Scenario Manager* at the drop-down list.
   b. Click the Summary button at the Scenario Manager dialog box.
   c. At the Scenario Summary dialog box, with the *Report type* set to *Scenario summary* and the *Result cells* displaying the address *D8*, click OK.

     Step 1c

2. Examine the Scenario Summary sheet added to the workbook. The summary report displays each changing cell with the input values for each scenario. Below the Changing Cells table, Excel displays the Result Cells' values given each scenario's input.

Scenario Summary worksheet created at Step 1

Scenario Summary	Current Values:	LowInflation	HighInflation	OriginalForecast
Changing Cells:				
WageInc	13,016	12,010	15,224	13,016
SuppliesInc	2,255	2,150	2,765	2,255
TrainingInc	6,385	5,276	7,236	6,385
AdminIncrease	2,479	1,998	3,195	2,479
Result Cells:				
TotalNewCosts	659,786	657,085	664,071	659,786

Notes: Current Values column represents values of changing cells at time Scenario Summary Report was created. Changing cells for each scenario are highlighted in gray.

3. Print the Scenario Summary worksheet.
4. Save and then close **EL2-C5-P3-NationalCSDeptBdgt.xlsx**.

Project 4   **Compare Impact of Various Inputs Related to Cost and Sales Pricing**   **2 Parts**

Using a one-variable and a two-variable data table, you will analyze the impact on the cost per unit and selling price per unit of a manufactured container.

Performing What-If Analysis Using Data Tables ■■■■■■■

Data Table

A ***data table*** is a range of cells that contains a series of input values. Excel calculates a formula substituting each input value in the data table range and places the result in the cell adjacent to the value. You can create a one-variable and a two-variable data table. A one-variable data table calculates a formula by modifying one input value in the formula. A two-variable data table calculates a formula substituting two input values. Data tables provide a means to analyze various outcomes in a calculation that occur as a result of changing a dependent value without creating multiple formulas.

▼ Quick Steps

Create One-Variable Data Table
1. Create variable data in column at right of worksheet.
2. Enter formula one row above and one cell right of variable data.
3. Select data range including formula cell.
4. Click Data tab.
5. Click What-If Analysis button.
6. Click *Data Table.*
7. Type cell address for variable data in source formula in *Column input cell* text box.
8. Press Enter or click OK.

Creating a One-Variable Data Table

Design a one-variable data table with the variable input data values either in a series down a column or across a row. Examine the worksheet shown in Figure 5.7. Assume that management wants to calculate the effects on the cost per unit for a variety of production volumes given a standard set of costs per factory shift. The worksheet includes the total costs for direct materials, direct labor, and overhead.

The formula in B8 sums the three cost categories. Based on a standard production volume of 500,000 units, the cost per unit is $3.21, calculated by dividing the total cost by the production volume (B8/B10). In E6:E12, the factory manager has input varying levels of production. The manager would like to see the change in the cost per unit for each level of production volume assuming the costs remain the same. In Project 4a, you will use a data table to show the various costs. This data table will manipulate one input value, production volume; therefore, the table is a one-variable data table.

Figure 5.7 Project 4a One-Variable Data Table

	A	B	C	D	E	F	G	H
1		**Precision Design and Packaging**						
2		**Cost Price Analysis**						
3		**"E" Container Bulk Cargo Box**						
4	**Factory costs per shift**				**Variable unit production impact on cost**			
5	Direct materials	$ 580,000						
6	Direct labor	880,552			425,000			
7	Overhead	145,350			450,000	In this area of the worksheet,		
8	Total cost	$ 1,605,902			475,000	you can calculate the change		
9					500,000	in cost per unit based on		
10	Standard production	500,000	units		525,000	varying the production		
11					550,000	volume using a data table.		
12	Cost per unit	$ 3.21			575,000			

1. Open **PrecisionEBoxCost.xlsx**.
2. Save the workbook with Save As and name it **EL2-C5-P4-PrecisionEBoxCost**.
3. Calculate the cost per unit for seven different production levels using a one-variable data table by completing the following steps:
   a. A data table requires that the formula for calculating the various outcomes be placed in the cell in the first row above and one column right of the table values. The data table's values have been entered in E6:E12; therefore, make F5 the active cell.

   b. The formula that calculates the cost per unit is =B8/B10. This formula has already been entered in B12. Link to the source formula by typing **=b12** and then pressing Enter.

			Variable unit production impact on cost
$	580,000		=b12
	880,552	425,000	
	145,350	450,000	
$	1,605,902	475,000	
		500,000	
	500,000	units	525,000
			550,000
$	3.21	575,000	

Step 3b

   c. Select E5:F12.
   d. Click the Data tab.
   e. Click the What-If Analysis button and then click *Data Table* at the drop-down list.

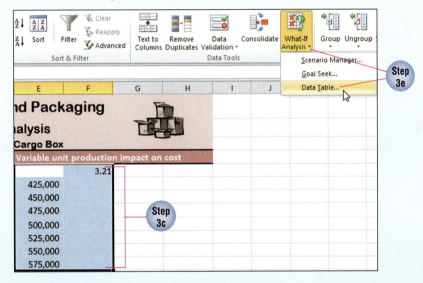

Step 3e

Step 3c

   f. At the Data Table dialog box, click in the *Column input cell* text box, type **b10**, and then press Enter or click OK. At the Data Table dialog box, Excel needs to know which reference in the source formula is the address for which the variable data is to be inserted. (The production volume is B10 in the source formula.)

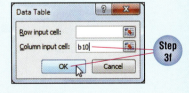

Step 3f

   g. Click in any cell to deselect the range.
4. Print the worksheet.
5. Save and then close **EL2-C5-P4-PrecisionEBoxCost.xlsx**.

Variable unit production impact on cost	
	3.21
425,000	3.78
450,000	3.57
475,000	3.38
500,000	3.21
525,000	3.06
550,000	2.92
575,000	2.79

Costs are calculated by the data table at each production volume. Notice the costs are higher at lower volumes and decrease as production volume increases.

Create Two-Variable Data Table

1. Create variable data at right of worksheet with one input series in a column and another in a row across the top of the table.
2. Enter formula in top left cell of table.
3. Select data table range.
4. Click Data tab.
5. Click What-If Analysis button.
6. Click *Data Table*.
7. Type cell address for variable data in source formula in *Row input cell* text box.
8. Press Tab.
9. Type cell address for variable data in source formula in *Column input cell* text box.
10. Press Enter or click OK.

Creating a Two-Variable Data Table

A data table can substitute two variables in a source formula. To modify two input cells, design the data table with a column along the left containing one set of variable input values and a row along the top of the table containing the second set of variable input values. In a two-variable data table, the source formula is placed at the top left cell in the table. In the worksheet shown in Figure 5.8, the source formula will be inserted in E5, which is the top left cell in the data table.

Figure 5.8 Project 4b Two-Variable Data Table

	A	B	C	D	E	F	G	H
1			**Precision Design and Packaging**					
2			**Selling Price Analysis at Variable Production and Markups**					
3			**"E" Container Bulk Cargo Box**					
4	Factory costs per shift				Variable unit production impact on sell price			
5	Direct materials	$ 580,000				50%	52%	55%
6	Direct labor	880,552			425,000			
7	Overhead	145,350			450,000			
8	Total cost	$ 1,605,902			475,000			
9					500,000			
10	Standard production	500,000	units		525,000			
11					550,000			
12	Cost per unit	$ 3.21			575,000			
13	Markup	52%						
14	Selling price per unit	$ 4.88						

This data table contains two input variables—production units and markup percentage. The data table will calculate a selling price at each production volume and at each markup percentage.

Project 4b   Creating a Two-Variable Data Table   Part 2 of 2

1. Open **PrecisionEBoxSell.xlsx**.
2. Save the workbook with Save As and name it **EL2-C5-P4-PrecisionEBoxSell**.
3. Calculate the selling price per unit for seven different production levels and three different markups using a two-variable data table by completing the following steps:
   a. In a two-variable data table, Excel requires the source formula in the top left cell in the data table; therefore, make E5 the active cell.
   b. Type **=b14** and press Enter. The formula that you want Excel to use to create the data table is in B14. The selling price is calculated by adding to the cost per unit (B12) an amount equal to the cost per unit times the markup percentage (B13).

			Variable unit
$	580,000		=b14
	880,552		425,000
	145,350		450,000
$	1,605,902		475,000
			500,000
	500,000	units	525,000
			550,000
$	3.21		575,000
	52%		
$	4.88		

Step 3b

   c. Select E5:H12.

d. Click the Data tab.

e. Click the What-If Analysis button and then click *Data Table* at the drop-down list.

f. At the Data Table dialog box with the insertion point positioned in the *Row input cell* text box, type **b13** and press Tab. Excel needs to know which reference in the source formula is the address relating to the variable data in the first row of the data table. (The markup value is in B13 in the source formula.)

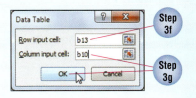

Step 3f

Step 3g

g. Type **b10** in the *Column input cell* text box and then press Enter or click OK. As in Project 4a, Excel needs to know which reference relates to the production volume in the source formula.

h. Click in any cell to deselect the range.

Variable unit production impact on sell price			
$ 4.88	50%	52%	55%
425,000	5.67	5.74	5.86
450,000	5.35	5.42	5.53
475,000	5.07	5.14	5.24
500,000	4.82	4.88	4.98
525,000	4.59	4.65	4.74
550,000	4.38	4.44	4.53
575,000	4.19	4.25	4.33

Selling prices are calculated by the data table at each production volume and at each percentage markup.

4. Print the worksheet.

5. Save and then close **EL2-C5-P4-PrecisionEBoxSell.xlsx**.

Project 5 Audit a Worksheet to View and Troubleshoot Formulas
3 Parts

You will use buttons in the Formula Auditing group to view relationships between cells that comprise a formula, identify error codes in a worksheet, and troubleshoot errors using error checking tools.

Using Auditing Tools

The Formula Auditing group in the Formulas tab shown in Figure 5.9 contains buttons that are useful for viewing relationships between cells in formulas. Checking a formula for accuracy can be difficult when the formula is part of a complex sequence of operations. Opening a worksheet created by someone else can also present a challenge in understanding the relationships between sets of data. When Excel displays an error message in a cell, viewing the relationships between the dependencies of cells assists with finding the source of the error.

▼ **Quick Steps**

Trace Precedent Cells
1. Open worksheet.
2. Make desired cell active.
3. Click Formulas tab.
4. Click Trace Precedents button.
5. Continue clicking until all relationships are visible.

Trace Dependent Cells
1. Open worksheet.
2. Make desired cell active.
3. Click Formulas tab.
4. Click Trace Dependents button.
5. Continue clicking until all relationships are visible.

Figure 5.9 Formula Auditing Group in Formulas Tab

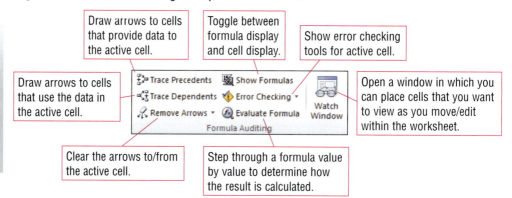

Draw arrows to cells that provide data to the active cell.

Toggle between formula display and cell display.

Show error checking tools for active cell.

Draw arrows to cells that use the data in the active cell.

Open a window in which you can place cells that you want to view as you move/edit within the worksheet.

Clear the arrows to/from the active cell.

Step through a formula value by value to determine how the result is calculated.

Trace Precedents and Trace Dependents

Trace Precedents

Trace Dependents

Remove Arrows

Show Formulas

Precedent cells are cells that provide data to a formula cell. For example, if cell B3 contains the formula =B1+B2, cell B1 and cell B2 are precedent cells. Dependent cells are cells that contain a formula that refers to other cells. In the previous example, cell B3 would be the dependent cell to cells B1 and B2 since B3 relies on the data from cells B1 and B2. Click a cell and click the Trace Precedents button to draw tracer arrows that show direct relationships to cell(s) that provide data to the active cell. Click the button a second time to show indirect relationships to cell(s) that provide data to the active cell at the next level. Continue clicking the button until no further arrows are drawn. Excel will sound a beep when you click the button if no more relationships exist.

Click a cell and click the Trace Dependents button to draw tracer arrows that show direct relationships to other cell(s) in the worksheet that use the active cell's contents. As with the Trace Precedents button, you can click a second time to show the next level of indirect relationships and continue clicking the button until no further tracer arrows are drawn.

Excel draws blue tracer arrows if no error is detected in the active cell and red tracer arrows if an error condition is detected within the active cell.

Project 5a **Viewing Relationships between Cells and Formulas** Part 1 of 3

1. Open **EL2-C5-P4-PrecisionEBoxSell.xlsx**.
2. View relationships between cells and formulas by displaying tracer arrows between cells by completing the following steps:
   a. Make B8 the active cell.
   b. Click the Formulas tab.
   c. Click the Trace Precedents button in the Formula Auditing group. Excel draws a blue tracer arrow that shows the cells that provide data to B8.
   d. Click the Remove Arrows button in the Formula Auditing group. The blue tracer arrow leading to B8 is cleared.
   e. Make B14 the active cell.

blue precedent arrow drawn to B8 at Step 2c

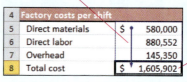

4	Factory costs per shift		
5	Direct materials	$	580,000
6	Direct labor		880,552
7	Overhead		145,350
8	Total cost	$	1,605,902

Step 2a

f. Click the Trace Precedents button.

g. Click the Trace Precedents button a second time to show the next level of cells that provide data to B14.

h. Click the Trace Dependents button to view other cell(s) dependent on B14.

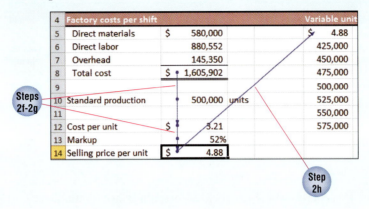

3. Click the Remove Arrows button to clear all of the arrows.

4. Click the Show Formulas button to display cell formulas. Click the Show Formulas button again to turn off the display of formulas.

5. Close **EL2-C5-P4-PrecisionEBoxSell.xlsx**. Click Don't Save when prompted to save changes.

Troubleshooting Formulas

Formulas in Excel can contain various types of errors. Some errors are obvious because Excel displays an error message such as *#VALUE!*. Other errors can occur that do not display error messages but are incorrect because the logic is flawed. For example, you could enter a formula in a cell which Excel does not flag as an error because the syntax is correct; however, the calculation could be incorrect for the data and the situation. Logic errors are difficult to find and require that you check a worksheet by entering proof formulas or by individually checking accuracy. A ***proof formula*** is a formula entered outside the main worksheet area that checks key figures within the worksheet. For example, in a payroll worksheet, a proof formula to check the total net pay column could add the total net pay to the totals of all of the deduction columns. The total displayed should be equal to the total gross pay amount in the worksheet.

Excel displays an error message code in a cell which is detected to have an error. Two types of error flags can occur. A green diagonal triangle in the upper left corner of a cell indicates an error condition. Activate the cell with the green triangle and an error checking button displays with which you can access error checking tools. Other cells indicate an error by displaying an entry such as *#NAME?*. Figure 5.10 displays a portion of the worksheet you will use in Project 5b to troubleshoot errors. Table 5.1 describes the three error codes that are displayed in Figure 5.10.

HINT

Reference errors can also occur—the formula uses correct syntax and logic but refers to the wrong data. These errors are difficult to find and only a thorough review and test of key figures reveal their existence.

▼ **Quick Steps**

Trace Errors
1. Click cell containing error message.
2. Click Formulas tab.
3. Click down-pointing arrow on Error Checking button.
4. Click *Trace Error*.

Figure 5.10 Project 5b Partial Worksheet

	A	B	C	D	E	F	G	H	I	J	K
1		**Precision Design and Packaging**									
2		Bulk Container 2014 Sales Target by Region (in millions)									
3	Model Number	Description	Base	East	West	North	South	Total		Sales Target Assumptions	
4	PD-1140	Gaylord with lid	2.75	#NAME?	#N/A	2.81	2.80	#NAME?		East	1.50%
5	PD-2185	Premium Gaylord with lid	2.14	#VALUE!	#VALUE!	#VALUE!	#VALUE!	#VALUE!		West	#N/A
6	PD-1150	Gaylord bottom	2.33	#NAME?	#N/A	2.38	2.37	#NAME?		North	2.15%
7	PD-1155	Gaylord lid	1.85	#NAME?	#N/A	1.89	1.88	#NAME?		South	1.75%
8	PD-3695	Telescoping top and bottom	2.45	#NAME?	#N/A	2.50	2.49	#NAME?			
9	PD-3698	Telescoping bottom	2.96	#NAME?	#N/A	3.02	3.01	#NAME?			

Table 5.1 Error Codes in Worksheet Shown in Figure 5.10

Error Code	Description of Error Condition
#N/A	A required value for the formula is not available.
#NAME?	This error code indicates the formula contains an unrecognized entry.
#VALUE!	A value within the formula is of the wrong type or is otherwise invalid.

Error Checking

Evaluate Formula

The Error Checking button in the Formula Auditing group can be used to assist with finding the source of an error condition in a cell by displaying the Error Checking dialog box or by drawing a red tracer arrow to locate the source cell that is contributing to the error. The Evaluate Formula button can be used to step through a formula value by value to determine the position within the formula where an error exists.

Project 5b Troubleshooting Formulas Part 2 of 3

1. Open **PrecisionSalesTrgt.xlsx**.
2. Save the workbook with Save As and name it **EL2-C5-P5-PrecisionSalesTrgt**.
3. Solve the #N/A error by completing the following steps:
   a. Make E4 the active cell.
   b. Point to the Trace Error button that displays next to the cell and read the ScreenTip that displays below the button.
   c. Look in the Formula bar at the formula that has been entered into the cell. Notice that the formula includes a reference to a named cell. You decide to use the tracer arrows to locate the source of the named cell.

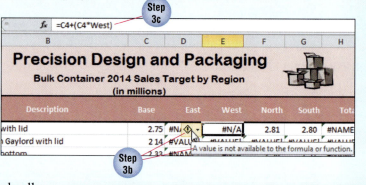

d. Click the down-pointing arrow to the right of the Error Checking button in the Formula Auditing group of the Formulas tab and then click *Trace Error* at the drop-down list. Excel moves the active cell to K5 and draws a red tracer arrow from K5 to E4. Look in the Formula bar and notice that *#N/A* displays as the entry in K5. Also notice the cell name *West* displayed in the *Name* text box. Since a value does not exist in the cell named *West*, which is K5, the dependent cell E4 was not able to calculate its formula.

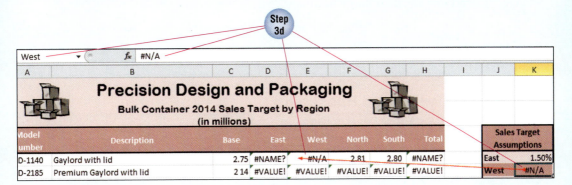

e. With K5 the active cell, type **1.25%** and press Enter. The red tracer arrow changes to blue now that the error is corrected and the #N/A error messages have disappeared.

f. Click the Remove Arrows button to clear the blue tracer arrow, and then right-align the entry in K5.

4. Solve the #NAME? error by completing the following steps:

   a. Make D4 the active cell, point to the Trace Error button that appears, and then read the ScreenTip that appears. The message indicates that the formula contains unrecognized text.

   b. Look at the entry in the Formula bar: *=C4+(C4*East)*. Notice the formula is the same as the formula you reviewed in Step 3c except that the named range is *East* instead of *West*. The formula appears to be valid.

   c. Click the down-pointing arrow to the right of the Name text box and view the range names in the drop-down list. Notice that a range named *East* is not in the list.

   d. Click *North* at the Name drop-down list. The active cell moves to K6. You know from this Step and from Step 3d that the named ranges should reference the percentage values within column K.

   e. Make K4 the active cell, type **East** in the Name text box, and press Enter. The #NAME? error is resolved.

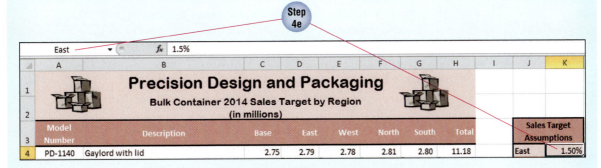

5. Solve the #VALUE! error by completing the following steps:

   a. Make D5 the active cell, point to the Trace Error button that appears, and then read the ScreenTip that appears. The message indicates that a value within the formula is of the wrong type.

b. Click the Trace Precedents button in the Formula Auditing group in the Formulas tab to display tracer arrows showing you the source cells that provide data to D5. Two blue arrows appear indicating two cells provide the source values: K4 and C5.

c. Make K4 the active cell and look at the entry in the Formula bar: *1.5%*. This value is valid.

d. Make C5 the active cell and look at the entry in the Formula bar: *2 14*. Notice there is a space instead of a decimal point between *2* and *1*.

e. Click in the Formula bar and then edit the formula to delete the space between *2* and *1* and type a period to insert a decimal point. Press Enter. The #VALUE! error is resolved.

f. Click the Remove Arrows button to clear the blue tracer arrows.

6. Save **EL2-C5-P5-PrecisionSalesTrgt.xlsx**.

▼ **Quick Steps**

Circle Invalid Data
1. Open worksheet containing validation rules.
2. Click Data tab.
3. Click down-pointing arrow on Data Validation button.
4. Click *Circle Invalid Data*.

Watch a Formula Cell
1. Click Formulas tab.
2. Click Watch Window button.
3. Click Add Watch button.
4. Click desired cell.
5. Click Add button.

Watch Window

Data Validation

Circling Invalid Data

Recall from Chapter 3 that Data Validation is a feature used to restrict entries entered into cells. If data validation rules have been set up after data has been entered, existing values are not tested against the new rules. In this situation, you can use the Circle Invalid Data feature to draw red circles around cells that do not conform to the new rule.

Watching a Formula

In a large worksheet, a dependent cell may not always be visible while you are making changes to other cells that affect a formula. You can open a Watch Window and add a dependent cell to the window so that you can view changes to the cell as you work within the worksheet. You can add multiple cells to the Watch Window providing a single window in which you can keep track of key formulas within a large worksheet.

Consider assigning a name to a cell that you want to track using the Watch Window. At the Watch Window, the cell's name will appear in the *Name* column providing you with a descriptive reference to the entry being watched. You can expand the width of the *Name* column if a range name is not entirely visible.

The Watch Window can be docked to the top, left, bottom, or right edge of the worksheet area by dragging the title bar of the window to the desired edge of the screen. Excel changes the window to a Watch Window task pane.

1. With **EL2-C5-P5-PrecisionSalesTrgt.xlsx** open, view the Data Validation rule in effect for column C by completing the following steps:
   a. If necessary, make any cell containing a value in column C active.
   b. Click the Data tab.
   c. Click the top of the Data Validation button in the Data Tools group. (Do not click the down-pointing arrow on the button.) The Data Validation dialog box opens.
   d. Review the parameters for data entry in the Settings tab. Notice the restriction is that values should be greater than or equal to 1.57.
   e. Click OK.

2. Click the Data Validation button down-pointing arrow and then click *Circle Invalid Data* at the drop-down list. Three cells are circled in the worksheet: C11, C13, and C16.

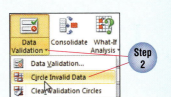

3. Watch the grand total cell update as you correct the invalid data by completing the following steps:
   a. Make H22 the active cell and then click the Formulas tab.
   b. Click the Watch Window button in the Formula Auditing group. A Watch Window opens.
   c. Click the Add Watch button in the Watch Window.
   d. At the Add Watch dialog box, move the dialog box out of the way if necessary to view cell H22. Notice H22 is entered by default as the watch cell. Click the Add button.

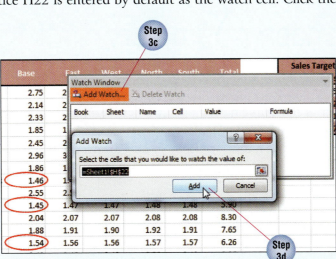

   e. Scroll up the worksheet if necessary until you can view C11. If necessary, drag the Watch Window to an out-of-the-way location in the worksheet.
   f. Make C11 the active cell, type 1.58, and press Enter. Notice the red circle disappears since you have now entered a value that conforms to the validation rule. Look at the value for H22 in the Watch Window. The new value is *153.67*.

g. Make C13 the active cell, type **1.61**, and press Enter. Look at the updated value for H22 in the Watch Window.

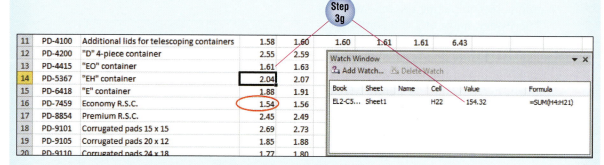

Step 3g

h. Make C16 the active cell, type **1.57**, and press Enter.
i. Click the Watch Window button to close the Watch Window.
4. Print the worksheet.
5. Save and then close **EL2-C5-P5-PrecisionSalesTrgt.xlsx**.

Checking a worksheet for accuracy using auditing and error checking tools is an important skill to develop. Worksheets provide critical information to decision-makers who rely on the validity of the data. After completing a worksheet, examine it carefully, looking for data entry mistakes, values that do not appear realistic, or other indications of potential errors that should be checked.

Chapter Summary

- Open the Paste Special dialog box to paste attributes of the source cell(s), or perform a mathematical operation during the paste.

- Transposing data during a paste routine means that data arranged in columns is converted to a row arrangement and rows are converted to columns.

- Click the Paste button arrow and then click *Paste Special* to access paste special options.

- The Goal Seek feature returns a value in a cell based on a target value you specify for another cell. The two cells must have a dependent relationship for Excel to calculate a value.

- Click the What-If Analysis button in the Data Tools group of the Data tab to locate the Goal Seek, the Scenario Manager, or the Data Table command.

- Scenario Manager allows you to save multiple sets of values for key cells in a worksheet. Switch between scenarios to view the impact of changing the input cells to one of the worksheet's saved data sets.

- A scenario summary report presents the input data for each key cell in a scenario in a tabular format with a results cell below each data set displaying the value if the data set is applied.

- A data table is a range of cells containing a series of input values with a calculated formula result adjacent to each input value.

- A one-variable data table modifies one input value within a formula.

- A two-variable data table modifies two input values within a formula.

- Design a one-variable data table with the input values in a columnar arrangement and the formula cell one row above and one column right of the input values.

- Design a two-variable data table with one set of input values in a columnar arrangement and the other set of input values starting in the first column right and first row above the first set of values. Add the formula cell to the top left cell within the input table.

- Buttons in the Formula Auditing group of the Formulas tab allow you to view relationships between cells and find and resolve errors.

- Use the Trace Precedents button to draw tracer arrows to cells that feed data into the active cell.

- Use the Trace Dependents button to draw tracer arrows to cells that use data from the active cell.

- Click the Trace Precedents or Trace Dependents button a second time to display an indirect set of relationship arrows at the next level.

- Logic errors occur when the formula is not correct for the data or the situation.

- Reference errors occur when a formula points to the wrong data cell.

- Use proof formulas to test the accuracy of key figures in a worksheet. A proof formula is entered outside the main worksheet area and double-checks data within the worksheet.

- Excel displays two types of error flags in a cell where an error has been detected.

- A green diagonal triangle in the upper left corner of the cell indicates an error is presumed. Click the active cell and use the Trace Error button to access error checking options.

- Error codes within a cell also indicate an error. For example, #NAME? means that the formula contains text that Excel cannot recognize.

- Other error codes include #VALUE?, which means a value within the formula is not valid, and #N/A, which means a value needed by the formula is not available.

- When a worksheet has data validation rules in force, data that was in existence before the rule was created is not tested. Use the Circle Invalid Data feature from the Data Validation button to place red circles around cells that do not test correct with the new rule.

- A Watch Window is a window that remains visible in the worksheet area while you scroll and edit other parts of a large worksheet. Add cells to the Watch Window that you want to keep an eye on while you make changes.

- After completing a worksheet, take time to examine the data carefully for data entry errors or logic errors that could impact the results.

Commands Review

FEATURE	RIBBON TAB, GROUP	BUTTON
Circle Invalid Data	Data, Data Tools	
Data Table	Data, Data Tools	
Goal Seek	Data, Data Tools	
Paste Special	Home, Clipboard	
Remove tracer arrows	Formulas, Formula Auditing	
Scenario Manager	Data, Data Tools	
Trace Dependents	Formulas, Formula Auditing	
Trace Error	Formulas, Formula Auditing	
Trace Precedents	Formulas, Formula Auditing	
Transpose	Home, Clipboard	
Watch Window	Formulas, Formula Auditing	

Concepts Check Test Your Knowledge

Completion: In the space provided at the right, indicate the correct term, command, or number.

1. This option from the Paste drop-down gallery will convert columns to rows and rows to columns.

2. Open this dialog box to perform a mathematical operation while pasting the copied range to the destination cells.

3. Use this feature if you know the end result you want to obtain but are not sure what input value you need to achieve the end value.

4. This feature allows you to store various sets of data for specified cells under a name.

5. This report compares various saved data sets side-by-side so you can view all of the results in one page.

6. A one-variable data table requires the formula to be entered at this location within the data table range.   _____

7. In a two-variable data table, the source formula is entered at this location within the data table range.   _____

8. The Data Table feature is accessed from this button.   _____

9. Click this button to draw arrows to cells that feed data into the active cell.   _____

10. Click this button to draw arrows to cells that use the data in the active cell.   _____

11. This button in the Formula Auditing group can be used to assist with locating the source cell that is causing an error code.   _____

12. This error code indicates that a value needed to calculate the formula result is not available.   _____

13. This type of error occurs when the formula has correct syntax but is not correct for the data or the situation.   _____

14. This type of formula is entered outside the main worksheet area and is used to check key figures within the worksheet.   _____

15. Use this feature to test existing data in a worksheet that has had a new data validation rule created.   _____

Skills Check Assess Your Performance

Assessment

1 CONVERT COLUMNS TO ROWS; ADD SOURCE CELLS TO DESTINATION CELLS; FILTER

1. Open **CutRateCars.xlsx**.
2. Save the workbook with Save As and name it **EL2-C5-A1-CutRateCars**.
3. Copy and paste A4:F12 below the worksheet, converting the data arrangement so that the columns become rows and vice versa.
4. Delete the original source data rows from the worksheet.
5. Adjust the merge and centering of the title rows across the top of the worksheet, adjust column widths as desired, and change any other formatting options you think would improve the appearance of the revised worksheet.
6. Copy the values in the *Shipping* column. Paste the values to the *Total Cost* values using an Add operation so that the Total Cost now includes the shipping fee.
7. Copy the values in the *Number of Cars* column. Paste the values to the *Total Cost* values using a Divide operation. Change the column heading from *Total Cost* to *Cost Per Car*. Adjust the column width as needed.

8. The values in the *Compact* column have a validation rule that you want to duplicate in the *Mid-Size* and *SUV* columns. Copy the *Compact* values and paste only the validation rule to the *Mid-Size* and *SUV* columns.
9. Save, print, and then close **EL2-C5-A1-CutRateCars.xlsx**.

Assessment

2 USE GOAL SEEK

1. Open **NationalCSDeptBdgt.xlsx**.
2. Save the workbook with Save As and name it **EL2-C5-A2-NationalCSDeptBdgt**.
3. Make D8 the active cell and open the Goal Seek dialog box.
4. Find the projected increase for *Wages and benefits* that will make the total cost of the new budget equal $655,000.
5. Accept the solution Goal Seek calculates.
6. Save, print, and then close **EL2-C5-A2-NationalCSDeptBdgt.xlsx**.

Assessment

3 USE SCENARIO MANAGER

1. Open **PrecisionCdnTarget.xlsx**.
2. Save the workbook with Save As and name it **EL2-C5-A3-PrecisionCdnTarget**.
3. Create scenarios to save various percentage data sets for the four regions using the following information:
   a. A scenario named *OriginalTarget* that stores the current values in K4:K7.
   b. A scenario named *LowSales* with the following values:

East	*.20*
West	*.32*
Ontario	*.48*
Quebec	*.37*

   c. A scenario named *HighSales* with the following values:

East	*.36*
West	*.58*
Ontario	*.77*
Quebec	*.63*

4. Apply the *LowSales* scenario and then print the worksheet.
5. Edit the *HighSales* scenario to change the Ontario value from *0.77* to *.73*. **Hint: After selecting the scenario name and clicking the Edit button, click OK at the Edit Scenario dialog box to show the scenario values.**
6. Create a scenario summary report displaying H18 as the result cell.
7. Print the Scenario Summary sheet.
8. Save and then close **EL2-C5-A3-PrecisionCdnTarget.xlsx**.

Assessment

4 CREATE A TWO-VARIABLE DATA TABLE

1. Open **NationalCSDeptHlpDsk.xlsx**.
2. Save the workbook with Save As and name it
   EL2-C5-A4-NationalCSDeptHlpDsk.
3. Create a two-variable data table that will calculate the average cost per
   call in the data table for each level of total call minutes logged and at each
   average cost per minute.
4. Format the average costs to display two decimal places.
5. Save, print, and then close **EL2-C5-A4-NationalCSDeptHlpDsk.xlsx**.

Assessment

5 FIND AND CORRECT FORMULA ERRORS

1. Open **NationalCSDeptCapital.xlsx**.
2. Save the workbook with Save As and name it
   EL2-C5-A5-NationalCSDeptCapital.
3. Make D19 the active cell and use the Trace Error feature to draw red tracer
   arrows to find the source cell creating the #N/A error.
4. The CS department manager advises the cost of a Pix firewall is $4,720.00.
   Enter this data in the appropriate cell to correct the #N/A error.
5. Remove the tracer arrows.
6. The worksheet contains a logic error in one of the formulas. Find and
   correct the error.
7. Save, print, and then close **EL2-C5-A5-NationalCSDeptCapital.xlsx**.

Visual Benchmark Demonstrate Your Proficiency

1 FIND THE BASE HOURLY RATE FOR DRUM LESSONS

1. Open **DrumStudioLessons.xlsx**.
2. Save the workbook with Save As and name it
   EL2-C5-VB1-DrumStudioLessons.
3. The current worksheet is shown in Figure 5.11. The hourly rates in
   B5:B13 are linked to the cell named *BaseRate* which is located in B16.
   Intermediate-level and advanced-level lessons have $4 and $8 added to the
   hourly base rate.
4. The drum teacher wants to earn $2,645.50 per month from drum lessons
   (instead of the current total of $2,292.00). Use Goal Seek to change the
   base hourly rate to the required value needed to reach the drum teacher's
   target.
5. Save, print, and then close **EL2-C5-VB1-DrumStudioLessons.xlsx**.

Figure 5.11 Visual Benchmark

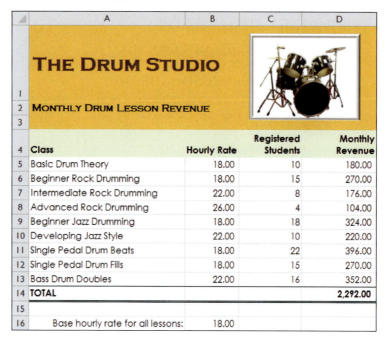

2 CREATE SCENARIOS FOR DRUM LESSON REVENUE

1. Open **DrumStudioLessons.xlsx**.
2. Save the workbook with Save As and name it **EL2-C5-VB2-DrumStudioLessons**.
3. The drum teacher has decided to create three models for an increase in the base hourly rate charged for drum lessons before she decides which base rate to use for next year. Examine the Scenario Summary report shown in Figure 5.12. Create three scenarios to save the hourly base rates shown: Low Rate Increase, Mid Rate Increase, and High Rate Increase.
4. Generate the Scenario Summary report to show the monthly revenue for all classes at the three hourly base rates.
5. Format the report by changing fill color and font color and adding the descriptive text in row 7. Use your best judgment to match the colors shown in Figure 5.12.
6. Edit the Notes text in B20 so that the sentence correctly references the highlighted color for changing cells.
7. Print the Scenario Summary worksheet.
8. Save and then close **EL2-C5-VB2-DrumStudioLessons.xlsx**.

Figure 5.12 Visual Benchmark

	A	B	C	D	E	F	G
1							
2		**Scenario Summary**					
3				Current Values:	Low Rate Increase	Mid Rate Increase	High Rate Increase
5		Changing Cells:					
6		BaseRate		18.00	20.00	22.00	24.00
7		Result Cells:		*Monthly revenue for each lesson assuming no change in number of registered students*			
8		BasicTheory		180.00	200.00	220.00	240.00
9		BegRock		270.00	300.00	330.00	360.00
10		IntRock		176.00	192.00	208.00	224.00
11		AdvRock		104.00	112.00	120.00	128.00
12		BegJazz		324.00	360.00	396.00	432.00
13		DevJazz		220.00	240.00	260.00	280.00
14		SinglePedalBeats		396.00	440.00	484.00	528.00
15		SinglePedalFills		270.00	300.00	330.00	360.00
16		BassDoubles		352.00	384.00	416.00	448.00
17		MonthlyRevTotal		2,292.00	2,528.00	2,764.00	3,000.00
18		Notes: Current Values column represents values of changing cells at					
19		time Scenario Summary Report was created. Changing cells for each					
20		scenario are highlighted in green.					

Case Study Apply Your Skills

Part 1

Yolanda Robertson is continuing her work on the marketing information package for prospective new franchise owners. She has sent you a workbook named **PizzaByMarioStartup.xlsx**. The workbook contains information on the estimated capital investment required to start up a new franchise along with estimated sales and profits for the first year. The workbook calculates the number of months in which a new franchisee can expect to recoup his or her investment based on estimated sales and profits for the first year. Yolanda wants you to apply what-if analysis to find out the value that is needed for projected sales in Year 1 in order to pay back the initial investment in 12 months (instead of 17). Accept the proposed solution and use Save As to name the revised workbook **EL2-C5-CS-P1-PizzaByMarioStartup**. Print the worksheet.

Part 2

After reviewing the printout from Part 1, Yolanda is concerned that the revised sales figure is not attainable in the first year. Restore the sales for year 1 to the original value of $485,000. Yolanda has created the following three models for the startup investment worksheet.

Item	Conservative	Optimistic	Aggressive
Projected Sales	$450,000	$590,000	$615,000
Profit Percent	20%	22%	18%

Yolanda would like you to set up the worksheet to save each of these models. *Hint: Use a comma to separate two cell references as the changing cells*. Create a report that shows Yolanda the input variables for each model and the impact of each on the number of months to recoup the initial investment. Save the revised workbook as **EL2-C5-CS-P2-PizzaByMarioStartup**. Print the summary report. Switch to the worksheet and show the model that reduces the number of months to recoup the initial investment to the lowest value. Print the worksheet. Save **EL2-C5-CS-P2-PizzaByMarioStartup**.

Part 3

Yolanda would like you to check each formula in the worksheet to make sure the formulas are accurate before submitting this worksheet to the client. Since you did not create this worksheet, you decide to check if there is a feature in Excel that navigates to formula cells automatically so that you do not miss any calculated cells. Use the Help feature to find out how to select cells that contain formulas. Based on the information you learned in Help, select the cells within the worksheet that contain formulas and then review each formula cell in the Formula bar to ensure the formula is logically correct. *Hint: When the formula cells are selected as a group, press the Enter key to move to the next formula cell without losing the selection*. When you are finished reviewing the formula cells, type the name of the feature you used in a blank cell below the worksheet and then print the worksheet. Save the revised workbook and name it **EL2-C5-CS-P3-PizzaByMarioStartup**.

Part 4

When meeting with a prospective franchise owner, Yolanda expects that the money required for the initial capital investment will present a challenge for some people that do not have an excellent credit rating. Assume that the owners of Pizza by Mario would be willing to finance the initial investment. Search the Internet for current lending rates for secured credit lines at the bank at which you have an account. In a new worksheet within the workbook, document the current loan rate that you found and the URL of the bank website from which you obtained the rate. Add two percentage points to the lending rate to compensate the owners for the higher risk associated with financing the startup. Create a linked cell in the new worksheet to the Total Estimated Initial Investment in Sheet1. Calculate the monthly loan payment for a term of five years. Add appropriate labels to describe the data and format the worksheet as desired to improve the worksheet appearance. Save the revised workbook and name it **EL2-C5-CS-P4-PizzaByMarioStartup**. Print the loan worksheet.

Protecting and Sharing Workbooks

PERFORMANCE OBJECTIVES

Upon successful completion of Chapter 6, you will be able to:

- Add information to a workbook's properties
- Add comments containing additional information or other notes to the reader
- Share a workbook with other people and view other users who have the shared workbook open at the same time
- Edit a shared workbook and resolve conflicts with changes
- Print a history of changes made to a shared workbook
- Stop sharing a workbook
- Protect cells within a worksheet to prevent changes
- Add a password to open a workbook
- Track changes made to a workbook
- Modify and resolve tracked changes

Tutorials

6.1 Inserting and Editing Comments
6.2 Adding Workbook Properties
6.3 Printing and Editing Comments
6.4 Sharing a Workbook
6.5 Resolving Conflicts in a Shared Workbook
6.6 Protecting and Unprotecting Worksheets
6.7 Protecting and Unprotecting Workbook Structure
6.8 Adding Password Protection to a Workbook
6.9 Tracking Changes

In today's electronic business environment, collaborating with other people on an Excel workbook is becoming commonplace. Excel includes several features and tools which are useful for working in a collaborative environment. Adding information to a workbook's properties provides descriptive information about the nature and purpose of the workbook to other editors. Attaching a comment to a cell allows you to add explanatory information or ask questions when collaborating with others. Sharing a workbook, locking and unlocking worksheets and ranges, and tracking changes are all vital features for managing data accessed by multiple individuals. Through completing the projects in this chapter, you will learn how to use the collaborative tools in Excel. Model answers for this chapter's projects appear on the following page.

Excel2010L2C6

Note: Before beginning the projects, copy to your storage medium the Excel2010L2C6 subfolder from the Excel2010L2 folder on the CD that accompanies this textbook and then make Excel2010L2C6 the active folder.

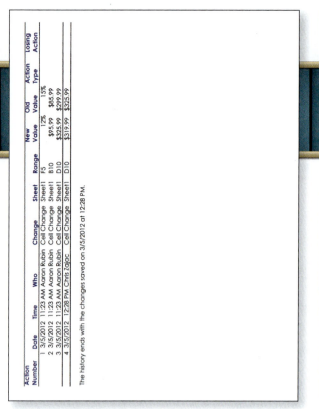

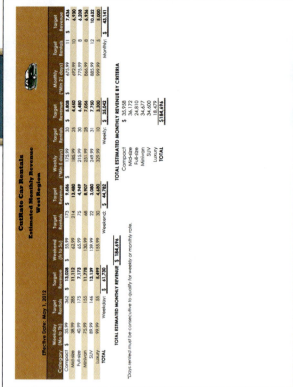

Project 1 Add Workbook Properties, Insert Comments, and Share a Workbook Project 1g, EL2-C6-P1-CutRatePricing-Shared.xlsx History Sheet

Project 3 Track and Resolve Changes Made to a Workbook Project 3c, EL2-C6-P3-CutRateWestRegion.xlsx

roject **1** **Add Workbook Properties, Insert Comments,** **7 Parts** **and Share a Workbook**

You will add the author's name and other descriptive information in a workbook's properties, insert comments with explanatory information, and then share the workbook with other users for editing purposes.

Adding Workbook Properties ■■■■■■■■■ ■■■■■ ■

▼ Quick Steps

Add Information to Properties
1. Click File tab.
2. Click *Add a [property]* next to desired property name.
3. Type desired text.
4. Click outside property box.

Workbook properties include information about the workbook such as the author's name, a title, a subject, a category to which the workbook is related (such as *Finance*), and general comments about the workbook. This information can be added to the file at the Info tab Backstage view shown in Figure 6.1 or by using the Document Information Panel shown in Figure 6.2.

Some information is added to file properties automatically by Microsoft Excel. For example, workbook statistics such as the date the workbook was created, the date the workbook was last modified, and the name of the last person to save the workbook are maintained by Excel. Workbook properties are sometimes referred to as *metadata*. Metadata is a term used to identify descriptive information about data.

Figure 6.1 Properties Pane in the Info Tab Backstage View

Figure 6.2 Document Information Panel

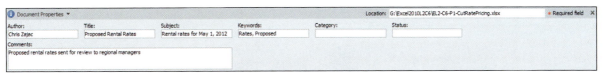

To add an author's name or other descriptive information about a workbook, click the File tab. By default, Excel displays the Info tab Backstage view with the workbook's properties displayed in the right pane. By default, Excel inserts in the *Author* property the name of the computer user (as defined when Microsoft Office is installed) when a new workbook is created. To add another author or make a change to a workbook property (such as Title), click the mouse to open the text box next to the property's name. For example, click over *Add a title* next to the Title property. A text box opens in which you can type the desired title. Click outside the text box to end the entry. Properties that do not display with a message *Add a [property]* cannot be edited. Click the hyperlink Show All Properties at the bottom of the right pane in the Info tab Backstage view to add more properties to the view.

The Document Information Panel shown in Figure 6.2 displays between the ribbon and the worksheet. If you prefer to add or edit properties while viewing the worksheet, open the panel by clicking the Properties button at the top of the right pane in the Info tab Backstage view and then click *Show Document Panel* at the drop-down list.

In Chapter 8, you will learn how to strip metadata including personal information from the file if you do not wish this information to be included when distributing a workbook outside your organization. Personal information can be useful, however, when you are browsing a list. The *Authors*, *Size*, and *Date Modified* appear in a ScreenTip when the mouse pointer rests on a workbook name in the Open dialog box. This information helps you select the correct file.

▼ **Quick Steps**

Add or Edit Properties Using Document Information Panel
1. Click File tab.
2. Click Properties button.
3. Click *Show Document Panel*.
4. Add or edit properties as required.
5. Close Document Information Panel.

1. Open **CutRatePricing.xlsx**.
2. Save the workbook with Save As and name it **EL2-C6-P1-CutRatePricing**.
3. Add an additional author's name, add a title, a subject, and comments to be associated with the workbook by completing the following steps:
   a. Click the File tab.
   b. At the Info tab Backstage view, click *Add an author* below the current author's name in the *Related People* section of the right pane to open an author property box.
   c. Type Chris Zajac.
   d. Click outside the author property box to close it.
   e. Click *Add a title* next to the *Title* property, type Proposed Rental Rates, and then click outside the title property box.
   f. Click the Show All Properties hyperlink at the bottom of the Properties pane to display additional properties.
   g. Click *Specify the subject* next to the *Subject* property, type Rental rates for May 1, 2012, and then click outside the subject property box.
   h. Click *Add comments* next to the *Comments* property, type Proposed rental rates sent for review to regional managers, and then click outside the comments property box.

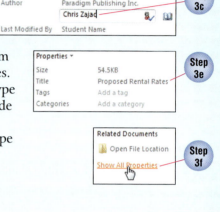

4. Right-click over *Paradigm Publishing Inc.* next to the *Author* property and then click *Remove Person* at the drop-down list.
5. Click the Show Fewer Properties hyperlink at the bottom of the Properties pane.
6. Compare your Properties pane with the one shown in Figure 6.1.

7. View the Document Information Panel and add text to a workbook property by completing the following steps:
   a. Click the Properties button at the top of the Properties pane (located below the miniature Excel worksheet) and then click *Show Document Panel* at the drop-down list. The Info tab Backstage view closes and the Document Information Panel displays between the ribbon and the worksheet. Using this panel you can view the worksheet while adding or modifying properties.
   b. Click in the *Keywords* property box, type Rates, Proposed, and then press Tab.
   c. Compare your Document Information Panel with the one shown in Figure 6.2.

d. Click the Close button located at the top right corner of the Document Information Panel. Be careful to click the Close button within the Document Information Panel and not the Close button located at the top right of the ribbon.

| G:\Excel2010L2C6\EL2-C6-P1-CutRatePricing.xlsx | * Required field | **Step 7d** |
| Status: | Close the Document Information Panel | |

8. Save **EL2-C6-P1-CutRatePricing.xlsx**.

Managing Comments

A *comment* is a pop-up box containing text that displays when the pointer is resting over a cell with an attached comment. Use a comment to provide instructions, identify critical information, or add other explanatory information about the cell entry. A comment is also useful when reviewing a worksheet with coworkers or other people with whom you are collaborating. Comments can be used by each reviewer to add his or her feedback or pose questions about a cell entry or layout.

Inserting a Comment

Insert a comment by clicking the Review tab and then clicking the New Comment button in the Comments group. This displays a shaded box with the user's name inside. Type the comment text and then click in the worksheet area outside the comment box. You can also insert a comment by right-clicking a cell and then clicking *Insert Comment* at the shortcut menu.

Viewing a Comment

A small, red diagonal triangle appears in the upper right corner of a cell alerting the reader that a comment exists. Rest the mouse pointer over a cell containing a comment and the comment box displays. Turn on the display of all comments by clicking the Show All Comments button in the Comments group of the Review tab. Navigate to cells containing a comment by clicking the Next button or the Previous button in the Comments group of the Review tab.

Printing a Comment

By default, comments do not print. If you want comments printed with the worksheet, click the Page Layout tab, click the Page Setup group dialog box launcher, and then click the Sheet tab at the Page Setup dialog box. Click the *Comments* down-pointing arrow and then click either *At end of sheet* to print comments on the page after cell contents, or *As displayed on sheet* to print the comments as they appear within the worksheet area.

Editing and Deleting a Comment

Click a cell containing a comment and then click the Edit Comment button in the Comments group of the Review tab. (The New Comment button changes to the Edit Comment button when the active cell contains a comment.) You can also edit a comment by right-clicking the cell containing the comment and then clicking *Edit Comment* at the shortcut menu. Insert or delete text as desired and then click in the worksheet area outside the comment box.

▼ **Quick Steps**

Insert Comment
1. Make desired cell active.
2. Click Review tab.
3. Click New Comment button.
4. Type comment text.
5. Click in worksheet area outside comment box.

New Comment

Show All Comments

Next

Previous

Edit Comment

Delete

▼ **Quick Steps**

Copy and Paste Comments
1. Select source cell containing comment.
2. Click Copy button.
3. Click destination cell(s).
4. Click Paste button arrow.
5. Click *Paste Special*.
6. Click *Comments*.
7. Click OK.

To delete a comment, click the cell containing the comment and then click the Delete button in the Comments group. You can also delete a comment by right-clicking the cell containing the comment and then clicking *Delete Comment* at the shortcut menu.

Copying and Pasting Comments

A comment that has been added to a cell can be copied and pasted to one or more cells. After copying the source cell, click the destination cell and then open the Paste Special dialog box. Click *Comments* in the *Paste* section and then click OK.

Project 1b **Inserting, Editing, Pasting, Viewing, and Deleting Comments** Part 2 of 7

1. With **EL2-C6-P1-CutRatePricing.xlsx** open, insert comments by completing the following steps:
   a. Make C10 the active cell.
   b. Click the Review tab and then click the New Comment button in the Comments group. A yellow shaded box with a black arrow pointing to C10 appears. The current user name is inserted in bold text at the top of the comment box followed by a colon and the insertion point is positioned at the left edge of the box on the second line.
   c. Type Most competitors charge 175.00 for weekend rentals of luxury vehicles.
   d. Click in the worksheet area outside the comment box. A small red diagonal triangle appears in the upper right corner of C10 indicating a comment exists for the cell.
   e. Right-click F8 and then click *Insert Comment* at the shortcut menu.
   f. Type Consider reducing the discount for minivans to 18% and then click in the worksheet area outside the comment box.
   g. Right-click F9, click *Insert Comment* at the shortcut menu, type Last year this discount was 12%, and then click in the worksheet area outside the comment box.
   h. Right-click F9, click *Copy* at the shortcut menu, right-click F10, point to *Paste Special*, and then click *Paste Special* at the shortcut menu.
   i. At the Paste Special dialog box, click *Comments* in the *Paste* section and then click OK.
   j. Press the Esc key to remove the moving marquee from F9.

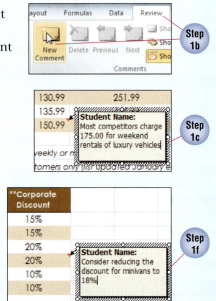

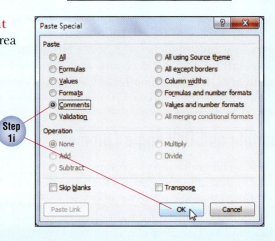

2. View comments by completing the following steps:

   a. Rest the mouse pointer on C10. The comment box pops up displaying the comment text.

   b. Rest the mouse pointer on F8 and then read the comment text that appears in the pop-up box.

   c. Rest the mouse pointer on F9, read the comment text that appears in the pop-up box, rest the mouse pointer on F10, and then read the pasted comment text in the pop-up box.

   d. Press Ctrl + Home to move the active cell to A1.

   e. Click the Next button in the Comments group of the Review tab. Excel displays the comment box in F8.

   f. Click the Next button in the Comments group of the Review tab. Excel displays the comment box in F9.

   g. Click the Next button to display the comment box in C10.

   h. Click Next to display the comment box in F10. Consider using the Next button to view comments in a large worksheet to ensure you do not miss any comment cells.

   i. Click the Show All Comments button in the Comments group of the Review tab. All comment boxes display in the worksheet area.

   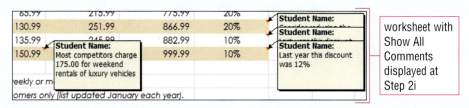

   j. Click the Show All Comments button again to turn off the display of all comments.

3. Edit and delete a comment by completing the following steps:

   a. Right-click C10 and then click *Edit Comment* at the shortcut menu. The comment box pops up with an insertion point positioned at the end of the existing comment text.

   b. Change *175.00* to *168.99* by moving the insertion point and then inserting and deleting text as required.

   c. Click in the worksheet area outside the comment box.

   d. Make F10 the active cell and then click the Edit Comment button in the Comments group of the Review tab.

   e. Change *12%* to *15%* and then click in the worksheet area outside the comment box.

   f. Right-click F8 and then click *Delete Comment* at the shortcut menu.

   g. Click F9 and then click the Delete Comment button in the Comments group in the Review tab.

4. Save **EL2-C6-P1-CutRatePricing.xlsx**.

Quick Steps

Share Workbook
1. Open workbook.
2. Click Review tab.
3. Click Share Workbook button.
4. Click *Allow changes by more than one user at the same time* check box.
5. Click OK to close Share Workbook dialog box.
6. Click OK to continue.

Share
Workbook

Sharing a Workbook

A workbook may need to be circulated among several people so they can review, add, delete, or edit data. One method that is available for collaborating with other users is to share a workbook. A shared workbook is generally saved to a network folder that is accessible by the other individuals that need the file. Excel tracks each person's changes and displays a prompt when conflicts to a cell occur if two people have the file open at the same time and make changes to the same data.

To share a workbook, click the Review tab and then click the Share Workbook button in the Changes group. At the Share Workbook dialog box with the Editing tab active shown in Figure 6.3, click the *Allow changes by more than one user at the same time* check box.

Figure 6.3 Share Workbook Dialog Box with Editing Tab Selected

Clicking this check box allows more than one person to edit a workbook.

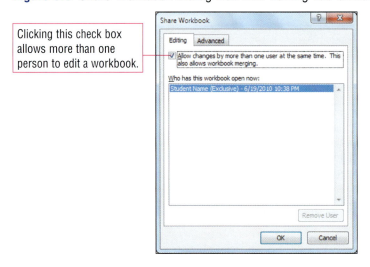

Figure 6.4 Share Workbook Dialog Box with Advanced Tab Selected

Select the options you want to use for tracking, updating, and resolving changes made to a shared workbook using the Advanced tab.

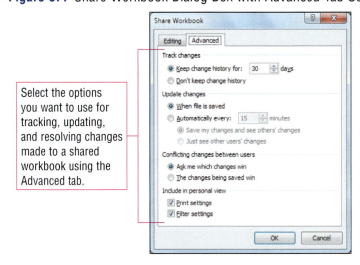

Click the Advanced tab in the Share Workbook dialog box to define the sharing options shown in Figure 6.4. A shared workbook should be saved to a network folder that is designated as a shared folder accessible by the other users. A network administrator is usually the person who creates a folder on a networked server designated with the read/write access rights for multiple accounts (referred to as a *network share*) and can assist you with navigating to and saving to a network share. All individuals with access to the shared network folder have full access to the shared workbook. One drawback of a shared workbook is that it cannot support all Excel features. If you need to use a feature that is unavailable or make a change to a feature that is not allowed, you will first need to remove shared access. In a later section you will learn how to lock/unlock worksheets and cells for editing if you want to protect the worksheet or sections of the worksheet from change before you share the workbook.

▼ Quick Steps

View Other Users of Shared Workbook
1. Open shared workbook.
2. Click Review tab.
3. Click Share Workbook button.
4. Review names in *Who has this workbook open now* list box.
5. Click OK.

Project 1c **Sharing a Workbook** *Part 3 of 7*

1. With **EL2-C6-P1-CutRatePricing.xlsx** open, use Save As to name the workbook **EL2-C6-P1-CutRatePricing-Shared**.
2. Assume that you are Chris Zajac, regional manager of CutRate Car Rentals. You want feedback on the proposed rental rates from another manager. Share the workbook so that the other manager can make changes directly within the file by completing the following steps:
   a. If necessary, click the Review tab.
   b. Click the Share Workbook button in the Changes group.
   c. At the Share Workbook dialog box with the Editing tab selected, click the *Allow changes by more than one user at the same time* check box to insert a check mark.
   d. Click OK.
   e. At the Microsoft Excel message box informing you that the workbook will now be saved and asking if you want to continue, click OK.

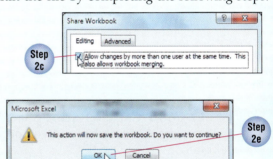

3. Notice that Excel adds *[Shared]* in the Title bar next to the workbook file name to indicate the workbook's status.

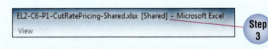

4. Close **EL2-C6-P1-CutRatePricing-Shared.xlsx**.

Changing the User Name

When a workbook is shared, Excel tracks the name of the user who edits a shared workbook. When Microsoft Office is installed, the user name information is entered by the person completing the installation. You can change the user name associated with the copy of Excel by opening the Excel Options dialog box.

▼ Quick Steps

Change User Name
1. Click File tab.
2. Click Options button.
3. Select current entry in *User name* text box.
4. Type new user name.
5. Click OK.

Excel Options

1. At a blank Excel screen, change the user name for the computer you are using to simulate an environment in which another manager is opening the shared workbook from a network share location by completing the following steps:

   a. Click the File tab.

   b. Click the Options button located near the bottom of the left pane at the Recent tab Backstage view.

   c. At the Excel Options dialog box with *General* selected in the left pane, make a note of the existing entry in the *User name* text box in the *Personalize your copy of Microsoft Office* section if the entry is a name other than your name. ***Note: You will be restoring the original user name in Project 1f. If necessary, write the user name down so you do not forget the correct entry.***

   d. Select the current entry in the *User name* text box, type **Aaron Rubin**, and then click OK.

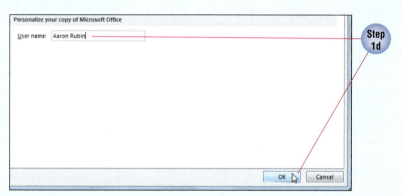

2. Open **EL2-C6-P1-CutRatePricing-Shared.xlsx**.

3. Assume you are Aaron Rubin and you decide to make a few changes to the proposed rental rates.

   a. Make F5 the active cell and change the entry from *15%* to *12%*.

   b. Make B10 the active cell and change the entry from *85.99* to *95.99*.

   c. Make D10 the active cell and change the entry from *299.99* to *325.99*.

4. Save **EL2-C6-P1-CutRatePricing-Shared.xlsx**.

---

1. Start a new copy of Excel by clicking the Start button, clicking *All Programs*, clicking *Microsoft Office*, and then clicking *Microsoft Excel 2010*. ***Note: You are opening another copy of Excel to simulate an environment in which multiple copies of the shared workbook are open. You will also change the user name to continue the simulation using a different identity.***

2. Open the Excel Options dialog box and change the *User name* in the new copy of Excel to *Chris Zajac*. Refer to Project 1d, Steps 1a–1d if you need assistance with this step.

3. In the new copy of Excel, open **EL2-C6-P1-CutRatePricing-Shared.xlsx**.

4. Assume you are Chris Zajac and want to see who else is working on the shared workbook. View other users working on the shared workbook by completing the following steps:

   a. Click the Review tab.

b. Click the Share Workbook button in the Changes group.

c. At the Share Workbook dialog box with the Editing tab selected, look at the names in the *Who has this workbook open now* list box.

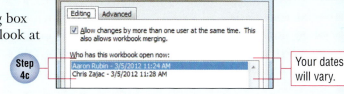

Step 4c

Your dates will vary.

d. Click OK.

5. Leave both copies of Excel open for the next project.

Resolving Conflicts in a Shared Workbook

When two users have a copy of a shared workbook open and each makes a change to the same cell, Excel prompts the second user to resolve the conflict by displaying the Resolve Conflicts dialog box shown in Figure 6.5. The cell address, original entry, and revised entry are shown for each user. You can choose to click the Accept Mine button to save your revision or the Accept Other button to remove your change and restore the cell to the entry made by the other user. Click the Accept All Mine button or the Accept All Others button to avoid being prompted at each individual cell that has a conflict.

▼ **Quick Steps**

Resolving Conflict in Shared Workbook
1. Open shared workbook.
2. Make desired edits.
3. Click Save button.
4. Click Accept Mine or Accept Other button at each conflict.
5. Click OK.

HINT

Open the Share Workbook dialog box and click the Advanced tab to instruct Excel not to display the Resolve Conflicts dialog box by selecting *The changes being saved win* in the *Conflicting changes between users* section.

Figure 6.5 Resolve Conflicts Dialog Box

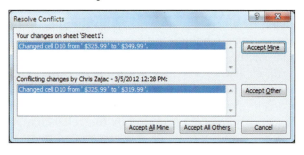

Project 1f **Resolving Conflicts in a Shared Workbook**   **Part 6 of 7**

1. With **EL2-C6-P1-CutRatePricing-Shared.xlsx** open, assume that you are still Chris Zajac and that you decide to make a change to a proposed rental rate which will conflict with a change made by Aaron Rubin.
   a. Make sure the copy of Excel that is active is the second copy you opened for Project 1e in which you viewed the users with the shared workbook open using the identity Chris Zajac.
   b. Make D10 the active cell and change *325.99* to *319.99*.
   c. Save **EL2-C6-P1-CutRatePricing-Shared.xlsx**.
2. Switch to the other copy of Excel using the Taskbar. Assume that Aaron Rubin has decided to change the weekly luxury rate again. Edit the worksheet and resolve the conflict by completing the following steps:
   a. Make D10 the active cell and change the entry to *349.99*.
   b. Click the Save button. Since this change conflicts with the change made by Chris Zajac in Step 1b, Excel prompts the second user with the Resolve Conflicts dialog box.

c. Click the Accept Other button to restore the cell to the value entered by Chris Zajac.

d. At the Microsoft Excel message box informing you that the workbook has been updated with changes saved by other users, click OK.

3. Notice that a cell in which a conflict was resolved is displayed with a colored border. Rest the mouse over D10 to view the pop-up box with the name, date, and time the cell change was saved as well as the original and revised data entries.

4. Exit the active copy of Excel.

5. With the other copy of Excel active, close **EL2-C6-P1-CutRatePricing-Shared.xlsx**.

6. Change the user name back to the name you recorded in Project 1d, Step 1c.

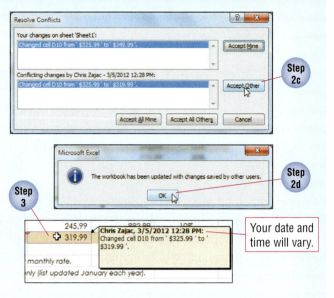

Printing History Sheet and Removing Shared Workbook Access

▼ **Quick Steps**

Print History Sheet
1. Open shared workbook.
2. Click Review tab.
3. Click Track Changes button.
4. Click *Highlight Changes*.
5. Change *When* to *All*.
6. If necessary, clear *Who* check box.
7. If necessary, clear *Where* check box.
8. Click *List changes on a new sheet* check box.
9. Click OK.
10. Print History sheet.

Track Changes

Before changing the status of a shared workbook to an exclusive workbook, consider printing the change history in order to have a record of the workbook's editing actions made by all users who worked on the file. To do this, click the Review tab, click the Track Changes button, and then click *Highlight Changes* at the drop-down list. At the Highlight Changes dialog box shown in Figure 6.6, change *When* to *All*, clear the *Who* and *Where* check boxes, click the *List changes on a new sheet* check box, and then click OK. By default, Excel displays a colored border in changed cells. When you rest the mouse pointer over a cell with a colored border, Excel displays in a pop-up box the cell's change history. Clear the *Highlight changes on screen* check box if you prefer not to highlight changed cells in the worksheet.

To stop sharing a workbook, open the shared workbook, click the Review tab, and then click the Share Workbook button. At the Share Workbook dialog box with the Editing tab selected, clear the check box for *Allow changes by more than one user at the same time*. When you click OK, Excel displays a message box informing you that changing the workbook to exclusive status will erase all of the change history in the workbook and prevent users who might have the workbook open from saving their changes. Consider copying and pasting the cells in the History sheet to a new workbook and saving the history as a separate file since the History sheet is removed when the shared workbook is saved.

Figure 6.6 Highlight Changes Dialog Box

Change this option to *All* to include in the History sheet changes made by all users who accessed the shared workbook.

Click this check box to create a sheet named *History* in the workbook with a list of changes made by each user.

By default, this option is selected, which causes a colored border to display in changed cells. Resting the mouse pointer over a highlighted cell causes a pop-up box to display with the change history.

Before changing a shared workbook's status to exclusive, make sure no one else is currently editing the workbook since once you remove shared access, users with the file open will not be able to save their changes.

▼ **Quick Steps**

Stop Sharing Workbook
1. Open shared workbook.
2. Click Review tab.
3. Click Share Workbook button.
4. Clear *Allow changes by more than one user at the same time* check box.
5. Click OK.
6. Click Yes.

Project 1g Printing the History Sheet and Removing Shared Access to a Workbook

1. Open **EL2-C6-P1-CutRatePricing-Shared.xlsx**.
2. Create a new sheet named *History* and print the record of changes made to the shared workbook by completing the following steps:
   a. If necessary, click the Review tab.
   b. Click the Track Changes button in the Changes group and then click *Highlight Changes* at the drop-down list.
   c. At the Highlight Changes dialog box, click the down-pointing arrow at the right of the *When* list box and then click *All* at the drop-down list.
   d. If necessary, clear the *Who* check box if a check mark is displayed in the box.
   e. If necessary, clear the *Where* check box if a check mark is displayed in the box.
   f. Click the *List changes on a new sheet* check box to insert a check mark and then click OK.
   g. Print the History sheet.

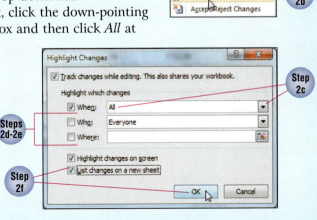

3. Stop sharing the workbook by completing the following steps:
   a. Click the Share Workbook button.
   b. Click the *Allow changes by more than one user at the same time* check box to clear the check mark.
   c. Click OK.

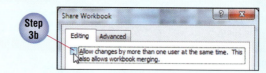

Step 3b

   d. At the Microsoft Excel message box informing you that the workbook will be removed from shared use, click Yes to make the workbook exclusive.

4. Close **EL2-C6-P1-CutRatePricing-Shared.xlsx**.

Step 3d

Project 2 Lock and Unlock a Workbook, a Worksheet, and Ranges

4 Parts

You will protect a worksheet, unlock ranges, prevent changes to the structure of a workbook, and add a password to open a workbook.

▼ Quick Steps

Protect Worksheet
1. Open workbook.
2. Activate desired sheet.
3. Click Review tab.
4. Click Protect Sheet button.
5. Type password to unprotect sheet.
6. Choose allowable actions.
7. Click OK.
8. Retype password.
9. Click OK.

Unlock Cells
1. Select cell(s) to be unlocked.
2. Click Home tab.
3. Click Format button.
4. Click *Lock Cell.*
5. Deselect cell(s).

Format

Protecting and Unprotecting Worksheets

Protecting a worksheet prevents another user from editing cells that you do not want accidentally deleted, modified, or otherwise changed. By default, when a worksheet is protected, each cell in the sheet is locked. This means no one can insert, delete, or modify the content. In most cases, some cells within the worksheet contain data that you want to allow another user to be able to change; therefore, in a collaborative environment, protecting the worksheet generally involves two actions:

1. Clear the lock attribute on those cells that will be allowed to be edited.
2. Protect the worksheet.

To clear the lock attribute (unlock) for the cells that will be allowed to be modified, select the cells, click the Home tab, and then click the Format button in the Cells group. Click *Lock Cell* in the *Protection* section at the drop-down list to turn off the lock attribute. Next, turn on worksheet protection by clicking the Review tab and then clicking the Protect Sheet button in the Changes group. At the Protect Sheet dialog box shown in Figure 6.7, select the actions you want to allow and then click OK. You can also choose to assign a password to unprotect the sheet. Be cautious if you add a password to remove protection since you will not be able to unprotect the worksheet if you forget the password. If necessary, write down the password and store it in a secure location.

Figure 6.7 Protect Sheet Dialog Box

You can choose to add a password that will need to be entered in order to unprotect the worksheet.

Select the actions that users of the protected worksheet can do in this list box.

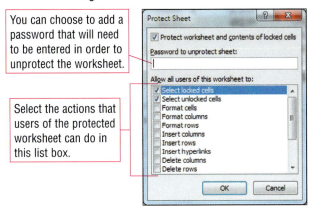

Project 2a Protecting an Entire Worksheet

Part 1 of 4

1. Open **CutRateFinalPrices.xlsx**.
2. Save the workbook with Save As and name it **EL2-C6-P2-CutRateFinalPrices**.
3. Protect the entire FinalPrices worksheet by completing the following steps:
   a. Make sure FinalPrices is the active sheet.
   b. Click the Review tab.
   c. Click the Protect Sheet button in the Changes group.
   d. At the Protect Sheet dialog box with the insertion point positioned in the *Password to unprotect sheet* text box, type **f4R$c** and then click OK.
   e. At the Confirm Password dialog box with the insertion point positioned in the *Reenter password to proceed* text box, type **f4R$c** and then press Enter or click OK.
   f. Make any cell active in the FinalPrices sheet and attempt to delete the data or type new data. Since the entire worksheet is now protected, all cells are locked and Excel displays a message that the cell is read-only. Click OK at the Microsoft Excel message indicating that you need to unprotect the sheet to modify the protected cell.

Step 3d

Step 3e

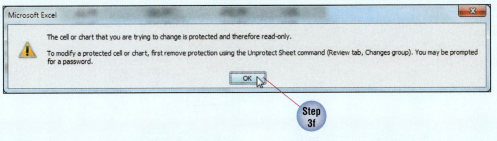

Step 3f

4. Notice the Protect Sheet button changes to the Unprotect Sheet button when a worksheet has been protected.
5. Save **EL2-C6-P2-CutRateFinalPrices.xlsx**.

1. With **EL2-C6-P2-CutRateFinalPrices.xlsx** open, make TargetRevenue the active sheet.
2. Unlock the weekday target rental data cells that you want to allow to be edited by completing the following steps:
   a. Select C5:C10.
   b. Click the Home tab.
   c. Click the Format button in the Cells group.
   d. At the Format button drop-down list, look at the icon next to *Lock Cell* in the *Protection* section. The highlighted icon indicates the lock attribute is turned on.
   e. Click *Lock Cell* at the Format button drop-down list to turn the lock attribute off for the selected range.
   f. Click any cell within the range C5:C10 and click the Format button in the Cells group. Look at the icon next to *Lock Cell* in the drop-down list. The icon is no longer highlighted, indicating the cell is unlocked.

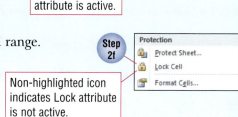

Step 2d — Protection: Protect Sheet..., Lock Cell, Format Cells...
Highlighted icon indicates Lock attribute is active.

Step 2f — Protection: Protect Sheet..., Lock Cell, Format Cells...
Non-highlighted icon indicates Lock attribute is not active.

   g. Click within the worksheet area outside the drop-down list to close the menu.
3. Unlock the remaining target rental ranges to allow the cells to be edited by completing the following steps:
   a. Select F5:F10, hold down the Ctrl key, select I5:I10 and L5:L10.
   b. Click the Format button in the Cells group and then click *Lock Cell* at the drop-down list.
   c. Click any cell to deselect the ranges.
4. Protect the TargetRevenue worksheet by completing the following steps:
   a. Click the Review tab.
   b. Click the Protect Sheet button in the Changes group.
   c. Type **f4R$c** in the *Password to unprotect sheet* text box.
   d. Click OK.
   e. Type **f4R$c** in the *Reenter password to proceed* text box and press Enter or click OK.
5. Save **EL2-C6-P2-CutRateFinalPrices.xlsx**.
6. Test the worksheet protection applied to the TargetRevenue sheet by completing the following steps:
   a. Make B8 the active cell and press the Delete key.
   b. Click OK at the Microsoft Office Excel message box indicating the protected cell is read-only.
   c. Make C8 the active cell and press the Delete key. Since C8 is unlocked, the contents of C8 are deleted and dependent cells are updated.

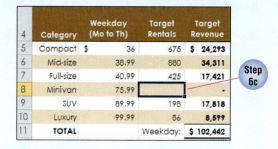

4	Category	Weekday (Mo to Th)	Target Rentals	Target Revenue
5	Compact	$ 36	675	$ 24,293
6	Mid-size	38.99	880	34,311
7	Full-size	40.99	425	17,421
8	Minivan	75.99		·
9	SUV	89.99	198	17,818
10	Luxury	99.99	86	8,599
11	TOTAL		Weekday:	$ 102,442

Step 6c

   d. Click the Undo button on the Quick Access toolbar to restore the contents of C8.
7. Save and then close **EL2-C6-P2-CutRateFinalPrices.xlsx**.

Figure 6.8 Unprotect Sheet Dialog Box

Protect Sheet

Unprotect Sheet

When a worksheet has protection turned on, the Protect Sheet button in the Changes group of the Review tab changes to the Unprotect Sheet button. To remove worksheet protection, click the Unprotect Sheet button. If a password was entered when the worksheet was protected, the Unprotect Sheet dialog box shown in Figure 6.8 appears. Type the password and press Enter or click OK.

Protecting and Unprotecting the Structure of a Workbook

The Protect Workbook button in the Changes group of the Review tab can be used to prevent changes to the structure of a workbook such as inserting a new sheet, deleting a sheet, or unhiding a hidden worksheet. At the Protect Structure and Windows dialog box shown in Figure 6.9 you can also turn on protection for the workbook's windows. Clicking the *Windows* check box prevents a user of the workbook from resizing or changing the position of the windows in the workbook.

As with protecting worksheets, an optional password can be entered that will be required to unprotect the workbook in the future.

▼ **Quick Steps**

Protect Workbook Structure
1. Open workbook.
2. Click Review tab.
3. Click Protect Workbook button.
4. Type optional password if desired.
5. Click OK.
6. Retype optional password if entered at Step 4.
7. Click OK.

Protect Workbook

Figure 6.9 Protect Structure and Windows Dialog Box

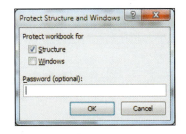

Project 2c **Protecting the Structure of a Workbook**   Part 3 of 4

1. Open **EL2-C6-P2-CutRateFinalPrices.xlsx**.
2. Protect the workbook structure by completing the following steps:
   a. If necessary, click the Review tab.
   b. Click the Protect Workbook button in the Changes group.
   c. At the Protect Structure and Windows dialog box with the insertion point positioned in the *Password (optional)* text box, type **w4R!c** and press Enter or click OK.

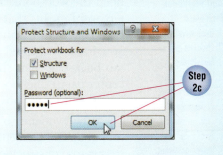

Step 2c

d. At the Confirm Password dialog box with the insertion point positioned in the *Reenter password to proceed* text box, type **w4R!c** and press Enter or click OK.

3. Test the workbook protection by attempting to insert a new worksheet by completing the following steps:

   a. Right-click the TargetRevenue sheet tab.

   b. Look at the shortcut menu. Notice that all of the options related to managing worksheets are dimmed, meaning the options are unavailable.

   c. Click within the worksheet area outside the pop-up list to close the menu.

4. Save **EL2-C6-P2-CutRateFinalPrices.xlsx**.

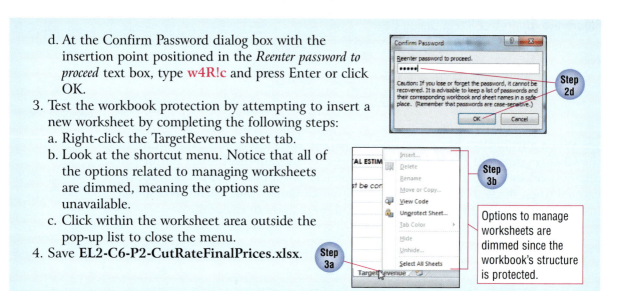

Options to manage worksheets are dimmed since the workbook's structure is protected.

Unprotecting a Workbook

Protected Workbook

When the structure of a workbook has been protected, the Protect Workbook button in the Changes group of the Review tab displays with an orange shaded background to indicate protection is turned on. To remove workbook protection, click the Protect Workbook button. If a password was entered when the workbook was protected, the Unprotect Workbook dialog box shown in Figure 6.10 appears. Type the password and press Enter or click OK.

Figure 6.10 Unprotect Workbook Dialog Box

Adding and Removing a Password to a Workbook ▪▪▪▪

▼ **Quick Steps**

Add Workbook Password
1. Open workbook.
2. Click File tab.
3. Click Protect Workbook button.
4. Click *Encrypt with Password.*
5. Type password.
6. Press Enter or click OK.
7. Retype password.
8. Press Enter or click OK.
9. Save the workbook.

You can prevent unauthorized access to Excel data by requiring a password to open the workbook. Passwords to open the workbook are encrypted. An *encrypted password* means that the plain text you type is converted into a scrambled format called *ciphertext* which prevents unauthorized users from retrieving the password. To add an encrypted password to an open workbook, click the File tab. At the Info tab Backstage view shown in Figure 6.11, click the Protect Workbook button in the center pane. Click *Encrypt with Password* at the drop-down list to open the Encrypt Document dialog box shown in Figure 6.12.

When you create passwords, a guideline to follow is to include a combination of four character elements: uppercase letters, lowercase letters, symbols, and numbers. Passwords constructed according to this model are considered secure and more difficult to crack. Note that if you forget the password, you will not be able to open the workbook. If necessary, write down the password and store it in a secure location.

Figure 6.11 Info Tab Backstage View with Protect Workbook Drop-Down List

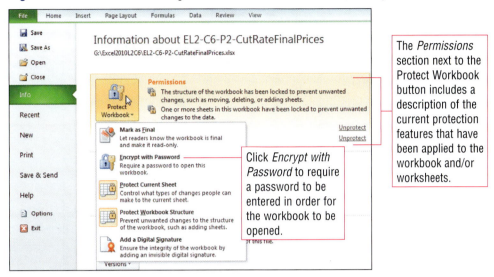

The *Permissions* section next to the Protect Workbook button includes a description of the current protection features that have been applied to the workbook and/or worksheets.

Click *Encrypt with Password* to require a password to be entered in order for the workbook to be opened.

Figure 6.12 Encrypt Document Dialog Box

Project 2d **Adding a Password to Open a Workbook** **Part 4 of 4**

1. With **EL2-C6-P2-CutRateFinalPrices.xlsx** open, add a password to open the workbook by completing the following steps:
   a. Click the File tab. The Backstage view opens with the Info tab selected.
   b. Read the information described in the *Permissions* section next to the Protect Workbook button. Since this workbook has protection features already applied, the existing features are described along with a hyperlink to unprotect each protected worksheet. In a workbook with no pre-existing protection, the *Permissions* section displays the text *Anyone can open, copy, and change any part of the workbook.*
   c. Click the Protect Workbook button.

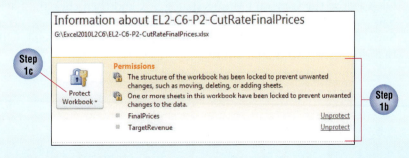

d. Click *Encrypt with Password* at the drop-down list.
e. At the Encrypt Document dialog box with the insertion point positioned in the *Password* text box, type **p4E#c** and then press Enter or click OK.

f. Type **p4E#c** at the Confirm Password dialog box with the insertion point positioned in the *Reenter password* text box and then press Enter or click OK.
g. Notice that Excel has added to the first line of the *Permissions* section next to the Protect Workbook button the text *A password is required to open this workbook.*
h. Click the Home tab to return to the worksheet.

2. Save and then close **EL2-C6-P2-CutRateFinalPrices.xlsx**.
3. Test the password security on the workbook by completing the following steps:
   a. Open **EL2-C6-P2-CutRateFinalPrices.xlsx**.
   b. At the Password dialog box with the insertion point positioned in the *Password* text box, type a password that is incorrect for the file and press Enter.

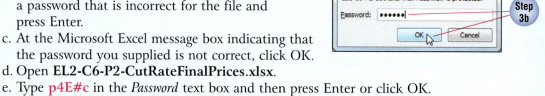

   c. At the Microsoft Excel message box indicating that the password you supplied is not correct, click OK.
   d. Open **EL2-C6-P2-CutRateFinalPrices.xlsx**.
   e. Type **p4E#c** in the *Password* text box and then press Enter or click OK.
4. Close **EL2-C6-P2-CutRateFinalPrices.xlsx**.

To remove a password from a workbook, open the workbook using your password and then open the Save As dialog box. Click the Tools button located near the bottom right of the Save As dialog box (next to the Save button) and then click *General Options* at the drop-down list. At the General Options dialog box, select and then delete the password in the *Password to open* text box. Click OK to close the General Options dialog box and then click the Save button at the Save As dialog box to save the file using the same name. Click Yes at the Confirm Save As dialog box to replace the password-protected workbook with a new copy that does not have the password.

Project **Track and Resolve Changes Made to a Workbook**   **3 Parts**

You will begin tracking changes made to a workbook, view changes made by two users, and accept and reject changes.

Tracking Changes to a Workbook ▪■■■■■■■■■■▪▪■■■■■▪

As you learned in Project 1, Excel automatically tracks changes made to the workbook by each user when you share a workbook. As you saw with the History sheet in Project 1g, you can display and print a record of the changes. If a workbook is not shared, you can turn on the Track Changes feature and Excel will automatically share the workbook. To do this, click the Track Changes button in the Changes group of the Review tab and click *Highlight Changes* at the drop-down list. At the Highlight Changes dialog box, click the *Track changes while editing* check box and click OK.

As the owner of a shared workbook you might need to view the worksheet with all cells highlighted that have had changes made to the data. Figure 6.13 displays the worksheet you will edit in Project 3 with all changes highlighted. As you rest the mouse pointer over a highlighted cell, a pop-up box displays the name of the person who changed the cell along with the date, time, original entry, and revised entry.

▼ **Quick Steps**

Track Changes
1. Open workbook.
2. Click Review tab.
3. Click Track Changes button.
4. Click *Highlight Changes*.
5. Click *Track changes while editing* check box.
6. Click OK twice.

Highlight Changes
1. Open tracked workbook.
2. Click Review tab.
3. Click Track Changes button.
4. Click *Highlight Changes*.
5. Change *When* to *Not yet reviewed*.
6. Make sure *Who* is *Everyone*.
7. Click OK.

Track Changes

Figure 6.13 Project 3 Worksheet with Changes Highlighted

	A	B	C	D	E	F	G	H	I	J	K	L	M
1							**CutRate Car Rentals**						
2							**Estimated Monthly Revenue**						
3							**West Region**						
4		Effective Date: May 1, 2012											
5	Category	Weekday (Mo to Th)	Target Rentals	Target Revenue	Weekend (Fr to Su)	Target Rentals	Target Revenue	Weekly (*Min 5 days)	Target Rentals	Target Revenue	Monthly (*Min 21 days)	Target Rentals	Target Revenue
6	Compact	$ 35.99	⊕ 391	Sam Forwell, 3/6/2012 2:47 PM: Changed cell C6 from '$362.00 ' to ' $391.00 '.			9,686	$ 175.99	46	$ 8,096	$ 675.99	11	$ 7,436
7	Mid-size	38.99	285				13,480	185.99	25	4,650	692.99	10	6,930
8	Full-size	40.99	175				4,949	215.99	30	6,480	775.99	8	6,208
9	Minivan	75.99	155	11,778	130.99	68	8,907	251.99	28	7,056	866.99	8	6,936
10	SUV	89.99	146	13,139	139.99	47	6,580	249.99	31	7,750	885.99	12	10,632
11	Luxury	99.99	55	5,499	155.99	30	4,680	329.99	10	3,300	999.99	5	5,000
12	TOTAL		Weekday:	$ 62,774		Weekend:	$ 48,282		Weekly:	$ 37,330		Monthly:	$ 43,141

Changed cells in a shared workbook can be displayed with a colored border to identify which cells were revised. Each person's changes are identified with a different color.

Figure 6.14 Select Changes to Accept or Reject Dialog Box

Choose to navigate to changes not yet reviewed or since a specific date.

You can restrict the review to changes made by a specific user name.

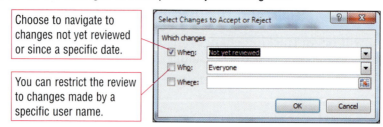

Accepting and Rejecting Tracked Changes

▼ **Quick Steps**

Accept and Reject Changes
1. Open tracked workbook.
2. Click Review tab.
3. Click Track Changes button.
4. Click *Accept/Reject Changes.*
5. Make sure *When* is *Not yet reviewed.*
6. Make sure *Who* is *Everyone.*
7. Click OK.
8. Click Accept or Reject button at each change.

As well as displaying the worksheet with the changes highlighted, you can elect to navigate to each change and accept or reject the revision. To do this, click the Track Changes button in the Changes group of the Review tab and then click *Accept/Reject Changes* at the drop-down list. At the Select Changes to Accept or Reject dialog box shown in Figure 6.14, define which changes you want to review and then click OK.

Excel navigates to the first cell changed and displays the Accept or Reject Changes dialog box shown in Figure 6.15. Review the information in the dialog box and click either the Accept or Reject button. If you reject a change, the cell is restored to its original value. As you respond to each changed cell, the colored border is removed since the cell has been reviewed. The dialog box also includes an Accept All button and a Reject All button to do a global review if desired. Be cautious with accepting and rejecting changes since Undo is not available after you review the cells.

Figure 6.15 Accept or Reject Changes Dialog Box

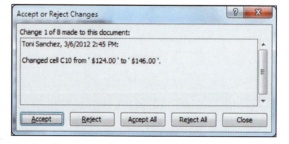

Project 3a | **Tracking Changes Made to a Workbook** | Part 1 of 3

1. Open **CutRateWestRegion.xlsx**.
2. Save the workbook with Save As and name it **EL2-C6-P3-CutRateWestRegion**.
3. Begin tracking changes made to the workbook by completing the following steps:
   a. If necessary, click the Review tab.
   b. Click the Track Changes button in the Changes group.
   c. Click *Highlight Changes* at the drop-down list.

d. At the Highlight Changes dialog box, click the *Track changes while editing* check box. Notice that turning on the Track Changes feature automatically shares the workbook.

e. With *When* set to *All* and *Who* set to *Everyone* by default, click OK.

f. At the Microsoft Excel message box indicating that this action will now save the workbook, click OK to continue.

4. Close **EL2-C6-P3-CutRateWestRegion.xlsx**.

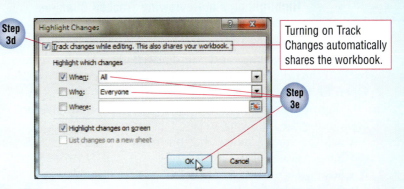

Step 3d

Step 3e

Turning on Track Changes automatically shares the workbook.

Step 3f

Project 3b   **Editing a Tracked Workbook** Part 2 of 3

1. Assume that you are Toni Sanchez, the SUV rental manager for the west region at CutRate Car Rentals. You have been asked to edit the target rental values for SUVs. At a blank Excel window, change the user name to *Toni Sanchez*. If necessary, refer to Project 1d, Step 1 if you need assistance with changing the user name. ***Note: Make sure you make a note of the original user name, which you will restore in Project 3c.***

2. Open **EL2-C6-P3-CutRateWestRegion.xlsx**.

3. Edit the SUV target data as follows:

C10 from	*124*	to	*146*
F10 from	*22*	to	*47*
I10 from	*22*	to	*31*
L10 from	*8*	to	*12*

4. Save and then close **EL2-C6-P3-CutRateWestRegion.xlsx**.

5. Assume that you are Sam Forwell, the compact rental manager for the west region at CutRate Car Rentals. You have been asked to edit the target rental values for compact cars. At a blank Excel window, change the user name to *Sam Forwell*.

6. Open **EL2-C6-P3-CutRateWestRegion.xlsx**.

7. Edit the compact target data as follows:

C6 from	*362*	to	*391*
F6 from	*165*	to	*173*
I6 from	*33*	to	*46*
L6 from	*15*	to	*11*

8. Save and then close **EL2-C6-P3-CutRateWestRegion.xlsx**.

1. Assume that you are the west region operations manager. You decide to review the changes made by Toni Sanchez and Sam Forwell. At a blank Excel window, change the user name back to the original user name for the computer that you are using.
2. Open **EL2-C6-P3-CutRateWestRegion.xlsx**.
3. Highlight cells with changes made by all users that have not yet been reviewed by completing the following steps:

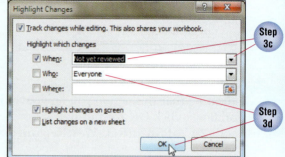

   a. Click the Track Changes button in the Changes group of the Review tab.
   b. Click *Highlight Changes* at the drop-down list.
   c. At the Highlight Changes dialog box, click the down-pointing arrow at the right of the *When* list box and then click *Not yet reviewed* at the drop-down list.
   d. With *Who* set to *Everyone* by default, click OK.

4. Accept and reject changes as you navigate the worksheet by completing the following steps:
   a. Press Ctrl + Home to move the active cell to A1.
   b. Click the Track Changes button and then click *Accept/Reject Changes* at the drop-down list.
   c. At the Select Changes to Accept or Reject dialog box, with *When* set to *Not yet reviewed*, and *Who* set to *Everyone* by default, click OK.
   d. Excel moves the active cell to C10 where the first change was made and displays the Accept or Reject Changes dialog box. Click the Accept button to leave C10 at 146.

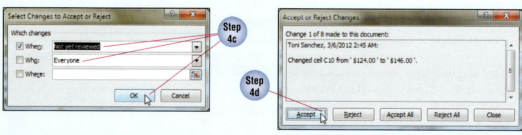

   e. Excel moves the active cell to F10. Click the Reject button to restore F10 to the original value of 22. ***Note: If necessary, drag the Accept or Reject Changes dialog box out of the way to see the cell being reviewed in the worksheet area.***

   f. Respond to the remaining changes as follows:

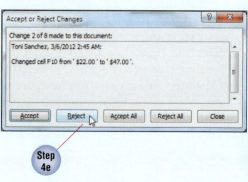

      Accept   I10
      Accept   L10
      Reject   C6
      Accept   F6
      Reject   I6
      Accept   L6

5. Print the worksheet.
6. Save and then close **EL2-C6-P3-CutRateWestRegion.xlsx**.

Stopping the Tracking of Changes in a Workbook

When you no longer need to track the changes made to a workbook, click the Track Changes button and click *Highlight Changes* at the drop-down list. At the Highlight Changes dialog box, clear the *Track changes while editing* check box and click OK. Excel displays the warning message that the workbook will no longer be shared and the change history will be erased. Click Yes to complete the action.

If you have not reviewed all changes made to the workbook, consider printing a copy of the History sheet before turning off the track changes feature. Refer to Project 1g, Step 2 for assistance with printing a history sheet.

Excel provides several methods to share and collaborate with other users of data in Excel. The method that you choose depends on factors such as the availability of a network share folder, the need to protect ranges or otherwise restrict access to sensitive data, and the resources available by the users who will receive the data. In Chapter 8 you will explore other features that are important to consider when you will be distributing a workbook which restrict access and remove personal information.

Chapter Summary

- Workbook properties include descriptive information about the workbook such as the author's name, title, subject, or comments.
- Workbook properties are sometimes referred to as *metadata*.
- Display the Info tab Backstage view or open the Document Information Panel to add information to a workbook's properties.
- Comments display text in a pop-up box when the cell pointer is resting on a cell to which a comment has been attached.
- Comments are useful to add explanatory notes, descriptions, or pose questions about a cell entry when a workbook is being created, edited, or shared with other reviewers.
- Insert, edit, view, or delete a comment using buttons in the Comments group of the Review tab. Comment text can be copied and pasted to another cell using the Paste Special dialog box.
- Sharing a workbook generally involves turning on the sharing feature and saving the workbook to a folder on a networked server that is accessible to the other users who need the file.
- Use the Share Workbook button in the Changes group of the Review tab to turn on the sharing feature.
- When Microsoft Office is installed, a user name is defined for the computer upon which the software has been copied. Excel automatically inserts this name in the *Author* workbook property as a new workbook is created.
- You can change the user name at the Excel Options dialog box.

- View other users who have a shared workbook open at the Share Workbook dialog box.

- When a workbook is shared, Excel automatically tracks the changes made by each person who accesses the file.

- If two users have a shared workbook open at the same time and each person makes a change to the same cell, a Resolve Conflicts dialog box appears when the second user saves the workbook.

- At the Resolve Conflicts dialog box, the second user can choose to accept the change made by him or her or restore the cell to the entry made by the last person to save the file.

- Print a History sheet that provides a detailed record of all changes made to a shared workbook before removing shared access to the workbook.

- When a shared workbook is changed to an exclusive workbook, all change history is removed from the file.

- An entire worksheet can be protected to prevent another person from accidentally inserting, deleting, or changing data that you do not want modified.

- Protect a worksheet using the Protect Sheet button in the Changes group of the Review tab.

- You can add a password that is required to unprotect a worksheet.

- Each cell in a worksheet has a lock attribute which activates when the worksheet is protected.

- To allow individual cells in a protected worksheet to be editable, select the cell(s) and turn off the lock attribute before protecting the worksheet.

- The Protect Workbook button in the Changes group of the Review tab is used to protect a workbook from a user inserting, deleting, renaming, or otherwise managing worksheets in the workbook.

- You can prevent unauthorized access to an Excel workbook by adding an encrypted password to open and/or modify the workbook.

- At the Info tab Backstage view, click the Protect Workbook button and then click *Encrypt with Password* to add a workbook password. Save the workbook after typing and confirming the password.

- Turn on or off the Track Changes feature or display changes in a shared workbook by opening the Highlight Changes dialog box.

- The Accept/Reject Changes feature is used to navigate to each changed cell in a worksheet and accept or reject the revision.

Commands Review

FEATURE	RIBBON TAB, GROUP	BUTTON	KEYBOARD SHORTCUT
Accept/Reject Changes	Review, Changes		
Add comment	Review, Comments		Shift + F2
Add password to a workbook	File, Info		
Change user name	File		
Delete comment	Review, Comments		
Document Information Panel	File, Info	Properties ▾	
Edit comment	Review, Comments		
Highlight Changes	Review, Changes		
Paste Copied Comment	Home, Clipboard		Ctrl + Alt + V
Protect Workbook	Review, Changes		
Protect Worksheet	Review, Changes		
Share Workbook	Review, Changes		
Track Changes	Review, Changes		
Unlock cells	Home, Cells		

Concepts Check Test Your Knowledge

Completion: In the space provided at the right, indicate the correct term, command, or number.

1. Open this view to add descriptive information about a workbook such as a title or subject heading. _____

2. This panel displays the workbook's properties between the ribbon and the worksheet. _____

3. A diagonal red triangle in the upper right corner of a cell indicates this box will pop up when the mouse pointer rests on the cell. _____

4. Open this dialog box to turn on the feature that allows changes by more than one user at the same time.

_____

5. Change the user name for the computer that you are using by opening this dialog box.

_____

6. When two users have the same workbook open at the same time and each makes a change to the same cell, this dialog box appears when the second person saves the workbook.

_____

7. Open this dialog box to create a History sheet that includes a record of all changes made to a shared workbook.

_____

8. Add a password that is required to unprotect a worksheet at this dialog box.

_____

9. Select a cell that you want to allow changes to and then click this button and menu option to unlock the cell before protecting the worksheet.

_____

10. Prevent users from inserting or deleting worksheets in a workbook by opening this dialog box.

_____

11. Click this option from the Protect Workbook drop-down list at the Info tab Backstage view to assign a password to open a workbook.

_____

12. Turn this feature on and Excel automatically changes the workbook to a shared workbook if it is not already shared.

_____

13. Excel applies this formatting to cells in a shared workbook that have been modified in order to make the revised cells stand out.

_____

14. Use this feature to navigate to each changed cell in a shared workbook and decide whether to keep the change or restore the cell back to its previous value.

_____

15. This feature is not available to restore cells to their previous values after you have finished reviewing tracked changes.

_____

Skills Check Assess Your Performance

Assessment

1 ENTER AND DISPLAY WORKBOOK PROPERTIES; INSERT COMMENTS

1. Open **NationalCSDeptLicenses.xlsx**.
2. Save the workbook with Save As and name it
   EL2-C6-A1-NationalCSDeptLicenses.
3. Type the following text in the appropriate workbook properties:

Add an Author	Student Name (Substitute your name for *Student Name*.)
Title	MSO 2010 License Chargeback
Subject	Journal entry by department
Category	JE supporting document
Status	Posted
Comments	Audit worksheet for Office 2010 site license with internal chargebacks

4. Remove the existing author *Paradigm Publishing Inc.*
5. Display the Document Information Panel.
6. Insert a screen image of the worksheet showing the Document Information Panel in a new Microsoft Word document using either Print Screen with Paste, the Screenshot feature (Insert tab, Screenshot button in Illustrations group), or the Windows Snipping tool (Start button, All Programs, Accessories). Type your name a few lines below the screen image.
7. Save the Microsoft Word document and name it
   EL2-C6-A1-NationalCSDeptLicenses.docx.
8. Print **EL2-C6-A1-NationalCSDeptLicenses.docx** and then exit Word.
9. At the Microsoft Excel worksheet, close the Document Information Panel.
10. Make B8 the active cell and insert a new comment. Type **Check this quantity with Marty. The number seems high.** in the comment box.
11. Make B14 the active cell and insert a new comment. Type **Make a note in the budget file for next year. This quantity will increase by 5.** in the comment box.
12. Print the worksheet with the comments as displayed on the sheet.
13. Save and close **EL2-C6-A1-NationalCSDeptLicenses.xlsx**.

Assessment

2 SHARE A WORKBOOK; EDIT A SHARED WORKBOOK; PRINT A HISTORY SHEET

1. Open **PrecisionMfgTargets.xlsx**.
2. Save the workbook with Save As and name it
   EL2-C6-A2-PrecisionMfgTargets.
3. Share the workbook.
4. Change the user name to *Lorne Moir* and then edit the following cells:

C11	from	*4,352*	to	*5520*
C18	from	*15,241*	to	*15960*

5. Save the workbook.
6. Change the user name to *Gerri Gonzales* and then edit the following cells:

F4	from	*3,845*	to	*5126*
F9	from	*7,745*	to	*9320*

7. Save the workbook.
8. Create a History sheet with a record of the changes made to the data by all users.
9. Print the History sheet. *Note: If you submit your assignment work electronically, create a copy of the History worksheet in a new workbook since the History worksheet is automatically deleted when the file is saved.*
10. Save and then close **EL2-C6-A2-PrecisionMfgTargets.xlsx**.
11. Change the user name back to the original user name for the computer you are using.

Assessment

3   REMOVE SHARED ACCESS

1. Open **EL2-C6-A2-PrecisionMfgTargets.xlsx**.
2. Save the workbook with Save As and name it **EL2-C6-A3-PrecisionMfgTargets**.
3. Remove the shared access to the workbook.
4. Close **EL2-C6-A3-PrecisionMfgTargets.xlsx**.

Assessment

4   PROTECT AN ENTIRE WORKSHEET; ADD A PASSWORD TO A WORKBOOK

1. Open **EL2-C6-A1-NationalCSDeptLicenses.xlsx**.
2. Save the workbook with Save As and name it **EL2-C6-A4-NationalCSDeptLicenses**.
3. Protect the entire worksheet using the password *L$07j* to unprotect.
4. Add the password *J07$e* to open the workbook.
5. Save and close **EL2-C6-A4-NationalCSDeptLicenses.xlsx**.
6. Open **EL2-C6-A4-NationalCSDeptLicenses.xlsx** and test the password to open the workbook.
7. Unprotect the worksheet to test the password to unprotect.
8. Close **EL2-C6-A4-NationalCSDeptLicenses.xlsx**. Click Don't Save when prompted to save changes.

Assessment

5   UNLOCK CELLS AND PROTECT A WORKSHEET; PROTECT WORKBOOK STRUCTURE

1. Open **PrecisionMfgTargets.xlsx**.
2. Save the workbook with Save As and name it **EL2-C6-A5-PrecisionMfgTargets**.
3. Select the range C4:F21 and unlock the cells.
4. Deselect the range and then protect the worksheet using the password *Mt14#* to unprotect.
5. Rename Sheet1 to *2014MfgTargets*.
6. Delete Sheet2 and Sheet3.
7. Protect the workbook structure to prevent users from inserting, deleting, or renaming sheets using the password *Mt14!shts* to unprotect.
8. Save and then close **EL2-C6-A5-PrecisionMfgTargets.xlsx**.

6 TRACK CHANGES; ACCEPT/REJECT CHANGES; PRINT A HISTORY SHEET

1. Open **EL2-C6-A5-PrecisionMfgTargets.xlsx**.
2. Save the workbook with Save As and name it
   EL2-C6-A6-PrecisionMfgTargets.
3. Unprotect the workbook structure so that new sheets can added, deleted,
   renamed, or copied.
4. Turn on the Track Changes feature.
5. Change the user name to *Grant Antone* and then edit the following cells:

D4	from	*3,251*	to	*3755*
D17	from	*5,748*	to	*6176*
6. Save the workbook, change the user name to *Jean Kocsis*, and then edit the
   following cells:

E6	from	*6,145*	to	*5748*
E11	from	*2,214*	to	*3417*
7. Save the workbook and then change the user name back to the original user
   name for the computer you are using.
8. Accept and Reject changes as follows:

Accept	D4
Reject	D17
Reject	E6
Accept	E11
9. Create and print a History sheet of the changes made to the worksheet. *Note:
   If you submit your assignment work electronically, create a copy of the History
   worksheet in a new workbook since the History worksheet is automatically
   deleted when the file is saved.*
10. Print the 2014MfgTargets worksheet.
11. Save and then close **EL2-C6-A6-PrecisionMfgTargets.xlsx**.

Visual Benchmark Demonstrate Your Proficiency

TRACK CHANGES; INSERT COMMENTS

1. Open **PawsParadise.xlsx**.
2. Save the workbook with Save As and name it **EL2-C6-VB-PawsParadise**.
3. Figure 6.16 illustrates the worksheet after the owner and operator reviewed
   the worksheet created by her kennel manager. While reviewing the service
   price list, the owner made comments and changed cells. Using Figure 6.16 and
   Figure 6.17 make the same changes to your copy of the worksheet making
   sure the changes are associated with the owner's name.
4. Create and print a History worksheet scaled to fit on one page. *Note: If
   you submit your assignment work electronically, create a copy of the History
   worksheet in a new workbook since the History worksheet is automatically
   deleted when the file is saved.*
5. Print the worksheet with the changes highlighted and the comments as
   displayed on the worksheet.

6. Save and then close **EL2-C6-VB-PawsParadise.xlsx**.
7. Change the user name back to the original user name for the computer you are using.

Figure 6.16 Visual Benchmark Worksheet with Comments

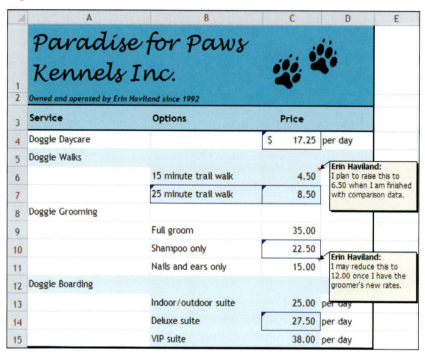

Figure 6.17 Visual Benchmark History Worksheet

	Action Number	Date	Time	Who	Change	Sheet	Range	New Value	Old Value	Action Type	Losing Action
2	1	3/6/2012	10:46 AM	Erin Haviland	Cell Change	Sheet1	C4	$17.25	$16.50		
3	2	3/6/2012	10:46 AM	Erin Haviland	Cell Change	Sheet1	C7	$8.50	$8.25		
4	3	3/6/2012	10:46 AM	Erin Haviland	Cell Change	Sheet1	C10	$22.50	$20.00		
5	4	3/6/2012	10:46 AM	Erin Haviland	Cell Change	Sheet1	C14	$27.50	$28.50		
6	5	3/6/2012	10:46 AM	Erin Haviland	Cell Change	Sheet1	B7	25 minute trail walk	30 minute trail walk		
7											
8	The history ends with the changes saved on 3/6/2012 at 10:46 AM.										

Case Study Apply Your Skills

Part 1

Yolanda Robertson of NuTrends Market Research is working with Nicola Carlucci of Pizza by Mario on a workbook with projected franchise startups for 2014. The workbook is currently in draft format in a file named **PizzaByMarioNewFranchises.xlsx**. Open the workbook and use Save As to name the workbook **EL2-C6-CS-P1-PizzaByMarioNewFranchises**. Add an appropriate title and subject to the workbook's properties and include comment text to explain that the draft workbook was created in consultation with Nicola Carlucci. Yolanda has asked for your assistance with protecting the workbook to prevent accidental data modifications or erasure when the workbook is shared with others. Yolanda and Nicola have agreed that the city, state, and store numbers should be protected; however, the month a new store is planned to open and the names of prospective franchisees could change. Share the workbook. Yolanda and Nicola have agreed on the following passwords:

- Password to unprotect the worksheet is *U14@s*.
- Password to open the workbook is *SbM@14*.

Part 2

Use Save As to name the workbook **EL2-C6-CS-P2-PizzaByMarioNewFranchises**. Yolanda has reviewed her research files and meeting notes and has the following changes to make to the data. Make sure the user name is correct so that the following changes are associated with Yolanda:

Store 138	Franchisee is Jae-Dong Han
Store 149	Franchisee is Leslie Posno

Save the workbook. Nicola is in charge of logistics planning and has two changes to make to the months that stores are scheduled to open. Make sure the user name is correct so that the following changes are associated with Nicola:

Store 135	Open in February
Store 141	Open in December

Save the workbook and then display the worksheet with all of the changes made by Yolanda and Nicola highlighted. Create a History sheet. Print the worksheet with the cells highlighted and also print the History sheet. *Note: If you submit your assignment work electronically, create a copy of the History worksheet in a new workbook since the History worksheet is automatically deleted when the file is saved.* Restore the worksheet to exclusive use. Close **EL2-C6-CS-P2-PizzaByMarioNewFranchises.xlsx**. Change the user name back to the original user name for the computer you are using.

Part 3

Yolanda will be sending the shared workbook from Part 1 to Leonard Scriver, a colleague at the Michigan office of NuTrends Market Research. Yolanda wants Leonard to review the data and add his recommendations; however, Yolanda would prefer that Leonard save his copy using a different name so that the original shared version is not disrupted. Open **EL2-C6-CS-P1-PizzaByMarioNewFranchises.xlsx**. Unprotect the worksheet, remove the password to open the workbook, and then save the workbook using the name **EL2-C6-CS-P3-PizzabyMario-LScriver**. Based on Leonard's experience with franchise startups, he has the following recommendations which he prefers to show in comments within the worksheet.

Make sure the user name is correct so that the comment boxes display Leonard's name:

Store 136 Opening a second store in Chicago is more likely to occur in April

Store 144 Move this opening to June as resources at head office will be stretched in May

Store 152 Try to open this franchise at the same time as store 151

Show all comments within the worksheet and then print the worksheet making sure the comments print as displayed. Save and then close **EL2-C6-CS-P3-PizzabyMario-LScriver.xlsx**. Change the user name back to the original user name for the computer that you are using.

Part 4

Mario Carlucci has commented that the password to open the workbook is not intuitive for him and he has had trouble remembering the password. He wants to change the workbook password to something more user-friendly such as *Target14*. Yolanda and Nicola chose the passwords they have used in the workbook carefully based on their understanding of strong passwords that are more difficult to crack by unauthorized users. Yolanda has asked you to assist with a training package for Mario that will educate him on strong passwords. Research on the Internet the guidelines for creating strong passwords. Based on what you have learned from your research, create a document in Microsoft Word that highlights the components of a strong password. Include a table of dos and don'ts for creating strong passwords in a user-friendly easy-to-understand format for Mario. Finally, create a minimum of three examples that show a weak password improved by a stronger password. Include a suggestion for how to use the phrasing technique to create strong passwords so that they are easier to remember. Save the document and name it **EL2-C6-CS-P4-PizzaByMarioPasswords**. Print and then close **EL2-C6-CS-P4-PizzaByMarioPasswords.docx**.

Microsoft Excel

Automating Repetitive Tasks and Customizing Excel

PERFORMANCE OBJECTIVES

Upon successful completion of Chapter 7, you will be able to:

- Record, run, and edit a macro
- Save a workbook containing macros as a macro-enabled workbook
- Create a macro that is run using a shortcut key combination
- Pin and unpin a frequently used file to the Recent Workbooks list
- Add and remove buttons for frequently used commands to the Quick Access toolbar
- Hide the ribbon to increase space in the work area
- Customize the display options for Excel
- Customize the ribbon by creating a custom tab and adding buttons
- Create and apply custom views
- Create and use a template
- Customize save options for AutoRecover files

Tutorials

7.1 Using Macros
7.2 Managing Macros
7.3 Editing a Macro
7.4 Pinning Workbooks to the Recent Workbooks List
7.5 Customizing the Quick Access Toolbar
7.6 Customizing the Work Area
7.7 Customizing the Ribbon
7.8 Using Custom Templates

Automating and customizing the Excel environment can increase your efficiency and allow you to change the environment to accommodate your preferences. Create a macro when you find yourself repeating the same task frequently to save time and ensure consistency. Customize the Excel environment by adding a button for a frequently used command to the Quick Access toolbar to provide single-click access to the feature. Other ways to customize can involve tasks such as pinning frequently used files to the Recent Workbooks list, creating a custom template, ribbon tab, or custom view, or by modifying display and save options. Through completing the projects in this chapter, you will learn how to effectively automate and customize the Excel environment. Model answers for this chapter's projects appear on the following page.

Excel2010L2C7

Note: Before beginning the projects, copy to your storage medium the Excel2010L2C7 subfolder from the Excel2010L2 folder on the CD that accompanies this textbook and then make Excel2010L2C7 the active folder.

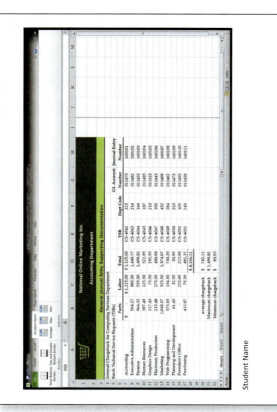

Project 2 Customize the Excel Work Environment

Project 2f, EL2-C7-P2-NationalAcctgDeptJE.docx

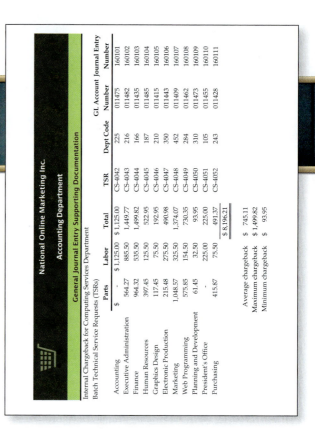

Project 2f, EL2-C7-P2-NationalAcctgDeptJE.xlsx

Noranda Sportsplex					
Swimming Schedule					
Winter 2012					
Day	**Start time**	**End time**	**Pool**	**Activity**	
MORNINGS					
Monday, Wednesday	6:30	7:50	Red pool	Aquafit	
Tuesday, Thursday, Friday	6:30	7:50	Blue pool	Moms and tots	
Monday, Wednesday	8:00	8:45			
Tuesday, Thursday, Friday	8:00	8:45			
Monday, Wednesday	8:00	8:45			
Tuesday, Thursday, Friday	8:00	8:45			
Monday, Wednesday	9:00	9:45			
Tuesday, Thursday, Friday	9:00	9:45			
Monday, Wednesday	9:00	9:45			
Tuesday, Thursday, Friday	9:00	9:45			
Monday, Wednesday	10:00	11:45			
Tuesday, Thursday, Friday	10:00	11:45			
Tuesday, Thursday, Friday	10:00	11:45			
Saturday, Sunday	9:00	11:45			
AFTERNOONS					
Monday, Wednesday	1:00	1:45			
Tuesday, Thursday, Friday	1:00	1:45			
Monday, Wednesday	1:00	1:45			
Tuesday, Thursday, Friday	1:00	1:45			
Monday, Wednesday	2:00	3:45			
Tuesday, Thursday, Friday	2:00	3:45			
Tuesday, Thursday, Friday	2:00	3:45			
Monday, Wednesday	2:00	3:45			
Tuesday, Thursday, Friday	2:00	3:45			
Monday, Wednesday	4:00	4:45			
Tuesday, Thursday, Friday	4:00	4:45			
Saturday, Sunday	2:00	4:45			
EVENINGS					
Monday, Wednesday	5:00	5:45			
Tuesday, Thursday, Friday	5:00	5:45			
Monday, Wednesday	5:00	5:45			
Tuesday, Thursday, Friday	5:00	5:45			
Monday, Wednesday	6:00	6:45			
Tuesday, Thursday, Friday	6:00	6:45			
Monday, Wednesday	7:00	7:45			
Tuesday, Thursday, Friday	7:00	7:45			
Monday, Wednesday	8:00	9:45			
Tuesday, Thursday, Friday	8:00	9:45			
Monday, Wednesday	8:00	9:45			
Tuesday, Thursday	8:00	9:45			
Friday	8:00	8:45			

Project 3 Save a Workbook as a Template

Project 3b, EL2-C7-P3-SwimSchWinter2012.xlsx

Project 1 Create Macros

4 Parts

You will create, edit, run, and delete macros to automate tasks including assigning a macro to a shortcut key and storing frequently used macros in a macro workbook.

Automating Tasks Using Macros ■■■■■■■ ■ ■■■■■

A *macro* is a series of instructions stored in sequence that can be recalled and carried out whenever the need arises. Macros are generally created when a task that is never varied is repeated frequently. Saving the instructions in the macro not only saves time but ensures that the steps are consistently reapplied, which can avoid errors in data entry, formatting, or other worksheet options.

Take a few moments before you record a new macro to plan the steps you will need to perform. Also consider if the active cell location at the time the macro is run will be a factor. For example, will the first step in the macro involve positioning the cell at a specific location? If yes, during recording, you can position the active cell using a shortcut key or Go To command.

To create a macro, you begin by turning on the macro recorder. A macro is identified by assigning a unique name to the steps that will be saved. Macro names must begin with a letter and can be a combination of letters, numbers, and underscore characters. A macro name cannot include spaces—use the underscore character if you want to separate words in a macro name. At the Record Macro dialog box shown in Figure 7.1, you also choose the location in which to save the macro. By default, Excel saves the macro within the current workbook.

Macros can be assigned to a Ctrl shortcut key combination, which allows the macro to be run more quickly by pressing Ctrl plus the chosen lowercase or uppercase letter. Entering a description of the macro's purpose provides information to other users who might use or edit the macro. In a macro workbook that will be shared, also consider entering the creator's name and date into the description box for reference purposes. Do not be concerned if you make a typing mistake or have to cancel a dialog box while recording—correct your mistakes as you go

▼ **Quick Steps**

Record Macro
1. Click View tab.
2. Click down-pointing arrow on Macros button.
3. Click *Record Macro*.
4. Type macro name.
5. Click in *Description* text box.
6. Type description text.
7. Click OK.
8. Perform desired actions.
9. Click Stop Recording button.

H I N T

While creating the macro, mouse clicks to select tabs within the ribbon are not saved.

Macros

Figure 7.1 Record Macro Dialog Box

Macro names begin with a letter and can include a combination of letters, numbers, and underscore characters.

Assigning a macro to a Ctrl key combination enables the macro to be run by pressing Ctrl plus the letter.

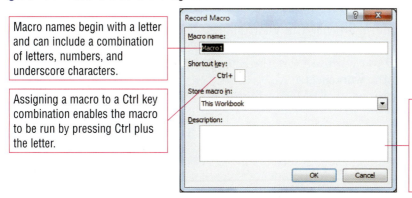

Including a description of the macro's purpose, the name of the person who created the macro, and the date recorded is useful for others who might need to run or edit the macro.

Stop Recording
Macro

since only the end result is saved. Click OK when you are finished identifying the macro and the recorder begins saving the text and/or steps that you perform. Once you have completed the tasks you want saved, click the Stop Recording button in the Status bar to end recording.

Saving Workbooks Containing Macros

▼ **Quick Steps**

Save Macro-Enabled Workbook
1. Click File tab.
2. Click Save As.
3. If necessary, navigate to desired drive and/ or folder.
4. Type file name in *File name* text box.
5. Click *Save as type* list arrow.
6. Click *Excel Macro-Enabled Workbook (*.xlsm)*.
7. Click Save.

A workbook that contains a macro should be saved using the macro-enabled file format. The default XML-based file format (.xlsx) cannot store VBA macro code. (VBA stands for Visual Basic for Applications.) When a macro is created in Excel, the commands are written and saved in Microsoft Visual Basic. The macro recorder that you use when creating a macro converts your actions to Visual Basic statements for you behind the scenes. You can view and edit the Visual Basic code, or you can create macros from scratch by using the Visual Basic Editor in Microsoft Visual Basic. In Project 1e you will look at the Visual Basic statements created when the AcctgDocumentation macro was recorded and edit an instruction.

To save a workbook as a macro-enabled workbook, do one of the following actions:

- *New workbook.* Click the Save button on the Quick Access toolbar. Type the file name and change *Save as type* to *Excel Macro-Enabled Workbook (*.xlsm)*. Click the Save button.

- *Existing workbook.* Click the File tab and then click Save & Send. Click *Change File Type* in the File Types category in the center pane, click *Macro-Enabled Workbook (*.xlsm)* in the *Workbook File Types* section of the right pane, and then click the Save As button. At the Save As dialog box, type the file name and then click the Save button.

Project 1a   **Creating a Macro and Saving a Workbook as a Macro-Enabled Workbook**   Part 1 of 4

1. Assume that you work in the Accounting department at a large company. The company has a documentation standard for all Excel workbooks that requires each worksheet to show the department name, the author's name, the date the workbook was created, and a revision history. You decide to create a macro that will insert row labels for this data to standardize the documentation. Begin by starting a new blank workbook.

2. Create the documentation macro by completing the following steps:

    a. Make C4 the active cell and then click the View tab. (You are making a cell other than A1 the active cell because within the macro you want to move the active cell to the top left cell in the worksheet.)

    b. Click the down-pointing arrow on the Macros button in the Macros group.

    c. Click *Record Macro* at the drop-down list.

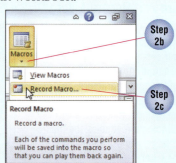

Step 2b

Step 2c

d. At the Record Macro dialog box with the insertion point positioned in the *Macro name* text box, type **AcctgDocumentation**.

e. Click in the *Description* text box and then type **Accounting department documentation macro. Created by [Student Name] on [Date].** where your name is substituted for *[Student Name]* and the current date is substituted for *[Date]*.

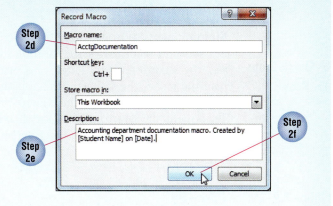

Step 2d

Step 2e

Step 2f

f. Click OK. The macro recorder is now turned on as indicated by the Stop Recording button in the Status bar (displays as a blue square next to *Ready*).

g. Press Ctrl + Home to move the active cell to A1. Including this command in the macro ensures that the documentation will always begin at A1 in all workbooks.

h. Type **Accounting department** and press Enter.

i. With the active cell in A2, type **Author** and press Enter.

j. With the active cell in A3, type **Date created** and press Enter.

k. With the active cell in A4, type **Revision history** and then press Enter three times to leave two blank rows before the worksheet will begin.

Steps 2h-2k

Step 2l

l. Click the Stop Recording button located near the left side of the Status bar next to *Ready*.

3. Save the workbook as a macro-enabled workbook by completing the following steps:
a. Click the File tab and then click Save As.
b. If necessary, navigate to the drive and/or folder for your student data files.
c. Click in the *File name* text box and type **EL2-C7-P1-Macros**.
d. Click the Save as type button, scroll up or down the pop-up list, and then click *Excel Macro-Enabled Workbook (*.xlsm)*.
e. Click the Save button.

Step 3c

Step 3d

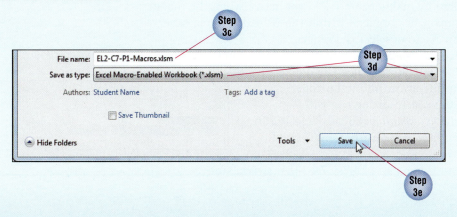

Step 3e

Running a Macro

Quick Steps

Run Macro
1. Click View tab.
2. Click Macros button.
3. Double-click macro name.

Running a macro is also sometimes referred to as playing a macro. Since a macro is a series of recorded tasks, running the macro involves instructing Excel to *play back* the recorded tasks. Think of a macro as a video you have made. When you play the video, the same thing happens every time. To run (play) a macro, view a list of macros by clicking the Macros button in the Macros group of the View tab. This opens the Macro dialog box shown in Figure 7.2. Click the macro name you want to run and then click the Run button, or double-click the macro in the *Macro name* list box.

Figure 7.2 Macro Dialog Box

By default, all macros within all open workbooks are displayed in this list box. Double-click the macro name to run it.

If the currently selected macro contains a description, the text displays here.

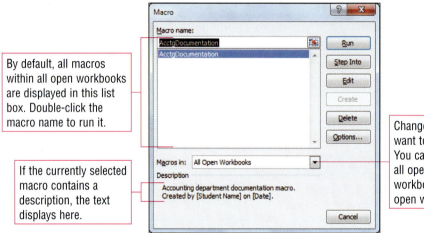

Change the list of macros you want to view using this list arrow. You can view macros contained in all open workbooks, the current workbook only, or select a specific open workbook name.

Project 1b Running a Macro   Part 2 of 4

1. With **EL2-C7-P1-Macros.xlsm** open, run the AcctgDocumentation macro to test that the macro works correctly by completing the following steps:
   a. Select A1:A4 and press the Delete key to erase the cell contents.
   b. You want to test the Ctrl + Home command in the macro by making sure A1 is not active when the macro begins. Click any cell within the worksheet area other than A1 to deselect the range.
   c. Click the Macros button in the Macros group of the View tab. Do not click the down-pointing arrow on the button.
   d. At the Macro dialog box with *AcctgDocumentation* already selected in the *Macro name* list box, click the Run button.
2. Save and then close **EL2-C7-P1-Macros.xlsm**.

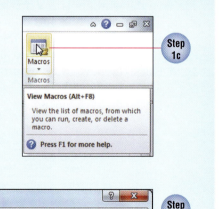

Step 1c

Step 1d

Assigning a Macro to a Shortcut Key

When you record a macro you have the option of assigning the macro to a Ctrl key combination. A macro that is assigned to a shortcut key can be run without displaying the Macro dialog box. You can choose any lowercase letter or uppercase letter for the macro. Excel distinguishes the case of the letter you choose when you type the letter at the *Shortcut key* text box at the Record Macro dialog box. For example, if you type an uppercase O, Excel defines the shortcut key as *Ctrl + Shift + O* as shown in Figure 7.3.

If an Excel feature is assigned to the key combination that you choose, your macro will override Excel's shortcut. For example, pressing Ctrl + p in Excel causes the Print dialog box to appear. If you create a macro and assign the macro to Ctrl + p, your macro's instructions are invoked instead of the Print dialog box. You can view a list of Excel-assigned keyboard shortcuts in Help by typing *keyboard shortcuts* in the Search text box of the Excel Help window. Select *Keyboard shortcuts in Excel 2010* in the Results list.

▼ Quick Steps

Assign Macro to Shortcut Key
1. Click View tab.
2. Click down-pointing arrow on Macros button.
3. Click *Record Macro*.
4. Type macro name.
5. Click in *Shortcut key* text box.
6. Type desired letter.
7. Click in *Description* text box.
8. Type description text.
9. Click OK.
10. Perform desired actions.
11. Click Stop Recording button.

Record
New Macro

Figure 7.3 Record Macro Dialog Box with Shortcut Key Assigned

Typing an uppercase letter in the *Shortcut key* text box defines the shortcut key as Ctrl + Shift + the letter; a lowercase letter is defined as Ctrl + the letter.

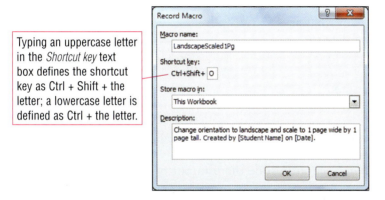

Project 1c   **Creating and Running a Macro Using a Shortcut Key**   Part 3 of 4

1. Open **EL2-C7-P1-Macros.xlsm**.
2. The default security setting for any workbook that is opened containing a macro is *Disable all macros with notification*. This causes a security warning to appear in the message bar (between the ribbon and the formula bar) notifying you that macros have been disabled. Enable the macros in the workbook by clicking the Enable Content button in the Security Warning message bar.

3. Create a macro assigned to a keyboard shortcut that changes print options for a worksheet by completing the following steps:

a. Once a macro has been recorded and stopped in an Excel session, the Stop Recording button in the Status bar changes to the Record New Macro button.

Step 3a

Click the Record New Macro button located at the left side of the Status bar next to *Ready*. If you exited Excel before starting this project, start a new macro by clicking the View tab, clicking the down-pointing arrow on the Macros button, and then clicking *Record Macro*.

b. Type **LandscapeScaled1Pg** in the *Macro name* text box.

c. Click in the *Shortcut key* text box, hold down the Shift key, and press the letter o.

d. Click in the *Description* text box and then type **Change orientation to landscape and scale to 1 page wide by 1 page tall. Created by [Student Name] on [Date].** Substitute your name for *[Student Name]* and the current date for *[Date]*.

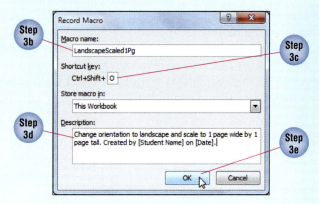

Step 3b

Step 3c

Step 3d

Step 3e

e. Click OK.

f. Click the Page Layout tab.

g. Click the Page Setup Dialog Box launcher located at the bottom right of the Page Setup group.

h. At the Page Setup dialog box with the Page tab selected, click *Landscape* in the *Orientation* section.

i. Click *Fit to* in the *Scaling* section to scale the printout to 1 page wide by 1 page tall.

j. Click OK.

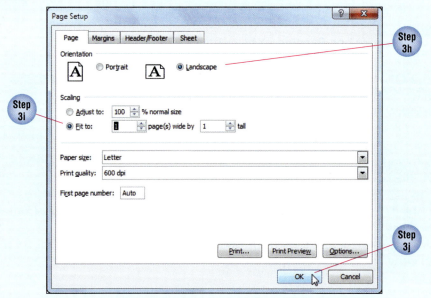

Step 3h

Step 3i

Step 3j

k. Click the Stop Recording button.

4. Press Ctrl + N to start a new blank workbook.
5. Press Ctrl + Shift + o to run the LandscapeScaled1Pg macro.
6. Type your name in A1, press Enter, and then press Ctrl + F2 to display the worksheet in the Print tab Backstage view. Notice in the Print Preview pane the page orientation is landscape. Review the options in the Settings category in the center pane. Notice that *Landscape Orientation* and *Fit Sheet on One Page* have been set by the macro.
7. Click the Home tab to return to the worksheet and then close the new workbook. Click Don't Save when prompted to save changes.
8. Save **EL2-C7-P1-Macros.xlsm**.

Editing a Macro

The actions that you performed while recording the macro are stored in Visual Basic for Applications program code. Each macro is saved as a separate module within a VBAProject for the workbook. A module can be described as a receptacle for the instructions. Each macro is contained within a separate module within the workbook. Figure 7.4 displays the Visual Basic macro code for the macro created in Project 1a.

Edit a macro if you need to make a change that is easy to decipher within the Visual Basic statements. If you need to make several changes to a macro or do not feel comfortable with the Visual Basic for Applications code window, you can re-record the macro. When you record a new macro that has the same name as an existing macro, Excel prompts you to replace the existing macro. You can then record the correct steps by overwriting the original macro.

▼ **Quick Steps**
Edit Macro
1. Open workbook containing macro.
2. Click View tab.
3. Click Macros button.
4. Click desired macro name.
5. Click Edit button.
6. Make desired changes in Visual Basic code window.
7. Click Save button.
8. Click File.
9. Click *Close and Return to Microsoft Excel.*

Figure 7.4 Microsoft Visual Basic for Applications Window for Project 1a AcctgDocumentation Macro

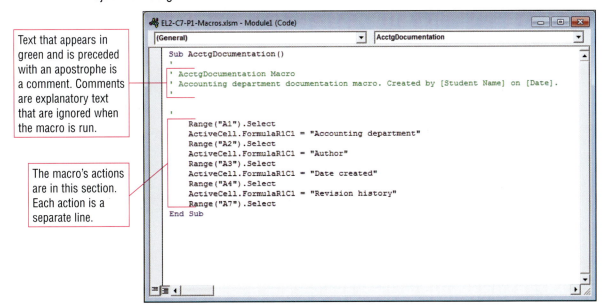

Text that appears in green and is preceded with an apostrophe is a comment. Comments are explanatory text that are ignored when the macro is run.

The macro's actions are in this section. Each action is a separate line.

Editing a Macro

1. With **EL2-C7-P1-Macros.xlsm** open, edit the AcctgDocumentation macro to leave only one blank row after the last entry by completing the following steps:
   a. If necessary, click the View tab.
   b. Click the Macros button in the Macros group.
   c. At the Macro dialog box with *AcctgDocumentation* already selected in the *Macro name* list box, click the Edit button. A Microsoft Visual Basic for Applications window opens with the program code displayed for EL2-C7-P1-Macros.xlsm Module1 (Code).

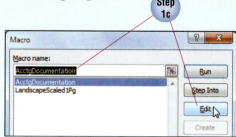

   d. Read the statements between the blue *Sub* and *End Sub* statements. *Sub* indicates the beginning of a procedure and *End Sub* indicates the end of the procedure. A procedure is a set of Visual Basic statements that perform actions. The name of the procedure is placed after the opening *Sub* statement and is the macro name. The lines beginning with a single apostrophe (') are comments. Comments are used in programming to insert explanatory text that describes the logic or purpose of a statement. Statements that begin with the apostrophe character are ignored when the macro is run. The commands that are executed when the macro is run are the indented lines of text below the comment lines.
   e. Position the insertion point at the beginning of the last statement before *End Sub* that reads *Range("A7").Select* and click the left mouse button. This is the last action in the macro that makes A7 the active cell. Notice the entry two lines above reads *Range("A4").Select*. To edit the macro and leave only one blank row you need to change the address from *A7* to *A6*.
   f. Use the Right Arrow key to move the insertion point, delete *7*, and type **6** so that the edited line reads *Range("A6").Select*.

```
EL2-C7-P1-Macros.xlsm - Module1 (Code)
(General)                              AcctgDocumentation

Sub AcctgDocumentation()
'
' AcctgDocumentation Macro
' Accounting department documentation macro. Created by [Student Name] on [Date].
'
'
    Range("A1").Select
    ActiveCell.FormulaR1C1 = "Accounting department"
    Range("A2").Select
    ActiveCell.FormulaR1C1 = "Author"
    Range("A3").Select
    ActiveCell.FormulaR1C1 = "Date created"
    Range("A4").Select
    ActiveCell.FormulaR1C1 = "Revision history"
    Range("A6").Select
End Sub
```

Step 1f

   g. Click the Save button on the toolbar.

2. Click File and then click *Close and Return to Microsoft Excel*.
3. Test the edited macro to make sure only one blank row is left before the active cell by completing the following steps:
   a. Select A1:A4 and press the Delete key.
   b. Make any cell other than A1 the active cell.
   c. Click the Macros button in the Macros group of the View tab. Do not click the down-pointing arrow on the button.
   d. At the Macro dialog box, double-click *AcctgDocumentation* in the *Macro name* list box.
4. Save and close **EL2-C7-P1-Macros.xlsm**.

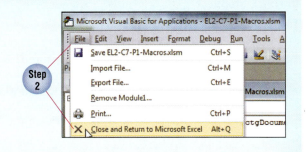

Step 2

Deleting a Macro

If you no longer need a macro, the macro can be deleted at the Macro dialog box. Open the Macro dialog box, select the macro name in the *Macro name* list box, and then click the Delete button.

Managing Macros

By default, macros are stored within the workbook that is active when the macro is recorded. When you close the workbook, the macros within the file are no longer available. For example, if you close the EL2-C7-P1-Macros.xlsm file, the AcctgDocumentation macro you created is not available to you in a new workbook. If you create macros that you want to use in other workbooks, one solution is to leave the workbook containing the macros open since the Macro dialog box, by default, displays macros in the *Macro name* list box from all open workbooks.

Consider creating a macros workbook with a set of standard macros that you wish to use in any file similar to the macros workbook you have created in Projects 1a through 1d. Open this workbook whenever you are working in Excel and the macros stored within the workbook will be available to you for all other files that you create or edit during an Excel session. Using this method, you can also copy the macros workbook to any other computer so that a set of standard macros can be distributed to others for their use.

Quick Steps
Delete Macro
1. Open Macro dialog box.
2. Click macro name.
3. Click Delete button.
4. Click Yes.

Project **2** **Customize the Excel Work Environment**   **8 Parts**

You will customize the Excel environment by pinning a frequently used workbook to the *Recent Workbooks* list, add buttons to the Quick Access toolbar to make features more accessible, minimize the ribbon to create more space in the work area, change display options, create a custom ribbon tab, and create custom views.

Pin Workbook to
Recent Workbooks
List
1. Make sure workbook has been opened recently.
2. Click File tab.
3. If necessary, click Recent.
4. Click pin icon next to workbook name.

Unpin Workbook
from *Recent*
***Workbooks* List**
1. Click File tab.
2. If necessary, click Recent.
3. Click blue pin icon next to workbook name.

Pinning Workbooks to the *Recent Workbooks* List ■■■■

The Recent tab Backstage view displays by default the 20 most recently opened workbook file names in the *Recent Workbooks* section in the left pane. The right pane displays a list of folders to which you have recently navigated in a section titled *Recent Places*. To open a workbook you used recently, click the workbook name in the *Recent Workbooks* list. A workbook that you use frequently can be permanently added to the *Recent Workbooks* list. To do this, make sure you have recently opened the workbook, click the File tab, click Recent if the Recent tab is not already displayed, and then click the pin icon next to the workbook name. A workbook that is permanently pinned to the list displays with a blue push pin icon. Clicking the blue push pin icon unpins a workbook from the list.

To change the number of workbooks shown in the *Recent Workbooks* list, open the Excel Options dialog box and click *Advanced* in the left pane. Change the number in *Show this number of Recent Documents* text box in the *Display* section to the desired number of workbooks.

Pinned
Workbook

Unpinned
Workbook

Project 2a **Pinning a Frequently Used Workbook to the *Recent Workbooks* List**   Part 1 of 8

1. Open **NorandaWinterSwimSch.xlsx**.
2. Scroll down the worksheet to review the winter swimming schedule and then close the workbook.
3. At a blank Excel screen, pin two workbooks to the *Recent Workbooks* list by completing the following steps:
   a. Click the File tab.
   b. By default the Recent tab Backstage view displays if no workbooks are currently open.
   c. Click the pin icon to the right of **NorandaWinterSwimSch.xlsx** in the *Recent Workbooks* list.
   d. Click the pin icon to the right of **EL2-C7-P1-Macros.xlsm**.

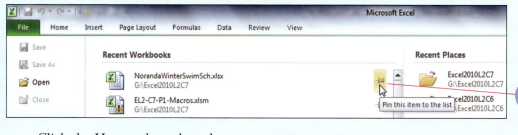

   e. Click the Home tab to close the Recent tab Backstage view.

4. Click the File tab and then click **EL2-C7-P1-Macros.xlsm** in the *Recent Workbooks* list to open the workbook.
5. Close **EL2-C7-P1-Macros.xlsm**.
6. Unpin the two workbooks by completing the following steps:
   a. Click the File tab.
   b. Click the blue push pin icon to the right of **EL2-C7-P1-Macros.xlsm**.
   c. Click the blue push pin icon to the right of **NorandaWinterSwimSch.xlsx**.
   d. Click the Home tab to close the Recent tab Backstage view.

Customizing the Quick Access Toolbar

As you work with Excel you may find that some features that you use frequently you would prefer to access from the Quick Access toolbar to save time and mouse clicks. Click the Customize Quick Access Toolbar button located at the right end of the toolbar to open the Customize Quick Access Toolbar drop-down list shown in Figure 7.5.

Click *More Commands* at the drop-down list to open the Excel Options dialog box with *Quick Access Toolbar* selected in the left pane as shown in Figure 7.6. Change the list of commands shown in the left list box by clicking the down-pointing arrow to the right of *Choose commands from* and then clicking the desired category. Scroll the list box to locate the command and then double-click the command name to add it to the Quick Access toolbar.

A few less popular features are only available by adding a button to the Quick Access toolbar. If a feature you are trying to locate is not available in any tab of the ribbon, search for the feature in the *All Commands* list.

Customize Quick Access Toolbar

▼ **Quick Steps**

Add Button to Quick Access Toolbar
1. Click Customize Quick Access Toolbar button.
2. Click desired button.
OR
1. Click Customize Quick Access Toolbar button.
2. Click *More Commands.*
3. Click down-pointing arrow at right of *Choose commands from.*
4. Click desired category.
5. Double-click desired command in commands list box.
6. Click OK.

Remove Button from Quick Access Toolbar
1. Click Customize Quick Access Toolbar button.
2. Click desired button.
OR
1. Click Customize Quick Access Toolbar button.
2. Click *More Commands.*
3. Click desired command in right list box.
4. Click Remove button.
5. Click OK.

Figure 7.5 Customize Quick Access Toolbar Drop-down List

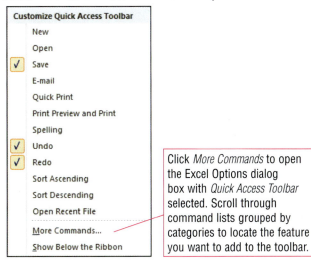

Click *More Commands* to open the Excel Options dialog box with *Quick Access Toolbar* selected. Scroll through command lists grouped by categories to locate the feature you want to add to the toolbar.

Figure 7.6 Excel Options Dialog Box with *Quick Access Toolbar* Selected

Begin by selecting the category from which to choose commands.

Next, double-click the command you wish to add from this list box.

Excel Options

General
Formulas
Proofing
Save
Language
Advanced
Customize Ribbon
Quick Access Toolbar
Add-Ins
Trust Center

Customize the Quick Access Toolbar.

Choose commands from:
Popular Commands

Customize Quick Access Toolbar:
For all documents (default)

<Separator>
Borders
Calculate Now
Center
Conditional Formatting
Connections
Copy
Create Chart
Custom Sort...
Cut
Datasheet Formatting
Decrease Font Size
Delete Cells...
Delete Sheet Columns
Delete Sheet Rows
E-mail
Fill Color
Filter
Font
Font Color
Font Size
Format Painter
Freeze Panes
Increase Font Size

Save
Undo
Redo

Add >>
<< Remove

Show Quick Access Toolbar below the Ribbon

Modify...

Customizations: Reset ▼
                    Import/Export ▼

OK   Cancel

Project 2b   Adding Commands to the Quick Access Toolbar   Part 2 of 8

1. Press Ctrl + N to start a new blank workbook and then add the Print Preview and Print and Sort commands to the Quick Access toolbar by completing the following steps:
   a. Click the Customize Quick Access Toolbar button located at the right end of the Quick Access toolbar.
   b. Click *Print Preview and Print* at the drop-down list. Print Preview and Print is added to the end of the Quick Access toolbar. **Note: Go to Step 1d if Print Preview and Print is already present on your Quick Access toolbar**.
   c. Click the Customize Quick Access Toolbar button.
   d. Click *More Commands* at the drop-down list.

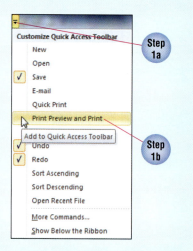

Customize Quick Access Toolbar
New
Open
✓ Save
E-mail
Quick Print
Print Preview and Print
Add to Quick Access Toolbar
✓ Undo
✓ Redo
Sort Ascending
Sort Descending
Open Recent File
More Commands...
Show Below the Ribbon

Step 1a

Step 1b

e. At the Excel Options dialog box with *Quick Access Toolbar* selected in the left pane, click the down-pointing arrow next to *Choose commands from* and then click *All Commands*.

f. Scroll down the *All Commands* list box and then double-click the *Sort* option that displays the ScreenTip *Data Tab | Sort & Filter | Sort....* (*SortDialog*). **Note: The commands are organized in alphabetical order—you will need to scroll far down the list**.

g. Click OK. The Sort button is added to the end of the Quick Access toolbar.

2. Type your name in A1, press Enter, and then click the Print Preview and Print button on the Quick Access toolbar to display the worksheet in Print Preview.

3. Click the Home tab to close the Print tab Backstage view.

4. Click the Sort button on the Quick Access toolbar to open the Sort dialog box.

5. Click the Cancel button at the Sort dialog box.

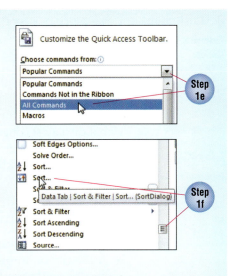

Project 2c   **Removing Buttons from the Quick Access Toolbar**   Part 3 of 8

1. Remove the Print Preview and Print and Sort buttons from the Quick Access toolbar by completing the following steps:

a. Click the Customize Quick Access Toolbar button.

b. Click *Print Preview and Print* at the drop-down list. **Note: Check with your instructor if Print Preview and Print was already present on the Quick Access toolbar before Project 2b. Your school may want the customized Quick Access toolbar to remain unchanged; go to Step 1d in this case**.

c. Click the Customize Quick Access Toolbar button.

d. Click *More Commands* at the drop-down list.

e. At the Excel Options dialog box with *Quick Access Toolbar* selected in the left pane, click *Sort* in the right list box and then click the Remove button.

f. Click OK.

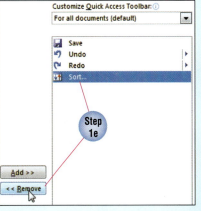

2. Close the workbook. Click Don't Save when prompted to save changes.

Changing Display Options to Customize the Work Area

The Excel Options dialog box contains many options for customizing the environment when the default options do not suit your needs. As shown in Figure 7.7, Excel groups options that affect the display of Excel by those that are global display settings, those that affect the entire workbook, and those that affect the active worksheet. Changes to workbook and/or worksheet display options are saved with the workbook.

Minimizing the Ribbon

When you are working with a large worksheet, you may find it easier to work with the ribbon minimized to provide more space within the work area. Figure 7.8 shows the worksheet you will use in Project 2d to customize the display options and minimize the ribbon. With the ribbon minimized, clicking a tab temporarily redisplays the ribbon to allow you to select a feature. As soon as you select the feature, the ribbon returns to the minimized state. Click the Minimize the Ribbon button located at the right end of the tab names (left of the Help button), or press Ctrl + F1, to toggle on or off the ribbon.

Figure 7.7 Excel Options Dialog Box with Display Options Shown

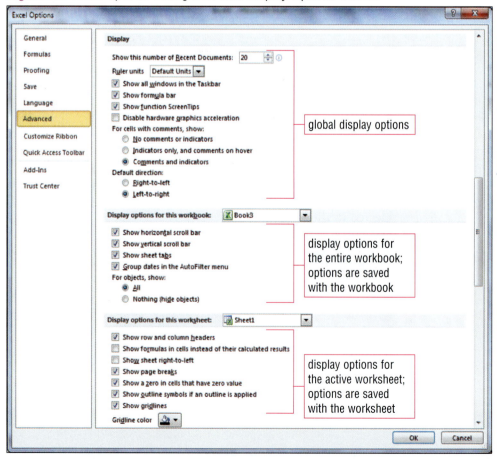

Figure 7.8 Project 2d Worksheet with Customized Display Options and Minimized Ribbon

Double-click a tab to show or hide the ribbon.

Project 2d   **Customizing Display Options and Minimizing the Ribbon**   **Part 4 of 8**

1. Open **NorandaWinterSwimSch.xlsx**.
2. Save the workbook with Save As and name it **EL2-C7-P2-NorandaWinterSwimSch**.
3. Turn off the display of the Formula bar since no formulas exist in the workbook, turn off the display of sheet tabs since only one sheet exists in the workbook, and turn off the display of row and column headers and gridlines by completing the following steps:
   a. Click the File tab.
   b. Click the Options button.
   c. Click *Advanced* in the left pane.
   d. Scroll down the Excel Options dialog box to the *Display* section and then click the *Show formula bar* check box to clear the check mark.
   e. Scroll down to the *Display options for this workbook* section and then click the *Show sheet tabs* check box to clear the check mark.

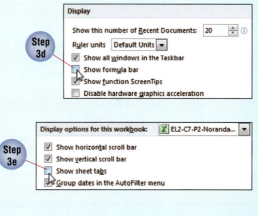

Step 3d

Step 3e

f. Scroll down to the *Display options for this worksheet* section and then click the *Show row and column headers* check box to clear the check mark.

g. Click the *Show gridlines* check box to clear the check mark.

h. Click OK.

4. Click the Minimize the Ribbon button located at the right end of the ribbon tabs (next to the Help button) to hide the ribbon.

5. Compare your screen with the one shown in Figure 7.8 on page 231.

6. Save and then close **EL2-C7-P3-NorandaWinterSwimSch.xlsx**.

Step 3f

Step 3g

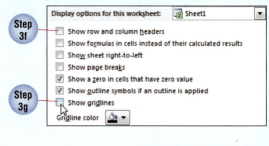

Step 4

Project 2e   **Restoring Default Display Options**   Part 5 of 8

1. Press Ctrl + N to start a new blank workbook.

2. Notice the display options that were changed in Project 2d that affect the workbook and the worksheet are restored to the default options. The Formula bar remains hidden since this option is a global display option. The ribbon remains minimized since the display of the ribbon is a toggle on/off option.

3. Open **EL2-C7-P2-NorandaWinterSwimSch.xlsx**.

4. Notice the sheet tabs, the row and column headers, and the gridlines remain hidden since these display option settings are saved with the workbook.

5. Close **EL2-C7-P3-NorandaWinterSwimSch.xlsx**.

6. Click the Expand the Ribbon button (previously the Minimize the Ribbon button) to redisplay the ribbon.

7. Redisplay the Formula bar by completing the following steps:
   a. Open the Excel Options dialog box.
   b. Click *Advanced* in the left pane.
   c. Scroll down the Excel Options dialog box to the *Display* section, click the *Show formula bar* check box to insert a check mark, and then click OK.

8. Close the workbook.

Step 6

Customizing the Ribbon ▪▪▪▪▪▪▪▪▪ ▪▪▪▪▪▪▪▪▪▪ ▪▪▪▪

HINT

Consider creating a custom tab with the buttons you use on a regular basis to save mouse clicks from frequently switching tabs and/or choosing options from drop-down lists (such as borders).

In addition to customizing the Quick Access toolbar, you can also customize the ribbon by creating a new tab. Within the new tab you can add groups and then add buttons within the groups. To customize the ribbon, click the File tab and then click the Options button. At the Excel Options dialog box, click *Customize Ribbon* in the left pane to open the dialog box shown in Figure 7.9.

The commands shown in the left list box are dependent on the current option for *Choose commands from*. Click the down-pointing arrow at the right of the current option (displays *Popular Commands*) to select from a variety of command lists such as *Commands Not In the Ribbon* or *All Commands*. The tabs shown in the right list box are dependent on the current option for *Customize the Ribbon*. Click the down-pointing arrow at the right of the current option (displays *Main Tabs*) to select *All Tabs*, *Main Tabs*, or *Tool Tabs*.

Figure 7.9 Excel Options Dialog Box with *Customize Ribbon* Selected

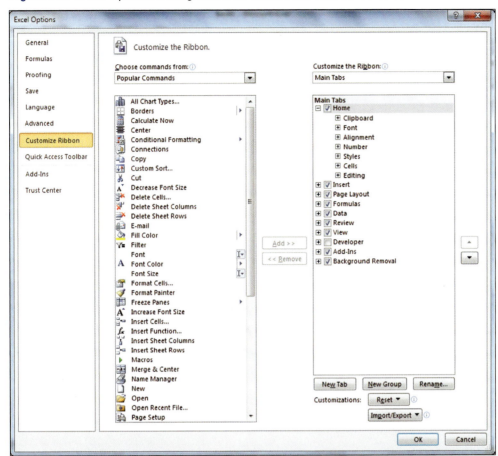

▼ **Quick Steps**

Create a New Tab and Group
1. Click File tab.
2. Click Options.
3. Click *Customize Ribbon* in left pane.
4. Click tab name to precede new tab.
5. Click New Tab button.

Add New Group to Existing Tab
1. Click File tab.
2. Click Options.
3. Click *Customize Ribbon* in left pane.
4. Click tab name with which the new group is associated.
5. Click New Group button.

Rename a Tab or Group
1. Click File tab.
2. Click Options.
3. Click *Customize Ribbon* in left pane.
4. Click tab or group to be renamed.
5. Click Rename button.
6. Type new name.
7. Press Enter or click OK.

Add Buttons to Group
1. Click File tab.
2. Click Options.
3. Click *Customize Ribbon* in left pane.
4. Click group name in which to insert new button.
5. Change *Choose commands from* to desired command list.
6. Scroll down and click desired command.
7. Click Add button.

You can create a new group in an existing tab and add buttons within the new group, or you can create a new tab, create a new group within the tab, and then add buttons to the new group.

Creating a New Tab

To create a new tab, click the tab name in the *Main Tabs* list box that you want the new tab positioned after and then click the New Tab button located below the *Main Tabs* list box. This inserts a new tab in the list box along with a new group below the new tab as shown in Figure 7.10. If you selected the wrong tab name before clicking the New Tab button, you can move the new tab up or down the list box by clicking *New Tab (Custom)* and then clicking the Move Up or the Move Down buttons that display at the right side of the dialog box.

Renaming a Tab or Group

Rename a tab by clicking the tab name in the *Main Tabs* list box and then clicking the Rename button located below the *Main Tabs* list box. At the Rename dialog box, type the desired name for the tab and then press Enter or click OK. You can also display the Rename dialog box by right-clicking the tab name and then clicking *Rename* at the shortcut menu.

Figure 7.10 New Tab and Group Created in the Customize Ribbon Pane at the Excel Options Dialog Box

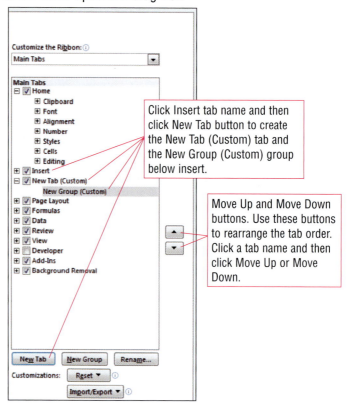

Complete similar steps to rename a group. The Rename dialog box for a group name or a command name contains a *Symbol* list as well as the *Display name* text box. Type the new name for the group in the *Display name* text box and press Enter or click OK. The symbols are useful for identifying new buttons rather than the group name.

Adding Buttons to a Tab Group

Add commands to a tab by clicking the group name within the tab, clicking the desired command in the list box at the left, and then clicking the Add button that displays between the two list boxes. Remove commands in a similar manner. Click the command you want to remove from the tab group and then click the Remove button that displays between the two list boxes.

Project 2f **Customizing the Ribbon**   Part 6 of 8

1. Open **NationalAcctgDeptJE.xlsx**.
2. Save the workbook with Save As and name it **EL2-C7-P2-NationalAcctgDeptJE**.
3. Customize the ribbon by adding a new tab and two new groups within the tab by completing the following steps:
   a. Click the File tab and then click the Options button.
   b. Click *Customize Ribbon* in the left pane of the Excel Options dialog box.

c. Click the Insert tab name in the *Main Tabs* list box located at the right of the dialog box.

d. Click the New Tab button located below the list box. (This inserts a new tab below the Insert tab and a new group below the new tab.)

e. With *New Group (Custom)* selected below *New Tab (Custom)*, click the New Group button that displays below the list box. (This inserts another new group below the new tab.)

4. Rename the tab and the groups by completing the following steps:

a. Click to select *New Tab (Custom)* in the *Main Tabs* list box.

b. Click the Rename button that displays below the list box.

c. At the Rename dialog box, type your first and last names and then press Enter or click OK.

d. Click to select the first *New Group (Custom)* group name that displays below the new tab.

e. Click the Rename button.

f. At the Rename dialog box, type **Borders** in the *Display name* text box and then press Enter or click OK. The Rename dialog box for a group or button displays symbols in addition to the *Display name* text box. You will apply a symbol to a button in a later step.

g. Right-click the New Group (Custom) group name below *Borders (Custom)* and then click *Rename* at the shortcut menu.

h. Type **Statistics** in the *Display name* text box at the Rename dialog box and then press Enter or click OK.

5. Add buttons to the *Borders (Custom)* group by completing the following steps:

a. Click to select *Borders (Custom)* in the *Main Tabs* list box.

b. Click the down-pointing arrow at the right of the *Choose commands from* list box (currently displays *Popular Commands*) and then click *All Commands* at the drop-down list.

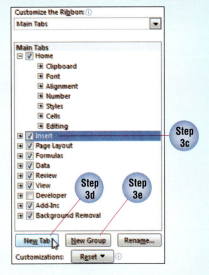

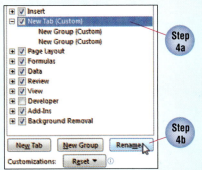

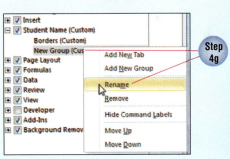

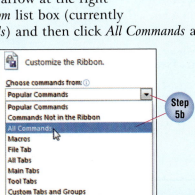

c. Scroll down the *All Commands* list box (the list displays alphabetically), click *Thick Bottom Border*, and then click the Add button located between the two list boxes. (This inserts the command below the Borders (Custom) group name.)

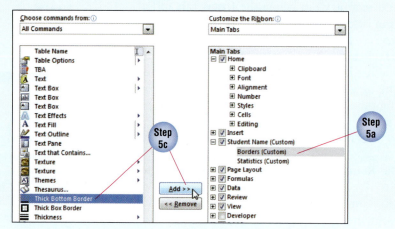

d. Scroll down the *All Commands* list box, click *Top and Double Bottom Border*, and then click the Add button.

6. Add buttons to the Statistics (Custom) group by completing the following steps:
a. Click to select *Statistics (Custom)* in the *Main Tabs* list box.

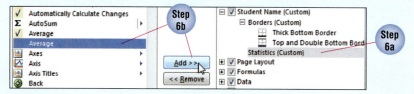

b. Scroll up the *All Commands* list box, click *Average* (choose the *Average* option that does not have a check mark), and then click the Add button.
c. Scroll down the *All Commands* list box, click *Max* (choose the *Max* option that does not have a check mark), and then click the Add button.
d. Scroll down the *All Commands* list box, click *Min* (choose the *Min* option that does not have a check mark), and then click the Add button.

7. Change the symbol for the Average, Max, and Min buttons by completing the following steps:
a. Right-click *Average* below *Statistics (Custom)* in the *Main Tabs* list box and then click *Rename* at the shortcut menu.
b. At the Rename dialog box, click the calculator icon in the *Symbol* list box (second icon in fifth row) and then click OK.
c. Right-click *Max* below *Statistics (Custom)*, click *Rename* at the shortcut menu, click the calculator icon in the *Symbol* list box at the Rename dialog box, and then click OK.

d. Change the symbol for *Min* to the calculator symbol by completing a step similar to Step 7c.

8. Click OK to close the Excel Options dialog box.

9. Use buttons in the custom tab to format and add formulas to the worksheet by completing the following steps:

a. Make A3 the active cell, click the custom tab with your name, and then click the Thick Bottom Border button in the Borders group.

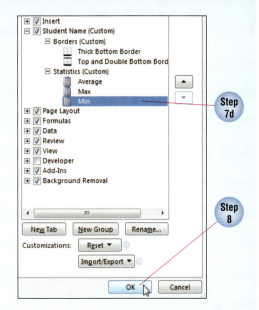

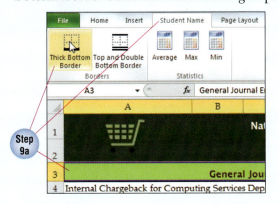

b. Select B6:H6 and click the Thick Bottom Border button in the Borders group.

c. Make D18 the active cell and then click the Top and Double Bottom Border button in the Borders group.

d. Make D20 the active cell and then click the Average button in the Statistics group.

e. With the range D7:D19 selected in the formula *=AVERAGE(D7:D19)*, drag to select D7:D17 and then press Enter.

f. With D21 the active cell, click the Max button in the Statistics group, drag to select the range D7:D17, and then press Enter.

g. With D22 the active cell, click the Min button in the Statistics group, drag to select the range D7:D17, and then press Enter.

10. Save **EL2-C7-P2-NationalAcctgDeptJE.xlsx**.

11. Insert a screen image of the worksheet showing the custom tab in a new Microsoft Word document using either Print Screen with Paste, the Screenshot feature (Insert tab, Screenshot button in Illustrations group), or the Windows Snipping tool (Start button, All Programs, Accessories). Type your name a few lines below the screen image.

12. Save the Microsoft Word document and name it **EL2-C7-P2-NationalAcctgDeptJE**.

13. Print **EL2-C7-P2-NationalAcctgDeptJE.docx** and then exit Word.

14. Print and then close **EL2-C7-P2-NationalAcctgDeptJE.xlsx**.

Resetting the Ribbon

Restore the original ribbon by clicking the Reset button that displays below the *Main Tabs* list box in the Excel Options dialog box with the Customize Ribbon pane selected. Clicking the Reset button displays two options—*Reset only selected Ribbon tab* and *Reset all customizations*. Click *Reset all customizations* to restore the ribbon to its original settings and then click Yes at the Microsoft Office message box that displays the message *Delete all Ribbon and Quick Access Toolbar customizations for this program?*

1. Open the Excel Options dialog box and click *Customize Ribbon* in the left pane.
2. Click the Reset button located below the *Main Tabs* list box.
3. Click *Reset all customizations* at the drop-down list.
4. Click Yes at the Microsoft Office message box that appears.
5. Click OK to close the Excel Options dialog box.

Step 2

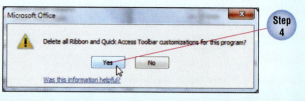
Step 3

Step 4

Creating and Applying a Custom View

A *custom view* saves display and print settings for the active worksheet. You can create multiple custom views for the same worksheet and apply a view by selecting a stored view name at the Custom Views dialog box. For example, in Project 2h you will create four custom views that store display settings, hidden rows, and a row height for a swimming schedule. You will switch between views to show different portions of the worksheet such as showing the morning swimming activities only.

In a custom view you can save settings such as column widths, row heights, hidden rows and/or columns, filter settings, cell selections, windows settings, page layout options, and a print area. Begin a custom view by applying the desired settings to the active worksheet. When finished, click the View tab, click the Custom Views button in the Workbook Views group, click the Add button, type a name for the custom view, and then click OK.

Change a worksheet to display a custom view's settings by opening the Custom Views dialog box, selecting the desired view name in the *Views* list box and then clicking the Show button. You can also double-click the desired view name to apply the saved display and print settings to the worksheet. If a worksheet other than the one in which the view was created is active, you will be switched to the worksheet for which the view applies.

1. Open **NorandaWinterSwimSch.xlsx**.
2. Save the workbook with Save As and name it
   EL2-C7-P2-NorandaWinterSwimSch-CustomViews.
3. Create a custom view with display settings for all swimming sessions by completing the following steps:
   a. Click the File tab, click the Options button, and then click *Advanced* in the left pane at the Excel Options dialog box.
   b. Scroll down the dialog box to the section titled *Display options for this worksheet*, click the *Show gridlines* check box to clear the check mark, and then click OK.
   c. Select rows 4 to 45, click the Format button in the Cells group in the Home tab, click *Row Height* at the drop-down list, type 25 in the *Row height* text box at the Row Height dialog box, and then press Enter or click OK.
   d. Click in any cell to deselect the rows.
   e. Click the View tab.
   f. Click the Custom Views button in the Workbook Views group.

   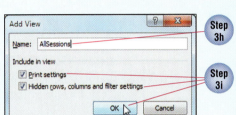

   g. Click the Add button at the Custom Views dialog box.
   h. With the insertion point positioned in the *Name* text box at the Add View dialog box, type **AllSessions**.
   i. With the *Print settings* and *Hidden rows, columns and filter settings* check boxes already selected, click OK.

4. Create a second custom view to display only the morning swimming activities by hiding the rows containing the afternoon and evening activities by completing the following steps:
   a. Select rows 19 to 45, click the Home tab, click the Format button in the Cells group, point to *Hide & Unhide* in the *Visibility* section, and then click *Hide Rows*.
   b. Click the View tab and then click the Custom Views button in the Workbook Views group.
   c. At the Custom Views dialog box click the Add button.
   d. At the Add View dialog box, type **MorningSessions** in the *Name* text box.
   e. With the *Print settings* and *Hidden rows, columns and filter settings* check boxes already selected, click OK.

   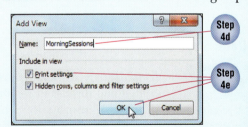

5. Click the Custom Views button in the Workbook Views group. With *AllSessions* currently selected in the *Views* list box, click the Show button to apply the custom view.

6. Create a third custom view to show only the afternoon swimming sessions by completing the following steps:
   a. Select rows 4 to 18 and hide the rows by completing a step similar to Step 4a.
   b. Hide rows 32 to 45.
   c. Create a custom view named *AfternoonSessions* by completing steps similar to Steps 4b through 4e.

7. Click the Custom Views button and then double-click *AllSessions* in the *Views* list box at the Custom Views dialog box.

8. Create a fourth custom view to show only the evening swimming sessions by completing the following steps:
   a. Hide rows 4 to 31.
   b. Create a custom view named *EveningSessions* by completing steps similar to Steps 4b through 4e.

9. Click the Custom Views button and then Show the *AllSessions* custom view.

10. Show the *MorningSessions* custom view.

11. Show the *AfternoonSessions* custom view.

12. Show the *EveningSessions* custom view.

13. Save and then close **EL2-C7-P2-NorandaWinterSwimSch-CustomViews.xlsx**.

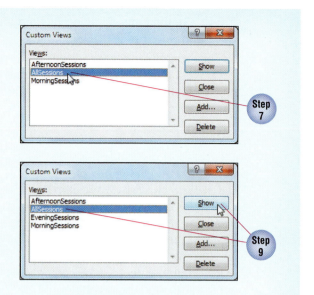

A custom view that is no longer needed can be deleted by opening the Custom Views dialog box, selecting the custom view name in the *Views* list box and then clicking the Delete button.

 **P**roject **3** **Save a Workbook as a Template** **3 Parts**

You will modify an existing workbook and save the revised version as a template.

▼ **Quick Steps**

Save Workbook as Template
1. Open workbook.
2. Make desired changes.
3. Click File tab.
4. Click Save As.
5. Change *Save as type* to *Excel Template (*.xltx)*.
6. Type desired file name.
7. Click Save button.

HINT

If macros exist in the template workbook, change the *Save as type* to *Excel Macro-Enabled Template (*.xltm)*.

Saving a Workbook as a Template

Templates are workbooks with standard text, formulas, and formatting. Cells are created and formatted for all of the entries that do not change. Cells are also created for variable information which has formatting applied but which are left empty since these cells will be filled in when the template is used to generate a worksheet. Examples of worksheets that would be suited to a template include an invoice, a purchase order, a time card, or an expense form. These templates would be reused often to fill in information that is different for each individual invoice, purchase order, time card, or expense.

Several templates have already been created and are available to you either installed on the computer or by download from Microsoft Office Online. New templates are made available through Microsoft Office Online frequently. Before creating a custom template, search the Microsoft Office Online website to see if a template already exists that is suited to your purpose.

If no template exists that meets your needs, you can create your own custom template. To do this, create a workbook that contains all of the standard data, formulas, and formatting. Leave cells empty for any information that is variable;

however, format these cells as required. When you are ready to save the workbook as a template, use the Save As dialog box and change *Save as type* to *Excel Template (*.xltx)*.

Consider protecting the worksheet by locking all cells except those that will hold variable data before saving the workbook as a template.

Project 3a　**Saving a Workbook as a Template**　　　　　　　　　　Part 1 of 3

1. Open **EL2-C7-P2-NorandaWinterSwimSch.xlsx**.
2. Redisplay the row and column headers in the worksheet. Refer to Project 2d if you need assistance with this step.
3. Assume that you work at the Noranda Sportsplex and have to publish swimming schedules often. The sportsplex manager never changes the days or times the pool operates; however, the activities and assigned pools will often change. You decide to modify this workbook and then save it as a template to be reused whenever the schedule changes. To begin, make the following changes to the worksheet:

   a. Clear the cell contents for the ranges D5:E18, D20:E31, and D33:E45.

   b. Make A2 the active cell, delete *Winter* in *Winter Swimming Schedule* so that the subtitle reads *Swimming Schedule*.

   c. Insert a new row between row 2 and row 3 and merge and center the cells in the new row to match the subtitle. (This will be used later to enter the timeframe for the new schedule.)

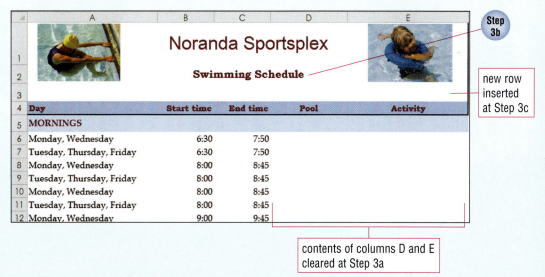

Step 3b

new row inserted at Step 3c

contents of columns D and E cleared at Step 3a

   d. Select and turn off the lock attribute for the following cells and ranges: A3, D6:E19, D21:E32, and D34:E46.

   e. Protect the worksheet. Do not assign a password to unprotect.

4. Save the revised workbook as a template by completing the following steps:
   a. Click the File tab.
   b. Click *Save As*.
   c. Click the Save as type button and then click *Excel Template (*.xltx)* at the pop-up list.
   d. Select the current text in the *File name* text box and then type **SwimSchTemplate-StudentName**, substituting your name for *StudentName*.
   e. Click the Save button.

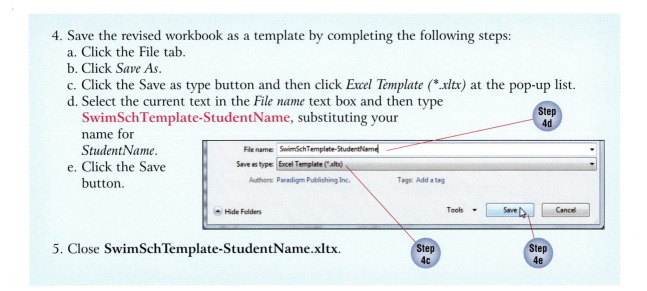

5. Close **SwimSchTemplate-StudentName.xltx**.

▼ **Quick Steps**

Use Custom Template
1. Click File tab.
2. Click New.
3. Click *My templates*.
4. Double-click desired template.

Using a Custom Template

To use a template that you created yourself, click the File tab and then click New. At the New tab Backstage view, click *My templates* in the Available Templates category at the top of the center pane. This opens the New dialog box shown in Figure 7.11. Double-click the desired template.

Figure 7.11 New Dialog Box

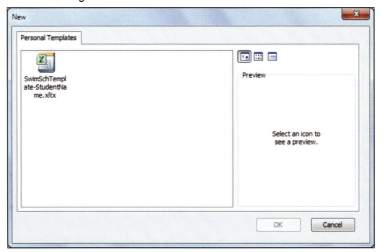

1. At a blank Excel screen, open the template created in Project 3a by completing the following steps:
   a. Click the File tab.
   b. Click *New*.
   c. At the New tab Backstage view, click *My templates* in the Available Templates category of the center pane.

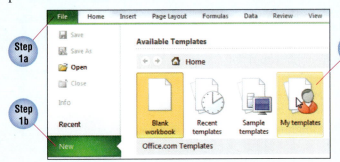

   d. At the New dialog box, double-click *SwimSchTemplate-StudentName.xltx,* where your name is substituted for *StudentName*.
2. Look at the workbook name in the title bar. Notice that Excel has added *1* to the end of the name.
3. Make A3 the active cell and then type Winter 2012.
4. Enter data for the first two rows in the MORNINGS section by making up a pool name and activity for each row.
5. Click the Save button on the Quick Access toolbar.
6. Excel opens the Save As dialog box and automatically changes the *Save as type* option to *Excel Workbook (*.xlsx)*. Type **EL2-C7-P3-SwimSchWinter2012** in the *File name* text box, navigate to the Excel2010L2C7 folder on your storage medium, and then click the Save button.
7. Print and then close **EL2-C7-P3-SwimSchWinter2012.xlsx**.

Deleting a Custom Template

To delete a custom template, click the File tab and then click *New*. At the New tab Backstage view, click *My templates* in the Available Templates category of the center pane. At the New dialog box, right-click the template you want to delete and then click *Delete* at the shortcut menu. At the Delete File dialog box, click Yes.

▼ **Quick Steps**

Delete Custom Template
1. Click File tab.
2. Click New.
3. Click *My templates*.
4. Right-click desired template name.
5. Click *Delete*.
6. Click Yes.
7. Close New dialog box.
8. Click Home tab.

1. At a blank Excel screen, delete the template created in Project 3a by completing the following steps:
   a. Click the File tab.
   b. Click *New*.
   c. At the New tab Backstage view, click *My templates* in the Available Templates category of the center pane.
   d. At the New dialog box, right-click *SwimSchTemplate-StudentName.xltx*, where your name is substituted for *StudentName*.
   e. Click *Delete* at the shortcut menu.
   f. At the Delete File dialog box, click Yes.
2. Close the New dialog box.
3. Click the Home tab.

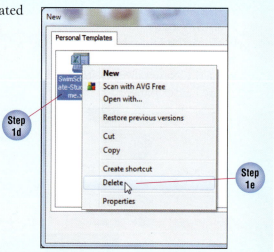

Project 4   Managing Excel's Save Options   2 Parts

You will review Excel's current save options, modify the AutoRecover options, and recover an unsaved workbook.

▼ Quick Steps

Customize Save Options
1. Click File tab.
2. Click Options button.
3. Click *Save* in left pane.
4. Change save options as required.
5. Click OK.

Do not rely on AutoRecover and AutoSave as you work. Saving regularly to minimize data loss as protection against unforeseen events is a best practice.

Options

Customizing Save Options ■■■■■■ ■■■■■■ ■ ■■

AutoRecover saves versions of your work at the time interval specified so that you can restore all or part of your data should you forget to save or otherwise experience a situation that causes Excel to close unexpectedly (such as a power outage). When you restart Excel, the Document Recovery task pane opens with a list of workbooks that have an AutoRecover file. By default, Excel's AutoRecover feature is turned on and will automatically save AutoRecover information every 10 minutes. You can adjust the time interval to meet your needs. Keep in mind that data loss can still occur even with AutoRecover turned on. If, for example, the time interval is 20 minutes and a power outage occurs, when you restart Excel the recovered file will not have the last 19 minutes of work if you did not save manually.

In conjunction with AutoRecover, Excel includes the **AutoSave** feature which will keep the last version of a workbook saved in a temporary file. You can recover the last version if you closed the workbook without saving or wish to return to the earlier version of the file. At the Recent tab Backstage view, you can view a listing of AutoSaved files.

Open the Excel Options dialog box with *Save* selected in the left pane to view and/or change the *AutoRecover* and *AutoSave* options.

Customizing Save Options

1. At a blank Excel screen, click the File tab and then click the Options button to open the Excel Options dialog box.
2. Click *Save* in the left pane of the Excel Options dialog box.
3. Take note of the current settings for *Save AutoRecover information every [ ] minutes* and *Keep the last autosaved version if I close without saving*. By default, both check boxes should be checked and the time interval is 10 minutes; however, the settings may have been changed on the computer you are using. In that case, write down the options so that you can restore the program to its original state.
4. If necessary, click the two check boxes to turn the AutoRecover and AutoSave features on.
5. Select the current value in the *Save AutoRecover information every [ ] minutes* text box and then type 2 to change the time interval to 2 minutes.
6. Click OK.

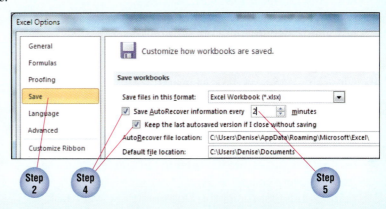

Recovering a Workbook

1. Open **EL2-C7-P2-NationalAcctgDeptJE.xlsx**.
2. Save the workbook with Save As and name it **EL2-C7-P4-NationalAcctgDeptJE**.
3. Note the system time at the bottom right corner of the screen. You want to make sure that more than two minutes elapses before you interrupt the Excel session.
4. Make the following changes to the worksheet:
   a. Select A7:A17 and change the font color to *Dark Red* (first color square in the *Standard Colors* section of the drop-down color palette).
   b. Select E7:E17 and change the font color to *Dark Red*.
   c. Delete rows 20 to 22 to remove the statistics from the workbook.

6		Parts	Labor	Total	TSR	Dept Code
7	Accounting	$ -	$ 1,125.00	$ 1,125.00	CS-4042	225
8	Executive Administration	564.27	885.50	1,449.77	CS-4043	216
9	Finance	964.32	535.50	1,499.82	CS-4044	166
10	Human Resources	397.45	125.50	522.95	CS-4045	187
11	Graphics Design	117.45	75.50	192.95	CS-4046	210
12	Electronic Production	215.48	275.50	490.98	CS-4047	350
13	Marketing	1,048.57	325.50	1,374.07	CS-4048	452
14	Web Programming	575.85	154.50	730.35	CS-4049	284
15	Planning and Development	61.45	32.50	93.95	CS-4050	310
16	President's Office	-	225.00	225.00	CS-4051	105
17	Purchasing	415.87	75.50	491.37	CS-4052	243
18				$ 8,196.21		
19						
20						
21						
22						

statistical data in rows 20 to 22 deleted at Step 4c

5. Make sure more than 2 minutes have elapsed since you checked the system time at Step 3. If necessary, wait until you are sure an AutoRecover file will have been saved.

6. Press Alt + Ctrl + Delete.

7. At the Windows screen, select *Start Task Manager*.

8. At the Windows Task Manager dialog box, click *Microsoft Excel - EL2-C7-P4-NationalAcctgDeptJE.xlsx* in the *Task* list box and then click the End Task button.

9. Click the End Now button at the End Program dialog box.

10. Close the Windows Task Manager dialog box.

11. Restart Microsoft Excel. When Excel opens the Document Recovery task pane will be open with two available files: the original version of the file used in this project and the AutoRecover version.

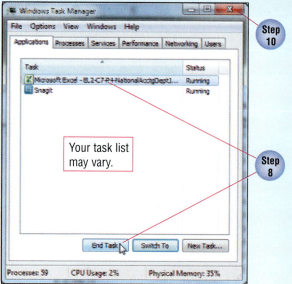

12. Point to the first file in the Document Recovery task pane. A ScreenTip displays informing you the first file is the AutoRecover version.

13. Point to the second file in the Document Recovery task pane. A ScreenTip displays informing you the second file is the original workbook.

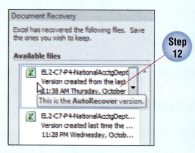

14. Click the first file in the Document Recovery task pane. Notice the edited version of the file appears. Look at the additional information displayed next to the file name in the Title bar. Excel includes *(version 1)* and *[Autosaved]* in the file name. Notice also that an Autosaved file has the file extension *.xlsb*.

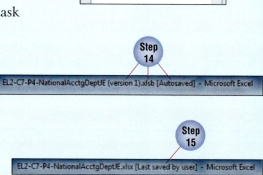

15. Click the second file in the Document Recovery task pane. Notice that the original workbook opens and the message *[Last saved by user]* is added to the file name in the Title bar.

16. Click the Close button located at the bottom of the Document Recovery task pane to close the pane.

17. Close both workbooks. Click Yes when prompted to save changes and then click *Save* at the Save As dialog box to accept the default name *EL2-C7-P4-NationalAcctgDeptJE (Autosaved).xlsx*.

18. Open the Excel Options dialog box. Restore the Save options to the settings you wrote down in Project 4a. If the Save options were the default options, change the time interval back to 10 minutes. Close the Excel Options dialog box.

The Save options at the Excel Options dialog box also allow you to specify the drive and/or folder in which the AutoRecover file is stored as well as the default file location for all new workbooks.

At the Recent tab Backstage View, click *Recover Unsaved Workbooks* at the bottom of the *Recent Places* pane to view a list of Autosaved files.

Chapter Summary

- Create a macro for a set of tasks that you repeat frequently in which the steps do not vary.
- Start creating a new macro by clicking the View tab, the down-pointing arrow on the Macros button in the Macros group, and then *Record Macro*.
- At the Record Macro dialog box, assign a name to the macro, an optional shortcut key, and a description.
- The macro recorder is turned on after you click OK to close the Record Macro dialog box. All commands and keystrokes are recorded until you click the Stop Recording button.
- Workbooks that contain macros are saved in the *Excel Macro-Enabled Workbook (*.xlsm) file format.
- Run a macro by opening the Macro dialog box and double-clicking the macro name.
- A macro assigned to a shortcut key is run by pressing Ctrl + the assigned letter.
- Excel differentiates the case of the letter typed in the *Shortcut key* text box at the Record Macro dialog box. An uppercase letter is assigned the shortcut key Ctrl + Shift + the assigned letter.
- If you assign a shortcut key to a macro that is the same as a shortcut key assigned to an Excel feature, the macro overrides the Excel shortcut.
- A macro's instructions are recorded in Visual Basic for Applications (VBA) program code. To edit a macro, open the Macro dialog box, click the macro name to be edited, and then click the Edit button. A Microsoft Visual Basic for Applications window opens with a code window in which you edit the macro's program code.
- After editing the macro, save the changes, click *File*, and then click *Close and Return to Microsoft Excel*.
- If you are not comfortable with editing a macro in Visual Basic for Applications, you can record a new macro to correct the steps using the same name to replace the existing macro.
- Delete a macro at the Macro dialog box.
- Macros are stored in the workbook in which they are created. When you open the Macro dialog box, all macros from all open workbooks are made accessible; therefore, to use a macro stored in another workbook you will need to open the other workbook first.
- Another option to make macros accessible to other workbooks is to create a macros workbook with all of your standard macros and open the macros workbook each time you start Excel.

- Pin a workbook that you want to make permanently available in the *Recent Workbooks* list at the Recent tab Backstage view.

- A pinned workbook displays with a blue push pin icon. Clicking the blue push pin icon unpins the workbook from the list.

- Add or delete a button to the Quick Access toolbar using the Customize Quick Access Toolbar button. Click *More Commands* from the drop-down list to open the Excel Options dialog box with *Quick Access Toolbar* selected to locate a feature you want to add in the commands list box.

- Display options in Excel are grouped by global display options, options that affect the current workbook, and options that affect the current worksheet.

- Customized workbook and worksheet display options are saved with the file.

- Minimize the ribbon to open more space in the work area when working with a large worksheet. The minimized ribbon displays only the tabs. Clicking a tab temporarily redisplays the ribbon to allow you to select a feature.

- You can customize the ribbon by creating a new tab, creating a new group within the new tab, and then adding buttons within the new group.

- To customize the ribbon, open the Excel Options dialog box and click *Customize Ribbon* in the left pane.

- Create a new ribbon tab by clicking the tab name that will precede the new tab and then clicking the New Tab button. A new group is automatically added with the new tab.

- Rename a custom tab by clicking to select the tab name, clicking the Rename button, typing a new name, and then pressing Enter or clicking OK. Rename a group using a similar process.

- Add buttons within a group by clicking the group name, selecting the desired command in the commands list box, and then clicking the Add button located between the two list boxes.

- Restore the ribbon to the default by clicking the Reset button located near the bottom right of the Excel Options dialog box with *Customize Ribbon* selected and then clicking *Reset all customizations* at the drop-down list.

- A custom view saves display settings so that you can apply the saved settings to a worksheet when needed. Multiple custom views can be created for the same worksheet at the Custom Views dialog box accessed by clicking the Custom Views button in the Workbook Views group of the View tab.

- Templates are workbooks with standard text, formatting, and formulas.

- A custom template is created from an existing workbook by saving the workbook as an *Excel template (*.xltx)* at the *Save as type* list at the Save As dialog box.

- To use a custom template, open the New tab Backstage view, click *My templates* to open the New dialog box and then double-click the custom template name.

- Delete a custom template at the New dialog box by right-clicking the template name and selecting *Delete* at the shortcut menu.

- By default, Excel saves your work every 10 minutes to an AutoRecover file. If your Excel session is unexpectedly terminated or you close the file without saving, you can recover the file when you restart Excel at the Document Recovery task pane.

Commands Review

FEATURE	RIBBON TAB, GROUP	BUTTON	KEYBOARD SHORTCUT
Custom Views	View, Workbook Views		
Customize Quick Access toolbar	File, Options		
Customize ribbon	File, Options		
Customize save options	File, Options		
Delete macro	View, Macros		Alt + F8
Display options	File, Options		
Edit macro	View, Macros		Alt + F8
Expand ribbon			
Minimize ribbon			Ctrl + F1
Record macro	View, Macros	OR	
Save as a macro-enabled workbook	File, Save As		F12
Use custom template	File, New		

Concepts Check Test Your Knowledge

Completion: In the space provided at the right, indicate the correct term, command, or number.

1. Macro names must begin with a letter and can contain a combination of letters, numbers, and this other character. _____

2. Click this button to indicate you have finished the tasks or keystrokes you want saved in the macro. _____

3. A workbook containing a macro is saved in this file format. _____

4. A macro can be assigned to a shortcut key that is a combination of a lowercase or uppercase letter and this other key. _____

5. Macro instructions are stored in this program code. _____

6. A workbook that you use frequently can be permanently added to the *Recent Workbooks* list by clicking this icon next to the workbook name. _____

7. Click this option at the Customize Quick Access Toolbar drop-down list to locate a feature to add to the toolbar from a commands list box. _____

8. Display options are shown in the Excel Options dialog box with this option selected in the left pane. _____

9. Click this button to minimize the ribbon to provide more space in the work area. _____

10. Click this option in the left pane at the Excel Options dialog box to create a custom ribbon tab. _____

11. Click this button at the Custom Views dialog box to create a new custom view that will save the current display settings for the active worksheet. _____

12. Change *Save as type* to this option at the Save As dialog box to save the current workbook as a standard workbook that can be opened from the New dialog box. _____

13. This task pane opens when Excel is restarted after the previous session ended abnormally. _____

Skills Check Assess Your Performance

Assessment

1 CREATE MACROS

1. At a new blank workbook, create the following two macros:
   a. Create a macro named *Landscape* that changes the page orientation to landscape, sets custom margins at top = 1 inch; bottom, left, and right = 0.5 inch; and centers the worksheet horizontally. Assign the macro to the shortcut key Ctrl + Shift + Q. Enter an appropriate description that includes your name and the date the macro was created.
   b. Create a macro named *Technic* that applies the theme named *Technic* and turns off the display of gridlines in the active worksheet. Assign the macro to the shortcut key Ctrl + t. Enter an appropriate description that includes your name and the date the macro was created.
2. Save the workbook as a macro-enabled workbook named **MyMacros-StudentName**, with your name substituted for *StudentName*.
3. Leave the **MyMacros-StudentName.xlsm** workbook open for the next assessment.

Assessment

2 RUN MACROS

1. Open **NationalAcctgDeptCS.xlsx**.
2. Save the workbook with Save As and name it
   EL2-C7-A2-NationalAcctgDeptCS.
3. Press Ctrl + t to run the Technic macro.
4. Press Ctrl + Shift + Q to run the Landscape macro.
5. Save, print, and then close **EL2-C7-A2-NationalAcctgDeptCS.xlsx**.
6. Close **MyMacros-StudentName.xlsm**.

Assessment

3 CREATE MACROS; SAVE AS A MACRO-ENABLED WORKBOOK

1. Open **EL2-C7-A2-NationalAcctgDeptCS.xlsx**.
2. Create the following two macros within the current workbook:
   a. Create a macro named *FormulaBarOff* that turns off the display of the Formula
      bar and protects the worksheet. Do not enter a password to unprotect the sheet.
      Assign the macro to the shortcut key Ctrl + Shift + M. Enter an appropriate
      description that includes your name and the date the macro was created.
   b. Create a macro named *FormulaBarOn* that turns on the display of the
      Formula bar and unprotects the worksheet. Assign the macro to the shortcut
      key Ctrl + Shift + B. Enter an appropriate description that includes your
      name and the date the macro was created.
3. Test each macro to make sure the shortcut key runs the correct commands.
4. Save the revised workbook as a macro-enabled workbook and name it
   EL2-C7-A3-NationalAcctgDeptCS.
5. Close **EL2-C7-A3-NationalAcctgDeptCS.xlsm**.

Assessment

4 PRINT MACROS

1. Open **EL2-C7-A3-NationalAcctgDeptCS.xlsm** and enable content.
2. Open the Macro dialog box and edit the FormulaBarOff macro.
3. At the Microsoft Visual Basic for Applications window with the insertion point
   blinking in the code window, click File on the Menu bar and then click *Print*.
   At the Print - VBAProject dialog box, click OK. ***Note: The FormulaBarOn
   macro code will also print since both macros are stored within the VBA Project.***
4. Click File on the Menu bar and then click *Close and Return to Microsoft Excel*.
5. Close **EL2-C7-A3-NationalAcctgDeptCS.xlsm**.
6. Open **MyMacros-StudentName.xlsm** and enable content.
7. Open the Macro dialog box and edit the Landscape macro.
8. At the Microsoft Visual Basic for Applications window with the insertion
   point blinking in the code window, click File on the Menu bar and then click
   Print. At the Print - VBAProject dialog box, click OK. ***Note: The Technic macro
   code will also print since both macros are stored within the VBA Project.***
9. Click File on the Menu bar and then click *Close and Return to Microsoft Excel*.
10. Close **MyMacros-StudentName.xlsm**.

Assessment

5 CUSTOMIZE THE EXCEL ENVIRONMENT

1. Open **BillingsDec21.xlsx**.
2. Save the workbook with Save As and name it **EL2-C7-A5-BillingsDec21**.
3. Make the following changes to the Display options:
   a. Turn off the horizontal scroll bar.
   b. Turn off sheet tabs.
   c. Turn off row and column headers.
   d. Turn off gridlines.
4. Change the current theme to Origin.
5. Freeze the first four rows in the worksheet.
6. Create a screen image of the worksheet with the modified display options and paste the image into a new Word document. Type your name a few lines below the screen image.
7. Save the Word document and name it **EL2-C7-A5-BillingsDec21**.
8. Print **EL2-C7-A5-BillingsDec21.docx** and then exit Word.
9. Save and close **EL2-C7-A5-BillingsDec21.xlsx**.

Assessment

6 CREATE CUSTOM VIEWS

1. Open **BillingsDec21.xlsx**.
2. Save the workbook with Save As and name it **EL2-C7-A6-BillingsDec21**.
3. Select A4:I23 and custom sort in ascending order by *Attorney* and then by the client's *Last Name*.
4. With A4:I23 still selected turn on filter arrows.
5. Deselect the range and then filter the *Attorney* column to show only those rows with the attorney name *Kyle Williams*.
6. Create a custom view named *Williams* to save the filter settings.
7. Clear the filter in the *Attorney* column.
8. Filter the list by the *Attorney* named *Marty O'Donovan*.
9. Create a custom view named *O'Donovan* to save the filter settings.
10. Clear the filter in the *Attorney* column.
11. Create a custom view named *Martinez* by completing steps similar to those in Steps 8 and 9 and then clear the filter from the *Attorney* column.
12. Create a custom view named *Sullivan* by completing steps similar to those in Steps 8 and 9 and then clear the filter from the *Attorney* column.
13. Open the Custom Views dialog box. If necessary, drag the Custom Views dialog box Title bar to move the dialog box to the right of the worksheet. Create a screen image of the worksheet with the dialog box open and paste the image into a new Word document. Type your name a few lines below the screen image.
14. Save the Word document and name it **EL2-C7-A6-BillingsDec21**.
15. Print **EL2-C7-A6-BillingsDec21.docx** and then exit Word.
16. Close the Custom Views dialog box and then save and close **EL2-C7-A6-BillingsDec21.xlsx**.

7 CREATE AND USE A TEMPLATE

1. Open **EL2-C7-A5-BillingsDec21.xlsx** and turn on the display of row and column headers.
2. Make the following changes to the workbook:
   a. Select and delete all of the data below the column headings in row 4.
   b. Delete the text in A3.
   c. Edit the subtitle in A2 to *Associate Weekly Billing Summary*.
3. Save the revised workbook as a template named **Billings-StudentName** with your name substituted for *StudentName*.
4. Close **Billings-StudentName.xltx**.
5. Start a new workbook based on the **Billings-StudentName.xltx** template.
6. Type the dates for Monday to Friday of the current week in A3 in the format *November 12 to 16, 2012*.
7. Enter the following two billings using Monday's date of the current week. Enter dates in the format mm/dd/yyyy. For example, *11/12/2012*.

| IN-774 | 10665 | [Monday's date] | Rankin | Jan | Maureen Myers | Insurance | 4.50 | 100.00 |
| EP-895 | 10996 | [Monday's date] | Knox | Velma | Rosa Martinez | Estate | 3.50 | 100.00 |

8. Save the worksheet as an Excel workbook named **EL2-C7-A7-Billings**.
9. Print and then close **EL2-C7-A7-Billings.xlsx**.
10. Display the New dialog box and right-click the template **Billings-StudentName.xltx**. Select *Copy* at the shortcut menu. Open a Computer window and navigate to the Excel2010L2C7 folder on your storage medium and then paste the template. Close the Computer window.
11. At the New dialog box, delete the custom template named **Billings-StudentName.xltx**.
12. Close the New dialog box and then click the Home tab.

Visual Benchmark Demonstrate Your Proficiency

1 CUSTOMIZE THE RIBBON

1. Create the custom tab including the groups and buttons shown in Figure 7.12. Substitute your name for *Student Name* in the tab. You can locate all of the buttons using the *All Commands* list.
2. Insert a screen image in a new Word document that shows the ribbon with the custom tab displayed in Microsoft Excel.
3. Save the Word document and name it **EL2-C7-VB1-MyRibbon**.
4. Print **EL2-C7-VB1-MyRibbon.docx** and then exit Word.
5. Restore the ribbon in Excel to its original settings.

Figure 7.12 Visual Benchmark 1

2 CREATE A CUSTOM TEMPLATE

1. Create a custom template that could be used to generate a sales invoice similar to the one shown in Figure 7.13. Use your best judgment to match the column widths, row heights, and color formatting. The font used in A1 is *Footlight MT Light 36-point* and *Garamond* for the remaining cells (18-point in A2 and 12-point elsewhere). Substitute an appropriate clip art image if the one shown is not available on the computer you are using. Recall that a template should only contain text, formulas, and formatting that is not variable from one invoice to another.
2. Save the workbook as a template and name it **EL2-C7-VB2-AudennitaSalesInv**.
3. Using the template, fill out a sales invoice using the data shown in Figure 7.13.
4. Save the completed invoice and name it **EL2-C7-VB2-AudennitaInvToVanderwyst**.
5. Print the invoice and then close **EL2-C7-VB2-AudennitaInvToVanderwyst.xlsx**.
6. Make a copy of the custom template at the New dialog box saving the copy to your storage medium in the Excel2010L2C7 folder.
7. Delete the custom template from the computer you are using at the New dialog box.

Figure 7.13 Visual Benchmark 2

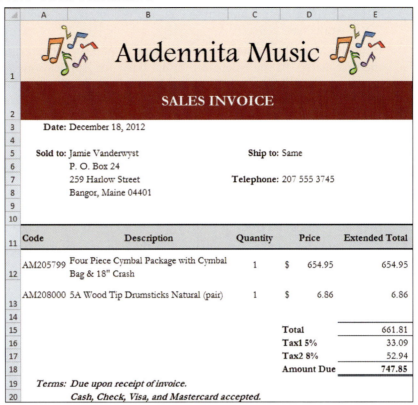

Case Study   Apply Your Skills

Part

1

Yolanda Robertson of NuTrends Market Research would like you to help her become more efficient by creating macros for the frequently performed tasks in the list below. In order to share the macros with colleagues in the office you decide to save all of the macros in a macro-enabled workbook named **EL2-C7-CS-P1-NuTrendMacros**. Delete Sheet2 and Sheet3 from the workbook. Rename Sheet1 to *MacroDocumentation*. Document the macros in the workbook by typing the macro names, the shortcut keys you assigned to each macro, and descriptions of the actions each macro performs. This documentation will assist your colleagues by informing them about the macros in the file. For example, in column A type the name of the macro, in column B type the macro's shortcut key, and in column C enter a description of the actions the macro performs.

Create a separate macro for each of the following tasks. At the Record Macro dialog box, type your name and the current date in the *Description* text box for each macro.

- Apply the theme named *Equity* and show all comments.
- Set the active column's width to 20.
- Apply conditional formatting to highlight the top 10 in a selected list. Accept the default formatting options.

- Apply the Accounting format with zero decimals.
- Create a footer that prints your name centered at the bottom of the worksheet.

Print the MacroDocumentation worksheet. Open the Macro dialog box and edit the first macro. At the Microsoft Visual Basic for Applications window, print the macros in the VBAProject. Close the Visual Basic for Applications window to return to the worksheet. Save **EL2-C7-CS-P1-NuTrendsMacros.xlsm**.

Part 2

Yolanda has received the file named **PizzaByMarioNewFranchiseRev.xlsx** from Nicola Carlucci. She wants you to format the workbook using the macros created in Part 1. Open the workbook and use Save As to name it **EL2-C7-CS-P2-PizzaByMarioNewFranchiseRev**. Run each macro created in Part 1 using the following information:

- Set all of the column widths to 20 except column C.
- Run the number formatting and the conditional formatting with the values in column E selected.
- Run the theme and footer macros.

Print the worksheet making sure the comments print as displayed. Save and then close **EL2-C7-CS-P2-PizzaByMarioNewFranchiseRev.xlsx**. Close **EL2-C7-CS-P1-NuTrendsMacros.xlsm**.

Part 3

Yolanda would like to customize the Quick Access toolbar but finds the process cumbersome using the Excel Options dialog box to locate commands. Use Excel Help to learn how to add a button to the Quick Access toolbar directly from the ribbon. Test the information you learned by adding two buttons of your choosing to the Quick Access toolbar using the ribbon. For example, add the Orientation button from the Page Layout tab and the New Comment button from the Review tab. Using Microsoft Word, compose a memo to Yolanda that describes the steps to add a button to the Quick Access toolbar directly from the ribbon. Insert a screen image of the Quick Access toolbar in Excel that displays the buttons you added below the memo text. Save the Word memo and name it **EL2-C7-C3-P3-CustomizeQATMemo**. Print **EL2-C7-CS-P3-CustomizeQATMemo.docx** and then exit Word. Remove the two buttons you added to the Quick Access toolbar.

Part 4

Yolanda has mentioned that sometimes she sees a task pane named Document Recovery appear when she starts Excel. She has asked you to explain why the task pane appears and what she should do when she sees the task pane. Compose a memo to Yolanda using Microsoft Word in which you explain the AutoRecover and AutoSave features in your own words. Include an explanation that the Document Recovery task pane appears after Excel has not been properly closed and provide advice for Yolanda on how to review the files in the pane to make sure she has not lost data.

Excel Microsoft®

Importing, Exporting, and Distributing Data

PERFORMANCE OBJECTIVES

Upon successful completion of Chapter 8, you will be able to:

- Import data from an Access table, a website, and a text file
- Append data from an Excel worksheet to an Access table
- Embed and link data in an Excel worksheet to a Word document
- Copy and paste data in an Excel worksheet to a PowerPoint presentation
- Export data as a text file
- Scan and remove private or confidential information from a workbook
- Mark a workbook as final
- Check a workbook for features incompatible with earlier versions of Excel
- Save an Excel worksheet as a PDF or XPS file
- Save an Excel worksheet as a web page
- Send an Excel worksheet via an email message
- Save an Excel worksheet to SkyDrive

Tutorials

8.1 Importing Data from Access, a Text File, or a Website
8.2 Exporting Data from Excel
8.3 Copying and Pasting Worksheet Data between Programs
8.4 Copying and Pasting Worksheet Data to a Word Document
8.5 Exporting Data as a Text File
8.6 Preparing a Worksheet for Distribution
8.7 Converting a Workbook to a Different Format
8.8 Creating a PDF/XPS Copy of a Worksheet
8.9 Publishing a Worksheet as a Web Page
8.10 Sending a Workbook via Email; Saving a Workbook to Windows Live SkyDrive

Exchanging data contained in one program with another by importing or exporting eliminates duplication of effort and reduces the likelihood of data errors or missed entries that would arise if the data was retyped. One of the advantages of working with a suite of programs such as Word, Excel, Access, and PowerPoint is the ability to easily integrate data from one program to another. In this chapter you will learn how to bring data into an Excel worksheet from sources external to Excel and how to export data in a worksheet for use with other programs. You will also learn to use features that allow you to send Excel data using a variety of distribution methods. Model answers for this chapter's projects appear on the following pages.

Excel
Excel2010L2C8

Note: Before beginning the projects, copy to your storage medium the Excel2010L2C8 subfolder from the Excel2010L2 folder on the CD that accompanies this textbook and then make Excel2010L2C8 the active folder.

NuTrends Market Research
U.S. Population Estimates by State

Source: U.S. Census Bureau

ID	State	July2009	July2008	July2007	July2006
1	Alabama	4,708,708	4,677,464	4,637,904	4,597,688
2	Alaska	698,473	688,125	682,297	677,325
3	Arizona	6,595,778	6,499,377	6,362,241	6,192,100
4	Arkansas	2,889,450	2,867,764	2,842,194	2,815,097
5	California	36,961,664	36,580,371	36,226,122	35,979,208
6	Colorado	5,024,748	4,935,213	4,842,259	4,753,044
7	Connecticut	3,518,288	3,502,932	3,488,633	3,485,162
8	Delaware	885,122	876,211	864,896	853,022
9	District of Columbia	599,657	590,074	586,409	583,978
10	Florida	18,537,969	18,423,878	18,277,888	18,088,505
11	Georgia	9,829,211	9,697,838	9,533,761	9,330,086
12	Hawaii	1,295,178	1,287,481	1,276,832	1,275,599
13	Idaho	1,545,801	1,527,506	1,499,245	1,464,413
14	Illinois	12,910,409	12,842,954	12,779,417	12,718,011
15	Indiana	6,423,113	6,388,309	6,346,113	6,301,700
16	Iowa	3,007,856	2,993,987	2,978,719	2,964,391
17	Kansas	2,818,747	2,797,375	2,775,586	2,755,700
18	Kentucky	4,314,113	4,287,931	4,256,278	4,219,374
19	Louisiana	4,492,076	4,451,513	4,376,122	4,240,327
20	Maine	1,318,301	1,319,691	1,317,308	1,314,963
21	Maryland	5,699,478	5,658,655	5,634,242	5,612,196
22	Massachusetts	6,593,587	6,543,595	6,499,275	6,466,399
23	Michigan	9,969,727	10,002,486	10,050,847	10,082,438
24	Minnesota	5,266,214	5,230,567	5,191,206	5,148,346
25	Mississippi	2,951,996	2,940,212	2,921,723	2,897,150
26	Missouri	5,987,580	5,956,335	5,909,824	5,861,572
27	Montana	974,989	968,035	957,225	946,230
28	Nebraska	1,796,619	1,781,949	1,769,912	1,760,435
29	Nevada	2,643,085	2,615,772	2,567,752	2,493,405
30	New Hampshire	1,324,575	1,321,872	1,317,343	1,311,894
31	New Jersey	8,707,739	8,663,398	8,636,043	8,623,721
32	New Mexico	2,009,671	1,986,763	1,968,731	1,942,608
33	New York	19,541,453	19,467,789	19,422,777	19,356,564
34	North Carolina	9,380,884	9,247,134	9,064,074	8,866,977
35	North Dakota	646,844	641,421	638,202	636,771
36	Ohio	11,542,645	11,528,072	11,520,815	11,492,495
37	Oklahoma	3,687,050	3,644,025	3,612,186	3,574,334
38	Oregon	3,825,657	3,782,991	3,732,957	3,677,545
39	Pennsylvania	12,604,767	12,566,368	12,522,531	12,471,142
40	Rhode Island	1,053,209	1,053,502	1,055,009	1,060,196
41	South Carolina	4,561,242	4,503,280	4,424,233	4,339,399
42	South Dakota	812,383	804,532	797,035	788,519
43	Tennessee	6,296,254	6,240,456	6,172,862	6,089,453
44	Texas	24,782,302	24,304,290	23,837,701	23,369,024
45	Utah	2,784,572	2,727,343	2,663,796	2,583,724
46	Vermont	621,760	621,049	620,460	619,985
47	Virginia	7,882,590	7,795,424	7,719,749	7,646,996
48	Washington	6,664,195	6,566,073	6,464,979	6,372,243
49	West Virginia	1,819,777	1,814,873	1,811,198	1,807,237
50	Wisconsin	5,654,774	5,627,610	5,601,571	5,571,680
51	Wyoming	544,270	532,981	523,414	512,841
52	Puerto Rico	3,967,288	3,954,553	3,941,235	3,926,744

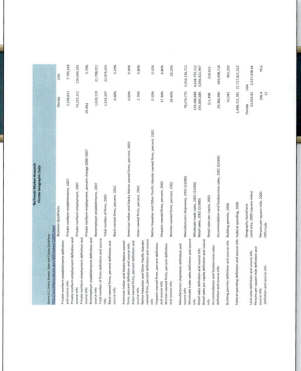

Project 1 Import Data from External Sources to Excel

Project 1a, EL2-C8-P1-NuTrendsCensusData.xlsx with PopulationEstimates Worksheet

Project 1b, EL2-C8-P1-NuTrendsCensusData.xlsx with FloridaGeographicData Worksheet

---

Housing Unit Estimates
100 Fastest Growing Counties
Change between July 1, 2008 and July 1, 2009

Source: Population Division, U.S. Census Bureau (HU-EST2005-06)

Rank	Geographic Area	Housing Unit Estimates		Change, 2008 to 2009	
		1-Jul-09	1-Jul-08	Number	Percent
1	Flagler County, FL	39,309	34,231	5,078	14.8
2	Sumter County, FL	35,786	31,715	4,071	12.8
3	Pinal County, AZ	108,777	98,666	10,111	10.2
4	Osceola County, FL	102,187	93,352	8,835	9.5
5	Franklin County, WA	20,433	18,681	1,752	9.4
6	Culpeper County, VA	16,154	14,775	1,379	9.3
7	Washington County, UT	48,777	44,908	3,869	8.6
8	Kendall County, IL	28,149	25,932	2,217	8.5
9	St. Lucie County, FL	117,020	108,130	8,890	8.2
10	Rockwall County, TX	22,103	20,528	1,575	7.7
11	Loudoun County, VA	93,374	86,915	6,459	7.4
12	Paulding County, GA	43,769	40,786	2,983	7.3
13	Walton County, FL	37,422	34,889	2,533	7.3
14	Yuba County, CA	25,437	23,749	1,688	7.1
15	Fannin County, GA	15,848	14,801	1,047	7.1
16	Jackson County, GA	21,072	19,690	1,382	7
17	St. Johns County, FL	74,850	69,964	4,886	7
18	Lee County, FL	312,724	292,830	19,894	6.8
19	Teton County, ID	3,693	3,460	233	6.7
20	Rutherford County, TN	90,147	84,753	5,394	6.4
21	Indian River County, FL	70,487	66,291	4,196	6.3
22	Henry County, GA	64,533	60,828	3,705	6.1
23	Forsyth County, GA	51,536	48,580	2,956	6.1
24	Barrow County, GA	23,141	21,841	1,300	6
25	Douglas County, CO	90,010	85,040	4,970	5.8
26	Newton County, GA	33,365	31,526	1,839	5.8
27	Cherokee County, GA	71,370	67,442	3,928	5.8
28	Brunswick County, NC	64,647	61,116	3,531	5.8
29	Iron County, UT	16,137	15,257	880	5.8
30	Deschutes County, OR	68,602	64,861	3,741	5.8
31	Lyon County, NV	16,647	15,750	897	5.7
32	Gallatin County, MT	34,097	32,266	1,831	5.7
33	Caroline County, VA	10,369	9,815	554	5.6
34	Nevada County, AR	5,600	5,305	295	5.6
35	Union County, NC	59,917	56,783	3,134	5.5
36	King George County, VA	8,283	7,859	424	5.4
37	Madison County, MS	34,109	32,388	1,721	5.3
38	Baldwin County, AL	89,900	85,380	4,520	5.3
39	Madison County, ID	10,412	9,890	522	5.3
40	Fayette County, TN	12,750	12,117	633	5.2

Page 1

11,860	11,272	588	5.2
29,896	28,427	1,469	5.2
718,358	683,244	35,114	5.1
15,248	14,515	733	5
12,475	11,877	598	5
127,656	121,564	6,092	5
140,596	133,916	6,680	5
52,979	50,465	2,514	5
26,591	25,335	1,256	5
44,427	42,331	2,096	5
65,570	62,501	3,069	4.9
44,673	42,591	2,082	4.9
42,578	40,624	1,954	4.8
7,189	6,860	329	4.8
14,871	14,194	677	4.8
2,529	2,415	114	4.7
17,108	16,337	771	4.7
42,277	40,373	1,904	4.7
250,452	239,179	11,273	4.7
203,449	194,333	9,116	4.7
147,207	140,628	6,579	4.7
91,613	87,521	4,092	4.7
40,220	38,427	1,793	4.7
125,667	120,072	5,595	4.7
17,505	16,734	771	4.6
17,369	16,606	763	4.6
60,524	57,874	2,650	4.6
39,522	37,802	1,720	4.6
15,082	14,427	655	4.5
12,005	11,484	521	4.5
10,162	9,722	440	4.5
10,743	10,278	465	4.5
76,074	72,788	3,286	4.5
4,175	3,995	180	4.5
29,050	27,801	1,249	4.5
40,240	38,513	1,727	4.5
699,474	669,785	29,689	4.4
31,140	29,823	1,317	4.4
5,759	5,516	243	4.4
46,574	44,611	1,963	4.4
94,768	90,778	3,990	4.4
6,293	6,029	264	4.4
44,733	42,859	1,874	4.4
56,686	54,314	2,372	4.4
30,294	29,028	1,266	4.4
89,761	86,013	3,748	4.4
86,749	83,141	3,608	4.3

Page 2

127,340	122,047	5,293	4.3
25,820	24,752	1,068	4.3
34,865	33,424	1,441	4.3
12,393	11,881	512	4.3
11,481	11,010	471	4.3
54,650	52,411	2,239	4.3
207,862	199,393	8,469	4.2
72,953	69,984	2,969	4.2
97,270	93,315	3,955	4.2
13,994	13,426	568	4.2
9,080	8,712	368	4.2
13,119	12,588	531	4.2
8,183	7,853	330	4.2

Page 3

Project 1c, EL2-C8-P1-NuTrendsCensusData.xlsx with HousingUnitData Worksheet

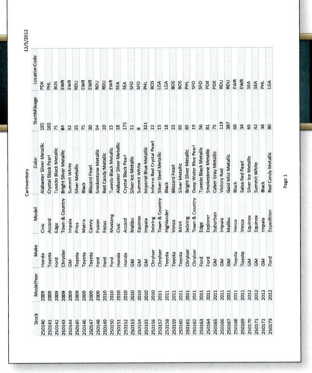

Project 2 Export Data in Excel

Project 2a, CarInventory Datasheet from CutRateInventory.accdb

Project 2b, EL2-C8-P2-CutRateCarRpt.docx

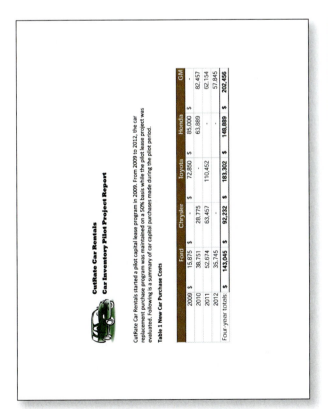

Project 2c, EL2-C8-P2-CutRateCarRptLinked.docx

Project 2e, EL2-C8-P2-CutRateCarRpt.pptx

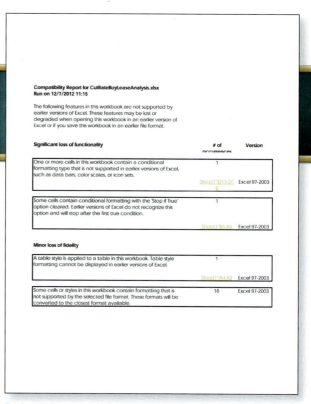

```
                        EL2-C8-P2-CutRateInventory.csv
CutRate Car Rentals,,,,,,
New Car Inventory,,,,,,

,,,,,,
Stock,ModelYear,Make,Model,Color,StartMileage,LocationCode
250145,2009,Toyota,Prius,Silver Metallic,25,RDU
250146,2009,Toyota,Matrix,Black,75,EWR
250147,2009,Toyota,Camry,Blizzard Pearl,30,EWR
250148,2009,Ford,Fusion,Smokestone Metallic,54,RDU
250149,2010,Ford,Focus,Red Candy Metallic,10,RDU
250150,2010,Ford,Mustang,Tuxedo Black Metallic,15,EWR
250151,2010,Honda,Civic,Alabaster Silver Metallic,18,SEA
250152,2010,Honda,Accord,Crystal Black Pearl,175,SEA
250153,2010,GM,Malibu,Silver Ice Metallic,11,SFO
250154,2010,GM,Equinox,Summit White,8,SFO
250155,2010,GM,Impala,Imperial Blue Metallic,321,PHL
250156,2010,Chrylser,Sebring,Inferno Red Crystal Pearl,22,BOS
250157,2011,Chrylser,Town & Country,Silver Steel Metallic,15,LGA
250158,2011,Toyota,Highlander,Black,18,LGA
250159,2011,Toyota,Venza,Blizzard Pearl,23,BOS
250160,2011,Toyota,RAV4,Silver Metallic,65,BOS
250161,2011,Chrylser,Sebring,Bright Silver Metallic,85,PHL
250162,2011,Chrylser,Town & Country,Deep Water Blue Pearl,19,SFO
250163,2011,Ford,Edge,Tuxedo Black Metallic,56,SFO
250164,2011,Ford,Explorer,Smokestone Metallic,81,PDX
250165,2011,GM,Suburban,Cyber Gray Metallic,75,PDX
250166,2011,GM,Impala,Victory Red,119,RDU
250167,2011,GM,Malibu,Gold Mist Metallic,387,RDU
250168,2011,Toyota,Venza,Black,68,EWR
250169,2011,Toyota,Venza,Salsa Red Pearl,34,EWR
250170,2012,GM,Equinox,Silver Ice Metallic,65,SEA
250171,2012,GM,Equinox,Summit White,42,SEA
250172,2012,GM,Impala,Black,38,PHL
250173,2012,Ford,Expedition,Red Candy Metallic,80,LGA
```

Page 1

Project 2f, EL2-C8-P2-CutRateInventory.csv

Project 3 Prepare a Workbook for Distribution
Project 3c, EL2-C8-P3-CutRateBuyLeaseAnalysisCompChk.xlsx

Compatibility Report for CutRateBuyLeaseAnalysis.xlsx
Run on 12/7/2012 11:15

The following features in this workbook are not supported by earlier versions of Excel. These features may be lost or degraded when opening this workbook in an earlier version of Excel or if you save this workbook in an earlier file format.

Significant loss of functionality	# of occurrences	Version
One or more cells in this workbook contain a conditional formatting type that is not supported in earlier versions of Excel, such as data bars, color scales, or icon sets. *Sheet1!D13:D16*	1	Excel 97-2003
Some cells contain conditional formatting with the 'Stop if True' option cleared. Earlier versions of Excel do not recognize this option and will stop after the first true condition. *Sheet1!B5:K8*	1	Excel 97-2003

Minor loss of fidelity

	# of occurrences	Version
A table style is applied to a table in this workbook. Table style formatting cannot be displayed in earlier versions of Excel. *Sheet1!A4:K8*	1	Excel 97-2003
Some cells or styles in this workbook contain formatting that is not supported by the selected file format. These formats will be converted to the closest format available.	16	Excel 97-2003

Model Answers

Project 1 Import Data from External Sources to Excel   3 Parts

You will import U.S. Census Bureau data related to a market research project from an Access database, from the U.S. Census Bureau's website, and from a text file previously downloaded from the Census Bureau.

Importing Data into Excel ■■■■■■■■■■■■■■■■■■■

The Get External Data group in the Data tab contains buttons used to import data from external sources into an Excel worksheet. During an import or export routine, the program containing the original data is called the *source*, and the program to which the data source is being copied, embedded, or linked is called the *destination*. Make the cell active at which you want the import to begin and click the button representing the source application, or click the From Other Sources button to select the source from a drop-down list. A connection can be established to an external data source to avoid having to repeat the import process each time you need to analyze the data in Excel. Once a connection has been created, you can repeat the import in another worksheet by simply clicking the connection file in the Existing Connections dialog box.

Importing Data from Access

Exchanging data between Access and Excel is a seamless process since data in an Access datasheet is structured in the same row and column format as an Excel worksheet. You can import the Access data as an Excel table, a PivotTable Report, or as a PivotChart and a PivotTable report. The imported data can be placed in a cell you identify in the active worksheet or in a new worksheet. To import an Access table, click the Data tab and then click the From Access button in the Get External Data group. At the Select Data Source dialog box, navigate to the drive and/or folder in which the source database resides and then double-click the Access database file name in the file list. If the source database contains more than one table, the Select Table dialog box opens in which you choose the table containing the data you want to import. If the source database contains only one table you are not prompted to select a table name. Once the table is identified, the Import Data dialog box shown in Figure 8.1 appears. Choose how you want to view the data and the location to begin the import and click OK.

▼ Quick Steps

Import Access Table
1. Make active cell at which to begin import.
2. Click Data tab.
3. Click From Access button.
4. Navigate to drive and/or folder.
5. Double-click source database file name.
6. If necessary, click desired table name and OK.
7. Select desired view format.
8. Click OK.

HINT

Only one table can be imported at a time. To import all of the tables in the source database, repeat the import process for each table.

From Access

Figure 8.1 Import Data Dialog Box

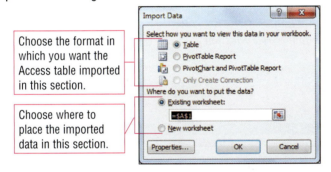

Choose the format in which you want the Access table imported in this section.

Choose where to place the imported data in this section.

Project 1a | **Importing Data from an Access Database** | Part 1 of 3

1. Open **NuTrendsCensusData.xlsx**.
2. Save the workbook with Save As and name it **EL2-C8-P1-NuTrendsCensusData**.
3. Import four years of U.S. state population estimates compiled by the U.S. Census Bureau that are stored in an Access database by completing the following steps:
   a. With PopulationEstimates the active worksheet, make A5 the active cell if A5 is not currently active.
   b. Click the Data tab.
   c. Click the From Access button in the Get External Data group.
   d. At the Select Data Source dialog box, navigate to the Excel2010L2C8 folder on your storage medium and then double-click **NuTrendsCensusData.accdb**.

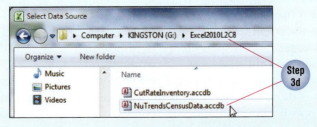

e. Since the source database contains more than one table, the Select Table dialog box appears. Click *PopByState* in the *Name* column and then click OK.

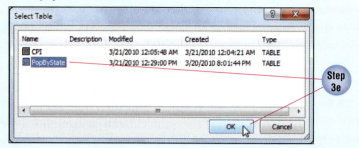

Step 3e

f. At the Import Data dialog box with *Table* selected in the *Select how you want to view this data in your workbook* section and with =$A$5 in the *Existing worksheet* text box in the *Where do you want to put the data?* section, click OK.

Step 3f

4. Scroll down the imported table data. Notice the data is formatted as a table with filter arrow buttons.
5. Make the following changes to the worksheet:
   a. Remove the filter arrow buttons.
   b. Change the table style to *Table Style Medium 1* (first from left in *Medium* section) at the Format as Table drop-down gallery.
   c. Format all of the values to display a comma in the thousands and zero decimals.

Steps 5a-5e

   d. Adjust the column widths of columns C to F to 15.
   e. Center-align the labels in C5:F5.
6. Print the PopulationEstimates worksheet scaled to fit 1 page in width and height and centered horizontally between the left and right margins.
7. Save **EL2-C8-P1-NuTrendsCensusData.xlsx**.

▼ **Quick Steps**

Import Data from Web Page
1. Make active cell at which to begin import.
2. Click Data tab.
3. Click From Web button.
4. Navigate to desired web page.
5. Click arrows next to tables to import.
6. Click Import button.
7. Click OK.

Importing Data from a Website

Tables in a website can be downloaded directly from the web source using the New Web Query dialog box shown in Figure 8.2. Make active the cell at which you want to begin the import, click the Data tab, and then click the From Web button in the Get External Data group. Use the Address bar and web navigation buttons to go to the page containing the data you want to use in Excel. At the desired page, Excel displays black right-pointing arrows inside yellow boxes next to elements on the page that contain importable tables. Point to an arrow and a blue border surrounds the data Excel will capture if you click the arrow. Click the arrow for those tables you want to bring into your Excel worksheet and then click the Import button. In Project 1b, you will import multiple sections of data about Florida from the U.S. Census Bureau QuickFacts web page.

Figure 8.2 New Web Query Dialog Box

Navigate to the desired website as you would in a browser window.

Point to an arrow in a yellow box to display a blue border around a table on the web page. Click the arrow to select the table and then click the Import button to copy the data into the active cell.

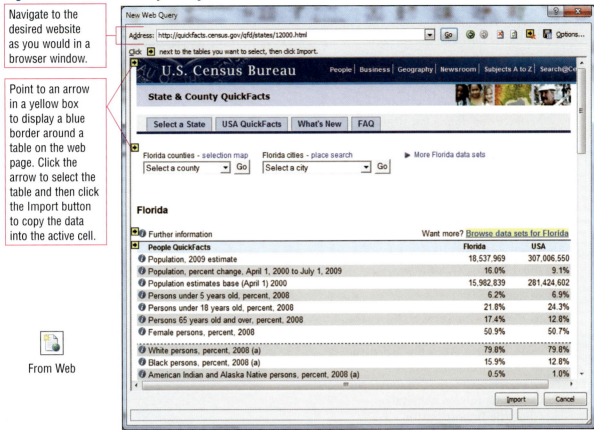

From Web

Project 1b   **Importing a Table from a Web Page**   Part 2 of 3

1. With **EL2-C8-P1-NuTrendsCensusData.xlsx** open, make FloridaGeographicData the active worksheet.
2. Import statistics related to Florida from the U.S. Census Bureau QuickFacts web page by completing the following steps:
   a. Make A6 the active cell if A6 is not currently active.
   b. Click the From Web button in the Get External Data group of the Data tab.
   c. At the New Web Query dialog box, select the current entry in the *Address* text box, type http://www.census.gov, and press Enter.
   d. Click the Data Tools link located near the top left of the web page.

e. At the Data Access Tools page, scroll down the page if necessary and then click the QuickFacts link in the *Interactive Internet Tools* section.

f. At the State & County QuickFacts page, resize the New Web Query dialog box until you can see the entire map of the United States.

g. Click over the state of Florida in the map. *Note: If a **Script Error dialog box displays, click** Yes **to continue running scripts on the page***.

h. At the Florida QuickFacts page, notice the black right-pointing arrows inside yellow boxes along the left edge of the page. Point to one of the arrows to see the blue border that surrounds a section of data; the border indicates the data that will be imported into Excel if you click the arrow.

i. Scroll down the page to the section titled *Business QuickFacts*.

j. Click the black right-pointing arrow inside the yellow box next to *Business QuickFacts* to select the table. The arrow changes to a check mark inside a green box when the table is selected for import.

k. Click the arrow next to *Geography QuickFacts* to select the table.

l. Click the Import button.

Step 2e

Step 2g

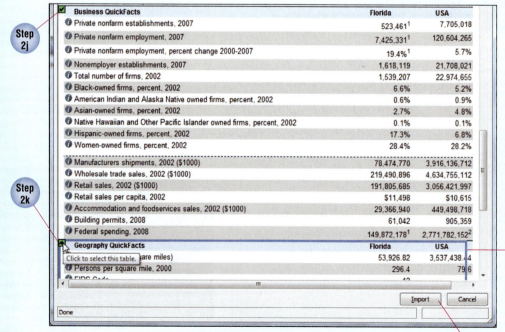

Step 2j

Step 2k

A blue border displays around the data that will be imported to Excel if the table is selected.

Step 2l

m. At the Import Data dialog box with *=$A$6* in the *Existing worksheet* text box in the *Where do you want to put the data?* section, click OK. Excel imports the data from the web page into the Excel worksheet starting in A6.

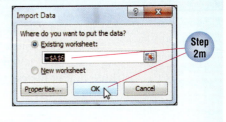

Step 2m

3. Make the following changes to the worksheet:
   a. Select the cells in Column A that contain imported text, click the Home tab, and then click the Wrap Text button in the Alignment group.
   b. Decrease the width of column A to 35.00 (250 pixels).
   c. Select the cells in Column A that contain imported text, click the Format button in the Cells group of the Home tab, and then click *AutoFit Row Height* at the drop-down list.
   d. Align the text in C6:D6 at the center.
   e. Change the page orientation to landscape.
4. Print the FloridaGeographicData worksheet scaled to fit 1 page width by 1 page height and centered between the left and right margins.
5. Save **EL2-C8-P1-NuTrendsCensusData.xlsx**.

Importing Data from a Text File

A text file is often used to exchange data between dissimilar programs since the file format is recognized by nearly all applications. Text files contain no formatting and consist of letters, numbers, punctuation symbols, and a few control characters only. Two commonly used text file formats separate fields with either a tab character (delimited file format) or a comma (comma separated file format). The text file you will use in Project 1c is shown in a Notepad window in Figure 8.3. If necessary, you can view and edit a text file in Notepad prior to importing.

Figure 8.3 Project 1c Text File Contents

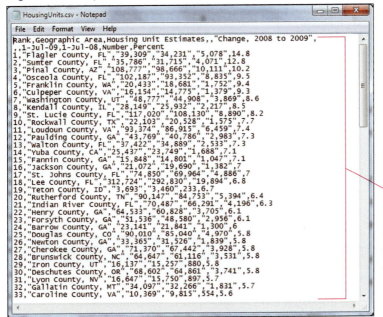

Text files contain no formatting codes. A comma separated file (.csv) contains a comma separating each field. During the import, Excel starts a new column at each comma. Notice also that quotes surround text data. Excel strips the quotes from the data upon importing.

Most programs can export data in a text file. If you need to use data from a program that is not compatible with Excel, check the source program's export options for a text file format.

To import a text file into Excel, use the From Text button in the Get External Data group of the Data tab and then select the source file at the Import Text File dialog box. Excel displays in the file list any file in the active folder that ends with a text file extension *.prn, .txt,* or *.csv.* Once the source file is selected, Excel begins the Text Import Wizard, which guides you through the import process through three dialog boxes.

Project 1c Importing Data from a Comma Separated Text File   Part 3 of 3

1. With **EL2-C8-P1-NuTrendsCensusData.xlsx** open, make HousingUnitData the active worksheet.
2. Import statistics related to the top-growing U.S. counties based on changes in housing units downloaded from the U.S. Census Bureau website in a text file by completing the following steps:
   a. Make A6 the active cell if A6 is not currently active.
   b. Click the Data tab.
   c. Click the From Text button in the Get External Data group.
   d. At the Import Text File dialog box, double-click the file named ***HousingUnits.csv*** in the file list.
   e. At the Text Import Wizard - Step 1 of 3 dialog box, with *Delimited* selected in the *Original data type* section, click Next. Notice the preview window in the lower half of the dialog box displays a sample of the data in the source text file. Delimited files use commas or tabs as separators, while fixed-width files use spaces.
   f. At the Text Import Wizard - Step 2 of 3 dialog box, click the *Comma* check box in the *Delimiters* section to insert a check mark and then click Next. Notice after you select the comma as the delimiter character, the data in the *Data*

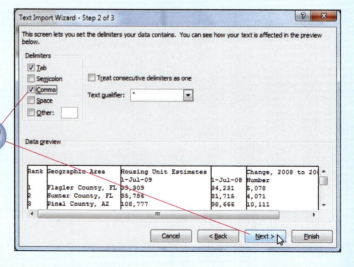

preview section updates to show the imported data arranged in Excel columns.

g. Click Finish at the Text Import Wizard - Step 3 of 3 dialog box to import all of the columns using the default *General* format. Formatting can be applied after the data has been imported into the worksheet.

h. At the Import Data dialog box with *=$A$6* in the *Existing worksheet* text box in the *Where do you want to put the data?* section, click OK.

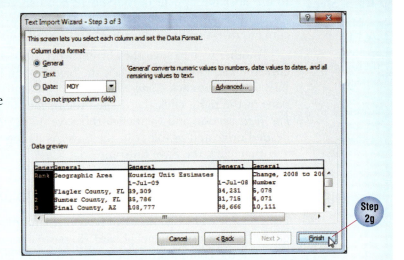

Step 2g

3. Scroll down the worksheet and view the imported data. The text file contained the top 100 counties in the United States ranked by change in housing units from 2008 to 2009. The number of housing units and the percent change are included.

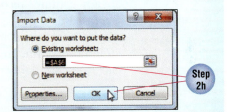

Step 2h

4. Make the following changes to the data:
   a. Select C6:D6, click the Home tab, and then click the Merge & Center button in the Alignment group.
   b. Merge and center E6:F6.
   c. Right-align E7.
   d. Change the width of columns C, D, and E to 14.00 (103 pixels).
5. Print the HousingUnitData worksheet centered between the left and right margins.
6. Save and then close **EL2-C8-P1-NuTrendsCensusData.xlsx**.

Project **2** **Export Data in Excel** **6 Parts**

You will copy and paste data related to car inventory from an Excel worksheet to integrate with an Access database, a Word report, and a PowerPoint presentation. You will also save a worksheet as a comma separated text file for use in a non-Microsoft program.

Exporting Data from Excel ■■■■■■■■ ■■■■■■■■■ ■■

Excel data can be exported for use in other programs by copying the cells to the clipboard and pasting into the destination document or by saving the worksheet as a separate file in another file format. To use Excel data in Word, PowerPoint, or Access, use the copy and paste routine since the programs within the Microsoft Office Suite are designed for integration. To export the Excel data for use in other programs, open the Save As dialog box and change the *Save as type* option to the desired file format. If the file format for the destination program that you want

Quick Steps

Append Excel Data to Access Table
1. Select cells.
2. Click Copy button.
3. Start Access.
4. Open database.
5. Open table in Datasheet view.
6. Click Paste button arrow.
7. Click *Paste Append*.
8. Click Yes.
9. Deselect pasted range.

to use does not appear in the *Save as type* list, you can try copying and pasting the data or go to the Microsoft Office Online website and search for a file format converter that you can download and install.

Another way to save the current worksheet in another file format is to click the File tab and then click the Save & Send tab. At the Save & Send tab Backstage view, click *Change File Type* in the center pane. In the Change File Type pane at the right, click the desired file format in the *Workbook File Types* or *Other File Types* section and then click the Save As button. If necessary, navigate to the desired drive and/or folder in the Save As dialog box. Type the desired file name and then click the Save button.

Copying and Pasting Worksheet Data to an Access Table

Data in an Excel worksheet can be copied and pasted to an Access table datasheet, query, or form using the clipboard. To paste data into a table datasheet, make sure that the column structure in the two programs match. If the Access datasheet already contains records, you can choose to replace the existing records or append the Excel data to the end of the table. If you want to export Excel data to an Access database that does not have an existing table in which to receive the data, perform an import routine from Access. To do this, start Access, open the desired database, click the External Data tab, and then click the Import Excel spreadsheet button.

Project 2a **Copying and Pasting Excel Data to an Access Datasheet** Part 1 of 6

1. Open **CutRateInventory.xlsx**.
2. Copy and paste the rows in the Inventory worksheet to the bottom of an Access table by completing the following steps:
   a. Make sure Inventory is the active worksheet.
   b. Select A5:G33 and click the Copy button in the Clipboard group in the Home tab.
   c. Start Microsoft Access 2010.
   d. Click File, then click New. At the New tab Backstage view, click the Open button.
   e. At the Open dialog box, navigate to the Excel2010L2C8 folder on your storage medium and then double-click the database named ***CutRateInventory.accdb***. If a Security Warning message displays below the ribbon stating that active content has been disabled, click the Enable Content button.

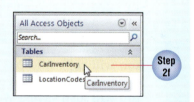

   f. Double-click the object named *CarInventory* in the Tables group of the Navigation pane at the left side of the Access window. This opens the CarInventory table in Datasheet view. Notice the structure of the columns in the datasheet is the same as the source worksheet in Excel.

   g. With the table open in Datasheet view, click the down-pointing arrow on the Paste button in the Clipboard group and then click *Paste Append* at the drop-down list.

h. At the Microsoft Access message box informing you that you are about to paste 29 records and asking if you are sure, click Yes.

i. Click any cell within the datasheet to deselect the pasted records.

Step 2h

3. Print the datasheet in Access in landscape orientation by completing the following steps:
   a. Click the File tab, click the Print tab, and then click Print Preview at the Print tab Backstage view.
   b. Click the Landscape button in the Page Layout group in the Print Preview tab.

Step 3b

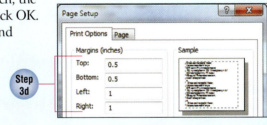

Step 3c

   c. Click the Page Setup button in the Page Layout group.
   d. At the Page Setup dialog box with the Print Options tab selected, change the Top and Bottom margins to 0.5 inch, the Left and Right margins to 1 inch, and then click OK.
   e. Click the Print button in the Print group and then click OK at the Print dialog box.
   f. Click the Close Print Preview button in the Close Preview group.

Step 3d

4. Click the File tab and then click the Exit button located at the bottom of the left pane in the Backstage view.
5. Click any cell to deselect the range in the Inventory worksheet and then press the Esc key to remove the moving marquee.
6. Leave the **CutRateInventory.xlsx** workbook open for the next project.

Copying and Pasting Worksheet Data to a Word Document

Using a process similar to the one in Project 2a, you can copy and paste Excel data, copy and embed Excel data as an object, or copy and link Excel data as an object in a Word document. Use the copy and paste method if the data being brought into Word is not likely to be updated or require editing once the source cells are pasted in the Word document. Copy and embed the data if you want to have the ability to edit the data once it is inserted in Word using Excel's editing tools and features. Copy and link the data if the information being pasted into Word is likely to be changed in the future and you want the document in Word updated if the data in the source file changes.

Embed Excel Data in Word Document
1. Select cells.
2. Click Copy button.
3. Open Word document.
4. Position insertion point at desired location.
5. Click Paste button arrow.
6. Click *Paste Special.*
7. Click *Microsoft Excel Worksheet Object.*
8. Click OK.

Link Excel Data in Word Document
1. Select cells.
2. Click Copy button.
3. Open Word document.
4. Position insertion point at desired location.
5. Click Paste button arrow.
6. Click *Paste Special.*
7. Click *Microsoft Excel Worksheet Object.*
8. Click Paste link.
9. Click OK.

Embedding Excel Data into Word

To embed copied Excel data into a Word document, open the desired Word document, move the insertion point to the location at which you want to insert the copied Excel data, and then open the Paste Special dialog box. At the Paste Special dialog box, click *Microsoft Excel Worksheet Object* in the *As* list box and then click OK.

To edit an embedded Excel object in Word, double-click over the embedded cells to open the cells for editing in a worksheet. Word's ribbon is temporarily replaced with Excel's ribbon. Click outside the embedded object to restore Word's ribbon and close the worksheet object in Word.

Linking Excel Data into Word

Linking Excel data to a Word document means that the source data exists only in Excel. Word places a shortcut to the source data file name and range in the Word document. When you open a Word document containing a link, Word prompts you to update the links. Since the data resides in the Excel workbook only, be careful not to move or rename the original workbook from which you copied the cells or the link will no longer work.

To paste copied Excel data as a link in a Word document, open the desired Word document, move the insertion point to the location at which you want to link the cells, open the Paste Special dialog box, click *Microsoft Excel Worksheet Object* in the *As* list box, click *Paste link*, and then click OK.

Project 2b   **Embedding Excel Data in a Word Document**   Part 2 of 6

1. With **CutRateInventory.xlsx** open, copy and embed the data in the CarCosts worksheet to a Word document by completing the following steps:
   a. Make CarCosts the active worksheet.
   b. Select A4:F9.
   c. Click the Copy button in the Clipboard group.
   d. Start Microsoft Word 2010.
   e. Open **CutRateCarRpt.docx** from the Excel2010L2C8 folder on your storage medium.
   f. Save the document with Save As and name it **EL2-C8-P2-CutRateCarRpt**.
   g. Press Ctrl + End to move the insertion point to the end of the document.
   h. Click the down-pointing arrow on the Paste button in the Clipboard group and then click *Paste Special* at the drop-down list.

Step 1h

i. At the Paste Special dialog box, click *Microsoft Excel Worksheet Object* in the *As* list box and then click OK.

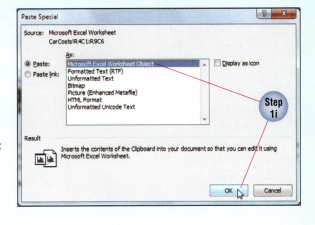

Step 1i

2. Save **EL2-C8-P2-CutRateCarRpt.docx**.
3. When you use Paste Special, the copied cells are embedded as an object in the Word document. Edit the embedded object using Excel's editing tools by completing the following steps:
   a. Double-click over any cell in the embedded worksheet object. The object is surrounded with a border and Excel's column and row headers appear with the cells. Word's ribbon is temporarily replaced with Excel's ribbon.
   b. Select B5:F9 and then click the Accounting Number Format button in the Number group.

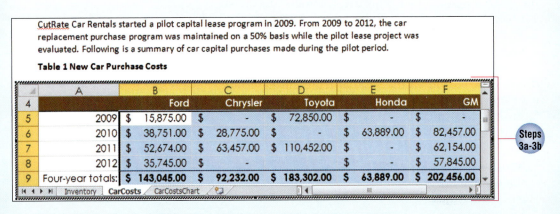

Steps 3a-3b

   c. Click in the document outside the embedded object to close the object and restore Word's ribbon.
4. Save and then print **EL2-C8-P2-CutRateCarRpt.docx**.
5. Click the File tab and then click the Exit button located at the bottom of the left pane in the Backstage view.
6. Click any cell to deselect the range in the CarCosts worksheet and leave the **CutRateInventory.xlsx** workbook open for the next project.

Project 2c   **Linking Excel Data in a Word Document**   Part 3 of 6

1. With **CutRateInventory.xlsx** open, copy and link the data in the CarCosts worksheet to a Word document by completing the following steps:
   a. With CarCosts the active worksheet, select A4:F9 and click the Copy button.
   b. Start Microsoft Word 2010.
   c. Open **CutRateCarRpt.docx**.
   d. Save the document with Save As and name it **EL2-C8-P2-CutRateCarRptLinked**.
   e. Press Ctrl + End to move the insertion point to the end of the document.

f. Click the down-pointing arrow on the Paste button and then click *Paste Special* at the drop-down list.

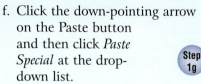

g. At the Paste Special dialog box, click *Microsoft Excel Worksheet Object* in the *As* list box and then click *Paste link*.

h. Click OK.

2. Save and then close **EL2-C8-P2-CutRateCarRptLinked.docx**. When data is linked, the data exists only in the source program. In the destination document, Word inserted a shortcut to the source range. Edit the source range and view the update to the Word document by completing the following steps:

a. Click the button on the Taskbar representing the Excel file named **CutRateInventory.xlsx**.

b. With CarCosts the active worksheet, press the Esc key to remove the moving marquee and then click any cell to deselect the copied range.

c. Make E5 the active cell, type 85000, and press Enter.

d. Click the button on the Taskbar representing Word.

e. Open **EL2-C8-P2-CutRateCarRptLinked.docx**.

f. At the Microsoft Word message box asking if you want to update the document with data from the linked files, click Yes.

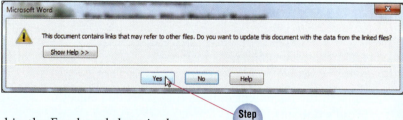

3. Notice the data inserted in the Excel worksheet is also shown in the linked Word document.

4. Save and then print **EL2-C8-P2-CutRateCarRptLinked.docx**.

5. Exit Word.

6. With CarCosts the active worksheet in **CutRateInventory.xlsx**, delete the contents of E5 and leave the workbook open for a later project.

▼ **Quick Steps**

Break Link to Excel Object
1. Open document.
2. Right-click linked object.
3. Point to *Linked Worksheet Object.*
4. Click *Links.*
5. Click Break Link button.
6. Click Yes.
7. Save document.

Breaking a Link to an Excel Object

If you linked Excel data to a Word document and later decide you no longer need to maintain the link, you can break the connection between the source and destination files so that you are not prompted to update the object each time you open the document. Breaking the link means that the data in the Word document will no longer be connected to the data in the Excel workbook. If you make a change to the original source in Excel, the Word document will not reflect the updated information. To break a link, open the document, right-click over the linked object, point to *Linked Worksheet Object,* and click *Links* at the shortcut menu. This opens the Links dialog box. If more than one linked object exists in the document, click the source object for the link you want to break and then click the Break Link button. Click Yes to confirm you want to break the link at the message box that appears.

1. Start Word and open **EL2-C8-P2-CutRateCarRptLinked.docx**.
2. At the message asking if you want to update links, click No.
3. Break the link between the Excel workbook and the linked object by completing the following steps:
   a. Right-click over the linked Excel worksheet object.
   b. Point to *Linked Worksheet Object* and then click *Links* at the shortcut menu.
   c. At the Links dialog box, with the linked object file name selected in the *Source file* list box, click the Break Link button.
   d. At the Microsoft Word dialog box asking if you are sure you want to break the selected link, click Yes.
4. Save **EL2-C8-P2-CutRateCarRptLinked.docx** and then exit Word.

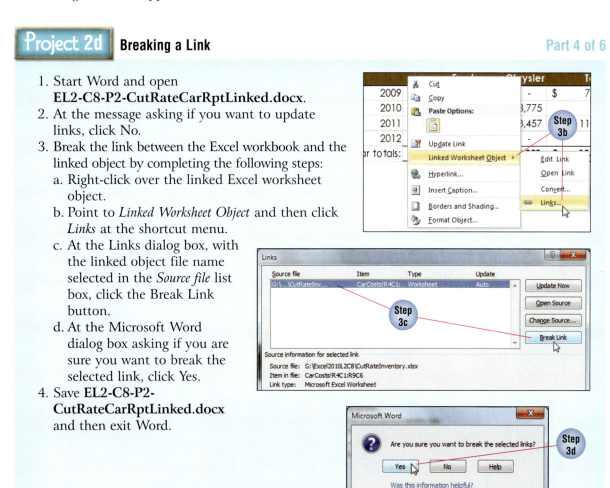

Copying and Pasting Worksheet Data to a PowerPoint Presentation

As with Word, you can copy and paste, copy and embed, or copy and link Excel data to slides in a PowerPoint presentation. Although you can create tables and charts in a PowerPoint slide, some people prefer to use Excel for these tasks and then copy and paste the data to PowerPoint. Presentations often incorporate charts to visually depict numerical data in a graph format that is easy to understand. In the Office 2010 suite, the charting system is fully integrated within Word, Excel, and PowerPoint. A chart inserted in a Word document or PowerPoint presentation is created as an embedded object with the source data used to generate the chart stored in an Excel worksheet; the Excel worksheet with the source data becomes part of the document or presentation file.

▼ **Quick Steps**

Embed Excel Data in PowerPoint
1. Select cells.
2. Click Copy button.
3. Open PowerPoint presentation.
4. Make desired slide active.
5. Click Paste button arrow.
6. Click *Paste Special*.
7. Make sure *Microsoft Excel Worksheet Object* is selected in *As* list box.
8. Click OK.

Since the chart feature is fully integrated within Word, Excel, and PowerPoint, you can edit a chart in a PowerPoint presentation using the same techniques you learned to edit a chart in Excel. Clicking a chart on a PowerPoint slide causes the contextual Chart Tools Design, Chart Tools Layout, and Chart Tools Format tabs to become active with the same groups and buttons available in Excel.

Project 2e **Embedding Excel Data in a PowerPoint Presentation** Part 5 of 6

1. With **CutRateInventory.xlsx** open, copy and embed the chart in the CarCostsChart worksheet to a slide in a PowerPoint presentation by completing the following steps:
   a. Make CarCostsChart the active worksheet.
   b. Click the Home tab and then click the Copy button.
   c. Start Microsoft PowerPoint 2010.
   d. Open **CutRateCarRpt.pptx**.
   e. Save the presentation with Save As and name it **EL2-C8-P2-CutRateCarRpt**.
   f. Click Slide 3 in the Slides pane.
   g. Click the Paste button in the Clipboard group. Since all charts are embedded by default, you do not need to use Paste Special.
2. Resize the chart to the approximate height and width shown and position the chart in the center of the slide horizontally.

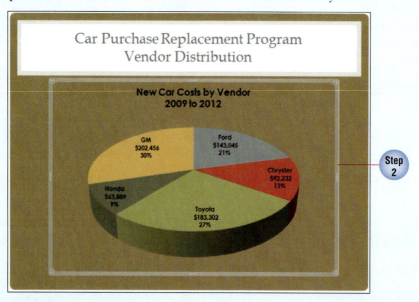

3. Copy and embed the table used to generate the chart in the CarCosts worksheet to the next slide in the PowerPoint presentation by completing the following steps:
   a. Click Slide 4 in the Slides pane.
   b. Click the button on the Taskbar representing the Excel workbook **CutRateInventory.xlsx**.
   c. Make CarCosts the active worksheet, select A1:F9, and click the Copy button.
   d. Click the button on the taskbar representing the PowerPoint presentation **EL2-C8-P2-CutRateCarRpt.pptx**.
   e. Click the down-pointing arrow on the Paste button and then click *Paste Special* at the drop-down list.

f. With *Microsoft Excel Worksheet Object* selected in the *As* list box, click OK.

4. Resize and position the embedded table to the approximate height, width, and position shown.

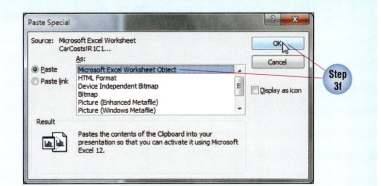

Step 3f

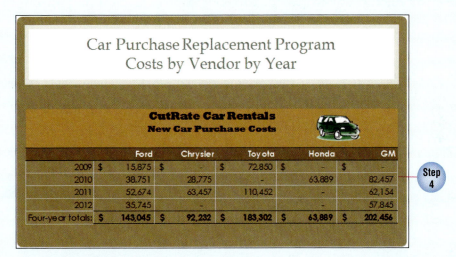

Step 4

5. Click the File tab and then click the Print tab. At the Print tab Backstage view, click the button in the Settings category of the center pane that currently reads *Full Page Slides*, and then click *4 Slides Horizontal* at the drop-down list. Click the Print button.

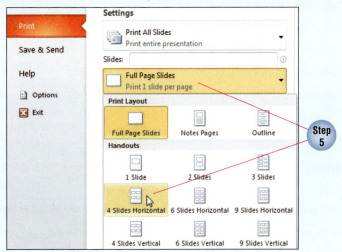

Step 5

6. Save **EL2-C8-P2-CutRateCarRpt.pptx** and then exit PowerPoint.
7. Press the ESC key to remove the moving marquee and then click any cell to deselect the range in the CarCosts worksheet. Leave the **CutRateInventory.xlsx** workbook open for the next project.

Export Worksheet as Text File
1. Make desired sheet active.
2. Click File tab.
3. Click Save & Send tab.
4. Click *Change File Type*.
5. Click desired text file type in *Other File Types* section.
6. Click Save As button.
7. If necessary, navigate to desired drive and/or folder.
8. Type file name.
9. Click Save button.
10. Click OK.
11. Click Yes.

Exporting Excel Data as a Text File

If you need to exchange Excel data with a person who is not able to import a Microsoft Excel worksheet or cannot copy and paste using the clipboard, you can save the data as a text file. Excel provides several text file options including file formats suitable for computers that use the Macintosh operating system as shown in Table 8.1. To save a worksheet as a text file, open the Save As dialog box and change *Save as type* to the desired option. Type a file name for the text file and then click the Save button. Click OK at the message box that informs you that only the active worksheet is saved and then click Yes at the next message box to confirm you want to save the data as a text file.

Another way to save the current worksheet in a text file format is to click the File tab and then click the Save & Send tab. At the Save & Send tab Backstage view, click *Change File Type* in the center pane. In the Change File Type pane at the right, click *Text (Tab delimited) (*.txt)*, *CSV (Comma delimited) (*.csv)*, or *Formatted Text (Space delimited) (*.prn)* in the *Other File Types* section and then click the Save As button. If necessary, navigate to the desired drive and/or folder in the Save As dialog box. Type the desired file name and then click the Save button.

Why so many text file formats? Although all systems support text files, differences occur across platforms. For example, a Macintosh computer denotes the end of a line in a text file with a carriage return character, Unix uses a linefeed character, and DOS inserts both a linefeed and a carriage return character code at the end of each line.

Table 8.1 Supported Text File Formats for Exporting

Text File Format Option	File Extension
Text (tab delimited)	.txt
Unicode text	.txt
CSV (Comma delimited)	.csv
Formatted text (Space delimited)	.prn
Text (Macintosh)	.txt
Text (MS-DOS)	.txt
CSV (Macintosh)	.csv
CSV (MS-DOS)	.csv

Project 2f   **Exporting a Worksheet as a Text File**   Part 6 of 6

1. With **CutRateInventory.xlsx** open, export the Inventory worksheet data as a text file by completing the following steps:
   a. Make Inventory the active worksheet.
   b. Click the File tab and then click the Save & Send tab.

c. Click *Change File Type* in the File Types category in the center pane in the Backstage view.

d. Click *CSV (Comma delimited) (*.csv)* in the *Other File Types* section in the right pane of the Backstage view.

e. Click the Save As button located below the *Other File Types* section in the right pane of the Backstage view.

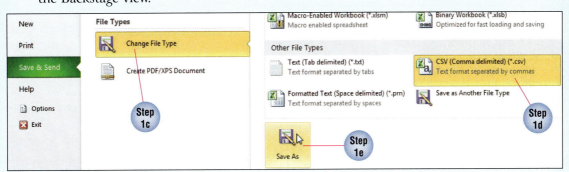

f. Type **EL2-C8-P2-CutRateInventory** in the *File name* text box.

g. Click the Save button.

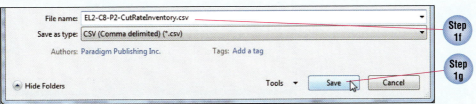

h. Click OK to save only the active sheet at the Microsoft Excel message box that informs you the selected file type does not support workbooks that contain multiple worksheets.

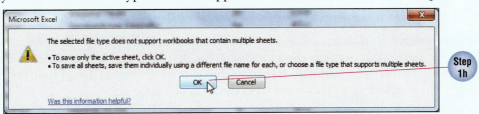

i. Click Yes to save the workbook in this format at the next message box that informs you **EL2-C8-P2-CutRateInventory.csv** may contain features that are not compatible with CSV (Comma delimited).

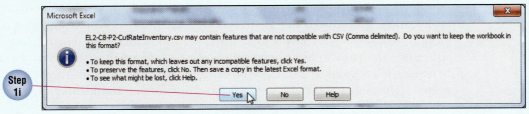

2. Close **EL2-C8-P2-CutRateInventory.csv**. Click Don't Save when prompted to save changes. (You do not need to save since no changes have been made since you changed the file type.)

3. Open Notepad and view the text file created in Step 1 by completing the following steps:
   a. Click the Start button, point to *All Programs*, click *Accessories*, and then click *Notepad*.
   b. Click File on the Notepad Menu bar and then click *Open*.
   c. Navigate to the Excel2010L2C8 folder on your storage medium.

d. Click the Text Documents (*.txt) button and then click *All Files (*.*)* at the drop-down list.

Step 3d

e. Double-click **EL2-C8-P2-CutRateInventory.csv**.

f. If necessary, scroll down to view all of the data in the text file. Notice that a comma has been inserted between each column's data.

4. Click File on the Notepad Menu bar and then click *Print*. Click the Print button at the Print dialog box.

5. Exit Notepad.

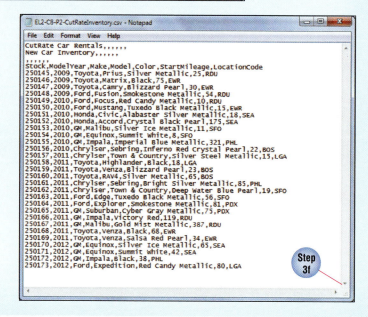

Step 3f

Project 3   Prepare a Workbook for Distribution   **3 Parts**

You will remove confidential information from a workbook and mark the workbook as final to prepare the workbook for distribution. In another workbook you will check for compatibility issues with earlier versions of Excel before sending the workbook to someone who uses Excel 2003.

Preparing a Workbook for Distribution ▪▪▪▪▪▪▪▪▪▪

In today's workplace, you often work as part of a team both within and outside your organization. Excel workbooks are frequently exchanged between workers via email message attachments; by saving to a shared network folder, a document management server, or a company website; or by other means of electronic distribution. Prior to making a workbook available for others to open, view, and edit, Excel provides several features that allow you to protect and/or maintain confidentiality.

Removing Information from a Workbook before Distributing

Prior to distributing a workbook electronically to others, you should consider using the Document Inspector feature to scan the workbook for personal or other hidden information that you would not want others to be able to view. Recall from Chapter 6 that a workbook's properties, sometimes referred to as *metadata,* include information that is tracked automatically by Excel such as the names of the individuals that accessed and edited a workbook. If a workbook will be sent electronically by email or made available on a document management server or other website, consider the implications of recipients of that workbook being able to look at some of this hidden information. Ask yourself if this information should remain confidential and if so, remove sensitive data and/or metadata before distributing the file. To do this, click the File tab. At the Info tab Backstage view, click the Check for Issues button located in the center pane and then click *Inspect Document* at the drop-down list. This opens the Document Inspector dialog box shown in Figure 8.4. By default, all check boxes are selected. Clear the check boxes for those items that you do not need or want to scan and remove and then click Inspect.

Note also that before removing sensitive data, you can save a copy of the original file that retains all content using password protection or other security measures to limit access. Another helpful use of the Document Inspector is as a tool to reveal the presence of headers, footers, hidden items, or other invisible items in a workbook for which you are not the original author.

The Document Inspector scans the workbook for the existence of any of the checked items. When completed, a dialog box similar to the one shown in Figure 8.5 appears. Excel displays a check mark in the sections for which no items were found and a red exclamation mark in the sections in which items were detected within the workbook. Click the Remove All button in the section that contains content you decide you want to remove. Click OK when finished and then distribute the workbook as needed.

▼ **Quick Steps**

Use Document Inspector to Remove Private Information
1. Open workbook.
2. Click File tab.
3. Click Check for Issues button.
4. Click *Inspect Document.*
5. Clear check boxes for those items you do not want to scan and remove.
6. Click Inspect button.
7. Click Remove All button in those sections with items you want removed.
8. Click Close button.

Figure 8.4 Document Inspector Dialog Box

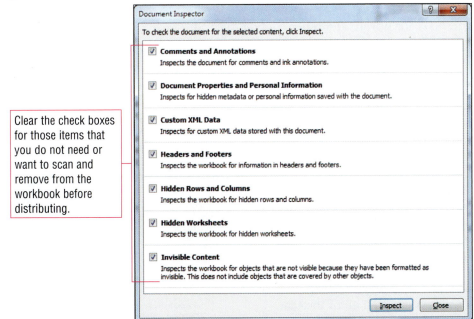

Clear the check boxes for those items that you do not need or want to scan and remove from the workbook before distributing.

Figure 8.5 Document Inspector Dialog Box with Inspection Results Shown

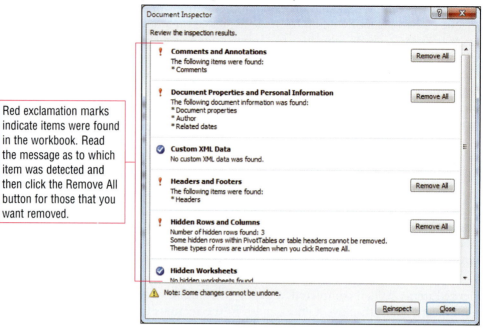

Red exclamation marks indicate items were found in the workbook. Read the message as to which item was detected and then click the Remove All button for those that you want removed.

Project 3a **Removing Private and Confidential Data from a Workbook** Part 1 of 3

1. Open **CutRatePilotPrjRpt.xlsx**.
2. Save the workbook with Save As and name it **EL2-C8-P3-CutRatePilotPrjRpt**.
3. Examine the workbook for private and other confidential information by completing the following steps:
   a. Click the File tab.
   b. Read the property information in the fields in the Properties pane located at the right of the Info tab Backstage view.
   c. Click the Properties button at the top of the Properties pane (located below the miniature Excel worksheet) and then click *Advanced Properties* at the drop-down list.
   d. Click the Custom tab in the **EL2-C8-P3-CutRatePilotPrjRpt.xlsx** Properties dialog box.
   e. Position the mouse pointer on the right column boundary for the *Value* column in the *Properties* list box until the pointer changes to a vertical bar with left- and right-pointing arrows and then drag the column width right until you can read all of the text within the column.
   f. Notice that the extra information added to the workbook properties contains names and other data that you might not want widely circulated.

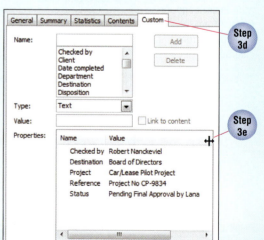

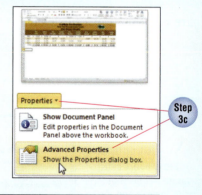

Step 3c

Step 3d

Step 3e

g. Click OK.

h. Click the Review tab and then click the Show All Comments button in the Comments group.

i. Read the two comments displayed in the worksheet area.

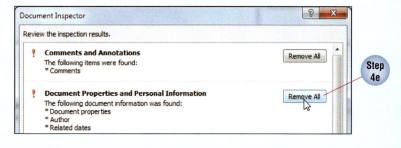

	Lease Toyota	Buy Honda	Lease Honda	Buy GM	Lease GM
	$ 71,856	$ -		-	$ -
	-	63,889		82,457	75,128
	90,653	-		62,154	36,412
		-		57,845	158,745
	$ 162,509	$ 63,889		202,456	$ 270,285

Francis Geddes: Let's try to negotiate a better lease contract with Toyota.

Whitney Simms: This was high due to excessive mileage. We can mitigate this in the future via earlier returns.

Step 3i

4. Scan the workbook for other confidential information using the Document Inspector by completing the following steps:

a. Click the File tab, click the Check for Issues button in the *Prepare for Sharing* section at the Info tab Backstage view, and then click *Inspect Document* at the drop-down list.

b. At the Microsoft Excel message box indicating the file contains changes that have not been saved, click Yes to save the file now.

c. At the Document Inspector dialog box with all check boxes selected, click the Inspect button to check for all items.

d. Read the messages in each section of the Document Inspector dialog box that display with a red exclamation mark.

e. Click the Remove All button in the *Document Properties and Personal Information* section. Excel deletes the metadata and the section now displays with a check mark indicating the information has been removed.

Document Inspector

Review the inspection results.

❗ **Comments and Annotations**
The following items were found:
* Comments

[Remove All]

❗ **Document Properties and Personal Information**
The following document information was found:
* Document properties
* Author
* Related dates

[Remove All]

Step 4e

f. Notice the inspection results indicate a header and three hidden rows were found. You decide to review these items before removing them. Click the Close button to close the Document Inspector dialog box.

5. Click the Home tab and then display the worksheet in Page Layout View and view the header.

6. Look at the row numbers in the worksheet area. Notice that after row 10, the next row number is 14. Select row numbers 10 and 14, right-click the selected rows, and then click *Unhide* at the shortcut menu to display rows 11 to 13.

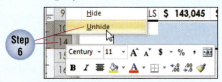

Step 6

9	Hide	LS $ 143,045
10	Unhide	
14		
1	Century ▾ 11 ▾ A A $ ▾ % ,	
1	B I ≡ 🖌 ▾ A ▾ 田 ▾	

7. Change to Normal view and click any cell to deselect the range. Review the information that was in the hidden rows.

8. You decide the rows that were initially hidden should remain displayed but want to remove the header and the comments from reviewers of the workbook. Use the Document Inspector to remove these items by completing the following steps:

a. Click the File tab, click the Check for Issues button, click *Inspect Document* at the drop-down list, and then click Yes to save the changes to the workbook.

b. Clear the check boxes for all items except *Comments and Annotations* and *Headers and Footers*.

c. Click the Inspect button.

d. Click the Remove All button in the *Comments and Annotations* section.

e. Click the Remove All button in the *Headers and Footers* section.

f. Click the Close button.

9. Click the Home tab. Notice the comments have been deleted from the worksheet. Switch to Page Layout view and check for the header text. Notice the header has been deleted. Switch back to Normal view.

10. Click the Show All Comments button in the Comments group of the Review tab to turn the feature off.

11. Save and then close **EL2-C8-P3-CutRatePilotPrjRpt.xlsx**.

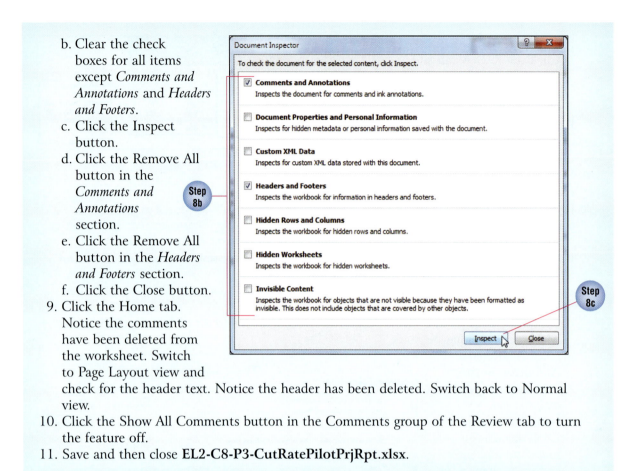

Step 8b

Step 8c

Marking a Workbook as Final before Distributing

A workbook that will be distributed to others can be marked as final which means the workbook is prevented from having additions, deletions, or modifications made to cells. The workbook is changed to read-only and the status property is set to *Final*. In addition to protecting the workbook, marking a workbook as final also serves to indicate to the recipient(s) of the workbook that you consider the content complete. To mark a workbook as final, click the File tab. At the Info tab Backstage view, click the Protect Workbook button in the *Permissions* section located in the center pane and then click *Mark as Final* at the drop-down list. Note that marking a workbook as final should not be considered as secure as using password-protected, locked ranges. A workbook marked as final displays with the ribbon minimized and with a message located above the Formula bar that informs the reader that an author has marked the workbook as final to discourage editing. You can click the Edit Anyway button in the message bar to remove the Mark as Final feature, redisplay the ribbon, and make changes to the workbook.

As an alternative to *Mark as Final*, consider distributing a workbook published as a PDF or XPS document. In the PDF or XPS format, readers are not able to make changes to the workbook. You will learn how to publish a workbook in these formats in a later section.

1. Open **EL2-C8-P3-CutRatePilotPrjRpt.xlsx**.
2. Save the workbook with Save As and name it **EL2-C8-P3-CutRatePilotPrjRptFinal**.
3. Mark the workbook as final to prevent changes and set the Status property to *Final* by completing the following steps:
   a. Click the File tab, click the Protect Workbook button in the *Permissions* section of the Info tab Backstage view, and then click *Mark as Final*.

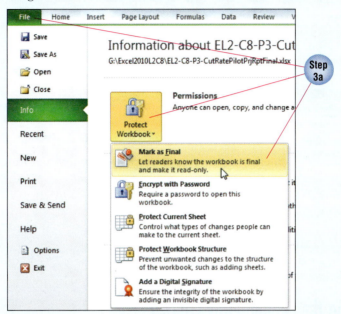

   b. Click OK at the message box that says the workbook will be marked as final and then saved.

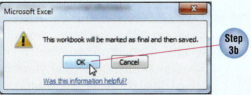

   c. Click OK at the second message box that says the workbook has been marked as final to indicate that editing is complete and that this is the final version of the document. ***Note: If this message box does not appear, it has been turned off by a previous user who clicked the*** **Don't show this message again** ***check box.***

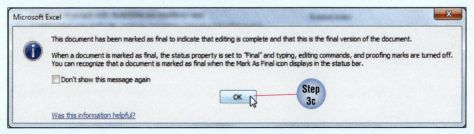

4. Notice the *Permissions* section of the Info tab Backstage view displays in orange and with a message indicating the workbook has been marked as final. Notice also the addition of *[Read-Only]* next to the file name in the Title bar.

5. Click the Home tab. The ribbon is minimized and a Marked as Final message displays above the Formula bar indicating that the workbook has been marked as final to discourage editing. Additionally, a *Marked as Final* icon displays in the Status bar next to *Ready*.

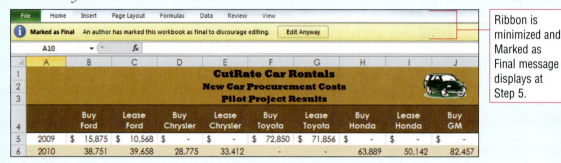

Ribbon is minimized and Marked as Final message displays at Step 5.

6. Click the File tab and then click the <u>Show All Properties</u> hyperlink located at the bottom of the Properties pane. Notice the *Status* property reads *Final*.

7. Click the the Home tab. Make any cell active and attempt to insert or delete text in the cell. Since the workbook is now read-only, you cannot open the cell for editing or delete the contents.

8. Close **EL2-C8-P3-CutRatePilotPrjRptFinal.xlsx**.

Using the Compatibility Checker

▼ **Quick Steps**

Check Workbook for Compatibility
1. Open workbook.
2. Click File tab.
3. Click Check for Issues button.
4. Click *Check Compatibility*.
5. Read information in *Summary* list box.
6. If desired, click *Copy to New Sheet* button.
OR
Click Close.

If you have a workbook that will be exchanged with other users that do not have Excel 2007 or Excel 2010, you can save the workbook in the Excel 97-2003 file format. When you save the file in the earlier version's file format, Excel automatically does a compatibility check and prompts you with information about loss of functionality or fidelity. If you prefer, you can run the compatibility checker before you save the workbook so that you know in advance areas of the worksheet that may need changes prior to saving.

In the Compatibility Checker Summary report, if an issue displays a <u>Fix</u> hyperlink, click <u>Fix</u> to resolve the problem. If you want more information about a loss of functionality or fidelity, click the <u>Help</u> hyperlink next to the issue. To return to the worksheet with the cells selected that are problematic for earlier Excel versions, click the <u>Find</u> hyperlink next to the issue.

1. Open **CutRateBuyLeaseAnalysis.xlsx**.
2. Run the Compatibility Checker to check the workbook in advance of saving in an earlier Excel file format by completing the following steps:
   a. Click the File tab.
   b. Click the Check for Issues button in the *Prepare for Sharing* section at the Info tab Backstage view.
   c. Click *Check Compatibility* at the drop-down list.
   d. At the Microsoft Excel - Compatibility Checker dialog box, read the information in the *Summary* box in the *Significant loss of functionality* section.
   e. Scroll down and read the information displayed in the *Minor loss of fidelity* section.
   f. Scroll back up to the top of the *Summary* box.
   g. Click the Copy to New Sheet button.

3. At the Compatibility Report sheet, read the information in the box with the hyperlink Sheet1'!D13:D16 and then click the hyperlink. Sheet1 becomes active with the cells selected that have conditional formatting applied that is not supported in the earlier version of Excel (D13:D16).

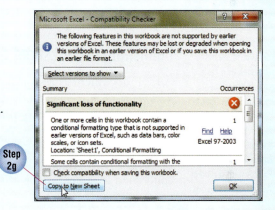

4. Make the Compatibility Report sheet active and then print the worksheet with the worksheet scaled to *Fit Sheet on One Page*.

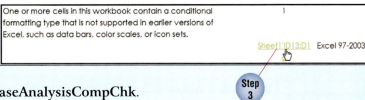

5. Use Save As to save the revised workbook and name it **EL2-C8-P3-CutRateBuyLeaseAnalysisCompChk**.
6. Make Sheet1 the active worksheet and deselect the range.
7. Click the File tab, click the Save & Send tab, click *Change File Type*, click *Excel 97-2003 Workbook (*.xls)* in the *Workbook File Types* section, and then click the Save As button located at the bottom of the Change File Type pane. Click the Save button at the Save As dialog box to accept the default file name. Click the Continue button at the Compatibility Checker dialog box.
8. Close **EL2-C8-P3-CutRateBuyLeaseAnalysisCompChk.xls**.

You will publish a worksheet as a PDF document, an XPS document, and as a web page. You will distribute a workbook via an email with a file attachment and save a workbook to Microsoft's SkyDrive website.

▼ **Quick Steps**

Publish Worksheet as PDF
1. Open workbook.
2. Click File tab.
3. Click Save & Send tab.
4. Click *Create PDF/XPS Document.*
5. Click Create PDF/XPS button.
6. Click Publish button.

If a workbook contains multiple sheets, you can publish the entire workbook as a multi-page PDF document by clicking the Options button in the Publish as PDF or XPS dialog box and then clicking *Entire workbook* in the *Publish what* section of the Options dialog box.

Distributing Workbooks ▪▪▪▪▪▪▪▪▪ ▪ ▪▪▪▪ ▪▪▪▪▪ ▪ ▪▪▪▪

Many organizations that need to make documents accessible by several users create a document management server or network share folder from which users can retrieve files. Alternatively, if you do not have access to these resources you can send a workbook via an email message by attaching the workbook file to the message. You can attach the workbook using your email program's file attachment feature, or you can initiate the email attachment feature directly from Excel.

A popular method of distributing documents that travel over the Internet is to publish the workbook as a PDF or XPS document. A workbook can also be published as a web page to make the content available on the Internet. Microsoft's SkyDrive web server allows you to store files on a web server that you can access from anywhere where you have an Internet connection.

Publishing a Worksheet as a PDF Document

A PDF document is a workbook saved in a fixed-layout format known as *portable document format*. The PDF standard was developed by Adobe and has become a popular choice for sharing files with people outside an organization. By creating a PDF copy of the workbook, you ensure that the workbook will look the same on most computers with all fonts, formatting, and images preserved, no one can easily make changes to the workbook content, and you do not need to be concerned if the recipient of the file has Microsoft Excel on his or her computer in order to read the file.

To open and view a PDF file, the recipient of the file must have Adobe Reader installed on his or her computer. The reader is a free application available from Adobe if the computer being used does not currently have the reader installed. Go to www.adobe.com and click Get Adobe Reader to download and install the latest version of the reader software.

Project 4a Publishing a Worksheet as a PDF Document Part 1 of 5

1. Open **EL2-C8-P3-CutRatePilotPrjRpt.xlsx**.
2. Publish the worksheet as a PDF document by completing the following steps:
   a. Click the File tab.
   b. Click the Save & Send tab.
   c. Click *Create PDF/XPS Document* in the File Types category of the Save & Send tab Backstage view.

d. Click the Create PDF/XPS button located at the bottom of the Create a PDF/XPS Document category in the right pane.

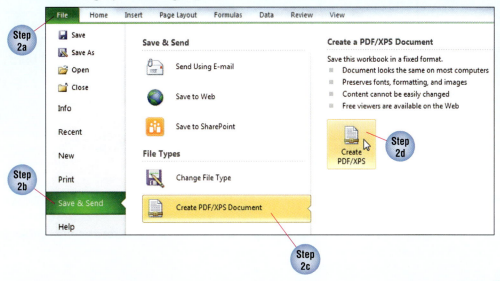

e. With *EL2-C8-P3-CutRatePilotPrjRpt.pdf* in the *File name* text box, click the Publish button in the Publish as PDF or XPS dialog box.

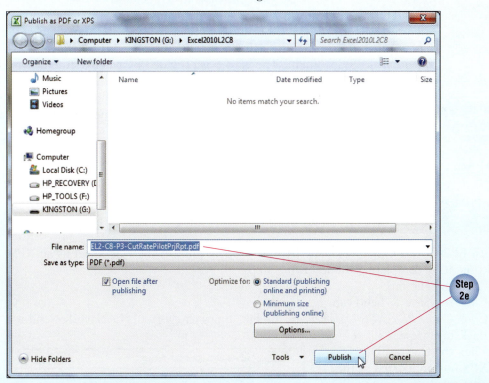

3. By default, an Adobe Reader (or an Adobe Acrobat) application window opens with the published worksheet displayed. Notice the worksheet has retained all of the Excel formatting and other visual features.

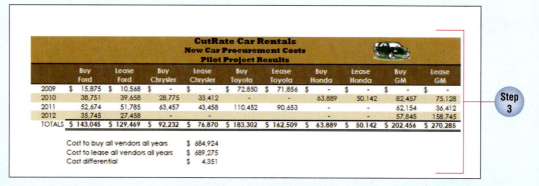

	Buy Ford	Lease Ford	Buy Chrysler	Lease Chrysler	Buy Toyota	Lease Toyota	Buy Honda	Lease Honda	Buy GM	Lease GM
2009	$ 15,875	$ 10,568	$ -	$ -	$ 72,850	$ 71,856	$ -	$ -	$ -	$ -
2010	38,751	39,658	28,775	33,412	-	-	63,889	50,142	82,457	75,128
2011	52,674	51,785	63,457	43,458	110,452	90,653	-	-	62,154	36,412
2012	35,745	27,458	-	-			-	-	57,845	158,745
TOTALS	$ 143,045	$ 129,469	$ 92,232	$ 76,870	$ 183,302	$ 162,509	$ 63,889	$ 50,142	$ 202,456	$ 270,285

Cost to buy all vendors all years	$ 684,924
Cost to lease all vendors all years	$ 689,275
Cost differential	$ 4,351

Step 3

4. Close the Adobe application window.
5. Leave the **EL2-C8-P3-CutRatePilotPrjRpt.xlsx** workbook open for the next project.

▼ **Quick Steps**

Publish Worksheet as XPS
1. Open workbook.
2. Click File tab.
3. Click Save & Send tab.
4. Click *Create PDF/XPS Document*.
5. Click Create PDF/XPS button.
6. Click Save as type button.
7. Click *XPS Document (*.xps)*.
8. Click Publish button.

Publishing a Worksheet as an XPS Document

XPS stands for *XML Paper Specification*, which is another fixed-layout format with all of the same advantages as a PDF document. XPS was developed by Microsoft with the Office 2007 suite. Similar to PDF files that require the Adobe Reader program in which to view documents, you need the XPS viewer in order to read an XPS document. The viewer is provided by Microsoft and is packaged with Windows 7 and Windows Vista; however, to view an XPS document using Windows XP, you may need to download the viewer application. Go to www.microsoft.com and search using the phrase View and Generate XPS to locate the download page.

Project 4b **Publishing a Worksheet as an XPS Document** Part 2 of 5

1. With **EL2-C8-P3-CutRatePilotPrjRpt.xlsx** open, publish the worksheet as an XPS document by completing the following steps:
   a. Click the File tab.
   b. Click the Save & Send tab.
   c. Click *Create PDF/XPS Document* in the File Types category of the Save & Send tab Backstage view.
   d. Click the Create PDF/ XPS button located at the bottom of the Create a PDF/ XPS Document category in the right pane.

File name:	EL2-C8-P3-CutRatePilotPrjRpt.pdf	
Save as type:	PDF (*.pdf)	
	PDF (*.pdf)	
	XPS Document (*.xps)	

Step 1e

   e. At the Publish as PDF or XPS dialog box, click the Save as type button located below the *File name* text box and then click *XPS Document (*.xps)* at the drop-down list.

f. With *EL2-C8-P3-CutRatePilotPrjRpt.xps* in the *File name* text box, click the Publish button.

2. By default, an XPS Viewer application window opens with the published worksheet displayed. Notice that similar to the PDF document format, the XPS document format has retained all of the Excel formatting and other visual features.

3. Close the XPS Viewer application window.

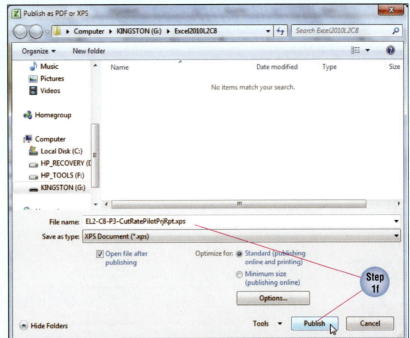

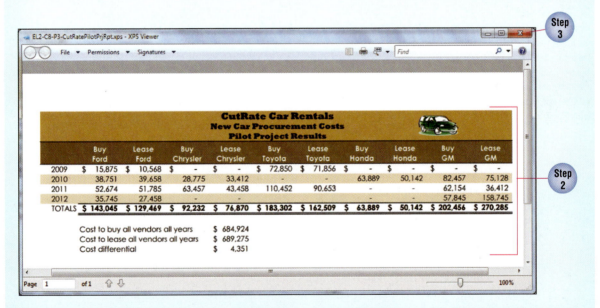

4. Leave the **EL2-C8-P3-CutRatePilotPrjRpt.xlsx** workbook open for the next project.

▼ Quick Steps

Publish Worksheet as Web Page
1. Open workbook.
2. Click File tab.
3. Click Save As.
4. Click Save as type button.
5. Click *Single File Web Page (*.mht; *.mhtml)*.
6. If necessary, change the drive and/or folder and/or file name.
7. Click Change Title button, type title, and click OK.
8. Click Publish button.
9. Set desired publishing options.
10. Click Publish.

HINT

Not all browsers support the single file (.mht) web page format. If you or others will not be viewing the page in Internet Explorer, consider using the traditional (.htm or .html) web page format.

Publishing a Worksheet as a Web Page

You can publish a worksheet as a single web page by changing the *Save as type* option to *Single File Web Page (*.mht; *.mhtml)*. In this format, all data in the worksheet such as graphics and other supplemental data is saved in a single file that can be uploaded to a web server. Alternatively, you can publish the worksheet in the traditional html (hypertext markup language) file format for web pages by changing the *Save as type* option to *Web Page (*.htm; *.html)*. In the *html* option, Excel creates additional files for supplemental data and saves the files in a subfolder.

When you choose a web page option at the *Save as type* list, the Save As dialog box changes as shown in Figure 8.6. At this dialog box, specify to publish the entire workbook or only the active sheet. Click the Change Title button if you want to add a title to the web page. The page title displays in the Title bar of the browser window and in the Internet Explorer tab when the page is viewed on the Internet. Click the Publish button and the Publish as Web Page dialog box appears as shown in Figure 8.7 with additional publishing options.

Figure 8.6 Save As Dialog Box with Save as Type Changed to Single File Web Page (*.mht; *.mhtml)

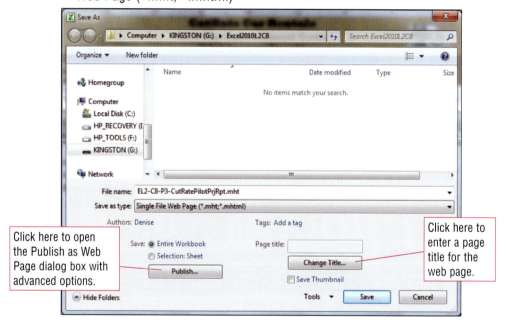

Click here to open the Publish as Web Page dialog box with advanced options.

Click here to enter a page title for the web page.

Figure 8.7 Publish as Web Page Dialog Box

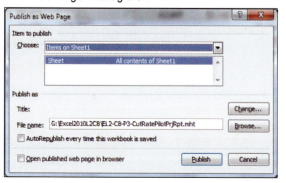

1. With **EL2-C8-P3-CutRatePilotPrjRpt.xlsx** open, publish the worksheet as a single file web page by completing the following steps:
   a. Click the File tab.
   b. Click the Save As button.
   c. Click the Save as type button and then click *Single File Web Page (*.mht; *.mhtml)* at the pop-up list.
   d. Click the Change Title button.

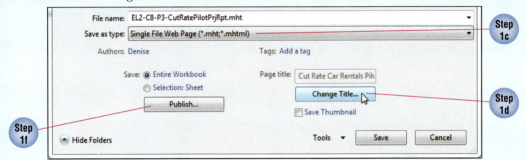

   e. At the Enter Text dialog box, type **CutRate Car Rentals Pilot Project Report** in the *Page title* text box and then click OK.

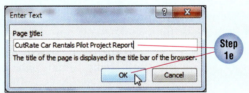

   f. Click the Publish button.
   g. At the Publish as Web Page dialog box, click the *Open published web page in browser* check box to insert a check mark and then click the Publish button. (This automatically displays the worksheet in your default web browser.)

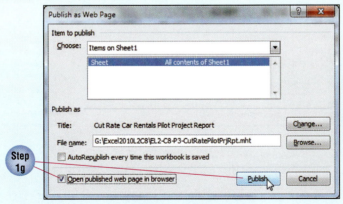

2. After viewing the web page, close the browser window.
3. Leave the **EL2-C8-P3-CutRatePilotPrjRpt.xlsx** workbook open for the next project.

Sending a Workbook via Email

Quick Steps

Send Workbook via Email
1. Open workbook.
2. Click File tab.
3. Click Save & Send tab.
4. Click Send as Attachment button.
5. Type recipient's email address in *To* text box.
6. If necessary, edit the *Subject* text.
7. Type message in message window.
8. Click Send.

A worksheet can be sent to others as a file attached to an email message. You can attach the workbook using your email program's file attachment feature, or you can choose to initiate the message from within Excel. To do this, click the File tab and then click the Save & Send tab. At the Save & Send tab Backstage view with *Send Using E-mail* already selected in the Save & Send category, click the Send as Attachment button located in the Send Using E-mail pane at the right side of the Backstage view. The default email program such as Microsoft Outlook launches an email message window with the workbook file already attached and the file name inserted in the *Subject* text box. Type the recipient's email address in the *To* text box, type the message text in the message window and then click the Send button. The message is sent to the email program's Outbox folder.

At the Save & Send tab Backstage view with *Send Using E-Mail* selected in the Save & Send category, the Send Using E-mail pane also contains buttons to attach the workbook to the email message as a PDF or as an XPS document instead of the default workbook file format.

Project 4d **Sending a Workbook via Email** Part 4 of 5

1. With **EL2-C8-P3-CutRatePilotPrjRpt.xlsx** open, send the workbook as a file attached to an email message by completing the following steps:
   a. Click the File tab and then click the Save & Send tab.
   b. With *Send Using E-mail* already selected in the Save & Send category, click the Send as Attachment button located in the Send Using E-mail pane at the right side of the Backstage view.

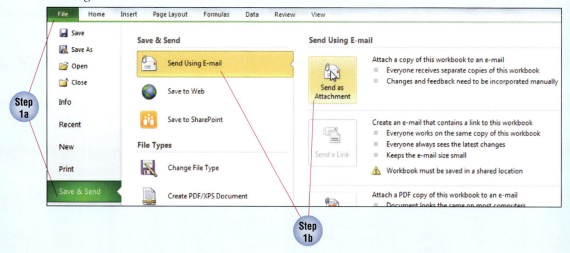

   c. With the insertion point positioned in the *To* text box at the message window, type your own email address.
   d. Click in the message window and type the following text:
   Here is the report on the new car procurement costs for the pilot project at CutRate Car Rentals. After four years, the cost differential between buying and leasing is $4,351 as shown in the attached worksheet.

e. Click the Send button. The message is sent and the message window closes.

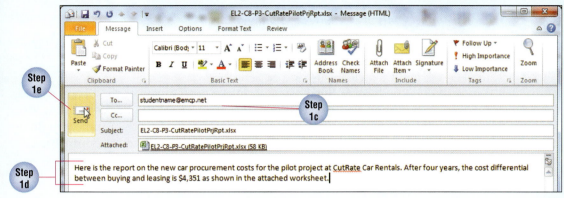

2. Open your email program (such as Microsoft Outlook).
3. Check your Inbox for the new message received and then open and view the message.
   Note: Depending on your mail server you may need to wait a few seconds for the message to be processed.
4. Close the message and then exit the email program.
5. Leave the **EL2-C8-P3-CutRatePilotPrjRpt.xlsx** workbook open for the next project.

Saving a Workbook to Windows Live SkyDrive

Windows Live SkyDrive is a feature in Office 2010 that allows one to save and share documents to a storage location on the Internet. You can save a workbook to your SkyDrive location and then access the file from any other location with Internet access. This means you do not have to make a copy of the workbook on a USB drive or some other storage medium in order to work on the workbook at another location. You can also share the workbook with others by sending people a link to the SkyDrive location rather than sending the workbook as an email attachment. With multiple people editing the workbook on SkyDrive, you do not need to manage multiple versions of the same file.

In order to save the workbook to SkyDrive you need to have a Windows Live account. If you use hotmail or MSN messenger, the account with which you sign in to these applications is your Windows Live ID. If you do not already have a Windows Live user name and password, you can sign up for a free account at windowslive.com by clicking the Sign Up button. Windows Live SkyDrive is free and includes 25 GB of storage on the SkyDrive server.

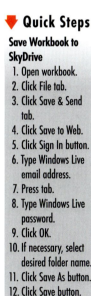

▼ **Quick Steps**

Save Workbook to SkyDrive
1. Open workbook.
2. Click File tab.
3. Click Save & Send tab.
4. Click Save to Web.
5. Click Sign In button.
6. Type Windows Live email address.
7. Press tab.
8. Type Windows Live password.
9. Click OK.
10. If necessary, select desired folder name.
11. Click Save As button.
12. Click Save button.

Note: Complete this project only if you have a Windows Live ID.

1. With **EL2-C8-P3-CutRatePilotPrjRpt.xlsx** open, save the workbook to Windows Live SkyDrive by completing the following steps:
   a. Click the File tab and then click the Save & Send tab.
   b. Click *Save to Web* in the Save & Send category in the center pane of the Backstage view.
   c. Click the Sign In button in the Save to Windows Live pane of the Backstage view. Excel establishes a connection to the Windows Live server and displays the Connecting to docs.live.net dialog box in which you enter your Windows Live account information.

d. With the insertion point positioned in the *E-mail address* text box, type the email address that you use for your Windows Live ID and then press tab.
e. Type your Windows Live ID password and then click OK.
f. With the *My Documents* folder name already selected in the *Personal Folders* list in the *Save to Windows Live SkyDrive* section of the Backstage view, click the Save As button.

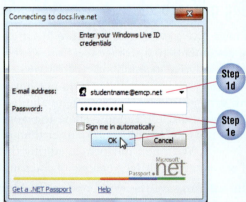

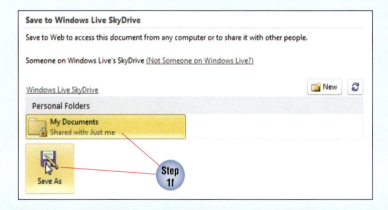

g. At the Save As dialog box with *EL2-C8-P3-CutRatePilotPrjRpt.xlsx* in the *File name* text box, click the Save button.

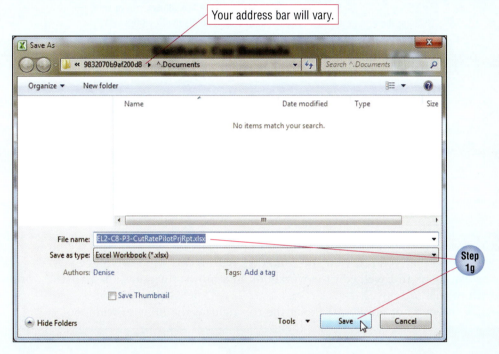

Your address bar will vary.

2. View the workbook stored on the Windows Live SkyDrive server by completing the following steps:
   a. Start Internet Explorer.
   b. Click in the Address bar and then type **http://live.com**.
   c. Sign in to Windows Live using your Windows Live ID email address and password.
   d. Point at the <u>Office</u> link located at the top of the Windows Live web page and then click *Your documents* at the drop-down list.

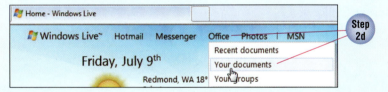

   e. Click the *My Documents* folder name in the *Personal* section.

f. Point at the Excel workbook name *EL2-C8-P3-CutRatePilotPrjRpt.xlsx* in the *Today* list to view the file options that display.

Clicking the Edit in browser link allows you to open the workbook for editing in Microsoft Office Web Apps.

Clicking the Share link allows you to send a link to someone else with whom you have given permission to view your My Documents folder in order to allow him or her access to the workbook.

Clicking the More link displays a drop-down list from which you can move, copy, rename, or download the workbook.

Step 2f

Step 2g

g. Click the Version history link. Windows Live opens the workbook in the browser window so that you can view the contents. Within this window you can elect to open the workbook in Excel, edit the workbook in a browser window, or share the workbook with others.

h. Click the sign out link located near the top right of the browser window.

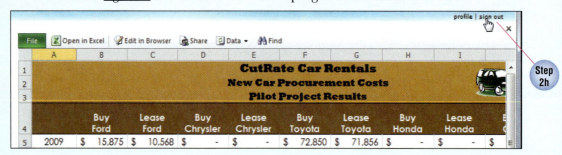

Step 2h

i. Close Internet Explorer.

3. Close **EL2-C8-P3-CutRatePilotPrjRpt.xlsx**.

Chapter Summary

- The Get External Data group in the Data tab contains buttons to use for importing data into an Excel worksheet from Access, from the Web, or from a text file.

- Only one Access table can be imported at a time.

- Tables in a website can be imported to Excel using the New Web Query dialog box.

- Text files are often used to exchange data between dissimilar programs since the file format is recognized by nearly all applications.

- Text files generally separate data between fields with either a tab character or a comma.

- The Text Import Wizard guides you through the process of importing a text file through three dialog boxes where you define the source file as delimited and select the delimiter character.

- Data in an Excel worksheet can be copied and pasted or copied and appended to an existing Access table.

- Worksheet data can be embedded or linked to a Word document. Embedding inserts a copy of the source data in the Word document and allows the object to be edited using Excel's tools within the Word environment, whereas linking the object inserts a shortcut to the Excel workbook from which the source data is retrieved.

- Breaking a link involves removing the connection between the source and destination programs so that the object is no longer updated in the destination document when the source data changes.

- You can embed and link objects to slides in a PowerPoint presentation using the same techniques as you would to embed or link cells to a Word document.

- In Office 2010, the charting tools are fully integrated. A chart copied and pasted from Excel to a PowerPoint presentation or a Word document is embedded by default.

- Save a worksheet as a text file by changing the file type at the Save & Send tab Backstage view.

- Excel includes several text file formats to accommodate differences that occur across operating system platforms that configure text files using various end of line character codes.

- The Document Inspector feature allows you to search for personal or hidden information and remove it before distributing a file.

- Once the workbook has been inspected, Excel displays a red exclamation mark in each section in which Excel detected the presence of the requested item. Clicking the Remove All button deletes the items from the workbook.

- Mark a Workbook as Final to change the workbook to a read-only file with the status property set to *Final*.

- Run the Compatibility Checker feature before saving a workbook in an earlier version of Excel to determine if a loss of functionality or fidelity will occur.

- The results of the compatibility check can be copied to a new worksheet for easy referencing and documentation purposes.

- A worksheet can be saved in PDF or XPS format, which are fixed-layout formats that preserve all of the Excel formatting and layout features.

- Adobe Reader is required in order to open and view a workbook saved as a PDF file.

- The XPS Viewer is included automatically with Windows Vista and Windows 7.

- If necessary, Adobe Reader or the XPS Viewer application can be downloaded from the Adobe or Microsoft websites. Both readers are free.

- Open the Save As dialog box and change the *Save as type* option to either *Single File Web Page* or *Web Page* to publish the current worksheet as a web page.

- An email message with the current workbook added as a file attachment can be generated from Excel using the Save & Send tab Backstage view. You can attach the workbook in the default .xlsx format, as a PDF, or as an XPS document.

- A workbook can be saved to a folder in your own personal storage location on Windows Live SkyDrive. From SkyDrive you can share, edit, or store the workbook from any location with Internet access.

Commands Review

FEATURE	RIBBON TAB, GROUP	BUTTON	KEYBOARD SHORTCUT
Compatibility checker	File, Info		
Copy	Home, Clipboard	📋	Ctrl + C
Document Inspector	File, Info		
Import from Access table	Data, Get External Data	📄	
Import from text file	Data, Get External Data	📄	
Import from web page	Data, Get External Data	📄	
Mark workbook as final	File, Info		
Paste Special	Home, Clipboard	📋	
Save As	File		F12
Save as PDF/XPS	File, Save & Send		
Save as web page	File, Save As		
Send workbook via email	File, Save & Send		
Save workbook to Skydrive	File, Save & Send		

Concepts Check Test Your Knowledge

Completion: In the space provided at the right, indicate the correct term, command, or number.

1. This group in the Data tab contains buttons for importing data from Access. _____

2. If the source database used to import data contains more than one table, this dialog box appears after you select the data source to allow you to choose the desired table. _____

3. To import tables from a web page, open this dialog box to browse to the website and click arrows next to tables on the page that you want to import. _____

4. These are the two commonly used delimiter characters in delimited text file formats.

_____

5. To add to the bottom of the active Access datasheet cells that have been copied to the clipboard, click this option at the Paste button drop-down list.

_____

6. Choosing *Microsoft Excel Worksheet Object* at the Paste Special dialog box in a Word document and then clicking OK inserts the copied cells as this type of object.

_____

7. If the Excel data you are pasting into a Word document is likely to be updated in the future and you want the Word document to reflect the updated values, paste the data as this type of object.

_____

8. A chart copied from Excel and pasted to a slide in a PowerPoint presentation is pasted as this type of object by default.

_____

9. Click this option in the *File Types* section of the Save & Send tab Backstage view to select the CSV file format in order to export the active worksheet as a text file.

_____

10. This feature scans the open workbook for personal and hidden information and provides you with the opportunity to remove the items.

_____

11. A workbook that has been marked as final is changed to this type of workbook to prevent additions, deletions, and modifications to cells.

_____

12. Use this feature to check the current workbook for formatting or features used that are not available with versions of Excel prior to Excel 2007 and that could cause loss of functionality if saved in the earlier file format.

_____

13. Save a worksheet in either of these fixed-layout formats that preserve Excel's formatting and layout features while allowing you to distribute the file to others who may not have Excel installed on their computer.

_____

14. Click this button in the Save As dialog box once the *Save as type* option has been changed to a web page file format in order to type a page title.

_____

15. This is the name of the free service from Microsoft which provides you with storage space on a Web server in order to save a workbook that you can share, edit, or download from any location with Internet access.

_____

Skills Check Assess Your Performance

Assessment

1 IMPORT DATA FROM ACCESS AND A TEXT FILE

1. Open **HillsdaleResearchServices.xlsx**.
2. Save the workbook with Save As and name it **EL2-C8-A1-HillsdaleResearchServices**.
3. Make A6 of the CPIData worksheet the active cell if A6 is not currently active. Import the table named CPI from the Access database named **NuTrendsCensusData.accdb**.
4. Make the following changes to the worksheet:
   a. Apply *Table Style Medium 15* to the imported cells.
   b. Format the values in all columns *except* column A to one decimal place.
   c. Remove the filter arrow buttons and then center the column headings.
   d. If necessary, adjust column widths to accommodate the data.
5. Print the CPIData worksheet.
6. Make UIRateMI the active worksheet.
7. Make A6 the active cell if A6 is not currently active. Import the comma delimited text file named **UIRateMI.csv**.
8. Make the following changes to the data:
   a. Change the width of column B to 8.00 (61 pixels).
   b. Change the width of columns C to F to 15.00 (110 pixels).
   c. Change the width of column G to 5.00 (40 pixels).
   d. Center the months in column B.
9. Print the UIRate-MI worksheet.
10. Save and then close **EL2-C8-A1-HillsdaleResearchServices.xlsx**.

Assessment

2 LINK DATA TO A WORD DOCUMENT

1. Open **HillsdaleOctSalesByDateByRep.xlsx**.
2. Save the workbook with Save As and name it **EL2-C8-A2-HillsdaleOctSalesByDateByRep**.
3. With SalesByDate the active worksheet, link A3:G27 a double-space below the paragraph in the Word document named **HillsdaleOctRpt.docx**.
4. Change the margins in the Word document to *Narrow* (Top, Bottom, Left, and Right to 0.5 inch).
5. Use Save As to name the revised Word document **EL2-C8-A2-HillsdaleOctRpt.docx**.
6. Switch to Excel and then press the Esc key to remove the moving marquee and then deselect the range.
7. Change the value in F4 to *525000*.
8. Change the value in F5 to *212000*.
9. Save **EL2-C8-P2-HillsdaleOctSalesByDateByRep.xlsx**.
10. Switch to Word, right-click the linked object, and then click *Update Link* at the shortcut menu.

11. Print the Word document.
12. Break the link in the Word document.
13. Save **EL2-C8-P2-HillsdaleOctRpt.docx** and then exit Word.
14. Save and then close **EL2-C8-A2-HillsdaleOctSalesByDateByRep.xlsx**.

Assessment

3 EMBED DATA IN A POWERPOINT PRESENTATION

1. Open **HillsdaleOctSalesByDateByRep.xlsx**.
2. Save the workbook with Save As and name it
   EL2-C8-A3-HillsdaleOctSalesByDateByRep.
3. Make SalesByRep the active worksheet.
4. Display the worksheet at outline level 2 so that only the sales agent names,
   sale prices, and commissions display.
5. Create a column chart in a separate sheet to graph the sales commissions
   earned by each sales agent. You determine an appropriate chart style, title, and
   other chart elements.
6. Start PowerPoint and open **HillsdaleOctRpt.pptx**.
7. Save the presentation with Save As and name it **EL2-C8-A3-HillsdaleOctRpt**.
8. Embed the chart created in Step 5 on Slide 3 of the presentation.
9. Print the presentation as Handouts with three slides per page.
10. Save **EL2-C8-A3-HillsdaleOctRpt.pptx** and then exit PowerPoint.
11. Save and then close **EL2-C8-A3-HillsdaleOctSalesByDateByRep.xlsx**.

Assessment

4 EXPORT DATA AS A TEXT FILE

1. Open **HillsdaleOctSalesByDateByRep.xlsx**.
2. With SalesByDate the active worksheet, save the worksheet as a CSV
   (Comma delimited) (*.csv) text file named
   EL2-C8-A4-HillsdaleOctSalesByDateByRep.
3. Close **EL2-C8-A4-HillsdaleOctSalesByDateByRep.csv**. Click Don't Save
   when prompted to save changes.
4. Start Notepad and open **EL2-C8-A4-HillsdaleOctSalesByDateByRep.csv**.
5. Delete the first three rows at the beginning of the file that contain the title
   text from the top of the worksheet. The first words in the file should begin at
   the first row with the heading *Hillsdale Realtors*.
6. Delete the bottom row in the file that contains the total commission value
   and the ending commas.
7. Print the document.
8. Save **EL2-C8-A4-HillsdaleOctSalesByDateByRep.csv** and then exit Notepad.

Assessment

5   PREPARE A WORKBOOK FOR DISTRIBUTION

1. Open **Hillsdale2012Sales.xlsx**.
2. Save the workbook with Save As and name it **EL2-C8-A5-Hillsdale2012Sales**.
3. Display the Info tab Backstage view and show all properties. Read the information in the *Author, Title,* and *Subject* properties. Open the Properties dialog box (click *Advanced Properties* from the Properties button drop-down list) and read the information in the Statistics and Custom tabs. Close the Properties dialog box and click the Review tab.
4. Turn on the display of all comments and then read the comments that appear.
5. Change to Page Layout view and check for a header or footer in the workbook.
6. Use the Document Inspector feature to check the workbook for private and hidden information. Leave all options selected at the Document Inspector dialog box.
7. Remove all items that display with a red exclamation mark and then close the dialog box.
8. Click the Review tab, turn off the Show All Comments feature, and switch to Normal view.
9. Click the File tab. With the Info tab Backstage view displayed showing all properties, paste a screen image into a new Word document using the PrintScreen key, the Screenshot feature, or the Windows Snipping tool. Type your name a few lines below the screen image. Print the Word document and then exit Word without saving.
10. Run the Compatibility Feature to check for loss of functionality or fidelity in the workbook if saved in an earlier Excel version. Save the Summary report to a new sheet and then print the Compatibility Report sheet.
11. Mark the workbook as final.
12. Close **EL2-C8-A5-Hillsdale2012Sales.xlsx**.

Assessment

6   PREPARE AND DISTRIBUTE A WORKBOOK

1. Open **Hillsdale2012Sales.xlsx**.
2. Save the workbook with Save As and name it **EL2-C8-A6-Hillsdale2012Sales**.
3. Use the Document Inspector feature to remove comments and annotations only from the worksheet.
4. Publish the worksheet as a PDF file named **EL2-C8-A6-Hillsdale2012Sales.pdf**.
5. Publish the worksheet as a single file web page named **EL2-C8-A6-Hillsdale2012Sales.mht** with a page title *Hillsdale Realtors*.
6. Save and close **EL2-C8-A6-Hillsdale2012Sales.xlsx**.
7. Display the contents of the Excel2010L2C8 folder on your storage medium. Make sure the folder is displaying file extensions. Paste a screen image of the folder's contents into a new Word document using the PrintScreen key, the Screenshot feature, or the Windows Snipping tool. Type your name a few lines below the screen image. Print the Word document and then exit Word without saving. Close the Computer or Documents window.

Optional: With **EL2-C8-A6-Hillsdale2012Sales.xlsx** open, email the workbook to yourself. Compose an appropriate message within the message window as if you were an employee of Hillsdale Realtors sending the file to the office manager. Open the message window from the Inbox in your email program and print the message. Close the message window and exit your email program.

Optional: With **EL2-C8-A6-Hillsdale2012Sales.xlsx** open, display the Save & Send tab Backstage view with the *Save to Web* option active. Sign in to Windows Live and create a new folder in your SkyDrive folder space named *Excel2010L2C8*. ***Hint: A New Folder button displays above and right of the My Documents folder in Backstage view once you are signed in to Windows Live. When you click this button, you will be redirected to the Windows Live web page and once you sign in again you will be at the Create folder web page.*** Within Windows Live SkyDrive, upload the three files you created in this assessment into the Excel2010L2C8 folder. Paste a screen image that shows the three files in the Excel2010L2C8 folder in Windows Live into a new Word document using the PrintScreen key, the Screenshot feature, or the Windows Snipping tool. Type your name a few lines below the screen image. Print the Word document and then exit Word without saving. Sign out of Windows Live and close the Internet Explorer window. Click the Home tab and then close **EL2-C8-A6-Hillsdale2012Sales.xlsx**.

Visual Benchmark Demonstrate Your Proficiency

IMPORT, ANALYZE, AND EXPORT POPULATION DATA

1. Look at the data in the worksheet shown in Figure 8.8. Create this worksheet by importing the PopByState table from the Access database named ***NuTrendsCensusData.accdb*** into a new worksheet. Once imported, rows and columns not shown in the figure were deleted and the filter arrows removed. The worksheet has *Table Style Light 2* style and the Solstice theme applied. Add the title rows at the top of the imported data and change the title in B4 as shown. Use your best judgment to match other formatting characteristics such as column width, row height, number formatting, alignment, and fill color.
2. Rename the worksheet *PopulationTable* and then print the worksheet.
3. Select A4:B19 and create the chart shown in Figure 8.9 in a new sheet named *PopulationChart*. The chart has the *Style 36* style applied. Use your best judgment to match other chart options and formatting with the chart shown.
4. Save the workbook and name it **EL2-C8-VB-PizzaByMarioPopData**.
5. Start Microsoft Word and then open **PizzaByMarioReport.docx**. Use Save As to name the workbook **EL2-C8-VB-PizzaByMarioReport**. Change *Student Name* on page 1 to your name. Copy and paste the Excel chart, positioning the chart between the last two paragraphs on page 2 of the document. Make any formatting adjustments to the chart you think are necessary once the chart has been inserted. Save, print, and then close **EL2-C8-VB-PizzaByMarioReport.docx**.
6. Close **EL2-C8-VB-PizzaByMarioPopData.xlsx**.

Figure 8.8 Visual Benchmark *PopulationTable* Worksheet

	A	B
1	U.S. Population Estimates as of July 1, 2009	
2	U.S. Census Bureau	
3	States Selected for Franchise Expansion	
4	**State**	**Population**
5	Illinois	12,910,409
6	Indiana	6,423,113
7	Iowa	3,007,856
8	Kansas	2,818,747
9	Kentucky	4,314,113
10	Michigan	9,969,727
11	Minnesota	5,266,214
12	Missouri	5,987,580
13	Montana	974,989
14	Nebraska	1,796,619
15	North Dakota	646,844
16	Ohio	11,542,645
17	South Dakota	812,383
18	Wisconsin	5,654,774
19	Wyoming	544,270

Figure 8.9 Visual Benchmark *PopulationChart* Chart

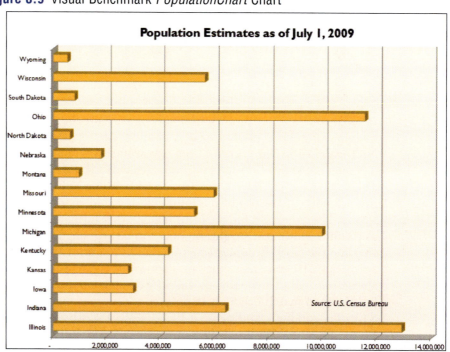

Case Study   Apply Your Skills

Part 1

Yolanda Robertson of NuTrends Market Research would like new research data from the U.S. Census Bureau for her Pizza by Mario franchise expansion project. The franchise expansion is planned for the states of Illinois, Indiana, and Kentucky. Start a new workbook and set up three worksheets named using the state names. In each sheet, using the New Web Query feature, display the web page http://quickfacts.census.gov/qfd/, and import the People Quickfacts table for the state. Once the data is imported, delete column A, which is the definitions information. Add an appropriate title merged and centered above the imported data and apply formatting enhancements to improve the appearance of the column headings. Save the workbook and name it **EL2-C8-CS-P1-PizzaByMarioResearch**. Print all three worksheets.

Part 2

To prepare for an upcoming meeting with Mario and Nicola Carlucci of Pizza by Mario, Yolanda would like you to copy selected information from each state to a Word report. Open **PizzaByMarioExpansionResearch.docx**. Save the document using Save As and name it **EL2-C8-CS-P2-PizzaByMarioExpansionResearch**. From the Excel workbook you created in Part 1, copy and paste to the Word document the following data for each state (do not include the data in the *USA* column). Do not embed or link since the data will not be changed or updated.

Households
Persons per household
Median household income

If the data you imported does not contain these headings, locate and copy information closely related to number of households and income for the state.

At the bottom of the document, create a reference for the data from the U.S. Census Bureau. Check with your instructor for the preferred format for the reference. Save, print, and then close **EL2-C8-CS-P2-PizzaByMarioExpansionResearch.docx**. Close **EL2-C8-CS-P1-PizzaByMarioResearch.xlsx**.

Part 3

Yolanda has noticed that when she opens the workbook created in Part 1, a message appears in the message bar that says *Data connections have been disabled*. Yolanda has asked what this message means and wonders what circumstances are acceptable to click the Enable Content button. Research in Help how to manage connections to external data using the Workbook Connections dialog box. Since the data that was imported does not need to be refreshed in the future, you decide to remove the connections so that Yolanda does not see the security message in the future. Open **EL2-C8-CS-P1-PizzaByMarioResearch.xlsx** and click the Enable Content button that appears in the message bar. Open the Workbook Connections dialog box and, using the information you learned in Help, remove all of the connections. Save the revised workbook as **EL2-C8-CS-P3-PizzaByMarioResearch** and then close the workbook.

Compose a memo to Yolanda using Microsoft Word that provides a brief explanation of why the security warning message about data connections appears when a workbook is opened that contains external content. Base the memo on the information you learned in Help, making sure that you compose the explanation using your own words. Explain that you have created a new copy of the workbook with the connections removed. Save the Word memo and name it **EL2-C8-CS-P3-DataConnectionsMemo**. Print and then close **EL2-C8-CS-P3-DataConnectionsMemo.docx** and then exit Word.

Part 4

Yolanda noticed the *Send as Internet Fax* option in the Send Using E-Mail pane at the Save & Send tab Backstage view. Yolanda wants to know how to send a worksheet as an Internet fax since NuTrends Market Research may need to distribute information via fax in the future. Research in Excel Help how to use the Internet Fax feature. Next, search the Internet for at least two fax service providers. Using Microsoft Word, compose a memo to Yolanda that briefly explains how to use the Internet Fax feature in Excel, making sure you compose the explanation using your own words. Include in the memo the URL of the two fax service providers you visited and add your recommendation for the provider you want to use. Save the memo and name it **EL2-C8-CS-P4-InternetFaxMemo**. Print and then close **EL2-C8-CS-P4-InternetFaxMemo.docx** and exit Word.

Performance Assessment

Excel2010L2U2

Note: Before beginning unit assessments, copy to your storage medium the Excel2010L2U2 subfolder from the Excel2010L2 folder on the CD that accompanies this textbook and then make Excel2010L2U2 the active folder.

Assessing Proficiency ▪▪▪▪▪▪▪▪▪▪▪▪▪▪▪

In this unit, you have learned to use features in Excel that facilitate performing what-if analysis, identifying relationships between worksheet formulas, collaborating with others by sharing and protecting workbooks, and automating repetitive tasks using macros. You also learned how to customize the Excel environment to suit your preferences and integrate Excel data by importing from and exporting to external resources. Finally, you learned how to prepare and distribute a workbook to others by removing items that are private or confidential, by marking the workbook as final, by checking for features incompatible with earlier versions of Excel, and by saving and sending a worksheet in various formats.

Assessment 1 Use Goal Seek and Scenario Manager to Calculate Investment Proposals

1. Open **HillsdaleInvtPlan.xlsx**.
2. Save the workbook with Save As and name it **EL2-U2-A1-HillsdaleInvtPlan**.
3. Use Goal Seek to find the monthly contribution amount the client must make in order to increase the projected value of the plan to $65,000 at the end of the term. Accept the solution Goal Seek calculates.
4. Assign the range name *AvgReturn* to E8.
5. Create three scenarios for changing E8 as follows:

Scenario name	Interest rate
Moderate	5.5%
Conservative	4.0%
Aggressive	12.5%

6. Apply the *Aggressive* scenario and then print the worksheet.
7. Edit the *Moderate* scenario's interest rate to 8.0% and then apply the scenario.
8. Create and then print a Scenario Summary report.
9. Save and then close **EL2-U2-A1-HillsdaleInvtPlan.xlsx**.

Calculate Investment Outcomes for a Portfolio Using a Two-Variable Data Table

1. Open **HillsdaleResearchInvtTbl.xlsx**.
2. Save the workbook with Save As and name it **EL2-U2-A2-HillsdaleResearchInvtTbl**.
3. Create a two-variable data table that calculates the projected value of the investment plan at the end of the term for each monthly contribution payment and at each interest rate in the range A11:G20.
4. Apply the Comma Style format to the projected values in the table and adjust column widths if necessary.
5. Make E8 the active cell and display precedent arrows.
6. Make A11 the active cell and display precedent arrows.
7. Remove the arrows.
8. Save, print, and then close **EL2-U2-A2-HillsdaleResearchInvtTbl.xlsx**.

Solve an Error and Check for Accuracy in Investment Commission Formulas

1. Open **HillsdaleModeratePortfolio.xlsx**.
2. Save the workbook with Save As and name it **EL2-U2-A3-HillsdaleModeratePortfolio**.
3. Solve the #VALUE! error in E19. Use formula auditing tools to help find the source cell containing the invalid entry.
4. Check the logic accuracy of the formula in E19 by creating proof formulas below the worksheet as follows:
   a. In row 21, calculate the amount from the customer's deposit that would be deposited into each of the six funds based on the percentages in column B. For example, in B21 create a formula to multiply the customer's deposit in B19 ($5,000.00) times the percentage recommended for investment in the DW Bond fund in B5 (40%). Create a similar formula for the remaining funds in C21:G21.
   b. In row 22, multiply the amount deposited to each fund by the fund's commission rate. For example, in B22, create a formula to multiply the value in B21 ($2,000.00) times the commission rate paid by the DW Bond fund in B17 (1.15%). Create a similar formula for the remaining funds in C22:G22.
   c. In B23, create a SUM function to calculate the total of the commissions for the six funds in B22:G22.
   d. Add appropriate labels next to the values created in rows 21 to 23.
5. Save, print, and then close **EL2-U2-A3-HillsdaleModeratePortfolio.xlsx**.

Document and Share a Workbook and Manage Changes in an Investment Portfolio Worksheet

1. Open **EL2-U2-A3-HillsdaleModeratePortfolio.xlsx**.
2. Save the workbook with Save As and name it **EL2-U2-A4-HillsdaleModeratePortfolio**.
3. Enter the following data into the workbook properties. *Note: Remove an entry for those properties shown below in which text may already exist*.

Author	Logan Whitmore
Title	Recommended Moderate Portfolio
Comments	Proposed moderate fund
Subject	Moderate Investment Allocation

4. Paste a screen image of the Info tab Backstage view showing all properties into a new Word document. Type your name a few blank lines below the image, print the document, and then exit Word without saving.
5. Click the Review tab and then share the workbook.
6. Change the user name to *Carey Winters* and then edit the following cells:

B7	from	*10%*	to	*15%*
B8	from	*15%*	to	*10%*

7. Save **EL2-U2-A4-HillsdaleModeratePortfolio.xlsx**.
8. Change the user name to *Jodi VanKemenade* and then edit the following cells:

D17	from	*2.15%*	to	*2.32%*
E17	from	*2.35%*	to	*2.19%*

9. Save **EL2-U2-A4-HillsdaleModeratePortfolio.xlsx**.
10. Create and then print a History sheet. *Note: If you submit your assignment work electronically, create a copy of the History worksheet in a new workbook named EL2-U2-A4-HillsdaleModeratePortfolioHistory.*
11. Change the user name back to the original name on the computer you are using.
12. Accept and reject changes made to the ModeratePortfolio worksheet as follows:

Reject	B7
Reject	B8
Accept	D17
Reject	E17

13. Save, print, and then close **EL2-U2-A4-HillsdaleModeratePortfolio.xlsx**.

Assessment 5 Insert Comments and Protect a Confidential Investment Portfolio Workbook

1. Open **EL2-U2-A4-HillsdaleModeratePortfolio.xlsx**.
2. Save the workbook with Save As and name it **EL2-U2-A5-HillsdaleModeratePortfolio.xlsx**.
3. Remove the shared access to the workbook.
4. Hide rows 20 to 23.
5. Make B17 the active cell and insert a comment. Type **Commission rate to be renegotiated in 2012** in the comment box.
6. Copy the comment in B17 and paste it to D17 and G17. Press the Esc key to remove the moving marquee from B17.
7. Edit the comment in G17 to change the year from *2012* to *2013*.
8. Protect the worksheet allowing editing to B19 only. Assign the password *hM$28* to unprotect the worksheet.
9. Encrypt the workbook with the password *Mod%82*.
10. Save and close **EL2-U2-A5-HillsdaleModeratePortfolio.xlsx**.
11. Test the security features added to the workbook by opening **EL2-U2-A5-HillsdaleModeratePortfolio.xlsx** using the password created in Step 9. Try to change one of the values in the range B5:B10 and B17:G17.
12. Make B19 the active cell and then change the value to *10000*.
13. Display all of the comments in the worksheet and then print the worksheet with the comments *As displayed on sheet* and with the worksheet scaled to fit on 1 page.
14. Save and then close **EL2-U2-A5-HillsdaleModeratePortfolio.xlsx**.

Assessment 6 Automate and Customize an Investment Portfolio Workbook

1. Open **EL2-U2-A5-HillsdaleModeratePortfolio.xlsx**.
2. Unprotect the worksheet, turn off the display of all comments, and then delete the comments in B17, D17, and G17.
3. Display the Custom Views dialog box. When a workbook has been shared, Excel automatically creates custom views (with the label *Personal View)* for each person who accessed the file as well as the original worksheet state before sharing was enabled. Delete all of the custom views in the dialog box and then add a new custom view named *ModeratePortfolioOriginalView*.
4. Create two macros to be stored in the active workbook as follows:
   a. A macro named *CustomDisplay* that applies the *Solstice* theme, and turns off the display of gridlines and row and column headers in the current worksheet. Assign the macro to the shortcut key Ctrl + Shift + T. Enter an appropriate description that includes your name and the date the macro was created.
   b. A macro named *CustomHeader* that prints the text *Private and Confidential* at the left margin. Assign the macro to the shortcut key Ctrl + Shift + H. Enter an appropriate description that includes your name and the date the macro was created.
5. Test the macros by opening **EL2-U2-A1-HillsdaleInvtPlan.xlsx**. Make InvestmentPlanProposal the active worksheet and then run the two macros created in Step 4. View the worksheet in Print Preview. Close Print Preview and then close **EL2-U2-A1-HillsdaleInvtPlan.xlsx** without saving the changes.
6. Print the Visual Basic program code for the two macros and then close the Microsoft Visual Basic window and return to Excel.
7. Create a custom view named *ModeratePortfolioTemplateView*.
8. Save the revised workbook as a macro-enabled workbook named **EL2-U2-A6-HillsdaleModeratePortfolio.xlsm** and remove the password to open the workbook.
9. Print the worksheet.
10. Display the Custom Views dialog box. Paste a screen image of the worksheet with the Custom Views dialog box open into a new Word document. Type your name a few blank lines below the image, print the document, and then exit Word without saving.
11. Close the Custom Views dialog box and then close **EL2-U2-A6-HillsdaleModeratePortfolio.xlsm**.

Assessment 7 Create and Use an Investment Planner Template

1. Open **EL2-U2-A2-HillsdaleResearchInvtTbl.xlsx**.
2. Make the following changes to the worksheet:
   a. Change the label in A3 to *Investment Planner*.
   b. Change the font color of A11 to white. This will make the cell appear to be empty. You want to disguise the entry in this cell because you think displaying the value at the top left of the data table will confuse Hillsdale customers.
   c. Clear the contents of E5:E7.
   d. Protect the worksheet allowing editing to E5:E7 only. Assign the password *H$pl@n* to unprotect the worksheet.
3. Save the revised workbook as a template named **HillsdaleInvPlan-StudentName** with your name substituted for *StudentName*.

4. Close **HillsdaleInvPlan-StudentName.xltx**.
5. Start a new workbook based on the **HillsdaleInvPlan-StudentName.xltx** template.
6. Enter the following information in the appropriate cells:
   a. *Monthly contribution*   -475
   b. *Number of years to invest*   5
   c. *Forecasted annual interest rate*   4.75%
7. Save the workbook as an Excel workbook named **EL2-U2-A7-HillsdaleInvPlan**.
8. Print and then close **EL2-U2-A7-HillsdaleInvPlan.xlsx**.
9. Display the New dialog box. Copy the template created in this assessment to the Excel2010L2U2 folder on your storage medium.
10. Delete the custom template created in this assessment from the hard disk drive on the computer you are using.

Assessment 8 Export a Chart and Prepare and Distribute an Investment Portfolio Worksheet

1. Open **EL2-U2-A6-HillsdaleModeratePortfolio.xlsm** and enable the content if the security warning message bar appears.
2. Start Microsoft PowerPoint 2010 and then open **HillsdalePortfolios.pptx**.
3. Save the presentation with Save As and name it **EL2-U2-A8-HillsdalePortfolios**.
4. Copy the pie chart from the Excel worksheet to Slide 7 in the PowerPoint presentation.
5. Resize the chart on the slide and edit the legend if necessary to make the chart consistent with the other charts in the presentation.
6. Print the PowerPoint presentation as *9 Slides Horizontal Handouts*.
7. Save **EL2-U2-A8-HillsdalePortfolios.pptx** and then exit PowerPoint.
8. Deselect the chart in the Excel worksheet.
9. Inspect the document, leaving all items checked at the Document Inspector dialog box.
10. Remove all items that display with a red exclamation mark and then close the dialog box.
11. Change the file type to a workbook with an .xlsx file extension and name it **EL2-U2-A8-HillsdaleModeratePortfolio**. Click Yes when prompted that the file cannot be saved with the VBA Project. Click OK at the privacy warning message box.
12. Mark the workbook as final. Click OK if the privacy warning message box reappears.
13. Send the workbook as an XPS document to yourself in an email initiated from Excel. Include an appropriate message in the message window assuming you work for Hillsdale Financial Services and are sending the portfolio file to a potential client. Open the message window from the Inbox in your email program and print the message. Close the message window and exit your email program.
14. Display the Info tab Backstage view showing all properties. Paste a screen image into a new Word document. Type your name a few blank lines below the image, print the document, and then exit Word without saving.
15. Close **EL2-U2-A8-HillsdaleModeratePortfolio.xlsx**.

Writing Activities

The Writing, Internet Research, and Job Study activities give you the opportunity to practice your writing skills while demonstrating an understanding of some of the important Excel features you have mastered in this unit. Use appropriate word choices and correct grammar, capitalization, and punctuation when setting up new worksheets. Labels should clearly describe the data that is presented.

Create a Computer Maintenance Template

The Computing Services department of National Online Marketing Inc. wants to create a computer maintenance template for Help Desk employees to complete electronically and save to a document management server. This system will make it easy for a technician to check the status of any employee's computer from any location within the company. The Help Desk department performs the following computer maintenance tasks at each computer twice per year.

- Delete temporary Internet files
- Delete temporary document files that begin with a tilde (~)
- Update hardware drivers
- Reconfirm all serial numbers and asset records
- Have employee change password
- Check that automatic updates for the operating system is active
- Check that automatic updates for virus protection is active
- Confirm that automatic backup to the computing services server is active
- Confirm that employee is archiving all email messages
- Clean the computer's screen, keyboard, and system unit

In a new workbook, create a template that can be used to complete the maintenance form electronically. The template should include information that identifies the workstation by asset ID number, the department in which the computer is located, the name of the employee using the computer, the name of the technician that performs the maintenance, and the date the maintenance is performed. In addition, include a column next to each task with a drop-down list with the options: *Completed, Not Completed, Not Applicable*. Next to this column include a column in which the technician can type notes. At the bottom of the template include a text box with the following message text:

Save using the file naming standard CM-StationID##-yourinitials where ## is the asset ID. Example CM-StationID56-JW

Protect the worksheet, leaving the cells unlocked that the technician will fill in as he or she completes a maintenance visit. Do not include a password for unprotecting the sheet. Save the template and name it **NationalCMForm-StudentName** with your name substituted for *StudentName*. Start a new workbook based on the custom template. Fill out a form as if you were a technician working on your own computer to test the template's organization and layout. Save the completed form as an Excel workbook named **EL2-U2-Act1-NationalCMForm**. Print the form scaled to fit one page in height and width. Copy the **NationalCMForm-StudentName.xltx** template file to your storage medium and then delete the template from the computer you are using.

Internet Research

Apply What-If Analysis to a Planned Move

Following graduation, you plan to move out of the state/province for a few years to gain experience living on your own. Create a new workbook to use as you plan this move to develop a budget for expenses in the first year. Research typical rents for apartments in the city in which you want to find your first job. Estimate other living costs in the city including transportation, food, entertainment, clothes, telephone, cable/satellite, cell phone, Internet, and so on. Calculate total living costs for an entire year. Next, research annual starting salaries for your chosen field of study in the same area. Estimate the take home pay at approximately 70% of the annual salary you decide to use. Using the take-home pay and the total living costs for the year, calculate if you will have money left over or have to borrow money to meet expenses.

Next, assume you want to save enough money to go on a vacation at the end of the year. Use Goal Seek to find the take-home pay you need to earn in order to have $2,000 left over at the end of the year. Accept the solution that Goal Seek provides and then create two scenarios in the worksheet as follows:

- A scenario named *LowestValues* in which you adjust each value down to the lowest amount you think is reasonable.
- A scenario named *HighestValues* in which you adjust each value up to the highest amount you think is reasonable.

Apply each scenario and watch the impact on the amount left over at the end of the year. Display the worksheet in the *HighestValues* scenario and then create a scenario summary report. Print the worksheet applying print options as necessary to minimize the pages required. Print the scenario summary report. Save the workbook as **EL2-U2-Act2-MyFirstYearBudget**. Close **EL2-U2-Act2-MyFirstYearBudget.xlsx**.

Research and Compare Smartphones

You work for an independent marketing consultant who travels frequently in North America and Europe for work. The consultant, Lindsay Somers, would like to purchase a smartphone. Lindsay will use the smartphone while traveling for conference calling, email, web browsing, text messaging, and making modifications to PowerPoint presentations, Word documents, or Excel worksheets. Using the Internet, research the latest smartphone from three different manufacturers. Prepare a worksheet that compares the three smartphones, organizing the worksheet so that the main features are shown along the left side of the page by category and each phone's specifications for those features are set in columns. At the bottom of each column, provide the hyperlink to the phone's specifications on the Web. Based on your perception of the best value, select one of the phones as your recommendation and note within the worksheet using a comment box in the price cell the phone you think Lindsay should select. Provide a brief explanation of why you selected the phone in the comment box. Make sure comments are displayed in the worksheet. Save the worksheet and name it **EL2-U2-Act3-Smartphones**. Publish the worksheet as a single file web page accepting the default file name and changing the page title to *Smartphone Feature and Price Comparison*. Print the web page from the Internet Explorer window. Close Internet Explorer and then close **EL2-U2-Act3-Smartphones.xlsx**.

Job Study

Prepare a Wages Budget and Link the Budget to a Word Document

You work at a small, independent, long-term care facility named Gardenview Place Long-Term Care. As assistant to the business manager, you are helping with the preparation of next year's hourly wages budget. Create a worksheet to estimate next year's hourly wages expense using the following information about hourly paid workers and the average wage costs in Table U2.1:

- The facility runs three 8-hour shifts, 7 days per week, 52 weeks per year.

  6 a.m. to 2 p.m.

  2 p.m. to 10 p.m.

  10 p.m. to 6 a.m.

- Each shift requires two registered nurses, four licensed practical nurses, and two health-care aid workers.

- At each shift, one of the registered nurses is designated as the charge nurse and is paid a premium of 15% of his or her regular hourly rate.

- The 6 a.m.-to-2 p.m. and 2 p.m.-to-10 p.m. shifts require one custodian; the 10 p.m.-to-6 a.m. shift requires two custodians.

- Each shift requires the services of an on-call physician and an on-call pharmacist. Budget for the physician and the pharmacist at 4 hours per shift.

- Add 14% to each shift's total wage costs to cover the estimated costs of benefits such as vacation pay, holiday pay, and medical care coverage plans for all workers *except* the on-call physician and on-call pharmacist, who do not receive these benefits.

Make use of colors, themes, or table features to make the budget calculations easy to read. Save the workbook and name it **EL2-U2-JS-GardenviewWageBdgt**. Print the worksheet, adjusting print options as necessary to minimize the pages required. Create a chart in a separate sheet to show the total hourly wages budget by worker category. You determine the chart type and chart options to present the information.

Start Word and open the document named **GardenviewOpBdgt.xlsx**. Edit the year on the title page to the current year. Edit the name and date at the bottom of the title page to your name and the current date. Link the chart created in the Excel worksheet to the end of the Word document. Save the revised document as **EL2-U2-JS-GardenviewOpBdgt**. Print and then close **EL2-U2-JS-GardenviewOpBdgt.docx**. Deselect the chart and close **EL2-U2-JS-GardenviewWageBdgt.xlsx**.

Table U2.1 Average Hourly Wage Rates

Wage Category	Average Wage Rate
Registered nurse	29.35
Licensed practical nurse	18.45
Health-care aid worker	13.91
Custodian	10.85
On-call physician	65.00
On-call pharmacist	47.00

Index

custom template
  deleting, 243–244
  using, 242–243
custom view, 238
  creating and applying, 238–240
Custom Views dialog box, 238

D

data
  circling invalid, 170
  converting from rows to columns, 153–154
  embedding Excel into Word, 270
  exporting, 267–278
  exporting, breaking link to an Excel object, 272–273
  exporting, copying and pasting worksheet data to Access table, 268–269
  exporting, copying and pasting worksheet data to PowerPoint presentation, 273–275
  exporting, copying and pasting worksheet data to Word document, 269–272
  exporting from Excel, 267–278
  exporting as text file, 276–278
  filtering and sorting, using conditional formatting or cell attributes, 24–27
  grouping and ungrouping, 92–93
  importing, 260–267
  importing from Access, 261–262
  importing from text file, 265–267
  importing from website, 262–265
  linking Excel into Word, 270–272
  looking up, 49–52
  pasting using paste special options, 151–155
  subtotal related, 88–92
  summarizing by linking to ranges in other worksheets or workbooks, 110–114
  summarizing in multiple worksheets using range names and 3-D references, 106–109
  summarizing with Sparklines, 128
  summarizing using Consolidate feature, 114–116
  in table, 71
  transposing, 152–154
data bars, conditional formatting using, 14
data entry, validating and restricting, 83–87
data tables
  creating one-variable, 162–163
  creating two-variable, 164–165
  defined, 162
  performing what-if analysis with, 162–165
Data Tools, 80–81
  removing duplicate records, 81–82
  validating and restricting data entry, 83–87
Data Validation, 170
Data Validation dialog box, 83
deleting
  comments, 185–186
  conditional formatting rules, 10–12

custom template, 243–244
  macros, 225
  range names, 48–49
  scenarios, 160
delimited file format, 265
dependent cells, 166
destination, 260
destination cells, multiplying source cells by, 154–155
destination files, breaking link between source files and, 272–273
display options, changing in customizing work area, 230
distribution
  marking workbook as final before, 282–284
  preparing workbook for, 278–286
  removing information from or before, 278–282
  of workbooks, 286–296
Document Inspector dialog box, 279–280
duplicate records, removing, 81–82

E

Edit Formatting Rule dialog box, 10
editing
  comments, 185–186
  conditional formatting rules, 10–12
  macros, 223–225
  range names, 48–49
  scenarios, 159
  tracked workbook, 203
Edit Links dialog box, 112
email, sending workbook via, 292–293
embedding
  Excel data in PowerPoint presentation, 274–275
  Excel data into Word, 270
Encrypt Document dialog box, 199
encrypted password, 198
error alerts, 83, 84
Excel Options dialog box, 230, 233
exporting data, 267–278
  breaking link to Excel object, 272–273
  copying and pasting worksheet data to Access table, 268–269
  copying and pasting worksheet data to PowerPoint presentation, 273–275
  copying and pasting worksheet data to Word document, 269–272
  as text file, 276–278
external link, updating, 112–113
external references
  maintaining, 111–112
  removing linked, 113–114

F

field names row, 74
fields, 74

rows
 banding, 76
 converting data, from and to columns, 153–154
rules
 creating new, 8–10
 formatting cells based on top/bottom, 8
running, macros, 220

S

Save & Send tab Backstage view, 276, 292
Save As dialog box, 267, 290
save options, customizing, 244–247
saving
 workbook as template, 240–244
 workbook to Windows Live SkyDrive, 293–296
Scenario Manager, 157
 creating assumptions for what-if analysis using, 157–161
scenarios
 applying, 159
 deleting, 160
 editing, 159
Scenario Summary dialog box, 160, 161
scenario summary report, compiling, 160–161
scientific formatting, 16–18
Select Changes to Accept or Reject dialog box, 202
shared workbook, 188–194
 changing user names in, 189–191
 printing history sheet and removing access, 192–194
 resolving conflicts in, 191–192
Share Workbook dialog box, 188–189
shortcut key, assigning macros to, 221–223
Show Detail button, 92–93
shrinking text to fit within cell, 22–23
Slicers, 121
 filtering PivotTable using, 121–123
Sort Dialog Box with Four-Color Sort Defined, 27
sorting
 by cell color, 26–27
 data using conditional filtering or cell attributes, 24–27
 tables, 78–80
source, 260
source cells, multiplying by destination cells, 154–155
source data, editing and updating external link, 112–113
source files, breaking link between destination files and, 272–273
space delimited file, 276
Sparklines, 103, 128
 customizing, 129–130
 summarizing data with, 128
special number formats, 18–19
standard formulas, 38
statistical functions, 39–45

AVERAGE, 39
AVERAGEIF, 43–44
AVERAGIF/AVERAGIFS, 43–45
AVERAGEIFS, 43, 44
COUNT, 39
COUNTA, 39
COUNTIF, 39–40
COUNTIF/COUNTIFS, 39–42
COUNTIFS, 40, 42
MAX, 39
MIN, 39
SUBSTITUTE, 59, 60–61
subtotals
 creating, 88–91
 modifying, 91–92
Sum function, 76, 88, 116
 changing, 123
SUMIF, 46–47
SUMIFS, 46
summarizing
 data by linking ranges in other worksheets or workbooks, 110–114
 data in multiple worksheets using range names and 3-D references, 106-109
 data using the Consolidate feature, 114–116
 data with Sparklines, 128–130

T

tab
 creating new, 233
 renaming, 233–234
tab delimited file, 276
tab group, adding buttons to, 234
table_array, 50
tables
 converting to normal range, 88
 converting range to, 75
 copying and pasting worksheet data to an Access, 268–269
 creating, 74–75
 data in, 71
 defined, 71
 field names row in, 74
 fields in, 74
 header rows in, 74
 importing from web page, 263–265
 lookup, 49, 50
 modifying, 75–76
 records in, 74
 sorting and filtering, 78–80
 styles of, 76–78
Table Tools Design tab, 76, 77
target value, using Goal Seek to return, 156–157
tasks, automating using macros, 217–225
templates, 240
 deleting custom, 243–244
 saving workbook as, 240–244
 using custom, 242–243

text, wrapping and shrinking to fit within cell, 22–23
text files, 265
    exporting Excel data as, 276–278
    importing data from, 265–267
text functions, 59–61
    LOWER, 59
    PROPER, 59, 60–61
    SUBSTITUTE, 59, 60–61
    UPPER, 59
Text Import Wizard, 266
Text to Columns feature, 80
3-D references, 106
    summarizing data in multiple worksheets using, 106–109
top/botton rules, formatting cells based on, 8
trace cells, 166
trace dependents, 166–167
trace precedents, 166–167
tracked changes
    accepting and rejecting, 202–203
    highlighting and reviewing, 204
tracked workbook, editing, 203
transposing data, 152–154
trigonometry functions. *See* math and trigonometry functions
troubleshooting, formulas, 167–170
two-variable data tables, creating, 164–165

U

ungrouping data, 92–93
unicode text, 276
Unprotect Sheet dialog box, 197
UPPER, 59
user name, changing, 189–191

V

value comparison, formatting cells based on, 7
VBA (Visual Basic for Applications), 218
viewing, comments, 185
Visual Basic, 218
VLOOKUP, 49–52
    argument parameters for, 50

W

web page, publishing worksheet as, 290–291
website, importing data from, 262–265
what-if analysis
    creating assumptions for using Scenario Manager, 157–161
    performing with data tables, 162–165
what-if analysis tools, 149
Windows Live SkyDrive, saving workbooks to, 293–296
Win/Loss Sparklines, 128
Word document
    breaking link to Excel object, 272–273

copying and pasting worksheet data to, 269–272
    embedding Excel data into, 270
    linking Excel data into, 270–272
work area, changing display options in customizing, 230
workbooks
    adding and removing password to, 198–201
    adding properties, 182–185
    changing user name, 189–191
    distribution of, 286–296
    marking as final before distribution, 282–284
    pinning to recent workbooks list, 226–227
    preparing for distribution, 278–286
    protecting and unprotecting the structure of, 197–198
    recovering, 245–247
    removing information from before distributing, 278–282
    saving containing macros, 218–219
    saving as template, 240–244
    saving to Windows Live SkyDrive, 293–296
    sending via email, 292–293
    sharing, 188–194
    stopping tracking of changes in, 205
    summarizing data by linking to ranges in other, 110–114
    tracking changes to, 201–205
    unprotecting, 198
workbooks list, pinning workbooks to recent, 226–227
worksheets
    copying and pasting data to Access table, 268–269
    copying and pasting data to PowerPoint presentation, 273–275
    copying and pasting data to Word document, 269–272
    filtering using custom AutoFilter, 23–24
    protecting and unprotecting, 194–197
    publishing as PDF document, 286–288
    publishing as web page, 290–291
    publishing as XPS document, 288–289
    summarizing data by linking to ranges in other, 110–114
    summarizing data in multiple, using range names and 3-D references, 106–109
    tables in, 71
    transposing data in, 152–154
wrapping text to fit within cell, 22–23

X

XML-based file format (.xlsx), 218
XML Paper Specification (XPS), 288
XPS document, 282
    publishing worksheet as, 288–289
    sending via email, 292–293
XPS viewer, 288

Excel 2010 Feature	Ribbon Tab, Group	Button	Shortcut
Accounting number format	Home, Number		
Align text left	Home, Alignment		
Align text right	Home, Alignment		
Bold	Home, Font		Ctrl + B
Borders	Home, Font		
Bottom align	Home, Alignment		
Cell styles	Home, Styles		
Center	Home, Alignment		
Change file type	File, Save & Send		
Clip Art	Insert, Illustrations		
Close workbook	File		Ctrl + F4
Comma style	Home, Number		
Comments	Review, Comments		
Conditional Formatting	Home, Styles		
Consolidate	Data, Consolidate		
Convert Text to Columns	Table Tools Design, Tools		
Copy	Home, Clipboard		Ctrl + C
Custom number format	Home, Number		
Cut	Home, Clipboard		Ctrl + X
Data Table	Data, Data Tools		
Data Validation	Data, Data Tools		

Excel 2010 Feature	Ribbon Tab, Group	Button	Shortcut
Decrease decimal	Home, Number		
Decrease indent	Home, Alignment		Ctrl + Alt + Shift + Tab
Delete cells	Home, Cells		
Document Inspector	File, Info		
Fill color	Home, Editing		
Financial functions	Formulas, Function Library		
Find & Select	Home, Editing		
Font color	Home, Font		
Format Painter	Home, Clipboard		
Goal Seek	Data, Data Tools		
Group and Ungroup	Data, Outline		Shift + Alt + Right Arrow key, Shift + Alt + Left Arrow key
Header & Footer	Insert, Text		
Help			F1
Hyperlink	Insert, Links		Ctrl + K
Import from Access, web page, or text file	Data, Get External Data		
Increase decimal	Home, Number		
Increase indent	Home, Alignment		
Insert cells	Home, Cells		
Insert Chart dialog box	Insert, Charts		
Insert function dialog box	Formulas, Function Library		
Italic	Home, Font		Ctrl + I

Excel 2010 Reference

Excel 2010 Feature	Ribbon Tab, Group	Button	Shortcut
Logical functions	Formulas, Function Library		
Lookup & Reference functions	Formulas, Function Library		
Macros	View, Macros		Alt + F8
Mark workbook as final	File, Info		
Math & Trigonometry functions	Formulas, Function Library		
Merge & Center	Home, Alignment		
Middle align	Home, Alignment		
Name Manager dialog box	Formulas, Defined Names		
New workbook	File, New		Ctrl + N
Number format	Home, Number	General	
Open dialog box	File	Open	Ctrl + O
Orientation	Home, Alignment		
Page orientation	Page Layout, Page Setup		
Paste	Home, Clipboard		Ctrl + V
Percent style	Home, Number	%	Ctrl + Shift + %
PivotTable or PivotChart	Insert, Tables or PivotTable Tools Options, Tools		
Print tab Backstage view	File, Print		Ctrl + P
Protect Worksheet	Review, Changes		
Remove Duplicates	Data, Data Tools or Table Tools Design, Tools		
Save or Save As	File	Save As	Ctrl + S, F12
Save as PDF/XPS	File, Save & Send		

Excel 2010 Feature	Ribbon Tab, Group	Button	Shortcut
Scenario Manager	Data, Data Tools		
Screenshot	Insert, Illustrations		
Share workbook	Review, Changes		
SmartArt	Insert, Illustrations		
Sort & Filter	Home, Editing		
Sparklines	Insert, Sparklines		
Spelling	Review, Proofing	ABC	
Statistical functions	Formulas, Function Library		
Subtotals	Data, Outline		
Sum	Home, Editing	Σ	Alt + =
Symbol dialog box	Insert, Symbols	Ω	
Text box	Insert, Text		
Text functions	Formulas, Function Library		
Themes	Page Layout, Themes		
Top align	Home, Alignment		
Trace Dependents or Trace Precedents	Formulas, Auditing		
Track Changes	Review, Changes		
Underline	Home, Font	U	Ctrl + U
Unlock cells	Home, Cells		
Wrap text	Home, Alignment		